ROGUE STATES

ROGUE STATES

The Making of America's
Global War on Terror

Matthew A. Frakes

CORNELL UNIVERSITY PRESS   ITHACA AND LONDON

Copyright © 2026 by Matthew A. Frakes

All rights reserved. Except for brief quotations in a review, this book, or parts thereof, must not be reproduced in any form without permission in writing from the publisher. For information, address Cornell University Press, Sage House, 512 East State Street, Ithaca, New York 14850. Visit our website at cornellpress.cornell.edu.

First published 2026 by Cornell University Press

Librarians: A CIP catalog record for this book is available from the Library of Congress.

ISBN 9781501785719 (hardcover)
ISBN 9781501785726 (paperback)
ISBN 9781501785733 (pdf)
ISBN 9781501785740 (epub)

GPSR EU contact: Sam Thornton, Mare Nostrum Group B.V., Mauritskade 21D, 1091 GC, Amsterdam, NL, gpsr@mare-nostrum.co.uk.

*For Brianna,
my inspiration throughout this journey
and all the journeys to come*

Contents

List of Illustrations	viii
Introduction: New World Order	1
1. Back to the Future: Challenging the Cold War Mindset of the Early Reagan Years	12
2. Act of War: Libya and the Struggle to Confront Terrorism	41
3. The Criminal Rogue: Panama and the Question of Regime Change	76
4. No Good Demon: Iraq, Iran, and the Emergence of the Quintessential Rogue	106
5. The Formative Precedent: The Gulf War and the Future of Global Security	137
Conclusion: New World Disorder	182
Acknowledgments	193
Notes	197
Bibliography	233
Index	241

Illustrations

1. Reagan, Bush, and Gorbachev on Governors Island, New York, December 7, 1988. Ronald Reagan Presidential Library (C50846-27). — 2

2. Reagan with advisors in the Cabinet Room of the White House, May 28, 1981. Ronald Reagan Presidential Library (C2164-14A). — 17

3. Reagan and Thatcher at 10 Downing Street, London, June 9, 1982. Ronald Reagan Presidential Library (C8575-32A). — 35

4. Cover of *Newsweek* featuring Muammar Qadhafi of Libya, July 20, 1981. Newsweek/EVG Media. — 48

5. Reagan, Bush, and Shultz in the White House Situation Room, June 16, 1985. Ronald Reagan Presidential Library (C29795-6). — 52

6. Reagan and Bush with advisors in the Oval Office, March 24, 1986. Ronald Reagan Presidential Library (C33990-15). — 59

7. Reagan with advisors in the White House Situation Room, April 15, 1986. Ronald Reagan Presidential Library (C34348-20). — 63

8. Cover of *Newsweek* featuring Manuel Noriega of Panama, February 15, 1988. Newsweek/EVG Media. — 82

9. Reagan, Shultz, and Powell in the Oval Office, June 13, 1988. Ronald Reagan Presidential Library (C47687-5). — 89

10. Reagan and Bush with advisors in the Yellow Oval Room of the White House, May 21, 1988. Ronald Reagan Presidential Library (C47131-30). — 92

11. Bush with advisors in the Treaty Room of the White
    House, December 17, 1989. George H. W. Bush
    Presidential Library (P8901-6).   102

12. Cover of *Newsweek* featuring Saddam Hussein
    of Iraq, August 13, 1990. Newsweek/EVG Media.   108

13. Reagan with advisors in the White House
    Situation Room, May 18, 1987. Ronald Reagan
    Presidential Library (C40764-24).   115

14. Bush with advisors in the White House
    Rose Garden, February 11, 1991. AP Photo/Dennis
    Cook (9102120160).   123

15. Bush and Thatcher in Aspen, Colorado,
    August 2, 1990. George H. W. Bush Presidential
    Library (P14921-30).   146

16. Bush with advisors in the White House Situation
    Room, October 30, 1990. George H. W. Bush
    Presidential Library (P17015-6).   163

17. Bush with advisors in the Oval Office,
    February 27, 1991. George H. W. Bush Presidential
    Library (P19782-6).   170

18. Reagan, Bush, and Gorbachev, New York,
    December 7, 1988. Paul F. Gero/Chicago
    Tribune/TCA.   192

ROGUE STATES

Introduction
NEW WORLD ORDER

It was a symbolic meeting, but just what it would come to symbolize was deeply uncertain.

In the waning days of Ronald Reagan's presidency, three world leaders came together for the last of five superpower summits between the US president and his Soviet counterpart, General Secretary Mikhail Gorbachev. This final meeting was unique for the addition of a third participant in the top-level discussions, President-elect George H. W. Bush. Though he had been elected as Reagan's successor just a month earlier, Bush insisted that he was attending the meeting only in his capacity as vice president, willing to support his current boss but not yet ready to tip his hand on the policies that his own administration would adopt.

The meeting between the three leaders took place on December 7, 1988, in the commandant's quarters of the US Coast Guard station on Governors Island in New York Harbor, chosen for its easy security arrangements and proximity to the United Nations, where Gorbachev had just delivered a major address that effectively announced an end to the Cold War. Though the meeting offered little in the way of substantial negotiations, its location and timing were rich with symbolism, some of which was intentional and obvious at the time and some of which would become apparent only years later.

The Cold War was clearly winding down. This brief summit meeting was meant to commemorate and showcase the partnership that Reagan and Gorbachev had built and the progress they had made toward lessening the threat of nuclear war and curtailing the tensions between the world's two superpowers that had defined and plagued the international landscape since the aftermath of

FIGURE 1. At the dawn of a new era: The Statue of Liberty provides a fitting backdrop for a symbolic end to the Cold War, as Ronald Reagan and Mikhail Gorbachev, accompanied by President-elect George Bush, meet for their final summit on December 7, 1988, on Governors Island in New York Harbor.

World War II. Gorbachev hoped to further this progress with Bush, the incoming president, to truly bring the Cold War to an end.[1] Asked by the press how their meeting had gone, a grinning Reagan replied, "Read our smiles." But just what lay ahead for the world was far less certain.

Following their meeting and a luncheon for the US and Soviet delegations, the three leaders made their way to a platform along the waterfront, where they lined up for the eagerly waiting photographers who were intent on capturing the historic scene of partnership representing the virtual end of the Cold War. Reagan directed Gorbachev's attention over the harbor toward the Statue of Liberty, a dramatic backdrop captured in pictures that reflected the world's hope for a dawning era of freedom and peace.[2]

But what would this new era hold for an international order that had been built over four decades earlier around the global competition and rivalry between the United States and the Soviet Union? How should the incoming administration reframe and reorient the role of the United States in the world to account for the end of the Cold War? How would it redefine US national security to meet the opportunities and challenges of the new era?

In fact, away from the headlines of US-Soviet summits and nuclear disarmament treaties, the process of reimagining US national security for a post–Cold War world was already well underway. For over a decade before the summit meeting on Governors Island, a series of emerging threats to global security that did not fit into the bounds of the Cold War—including terrorism, regional aggression, the proliferation of weapons of mass destruction (WMD), and narcotics trafficking—were evolving from mere peripheral nuisances in the US government's conception of national security to what the Reagan administration classified in 1986 as "a fundamental long-term security threat."[2] By the end of the 1980s, US officials and their key European allies began to recognize the convergence of these once-disparate dangers into a single growing phenomenon that they called "outlaw states," "renegade regimes," and eventually "rogue states." The Gulf crisis and war of 1990–1991 brought this new menace into such stark relief that it became the defining threat to the new global order that would come to replace the Cold War world.

This shift in the focus of US national security away from the Cold War anticommunist framework and toward rapidly emerging and poorly understood security threats was far from intentional. Ronald Reagan had entered the presidency in 1981 determined to double down on the traditional language of the Cold War that concentrated US foreign policy on the global competition with Soviet communism. But as the bipolar Cold War order began to fracture and collapse in the second half of the 1980s, what would come to replace anticommunism and containment of Soviet power as the defining framework for the role of the United States in the world was not yet settled. This book traces the formation and evolution of the idea of "rogue states" from the early Reagan years to the aftermath of the Gulf War as a new framework on which to build US national security as the Cold War was winding down.

This book argues that the strategies that grew out of the Reagan and Bush administrations' improvised responses to crises of terrorism, regional aggression, and WMD proliferation established a lasting enforcement role for the United States against rogue states in the post–Cold War world. Their approaches to the emerging rogue state threat did not leave a clear blueprint for future action. But Reagan and Bush set precedents and the parameters of debate that elevated the concepts of regime change and preemptive military action to the forefront of US strategic thinking. Their actions redefining the US understanding of national security around the rogue state threat ensured that when the United States faced future crises it instinctively looked to rogue states as the source of the problem.

Moreover, this story of the birth of a new geopolitical framework around which to orient US national security for the post–Cold War era lends significant insight into the making of US grand strategy. Scholars frequently debate whether leaders base their actions on the world stage on a broad "grand strategy" or whether they simply "muddle through," reacting to events as they occur.[4] The process through which rogue states came to define US involvement in the world following the end of the Cold War reveals that both are true. In each of the key crises that shaped US strategies toward rogue states, the Reagan and Bush administrations improvised to address unexpected developments, first reacting to attacks and then forming strategic principles to make sense of what had happened. In effect, the United States arrived at its post–Cold War grand strategy "in reverse." This book gives ample evidence that this grand strategy was hammered out through a process of improvisation and adaptation, and only then shaped into a doctrine that appeared to possess strategic coherence. Whether hamstrung by divisions among advisors over policy decisions or by a lack of consensus for action among allies, Congress, or the public, Reagan and Bush struggled repeatedly to get ahead of emerging security threats. Instead, crises involving early rogue states such as Libya, Panama, and Iraq forced their hands, spurring improvised responses that evolved into coherent strategies only in the crises' aftermath.

Regional aggressors and international troublemakers were nothing new. What made the rogue state threat different during the final decade of the Cold War and the first years of the 1990s were two factors: the unique cocktail of features that defined rogue states and the context in which they emerged as preeminent threats to international security.

The idea of "rogue states" emerged slowly and fitfully but with increasing urgency over the course of the final decade of the Cold War, percolating under the surface of more longstanding and clearly understood priorities for US foreign policy before emerging as a first-order priority in its own right. While the concept of "rogue states" took on greater clarity in the minds of US policymakers as the 1980s progressed, it was always a nebulous and elastic idea that did not lend itself to clear-cut definitions or rigid criteria, as not all rogue states shared the exact same set of characteristics—and others that did were not always considered rogues. Indeed, it was the fuzziness and adaptability of the concept that allowed US strategists to apply it with such lasting effect to a diverse range of crises in the late Cold War and post–Cold War world.

However, it was a shared band of threats to international security that emerged with increasing destructiveness over the course of the 1980s—terrorism, regional armed aggression, the proliferation of WMD, and narcotics trafficking—that ultimately converged to define the new phenomenon of rogue states. In a series of crises from 1981 to 1991, Libya, Panama, and Iraq emerged successively as the first poster children of the rogue state paradigm, each contributing different characteristics to this new security threat taking shape. Libya helped blend the emerging rogue paradigm with state-sponsored terrorism; Panama brought narcotics trafficking into the mix; and Iraq decisively fused rogues with the pursuit of WMD. All were led by dictators who destabilized their regions and threatened both their weaker neighbors as well as the United States and its allies with unpredictable aggressive impulses. International outlaws challenging the norms governing international behavior and security while sponsoring acts of terrorism, threatening military aggression, and pursuing WMD—especially nuclear weapons—gave this new menace a more acute and global reach than it could have had at a different moment in history.[5]

But what was it about these characteristics that made the threat of rogue states in the 1980s and early 1990s new and distinct from what came before? After all, pariah states in the international community had existed since ancient times, from the Gauls, the Vikings, and the Barbary states conducting raids and acts of piracy to Bolshevik Russia in the early twentieth century.[6] The rogue states that surfaced at the end of the Cold War shared many features with their earlier counterparts, reflecting important continuity as well as change on the international landscape. Examples of particular states that exhibited "rogue" behavior—engaging in regional conflicts or sponsoring terrorist acts or seeking WMD—can be traced to well before the Cold War's final decade. Indeed, the individual security threats that the rogue states of the 1980s and 1990s brought together and transformed from separate and lower-priority issues into a single phenomenon—particularly the state-sponsorship of terrorism, unpredictable regional aggression, and the proliferation of WMD—all had their own antecedents and earlier histories. Each of these threats had existed before the 1980s, and individual troublesome states exhibited certain characteristics or behavior of what would later become known as rogue states. The rogues at the end of the Cold War did not bubble to the surface of the international scene fully formed but rather had deep roots in earlier trends.[7]

Nevertheless, what made the emerging rogue state paradigm distinct in the 1980s and early 1990s was the ability of these pariahs to inflict outsize harm and pose disproportionate danger to the United States, its allies, and the international community as a whole. Rarely if ever had states brought together all of the ingredients that came to define rogues at the dawn of the post–Cold War world in such a potent and menacing way. Moreover, while each of the key rogue states of this era arose independently, never before had a *group* of states exhibiting such similar qualities—rather than individual examples—arisen to such a prominent place in US policymakers' hierarchy of security threats.

The second factor that differentiated the rogue state threat of the 1980s and early 1990s from what came before was the international context in which it arose. Rogue states were a product of the singular moment of historical transition to the new era that replaced the Cold War world, establishing their international standing in defiance of the global order that was in the process of being built.

The Cold War international system constricted each superpower's freedom of action by pitting two rival blocs of nations against one another: one committed to democratic capitalism and the other to Soviet communism. The vast nuclear arsenals of each side, threatening "mutual assured destruction" (MAD) against any potential aggressor, created the "balance of terror" underpinning the stability of this bipolar order. Though this MAD-based deterrence maintained an uneasy peace in Europe, it did not always stem the tide of conflict elsewhere in the world, including with the direct involvement of US or Soviet forces, as in Korea, Vietnam, and Afghanistan. However, the threat of direct confrontation between the superpowers kept either from exerting a free hand in addressing international dangers as it saw fit. Most visibly, the United States and the Soviet Union had veto powers over each other's ability to secure the backing of the United Nations Security Council for concerted international action. In practice, both sides were wary of becoming too deeply involved in regional conflicts that could escalate into wider US-Soviet wars. Moreover, the alignment of most of the world into two rival blocs helped to restrict the freedom of action of would-be regional troublemakers, whose need to look to one or the other superpower for support, supplies, or protection gave the United States and the Soviet Union a measure of influence in constraining their excesses.

The lessening of US-Soviet tensions from 1985 to 1991 and the disintegration of the Cold War international order that divided the world into two rival camps dramatically reduced the danger of a cataclysmic nuclear war but also opened the lid on a host of emerging security threats, from state-sponsored terrorism to the aggressive designs of regional dictators against their weaker neighbors. Without the constraints of the Cold War order, these emerging threats began to bubble over into more significant problems with consequences that reached beyond the immediate neighborhood in which they occurred. Meanwhile, though the winding down of the Cold War decreased the chances of nuclear catastrophe, the lessening of one threat made others seem proportionately larger than they had before: as the mountains of Soviet communism crumbled, the foothills of rogue states, terrorism, and WMD loomed larger in the eyes of US policymakers.

Just when these emerging threats to international security were growing—in both fact and US perception—the dissipation of Soviet power and eventual disintegration of the Soviet empire and the Soviet Union itself left the United States as the sole remaining superpower, wielding an unprecedented level of international power, prestige, and freedom of action to address threats and challenges as it deemed necessary. This freedom of action was far from absolute, but the "unipolar moment" that replaced the bipolar Cold War order offered the United States a unique opportunity to refashion its international role within the global system of the dawning era. This "unipolar" context would play a vital role in the creation of the rogue state framework for US strategy in the post–Cold War world. However, the idea of "rogue states" was not purely a US invention, but rather the reflection of a real and unique kind of threat to the security of the new world order that was rising out of the Cold War's ashes. Nevertheless, it was the choices that US decision-makers and their key allies made—often reluctantly and incrementally—that reoriented the focus of US national security strategy toward rogue states after the Cold War, elevating the threat to a place of central prominence in the era to come.

This is a story of perception and understanding—a study of not just how the world was changing at the end of the Cold War but also how policymakers in Washington and allied capitals in Europe *understood* and *interpreted* those changes, and how they sought to deploy US influence and power to counter what they felt posed the gravest threats to the new world order they were trying to build. Critically, this book does not seek to probe the theoretical depths of how the term "rogue states" should be defined and employed in the abstract. Rather, it examines how this concept actually was defined and employed by those forming the international strategies to combat it in the 1980s and early 1990s. This study is therefore primarily concerned with how US policymakers in the Reagan and Bush administrations and their allies understood and defined these emerging threats, and how their understanding changed over time.[8]

Inevitably, and contrary to the preferences of scholars who seek to impose order on the chaotic reality of the past, policymakers and strategists' understanding of the rogue state phenomenon during the final years of the Cold War was full of contradictions and inconsistencies. Not all of the regimes that would later become the most prominent and lasting rogue states were viewed as such during this period when the concept was first taking shape and becoming fixed in the minds of Reagan, Bush, and their teams of advisors. Some that played a critical role in establishing the idea of rogue states in the 1980s, such as Panama, would quickly fade from the scene, never to be considered rogues again by future administrations or scholars alike. Others, such as Iran and North Korea, that have since established positions for themselves as some of the most consistent and intractable rogue state foes of the West in the years after the Cold War played a surprisingly limited role in triggering and shaping the concept during its formative stage in the Reagan and Bush years.[9]

Iran, in particular, deserves closer scrutiny for its place in the story of the emergence of the rogue state paradigm in the Cold War's final decade—both for its prominence as a significant nemesis of the US government from the Iranian

Revolution of 1979 throughout the 1980s and for its centrality as a rogue state today. Indeed, Iran certainly qualified as a rogue regime in the 1980s, sponsoring terrorist attacks and exhibiting an aggressive and destabilizing influence in the Persian Gulf region, most notably during its titanic war with Iraq that raged throughout nearly the entire decade.

However, important differences between the Iranian regime and the other emerging rogue states generally kept it in a separate category in the thinking of US policymakers during the period in question. Iran's radical Islamist regime was of a fundamentally different character from the other rogue regimes that were rising to prominence in the 1980s. The threat that Iran posed to the region was based on its radical Islamist ideology, and US policymakers in the Carter and Reagan administrations viewed it as a significant threat in its own right from 1979 onward. By contrast, the rogue regimes in Libya, Panama, and Iraq did not share a common worldview or ideology, and the threat they posed was more tied to the erratic ambitions of individual dictators who sought to undermine the US-led global order coming into shape at the end of the Cold War. These other rogues were not ideologically opposed to the United States throughout the 1980s as was Iran, and US policymakers increasingly spoke of them as part of a single growing phenomenon as the decade progressed. They typically discussed Iran, by contrast, as a separate—and even opposing—regional problem, one that was certainly related to rogue states but not necessarily integral to their rise to a central place in threatening post–Cold War security. Indeed, just as the US perception of the threat posed by rogues such as Libya, Panama, and Iraq was growing in the mid and late 1980s, Iran's power and threat appeared to be waning and contained with the conclusion of the Iran-Iraq War. Secretary of State George Shultz concluded that by 1988 the need "to block Iran's threat was greatly diminished."[10] These other cases—Libya, Panama, and Iraq—are therefore more useful for understanding the strategic thinking of US policymakers toward rogue states at the end of the Cold War.[11]

Thus, it was not merely the features (terrorism, aggression, WMD, and narcotics trafficking) that made rogue states a unique threat but also, crucially, the context of the historical moment in which they took root. This book traces the birth of a paradigm to define international security after the Cold War, and the emergence of this rogue state paradigm occurred at a specific time; its history must therefore be grounded in a particular historical moment, the transition from the Cold War to the post–Cold War world. While in retrospect one might be able to find other earlier or later examples of rogue-like states, these cases did not play a role in the particular historical moment when the concept of "rogue states" was born in the minds of US policymakers and became the defining framework to guide US strategy. The cases that this book focuses on, unlike earlier or later pariah states, all played a critical role in *triggering* and *shaping* the idea of rogue states at the dawn of the post–Cold War world.

The recognition of the emerging threat and its component parts was a learning process for the Reagan and Bush administrations over the course of the 1980s and early 1990s. As their thinking evolved, President Reagan, Secretary of State Shultz, and President Bush played distinctive roles in crafting the strategies to confront the emerging threats to national security in the post–Cold War world. These three leaders grasped earlier than most of their contemporaries that the United States would have to construct new approaches to rogue states, terrorism, and WMD and would therefore need to reimagine national security to meet the dangers of the new era in world affairs. As Reagan, Bush, and their national security teams grappled with how to confront these emerging challenges, the strategies they fashioned—as well as their debates and disagreements over the merits of military intervention, negotiations, and regime change—laid the groundwork and set critical precedents for how the US government would handle similar crises from the aftermath of the Gulf War to the War on Terror after 9/11.

While most scholarship on the international history of the 1980s focuses on the summit meetings and negotiations between the US government and the Soviet Union, this book examines the 1980s as not the final decade of the Cold War world but rather the beginning of the post–Cold War world. It traces the rise of the threats that would come to define the 1990s and 2000s as US officials and their European allies first began to grapple with understanding a new framework on which to build Western foreign policy after the collapse of the bipolar Cold War order.

This book adds a new dimension to two emerging strands of scholarship on the Cold War and the advent of the post–Cold War world. The bulk of scholars of the Cold War and the Reagan presidency—like most policymakers at the time—have elevated the ideological and geopolitical rivalry between the Soviet Union and the United States, East and West, communism and democratic capitalism, to a place of dominance in understanding the era.[12] By contrast, a growing body of scholarship has revealed that many of the most critical international developments of the Cold War era actually lay outside the traditional US-Soviet standoff. These scholars have reframed the Cold War in global terms, illuminating processes such as decolonization and modernization that transformed the international landscape on a comparable or greater scale to the competition between East and West—and in regions far removed from the focal point of the Cold War in Central Europe. This scholarship on the "global Cold War" has emphasized that historians cannot properly understand the Cold War, especially by its final decade in the 1980s, in terms of a simple bipolar world order with the United States and its democratic allies on one side against the Soviet Union and its communist allies on the other—the "traditional Cold War framework" that defined the strategic thinking of many policymakers at the time.¹³

This book advances the historical push to reveal the transformations that were percolating underneath the surface of the Cold War's final years, away from the headlines of US-Soviet summits, tensions, and treaties. It exposes the origins of new types of threats to international security that were, as George H. W. Bush noted only after the fall of the Berlin Wall, "wholly unrelated to the earlier patterns of the U.S.-Soviet relationship."¹⁴ Even though the Reagan administration, particularly during its early years, viewed the Cold War through a bipolar, communism versus democracy framework, it increasingly—if reluctantly—had to adapt and evolve its conception of national security to meet the emerging challenges that lay outside the bounds of its understanding of the Cold War.

Indeed, the main historical actors at the heart of this story did not understand the Cold War in the same terms as the current generation of historians. The key figures in the Reagan administration, at least initially, saw the Cold War primarily as a bipolar struggle with Soviet communism. Their adherence to this framework and their early determination to view the world through a bipolar Cold War lens made them slow to recognize how the international order was evolving beneath their feet—and how new security challenges such as terrorism, WMD proliferation, and rogue states were emerging as first-order threats. The focus of this book is on the creation of a new paradigm for post–Cold War strategy, tracing how US policymakers and their allies understood the world and sought to figure out how to handle new threats during this period of enormous global change. But they did not hold the same perception of the Cold War as scholars do today, and for historians to impose upon them a "global Cold War" outlook would be to give them ideas that they did not have themselves.

While some works of history within the past decade reflect a greater openness to examining the impact of Ronald Reagan and his administration's international policies beyond the bounds of the Cold War, the scholarly consensus can still be summarized in the words of the historian Jussi Hanhimäki: "[Reagan's] grand strategy, much like that of other Cold War presidents, amounted to defining a foreign policy strategy towards the Soviet Union. The rest mattered to the extent that it related to that overarching concern." Reagan's strategy, therefore, "provided little useful guidance for future policymakers facing a dramatically altered international situation in the decades after the end of the Cold War."¹⁵ This book argues directly against this widely held view among scholars.¹⁶ While Reagan entered office determined to approach global issues primarily in terms of the Cold War struggle with Soviet communism, a distinctive series of crises over the course of the 1980s that did not fit neatly into the confines of the Cold War forced him to rethink his assumptions and devise new, more flexible strategies to address emerging threats to national security. Indeed, the impact and vision of Reagan, Bush, and key advisors such as George Shultz extended beyond the fall of communism to the shaping of the new global order that followed and the development of the strategies that would animate the US role in the world throughout the post–Cold War era.

This view aligns with a second strand of emergent scholarship that has begun to blur the bright line dividing the Cold War from the post–Cold War world. This line of historical research places greater emphasis on the transition between these two eras, noting continuities and efforts to build a new global order to replace the international norms and structures of the Cold War.[17] Likewise, this book departs from most previous scholarship in viewing the 1980s as more of a *beginning* than an ending, a period of *building* and not just dismantling. However, no other existing works of history, drawing on newly declassified records from archives in the United States and Europe, bring as broad of a scope in terms of both time and issues to specifically examine the reshaping of US national security strategy during this transformative era. This study of the origins of post–Cold War strategy brings together a wide spectrum of emerging security threats that contended for US strategic attention over the course of the entire final decade of the Cold War, with an eye toward understanding how US leaders reinvented their outlook toward international security to meet the uncertain challenges of a post–Cold War world.

Just as the nature of the threat of rogue states evolved over the course of a series of formative crises from 1981 to 1991, the strategies that the Reagan and Bush administrations constructed to combat it were the product of a process of learning and adapting, one that by its very nature required fits and starts, successes and failures, anticipation and reaction, vision and blindness. By the aftermath of the Gulf War, the strategies to address this new threat would come to replace anticommunism and containment of Soviet power as the defining framework for US foreign relations that would guide the United States' approach to global security for the coming decades.

1

BACK TO THE FUTURE
Challenging the Cold War Mindset
of the Early Reagan Years

Late in the afternoon of June 7, 1981, from his perch on his royal yacht in the Gulf of Aqaba, King Hussein of Jordan spotted eight US-made F-16 jets accompanied by six F-14 fighters racing by overhead. Heading eastward, their target was a French-built nuclear reactor known as Osirak, located at al-Tuwaitha, ten miles southwest of the Iraqi capital of Baghdad. Before the Iraqis could begin to fire their antiaircraft guns, two waves of jets descended on Osirak, reducing the reactor to ruins with what one French observer called "stupefying accuracy." Just as quickly, the planes were gone, disappearing with the setting sun into the western sky.[1]

This fire raining down from the skies over Baghdad was not, as a twenty-first-century observer might expect, part of the air campaign of Operation Desert Storm in the Gulf War or part of the later Iraq War—nor was it a US expedition at all. The day after the attack, Israeli prime minister Menachem Begin released a statement announcing that the raid on Osirak was an Israeli mission intended to keep nuclear weapons out of the hands of one of the most brutal dictators in the Middle East, Saddam Hussein, and thereby remove "a mortal danger to the people of Israel." The US government reacted with indifference and even condemnation to what it saw as a reckless and destabilizing act on the part of Israel that could "seriously add to the already tense situation in the area."[2]

Just ten months later, a military dictatorship launched an unprovoked invasion of a small, meagerly defended neighbor whose territory it claimed as its sovereign right. Faced with the universal enmity of the native inhabitants, the invaders imposed their control at the point of a gun. This brazen act of aggression was also completely unrelated to later US confrontations with Iraq, despite its similarities to the crisis sparked by Saddam Hussein's 1990 invasion of Kuwait that would give rise to the Gulf War. Rather, the military junta that governed Argentina had launched this invasion against the Falkland Islands in the South Atlantic, whose inhabitants had been part of the British Empire and Commonwealth since 1833. But where the United States would be willing to go to war to defend the principles of international law that were at stake in 1990–1991—in President George H. W. Bush's words, "This will not stand, this aggression against Kuwait"—it attempted to straddle the fence as an "honest broker" in response to the April 1982 crisis in the South Atlantic.[3]

Ronald Reagan entered the presidency in January 1981 with a determination to revive the resolve and capacity of the United States to wage and win the Cold War over Soviet communism. As the Reagan administration worked to form its international strategy during its early years in office, US officials and their European allies first began to grapple with understanding the emergence of new types of threats and challenges to global security that did not fit neatly into the Cold War framework on which Western foreign policy had been built since the aftermath of World War II. Crises such as the Osirak raid and the Falklands War complicated Reagan and his national security team's early desire to double down on the anticommunist focus of traditional US Cold War foreign policy. These key crises challenged the lens through which the Reagan administration initially viewed the world and its strategic priorities and mindset upon entering office—particularly its assumption that US foreign policy should be decided primarily in terms of the Cold War struggle, including in regions of the Third World more distant from the US-Soviet competition. The aggressive impulses and nuclear ambitions of regional rogue dictators had never previously stood out as central threats to US national security. The halting and uncertain US response to these emerging threats laid the contours for growing debates over what role the United States and its European allies should play in shaping and defending a new global order that would replace the Cold War world.

Doubling Down on the Cold War

From the moment his presidency began on January 20, 1981, Ronald Reagan saw the Cold War as the top priority of his administration's foreign policy—his central purpose and mission. During the 1980 campaign, one of Reagan's top advisors asked him, "Why are you doing this, Ron? Why do you want to be President?" He responded, "To end the Cold War."[4] Indeed, the US-Soviet rivalry stood central to Reagan's worldview. Since his days in Hollywood, Reagan had seen the Soviet

Union as "the focus of evil in the modern world," as he would later proclaim in his famous "Evil Empire" speech in 1983.[5] The world's most critical problems, he felt, all tied back to this source. With Soviet leaders' steadfast "determination that their goal must be the promotion of world revolution and a one-world Socialist or Communist state," the new president declared in his first press conference after taking office, they "reserve unto themselves the right to commit any crime, to lie, to cheat" in order to spread the tentacles of their noxious ideology to every corner of the globe.[6] The most crucial role of the United States on the world stage, Reagan believed, was to counter the spread of this global communist threat.

The experience of the previous four years, with President Jimmy Carter at the helm of US foreign policy, shaped the intellectual environment in which Reagan and his team of advisors developed their thinking, priorities, and the strategic approach they intended to take toward the world upon entering office. Carter became president in 1977 determined to set US foreign policy on a new course. He perceived that international affairs increasingly revolved around issues outside the US-Soviet superpower relationship and great power politics. He therefore set out to create the first "post–Cold War" agenda to pivot US foreign policy away from what he felt had been an excessive focus on the rivalry with the Soviet Union and reorient it toward an emerging set of global issues, particularly economic and energy interdependence and relations with the developing world. Unfortunately for Carter's ambitions, the Cold War was not yet over, and by 1980 the contradictions in his policies brought his international strategy crashing down. He sought to transcend the Cold War but instead became a prisoner of it.[7]

The tumultuous year of 1979 exposed the Carter administration's approach to the world to a host of crises that derailed its early aspirations to establish a post–Cold War American foreign policy. One of the most severe of these crises, which became a turning point for the direction of Carter's foreign policy, came in the closing days of 1979, when the Soviet Union launched an invasion of Afghanistan. Evidence from Soviet archives has since confirmed the reactive and defensive motives behind the move, based on a growing Soviet sense of threat over the security of the buffer states along its borders. To US analysts in the Carter administration, however, the military incursion appeared to reveal the first step of a potentially far-reaching strategic move to seize the resource- and oil-rich Persian Gulf.[8]

With the dawn of the new year of 1980, Carter jettisoned his earlier desire to move away from framing US foreign policy primarily in terms of the Cold War rivalry. He felt that the Soviet Union's "deliberate aggression" in Afghanistan "calls into question détente and the way we have been doing business with the Soviets for the past decade."[9] The crisis pushed Carter to swing toward a hawkish stance that reescalated Cold War tensions and revived the anticommunist containment policies of past administrations going back to Harry Truman. Carter's attempt to shape a "post–Cold War" foreign policy for the United States based around issues outside the realm of the US-Soviet standoff had foundered in significant measure because the Cold War was still very much ongoing.[10]

Upon assuming office in January 1981, Reagan wasted little time in implementing his vision of a robust US foreign policy in the form of a return to the traditional focus on the clear-eyed anticommunism of the early Cold War years. While Carter may have initiated the pivot toward a reinvigorated Cold War a year earlier after the Soviet invasion of Afghanistan, Reagan sought to greatly expand on his predecessor's initiatives and infuse them with the moral certainties that he felt defined the US cause. Surveying the international scene in the first days of his presidency, Reagan saw a situation that justified his intention to double down on a foreign policy based primarily around anticommunist measures that would challenge Soviet advances—in Europe, Afghanistan and the Persian Gulf, and Central America. He intended to use every available instrument of foreign policy to pressure the Soviet Union and eventually reduce Cold War tensions on US terms.[11] The importance Reagan invested in his plans to reshape the Cold War struggle against Soviet communism, along with his views of that ideology's pernicious global reach, fostered his expectation at the start of his presidency that challenges and conflicts that arose elsewhere in the world would be connected to the US-Soviet rivalry and should therefore be approached with Cold War priorities in mind.

Reagan would soon discover important exceptions to this rule, but most of the key members of his foreign policy team shared his initial Cold War–focused views. The new president assembled a national security team whose members had deep experience and wide-ranging views, but they shared his overarching goal of revamping US economic and military power for the purpose of waging the Cold War in a more robust and effective manner than had their predecessors.

The most important choice that Reagan made in assembling his team of foreign policy advisors was his selection of Alexander Haig as secretary of state. Haig's military career had been distinguished and brought him the rank of four-star general and the position of supreme allied commander of NATO from 1974 to 1979. Prior to this last assignment, Haig had also served as White House chief of staff during the Watergate crisis for President Richard Nixon, who in turn recommended him highly to Reagan. Nixon noted that Reagan's choice for secretary of state "must also share your general views with regard to the Soviet threat and foreign policy generally." Haig met this crucial requirement, Nixon asserted, and would "give pause to the Russians."[12] Nixon was correct on both counts. Haig who thought of himself as a product of the Cold War, had been shaped by the crises and conflicts that had marked the superpower confrontation. Upon accepting Reagan's offer to become the nation's top diplomat, Haig recollected, "I was certain that, in a broad way, the President-elect and I shared a certain view of the world." The two agreed that the Soviet Union lay at the heart of most of the world's critical problems, from Latin America to the Persian Gulf. Haig had advocated for several years prior to his appointment as secretary of state for the need to take a tougher stance that would "put the Soviet Union on notice," and he felt that "the weakness of the American will" under Carter and previous administrations had emboldened the Soviets to extend their influence across the globe. Haig believed firmly that "our primary adversary in Vietnam was the Soviet Union" and that the North Vietnamese and the Vietcong had been merely "Soviet surrogates." Similarly, he asserted that conflicts such as the one in Nicaragua were "not an isolated phenomenon but part of a global problem connected to the Soviet policy of supplying arms and tutors to guerrilla wars."[13]

President Reagan's choice for secretary of defense, Caspar Weinberger, shared both a warm friendship and a close ideological affinity with his boss. Weinberger agreed with Reagan wholeheartedly that the Soviet Union and the advance of communism represented the paramount threats facing the United States in the 1980s. As he later recounted, "For most of the 1980s, Soviet Communism constituted a very real—and indeed our greatest—threat, militarily and morally.... It seemed crystal clear to me that the USSR was bent on world domination, as evidenced by its writings, doctrines, and actions, particularly its acquisition of a huge military capability designed to achieve that domination." Weinberger's chief mission, which he set about with zeal, was to rebuild the country's military strength using an unprecedented boost in peacetime defense spending that the administration set out to secure from Congress. In keeping with Reagan and fellow conservative critics of détente, he sought to reverse what he viewed as "the general deterioration of our military during the Carter years" in order to close the "gap in strength between the Soviets' and our capabilities," which "had widened enormously." Weinberger's influence in the administration was rooted in his shared principles and priorities with the president, believing that the primary purpose of the military buildup was to deter Soviet aggression and roll back communist advances on the global chessboard.[14]

The other key members of the Reagan national security team likewise shared their chief's worldview that the Cold War competition with Soviet communism stood at the heart of international affairs, from developments in Europe to far-flung regional crises. As Reagan's chief foreign policy advisor during the 1980 campaign and then his first national security advisor in the White House, Richard Allen had a leading role in shaping the new administration's foreign policy goals and agenda during its first year in office. His ardent opposition to communism and hawkish views on US-Soviet relations reinforced Reagan's advocacy for

FIGURE 2. Reagan's first national security team: Surrounding President Reagan in the Cabinet Room of the White House in May 1981 are (L–R) Secretary of State Al Haig, speaking with National Security Advisor Richard Allen and Judge William Clark, who would replace Allen in that post in early 1982; and Secretary of Defense Caspar Weinberger, who shares a laugh with Reagan and White House chief of staff James Baker leaning overhead.

increased defense spending as part of a firm stance against Soviet communism.[15] After Allen's departure, William Clark assumed the role of national security advisor in the opening days of 1982, bringing with him even more fervently anti-communist views than his predecessor. Despite his lack of detailed knowledge of international affairs, Clark initiated the administration's first major studies to formulate a specific strategy to confront the Soviet Union. While his sharply ideological views brought him into conflict with members of Reagan's team who wanted to work toward arms control negotiations with the Soviet Union, Clark's close relationship with the president and strong support for his robust defense programs ensured him an influential role in framing a comprehensive anti-Soviet strategy that would guide the administration's overall approach to foreign policy.[16]

Finally, William Casey, a colorful corporate lawyer and businessman who had served in the Office of Strategic Services (OSS) during World War II, became the director of central intelligence (DCI). In the words of his future deputy, Robert Gates, "Bill Casey came to [the] CIA primarily to wage war against the Soviet

Union." In speeches throughout his tenure as DCI, Casey asserted the centrality of the Soviet threat: "The Soviet Union, of course, remains the principal threat to U.S. security and the primary concern of U.S. intelligence." Moreover, he was convinced that conflicts in the developing world were closely tied to the Cold War struggle and consequently approached them with Cold War concerns and priorities in mind. He argued that "the primary battlefield of this struggle is not on the missile test range or at the arms control negotiating table but in the countryside of the Third World."[17]

The staunchly anticommunist views of most key members of President Reagan's foreign policy team, emphasizing the need to robustly confront the Soviet and communist threat throughout the world, made the new administration's international priorities abundantly clear as it came into office: the Cold War would define America's approach to the world in the 1980s. Or so they expected.

"Bolt from the Blue": The Strike on Osirak, June 1981

Israel's raid that destroyed the Iraqi nuclear reactor known as Osirak on June 7, 1981, caught the Reagan administration completely by surprise. For the Americans as well as the Iraqis, the attack came as a "bolt from the blue," as scholars have since termed this type of precise preemptive attack.[18] Richard Allen, the president's national security advisor, later recalled that he received the news on the secure phone at his home in Arlington, Virginia, where he was spending that Sunday afternoon working through "my perpetually mounting paperwork." He immediately contacted President Reagan, who was boarding his Marine One helicopter at Camp David for the flight back to the White House. As the news sunk in, Reagan asked Allen why he thought the Israelis had launched the raid. After briefly considering Allen's response that the Israelis clearly did not want the reactor to become operational, Reagan responded simply, "Well, you know what? Boys will be boys!"[19]

Reagan's matter-of-fact response implied a certain acceptance and willingness to give this close US ally the benefit of the doubt, important intuitive factors that guided his approach to the crisis. But his reaction also revealed his lack of significant knowledge not only of plans for the raid itself but also of the reasons behind it. Indeed, in its first four and a half months in office, the issue of Israel's concerns over the Iraqi nuclear program had simply not found its way onto the desk of any senior members of the administration. The one possible exception was Secretary of State Al Haig, who had discussed the matter briefly with Prime Minister Begin during his trip to Israel that April, according to the principal history of the Osirak raid written by the journalist Shlomo Nakdimon, Begin's former media advisor.

Haig disputes this claim in his memoirs, stating unequivocally that "it was never discussed with the Reagan Administration" and emphasizing that he, too, was surprised when he received news of the raid at his home.[20]

The administration's official response to the raid was surprisingly negative, especially given the close relationship between the two countries and Reagan's particularly firm commitment to the US alliance with Israel. The day after the attack, the State Department released two official statements, both authored by Haig, which asserted that the US government "condemns the reported Israeli air strike on the Iraqi nuclear facility, the unprecedented character of which cannot but seriously add to the already tense situation in the area." Both statements emphasized that Israel had not consulted the United States or given it any prior knowledge of its plans. Moreover, Israel's use of US-made planes amounted to a "possible violation of the applicable agreement under which it was sold to Israel," which mandated the use of US equipment only for self-defense. The administration accordingly delayed a scheduled shipment of four F-16 aircraft to Israel.[21] Most significantly, the United States supported a resolution in the UN Security Council that condemned the raid, though it avoided calling for sanctions against Israel. The White House even permitted UN ambassador Jeane Kirkpatrick to consult her Iraqi counterpart while drafting the text of the resolution, despite the fact that the United States and Iraq had no formal diplomatic relations.[22]

Why did the Reagan administration react with such indifference and even opposition to such a dangerous, high-priority issue as nuclear proliferation in Iraq? The key players in fact saw different stakes and favored divergent priorities stemming from the Cold War lens through which they viewed the crisis.

In his numerous public statements after the attack and in his private deliberations beforehand, Israeli prime minister Menachem Begin left no doubt how he saw the stakes of this crisis. His reasoning for ordering the attack on Osirak was simple and reflected one of his most deeply held beliefs, as he explained in a letter to Reagan after the raid: "To prevent with all the means at our disposal another Holocaust."[23] Intelligence on Iraq's nascent nuclear program collected over the previous several years, combined with Saddam Hussein's blunt pronouncements that "the reactor is not intended against Iran but against the Zionist enemy," convinced Begin that the Iraqi regime intended to make nuclear weapons that it would not hesitate to use against Israel. Convening his cabinet ministers to inform them that the airstrike against Osirak was underway, Begin concluded that "Iraq's manufacture of atomic bombs constitutes an existential threat to the state of Israel." Indeed, his determination not to allow Israel's enemies to arm themselves with weapons of mass destruction (WMD)—articulated using this phrase in the Israeli government's official statement taking responsibility for the raid—became known thereafter as the "Begin Doctrine."[24]

The Americans, across the board, did not agree with Begin that the issue rose to such existential stakes, and a surprising level of hostility toward the Israeli raid emerged within the Reagan administration in the days immediately following. Haig recalled that the reaction inside the administration "combined astonishment with exasperation." When Reagan convened his top advisors for a long and animated meeting in the Oval Office the day after the attack, several different camps emerged. On one end lay the most sizable group who voiced their displeasure with Israel's action most stridently. Vice President George Bush urged the immediate publication of a sharp reprimand of Israel. Joining him were White House chief of staff James Baker and his deputy, Michael Deaver, along with Edwin Meese, the counselor to the president, and William Clark, who was then serving as Haig's deputy at the State Department. Leading this majority was Secretary of Defense Caspar Weinberger, "angry, but measured." This group "argued strongly for punitive actions against Israel, including taking back aircraft and delaying or canceling scheduled deliveries," recalled Allen.[25]

Urging a middle course of action were Haig, Allen, and Kirkpatrick (who was at the United Nations in New York and thus not personally at the meeting). Haig argued that "while some action must be taken to show American disapproval, our strategic interests would not be served by policies that humiliated and weakened Israel," as he recounted in his memoirs. On one hand, Haig had taken the lead in drafting the administration's public response, in which the raid was "condemned as an act that could not but worsen the tense and dangerous situation in the Middle East." He felt that "Israel's action had been shocking, and there would be consequences. Not only could the United States not condone the raid, it would have to take some action against Israel." Yet he also admitted to having mixed feelings, noting that Begin's suspicions of Iraq's intent to build nuclear weapons were "hardly unrealistic" and that the destruction of Osirak was therefore "understandable and might well be judged less severely by history than by the opinion of the day." His proposed course of action to balance these two strands—essentially the plan that the administration eventually adopted—was to issue firm verbal and written protests against the raid to head off any more severe drive to impose sanctions against Israel. Acceptance of sanctions against such a close ally, he argued, would be interpreted as an act of weakness on the part of the United States. Allen agreed with Haig's assessment, while Kirkpatrick, awaiting instructions at the United Nations, was personally sympathetic to the raid. DCI William Casey, meanwhile, remained neutral and "circumspect" during the Oval Office meeting, according to Allen's account.[26]

It is notable that none of the top members of the administration's national security team argued in favor of the Israeli action or suggested coming down definitively in Israel's camp to defend the airstrike and its objectives. This left

President Reagan himself, the final participant in the Oval Office meeting on June 8, isolated in his natural inclination to support both the Israeli military action and the reasoning behind it. Reagan stood at the opposite end of the spectrum from Weinberger and Bush—and even a significant distance from Haig—in favoring a less punitive approach toward Israel. But the president said little during the meeting, listening patiently without tipping his hand. Allen, perhaps sensing that Reagan's own views lay apart from those of his advisors, lingered behind after the meeting and commented on the wide range of viewpoints that had just been expressed. Confident in keeping his own counsel, Reagan simply smiled and turned to the papers on his desk.[27]

What were the key reasons behind the Reagan team's varying levels of opposition to the Osirak raid? Two of the more theoretical arguments—promoted most prominently at the United Nations, in Congress, and among the United States' European allies such as Britain, France, and Germany—asserted that the Israeli airstrike ran in violation of international law and that it would seriously impede the Middle East peace process.

The first of these arguments, that the raid violated international law, hinged on the question of whether the attack qualified as an act of legitimate self-defense. To Begin and his cabinet, not to mention the overwhelming majority of the Israeli people, this was the entire point: an unstable dictator who had a track record of launching wars against neighbors was actively seeking nuclear weapons while threatening their use against Israel—all while his country remained in a formal state of war with Israel.[28] To most of the international community, by contrast, Iraq was a signatory of the Nuclear Non-Proliferation Treaty (NPT) and its nuclear program was under the safeguard of inspections from the International Atomic Energy Agency (IAEA); an attack on its nominally peaceful nuclear program, therefore, amounted to a gross breach of Iraq's sovereignty.[29] The Reagan administration pointedly decided to keep its position on the legality of the Israeli attack ambiguous, preferring to distinguish between its "political" condemnation of the raid and the "legal" condemnation that would put Israel in violation of its agreement to use US-made equipment for only defensive purposes.[30] It is notable, though, that British prime minister Margaret Thatcher based her opposition to the raid on these grounds, declaring before Parliament that "armed attack in such circumstances cannot be justified. It represents a grave breach of international law." She maintained that national sovereignty was sacrosanct in international law and must not be breached unilaterally.[31]

While US officials noted the general dangers that the Osirak raid posed to the Middle East peace process, their concerns ran in two more specific directions, one immediate and tactical and the other long term and strategic. The tactical concern was that the raid would complicate the politics behind the administration's ongoing efforts to secure Congress's approval for the sale of aerial radar surveillance technology, known as the Airborne Warning and Control System (AWACS), to Saudi Arabia. Indeed, most accounts of the Osirak crisis in the memoirs of Reagan officials feature only as a brief interlude in chapters on the AWACS controversy.[32]

The broader concern, which lay at the heart of the Reagan team's opposition to the Israeli military action, connected to the administration's strategic goal of transforming the Middle East into a unified bulwark against Soviet expansion into the region. The Soviet invasion of Afghanistan had increased the wariness of many of the moderate Arab nations such as Saudi Arabia toward the further spread of communist influence in the Middle East. Officials in the incoming Reagan administration saw an opportunity to forge what Haig called a "strategic consensus" in a region known more for its animosities and divisions. The US government would seek to deepen its partnerships and alliances with moderate Arab states to complement its already-close relationship with Israel, thereby drawing as many allies as possible into the common cause of stymieing any Soviet or communist encroachments into the region. The AWACS sale to Saudi Arabia was a critical component of furthering this strategic plan and solidifying cooperation with the Arabs.[33]

The Osirak raid threw a wrench into Washington's attempt to forge its broad-based anticommunist coalition in the Middle East by forcing the US government to choose sides between Israel and an Arab state. The crisis jeopardized the evenhanded approach that the Reagan administration had been working so hard to prove to the skeptical leaders of Arab states who knew the depth of Reagan's commitment to Israel.[34] Some US officials even hoped to foster a closer relationship with Iraq and had held talks with Tariq Aziz, Iraq's deputy prime minister, to explore this possibility less than two weeks prior to the raid. Taking a clear stand alongside Israel in this unexpected dispute would clearly rule out the possibility of deepening ties with a mutual enemy of Iran.[35]

Why did the Reagan administration appear to give so little consideration to the dangers of the Iraqi nuclear program, especially when nuclear nonproliferation remained a stated international priority for the US government? For one thing, the United States did not share the same sense of threat as Israel. The idea of a direct nuclear threat to the United States that was not under the control of a major global power such as the Soviet Union or of a rational national leader susceptible to deterrence was unprecedented in its nature to US policymakers. Iraq's nuclear program, even if weaponized, was therefore more of an academic or theoretical threat than an existential one to US leaders, who thus did not share the pressing sense of urgency that weighed on Begin.[36] Perhaps US officials, like the wider international community, also held greater confidence in the ability of IAEA inspections to keep Iraq's nuclear program in check and for civilian purposes only, though this consideration figured little into the administration's discussions on how to respond to the Osirak crisis. Rather, the overriding reason for the Reagan administration's reluctance to support Israel's bold attempt to keep Iraq from acquiring nuclear weapons was the inconvenient conflict between this goal and the higher priority of US Cold War strategic interests in the Middle East. As Reagan stressed during a meeting with five Arab ambassadors the week after the raid, "We must not allow the Soviet Union to pick-up all the pieces."[37] When forced to choose between a nuclear-free Iraq and a "strategic consensus" against Soviet influence, the Americans chose the latter.

As an important wrinkle in this overall picture of US priorities during the Osirak crisis stood President Reagan himself. Reagan's diaries and public and private comments during the episode revealed a more intuitive reaction on the part of the president, less guided by calculated strategic considerations than the views of his advisors. Reagan's response to the crisis underscored both the weaknesses and the strengths of his policymaking leadership. On one hand, the president was caught unprepared to weigh the detailed implications of the conflict for his administration's Cold War goals in the Middle East and its nuclear nonproliferation goals.[38] On the other hand, however, his sense of empathy for Israel's vulnerability and his revulsion toward nuclear weapons allowed him to see beyond the muddle of diplomatic posturing in ways that advisors such as Haig and Weinberger—so concerned with preserving the regional "strategic consensus" against the Soviets—could not.

Reagan emphasized throughout the crisis, publicly and privately, to Arab as well as Israeli ambassadors, that his natural support for Israel remained undiminished and unabated. When faced with his advisors' demands that the United States take more punitive measures against Israel, Reagan wrote unequivocally in his diary that "we are not turning on Israel—that would be an invitation for the Arabs to attack." Nor would he allow any punitive measures from Congress, asserting that if Congress were to find Israel's actions in violation of the law barring the use of US-made equipment for offensive purposes, "frankly . . . I'll grant a Presidential waiver." More significantly, from the moment he heard the news of the raid, he shared Begin's fears of a nuclear holocaust and of Saddam Hussein as a dangerous rogue dictator. "I swear I believe Armageddon is near," he noted in his diary upon first receiving news of the airstrike. His views of Saddam and his treacherous intentions were similarly clear: "The truth is the Arab indignation on behalf of Iraq is a waste. Saddam Hussein is a 'no good nut' and I think he was trying to build a nuclear weapon." As he later summarized his views in his memoirs, "I sympathized with Begin's motivations and privately believed we should give him the benefit of the doubt. I had no doubt that the Iraqis were trying to develop a nuclear weapon." Indeed, Reagan came closest among all the senior members of the US government to sharing Begin's view of the stakes involved in the airstrike.[39]

However, these intuitive views were tempered by Reagan's isolation among all of his chief advisors, from the full-throated condemnation of the raid by Bush and Weinberger to Haig's more moderated opposition. Reagan made clear in both his diary and his press conference following the military action that the main reason for his opposition to the raid was the style in which it was launched, not the substance of the issues at stake: he objected to Israel's lack of consultation with its closest ally, concerned that Israel did not enlist diplomatic assistance from the United States or exhaust its diplomatic options prior to using force. As he told reporters, he "thought that there were other options that might have been considered—that we would have welcomed an opportunity, for example, to try and intervene with the French who were furnishing the nuclear fuel."[40]

It quickly became apparent, however, that this line of objection turned out not to be true at all, a fact that further softened Reagan's views toward the Israeli action once he became aware of the full picture. In fact, Begin *had* enlisted US aid in seeking diplomatic means for removing the Iraqi nuclear threat, consulting repeatedly with the Carter administration through 1980. The Carter administration had made overtures to the French and Italian governments, which were providing the materials for and overseeing the construction and technical training of Iraq's nuclear facilities, to cease their assistance, but these efforts were rebuffed. Moreover, US intelligence reports in 1980 concurred with Israel's assessment of the likelihood of Saddam's intention to build a nuclear bomb.[41]

However, all knowledge and awareness of this sensitive topic of cooperation had fallen through the cracks during the transition from the Carter to the Reagan administrations. In the midst of the other ongoing crises at the end of 1980, the Carter administration had not briefed any senior members of the incoming administration on the topic, creating what the US ambassador to Israel, Samuel Lewis, called "a gap in our institutional memory" of the matter.[42] Begin gave the go-ahead orders for the operation only once the diplomatic options had failed definitively, which Haig confirmed during his April 1981 trip to Israel—though he apparently did not appreciate the significance of his remarks.[43] The Israelis, for their part, were startled in listening to Reagan's press conference remarks to find that he clearly knew nothing of the long-running background to the US-Israeli diplomatic efforts to avert the need for military action. Reagan discovered this history of consultations and diplomacy later in the afternoon of June 16, following his press conference. Once this information became clear, the president essentially dropped his personal opposition and condemnation of the raid while seeing through his administration's current middle-ground course to as quiet and uneventful of a conclusion as possible. Once the international political firestorm subsided and the AWACS deal was completed with Saudi Arabia, the administration quietly lifted its suspension on the delivery of the F-16 aircraft to Israel.[44]

Nevertheless, Reagan never came out publicly in support of the Osirak mission. He even permitted Kirkpatrick to cast the US vote in support of UN Security Council Resolution 487, which "strongly condemns the military attack by Israel in clear violation of the Charter of the United Nations," on June 19.[45] Though the United States shared Israel's assessment of the Iraqi nuclear threat, the urgency and significance of the situation never seemed to sink in for the president and his team.

Why? Cold War priorities trumped all else. The episode had not changed the administration's policy that it was "absolutely essential that we maintain credibility with the more moderate Arab states," which would allow the United States "to promote a consensus of strategic concern on the threat posed by the Soviet Union and its surrogates."[46] The brief and decisive crisis nature of the event led all the US principals to form their views and reactions mainly on the basis of their *preexisting mindset* of the necessity to prevent the spread of Soviet influence in the Middle East. The administration had not had time to undertake significant strategic analysis of the wider options or implications of the issue before the raid occurred. By the time the raid was over, Iraq's nuclear program lay in ruins. The issue appeared to be resolved.

"The Robber Cannot Be Allowed to Get Away with His Swag": The Falklands War, April–June 1982

Less than a year later, the United States faced another, far more serious crisis that once again forced it to unwillingly choose sides between a traditional ally and a regional Cold War partner important to the administration's plans to confront communism in all corners of the globe. And once again, this crisis involved issues and threats that would become central to the post–Cold War world but that US officials dismissed at the time as second-tier distractions from more important Cold War priorities.

The crisis erupted when the military government, or junta, of Argentina launched an invasion of the sparsely populated and defended Falkland Islands on April 2, 1982. The Falklands lay about three hundred miles off the eastern coast of Argentina in the South Atlantic Ocean, approximately eight thousand miles from the United Kingdom, which had controlled the islands continuously since

1833. The archipelago had a complicated history with a labyrinth of competing claims to its proper sovereignty stemming from the exploits of European colonial powers since the 1700s. While Argentinians held as sacred to their national pride that the islands belonged to their country, the fact remained that the inhabitants of the Falklands were nearly all descended from British settlers and passionately wished to remain part of greater Britain. When over a decade of negotiations between the British and Argentine governments failed to produce a transfer of the islands' sovereignty, and with its political position imperiled at home, the Argentine junta chose to seize the Falklands by force, quickly overwhelming the few Royal Marines defending the capital, Port Stanley.[47]

Thus, depending on one's perspective, the Falklands crisis mixed antiquated colonialism with a brazen act of aggression and breach of international law, a combination that muddied the waters of the stakes involved. Unlike the later seizure of oil-rich Kuwait by Saddam Hussein's Iraq in 1990, the controversial nature of the competing claims in this case was not offset by any overriding strategic value of the territory in question, which was known primarily for its sheep farming. Nevertheless, the Falklands crisis revealed an early case of the behavior of a rogue state, with Argentina acting as a regional aggressor flouting international norms—and even seeking to clandestinely develop a nuclear weapons capability.[48]

As was the case following the bombing of Osirak, the United States reacted to the invasion of the Falkland Islands with indifference and hesitation to what officials in the Reagan administration viewed as a nuisance rather than a critical threat to Western security.[49] The contradictory nature of the response of the United States makes it difficult in retrospect to untangle the true thrust of US policy and aims over the duration of the conflict—precisely because these aims and policy papered over contradictory goals. Ultimately, US policy during the crisis and the viewpoints of virtually all of the key figures in the US administration were driven more by Cold War concerns than by a principled stand against aggression or a determination to enforce global norms and standards of international behavior.[50]

This stood in stark contrast to the central figure on the British side of the Falklands War: Prime Minister Margaret Thatcher. Thatcher recognized immediately the gravity of the stakes involved in Argentina's land-grab. Not only were Britain's honor and its prestige and standing as a major global power put in jeopardy, with British territory invaded and Thatcher's government in danger of falling, but Thatcher also knew instinctively that the more abstract but far more important issues at stake were the principles that the Argentine invasion endangered: that armed aggression must not pay and that self-determination should be paramount in deciding the government under which a democratic people would live.[51] As she stirringly declared to the House of Commons on April 14:

> The eyes of the world are now focused on the Falkland Islands. Others are watching anxiously to see whether brute force or the rule of law will triumph. Wherever naked aggression occurs it must be overcome. The cost now, however high, must be set against the cost we would one day have to pay if this principle went by default. That is why, through diplomatic, economic and, if necessary, through military means, we shall persevere until freedom and democracy are restored to the people of the Falkland Islands.[52]

Thatcher decided immediately that a naval task force should sail for the South Atlantic to reclaim the Falkland Islands. In this determination she found support from Admiral Sir Henry Leach, the First Sea Lord, who insisted that not only could the islands be retaken, but they must: "If we don't do it, if we pussyfoot . . . we'll be living in a totally different country whose word will count for little."[53] Thatcher laid out the stakes herself with words reminiscent of Winston Churchill's wartime addresses when she announced to the House of Commons her decision to send the task force:

> The people of the Falkland Islands, like the people of the United Kingdom, are an island race. . . . They are few in number, but they have the right to live in peace, to choose their own way of life and to determine their own allegiance. Their way of life is British; their allegiance is to the Crown. It is the wish of the British people and the duty of Her Majesty's Government to do everything that we can to uphold that right.[54]

She repeatedly reminded her US allies in the months to come that "the issue was far wider than a dispute between the United Kingdom and Argentina" because the "use of force to seize disputed territory set a dangerous precedent" that "mattered to many countries," including the communist-encircled city of West Berlin that lay at the heart of the Cold War standoff in Europe.[55]

At the very least, the armada heading south would provide a stiff backbone to the coercive diplomacy that Thatcher hoped would convince the Argentines to abandon the Falklands peacefully. But she was determined to fight for them if diplomacy proved unsuccessful. In both efforts, the prime minister knew she would need the United States on board for active support.

In this she would meet a continually perplexing mix of disappointment and satisfaction over the course of the two and a half months to come. Indeed, the response and policy of the US government toward the Falklands crisis was riddled with contradictions from the start. This stemmed from the two distinct elements that divided US policy—one that played out in public view and the other in private, each with different goals and based on quite different viewpoints toward the unfolding crisis. The public side of the approach of the United States was diplomatic, with Secretary of State Haig as the central public face of US involvement in the conflict and UN ambassador Kirkpatrick playing a prominent role as well. The private side of US policy, so quietly implemented that even many top leaders such as Thatcher herself were not completely aware of its full extent, was on the military front, with Secretary of Defense Weinberger leading the charge to supply British forces sufficiently to ensure their victory. President Reagan's role in both of these strands of US policy remains opaque but was in fact critical in framing his administration's nuanced and somewhat idiosyncratic approach to the crisis.

The administration's first critical decision point came immediately following the Argentine invasion, when Thatcher appealed to Reagan for his government's support in Britain's efforts to reclaim the Falklands. This request from the United States' closest ally was not as straightforward as it might have appeared at first glance, since Argentina had become a key player itself in the Reagan team's strategic efforts to curb communist influence in Latin America. Indeed, the Reagan administration had reversed President Carter's policy of distancing the United States from the Argentine junta due to its abuses of human rights. Adopting the distinctions between anticommunist "authoritarian" regimes and communist "totalitarian" regimes that Kirkpatrick had proposed as a leading academic on Latin America in her influential 1979 article "Dictatorships and Double Standards," the new administration sought to improve relations with potential allies in the fight against communist expansion in the region. Argentina emerged as a key partner in combating Soviet and communist subversion in what Reagan and his top advisors viewed as one of the most critical of Cold War battlegrounds: Central and South America. The administration courted Argentine president Leopoldo Galtieri and his predecessor in a series of high-level meetings in Washington, DC, from the time Reagan took office in 1981. Galtieri's regime had since agreed to contribute arms and personnel to the cause of the anticommunist rebels in Nicaragua and El Salvador, two of the highest-priority bastions of communism in the Western Hemisphere that Reagan hoped to roll back. Reversing this improvement of relations with Argentina—and jeopardizing relations with the whole of Latin America—by wholeheartedly backing Britain in the Falklands dispute would undermine the Reagan administration's entire Cold War strategy in the Western Hemisphere, risking any gains it had made in the region since Reagan entered office.[56]

During this early phase of the crisis, Haig emerged as the dominant orchestrator of the administration's policy. More than any other senior administration official, he sought to balance the web of competing US interests in the conflict by urging the government to take on the role of an "honest broker" to mediate a negotiated and peaceful resolution to the dispute in the South Atlantic. "While my sympathy was with the British," he later explained, "I believed that the most practical expression of that sympathy would be impartial United States mediation in the dispute. The honest broker must, above all, be neutral." He recounted in his memoirs the myriad of critical US interests caught up in the unfolding dispute, which included "the credibility of the already strained Western alliance, the survival or failure of a British government that was a staunch friend to the United States, the future of American policy and relations in the Western Hemisphere as well as in Europe, the possibility of yet another dangerous strategic incursion by the Soviet Union into South America, and most important of all, an unambiguous test of America's belief in the rule of law."[57]

Haig's approach favored straddling the fence to the greatest extent possible, thereby limiting the damage to either the US alliance with Britain or the newly formed anticommunist partnerships in Latin America. While he felt from the start that the United States would have to support Britain as a last resort, Haig sought to *avoid conflict* above all else—a constant theme in his communications throughout April and May. Conflict between these two allies of the United States, in Haig's view, would be the worst possible outcome of the crisis, as it would force the United States to choose sides and thus bring its Cold War interests in Europe and Latin America into conflict. Haig did understand and appreciate the principles involved in the crisis, of which Thatcher repeatedly reminded him in their frequent meetings during the month of April. But they never drove his response the way they did Thatcher's, in large part because he felt that US interests pulled elsewhere—especially when the Falkland Islands were such strategically inconsequential territory.[58]

Haig's messages to Reagan reveal these tensions in his views, asserting first that Thatcher's determination that aggression must not pay was critical for the United States as well as Britain: "It is virtually as important to us that she have that success, for the principle at stake is central to your vision of international order, in addition to being in our strategic interests." But then he added, "The consequences of hostilities would be devastating. Our interests through Latin America would be damaged, and the Soviets might even establish a foothold in the southern cone." Thus, Thatcher must succeed, but not through hostilities.[59]

Haig took the helm of the administration's mediation efforts, engaging in high-profile "shuttle diplomacy" between London and Buenos Aires throughout the month of April in an unsuccessful attempt to wrangle a mutually acceptable compromise that could avert war. Haig's diplomacy had double-edged effects on the British position during this crucial month when the task force was steaming south and before hostilities had broken out. On one hand, Haig's proposals and negotiations filled a diplomatic gap that the British government could not afford to ignore. Had Thatcher's government shunned diplomacy, it would have appeared intransigent and set on the use of armed force, for which it had so vociferously condemned Argentina. Haig provided the venue for the diplomatic side of Britain's coercive diplomacy, complementing the formidable task force and exposing the Argentine junta's intransigence against any meaningful compromise. Moreover, Haig's mission, coming from the perspective of a close ally, headed off any mediation efforts from other quarters that might have proved less friendly toward British interests. On the other hand, however, Haig used his closeness and leverage with the British to put firmer pressure on them than on Argentina, taking advantage of the greater reasonableness of a democratic government to craft a deal that he admitted was more advantageous to the Argentines—and which compromised key principles such as self-determination.[60]

Kirkpatrick, on the front lines of international opinion at the United Nations, went further than Haig in arguing for the importance of not favoring Britain in the crisis. She expressed more sympathy than most in the Reagan administration for the Argentine claims of sovereignty over the Falklands, and she was much less concerned with the abstract principles of opposing armed aggression and defending self-determination. As she explained at the time, "Armed aggression would take place in a clear-cut way against territory on which there was clear-cut ownership. If the Argentines own the Islands then moving troops into them is not armed aggression."[61] In her view, Latin America was the key battleground for the Cold War in the early 1980s—"the most important place in the world for us"—and should therefore take higher priority than placating the British desire to maintain control over outdated overseas territories. The United States should not undermine its promising anticommunist strategy and gains in Latin America, which were just beginning to bear fruit, for what she saw as a counterproductive cause.[62]

Caspar Weinberger could not have held a more starkly opposed view from his vantage at the Pentagon. In contrast to Haig's attempt to find an uneasy balance of each strategic consideration in framing the US response to the crisis, Weinberger saw it as a clear-cut and straightforward problem: "It would be unthinkable for the United States to remain neutral when our oldest friend had been attacked in such a fashion. We could not condone, by silence or inaction, naked aggression anywhere, certainly not in our own hemisphere and not by a corrupt military dictatorship against one of our NATO allies."[63]

Contributing to his steadfast determination to support Britain was a mix of Cold War concerns and principles of international conduct. It was clear to him that Britain represented the most important ally of the United States in waging the Cold War, and Margaret Thatcher's government—not least the personal leadership of the woman whom the Soviets had dubbed "the Iron Lady" for her staunch anticommunism—stood as a particularly irreplaceable friend in

Europe, which he saw as the unquestionable epicenter of the Cold War struggle. If Thatcher and her Conservative Party fell from power, the West's entire strategy for confronting the Soviets with a new deployment of nuclear missiles in Western Europe would be upended. Compared to this, Weinberger reasoned, any setbacks in South America were marginal. Yet Weinberger also immediately grasped the international principles at stake, to an extent that put his views closer to Thatcher's than any other senior US official, including Reagan himself. As he later explained, "The British success in the Falkland Islands told the world that aggression would not be allowed to succeed; that freedom and the rule of law had strong and effective defenders."[64]

Weinberger assumed the role of quiet facilitator of military assistance to Britain, streamlining and expediting British requests for supplies, intelligence, and facilities that would only increase as the crisis, and eventually the war, unfolded. Weinberger kept his part in the drama behind the scenes, avoiding the public limelight that Haig's shuttle diplomacy captured. The secretary of defense capitalized on the unique level of routine cooperation that already existed between the military and intelligence services of the United States and Britain, a key feature of the Anglo-American "special relationship" that had flourished since the Second World War. This longstanding collaborative partnership of the two countries allowed Weinberger to dial up the volume of aid without attracting excessive levels of public attention—and thus without technically contradicting Haig's assertions of US neutrality in the dispute. While Reagan did not personally approve each specific request, he did give his broad authorization to Weinberger's actions, which the secretary of defense likely interpreted somewhat liberally in turn. Yet each time he needed fresh presidential authorization he received it without delay. As one member of the administration put it, "Cap proposed, the President approved."[65]

President Reagan's views of and role in the Falklands crisis were rather ambiguous and challenging to untangle. He said little in the meetings of his national security team where the Falklands were discussed, and his diary entries on the crisis revealed little about his assessment of the stakes involved in the dispute or the merits and perils of backing each side. However, it would be a mistake to assume that the president was disengaged from the issue or was uninterested in its outcome. Indeed, Reagan made a point to ask for updates on the Falklands conflict during each morning's national security briefing. It was Reagan's preference to listen to a wide range of views from his advisors, often keeping his own to himself, before reaching a final decision, as he did in the Oval Office meeting following the Osirak raid. Reagan trusted Haig and Weinberger to oversee the specifics of the implementation of his administration's diplomatic and military policies during the crisis, relying on their assessments of the situation on the ground and allowing them the flexibility to adapt as needed. But there was no question that it was Reagan who set and approved the overall policy toward the Falklands crisis within which Haig and Weinberger operated.[66]

As during the Osirak crisis, Reagan's reaction to the Falklands conflict mixed a combination of intuitive and strategic views—a blend of Weinberger and Haig's viewpoints. Like Weinberger, there was no question in Reagan's mind but to support Britain and ensure the survival of Thatcher's government. Both Weinberger and Kirkpatrick, representing the polar opposite ends of opinion within the administration, agreed on one key point: in Kirkpatrick's words, "There wasn't any question about where President Reagan stood on this issue, from the start until the finish."[67] Reagan appreciated the principles that Thatcher sought to defend. As he noted to Thatcher even before the Argentines launched their invasion, "While we have a policy of neutrality on the sovereignty issue, we will not be neutral on the issue of Argentine use of military force."[68] He warned Galtieri before the invasion that "if armed force is involved we will not be able to side with you . . . you will be the guilty party."[69]

But Reagan could not bring himself to see the Falkland Islands—to which he dismissively referred in a press conference as "that little ice-cold bunch of land down there"—as a serious enough matter to warrant such a fuss or to risk broader strategic goals: Why should this inconsequential disagreement endanger Cold War alliances in either Europe or Latin America?[70] To Reagan, the Falklands were certainly not worth a war, so the United States should try its best to help the antagonists find a way out.[71] If this effort preserved the US Cold War strategy in South America, so much the better. After all, as Reagan explained in a press conference shortly after the Argentine invasion, "It's a very difficult situation for the United States, because we're friends with both of the countries engaged in this dispute."[72] Reagan also worried that armed conflict would give the Soviet Union opportunities to increase its influence in Latin American affairs, noting pointedly in a telephone conversation with Galtieri that "the only one who could profit from such a war would be the Soviet Union."[73] With this ranking of priorities in mind, the president lent his support to the initiatives of both Haig and Weinberger, genuinely backing policies that many saw as conflicting. As he would show again and again, Reagan was not troubled by wielding several prongs that seemed to point in opposing directions, displaying a flexibility that often resulted in a far more nuanced and effective policy than he received credit for.[74]

For Reagan and his chief advisors, despite their varying levels of appreciation for the international principles that Thatcher sought to defend, Cold War concerns stood paramount in influencing US policy toward the Falklands crisis. These concerns fell into three camps: first, the fate of the Reagan administration's anticommunist strategy in Latin America and its growing partnerships with countries such as Argentina; second, the potential that the Soviet Union would seize the opportunity of conflict in the South Atlantic to spread its influence in South America, perhaps through anti-US propaganda, military supplies, or even direct military aid; and third, the need to support Britain as a key NATO ally.[75]

Only a quick diplomatic solution that avoided armed conflict between Britain and Argentina would alleviate all of these concerns.[76] Yet even when Argentina rejected the final compromise plan that Haig's mediation produced, the Reagan administration persisted in its efforts to limit the damage that the conflict would cause to its Cold War interests. Following the failure of Haig's mission, Reagan and the National Security Council (NSC) decided on April 30 to publicly announce a policy "tilt" toward Britain—the second critical decision point during the crisis for the US government. Haig's statement to the press emphasized support for the principles undergirding the British position by noting that "we must take concrete steps to underscore that the United States cannot and will not condone the use of unlawful force to resolve disputes."[77]

This change of official policy, however, did not spur any significant change in views among Reagan's national security team. Haig continued to advocate for keeping the administration's options open—and continuing to straddle the fence—as much as possible. His fears that too much support for Britain would undermine US Cold War strategy in the Western Hemisphere remained unabated. In the NSC meeting before the announced change in policy, Haig expressed concern that the pro-US government in Argentina "may well be replaced by a left-wing, Peronist regime," and, therefore, "we need to be careful in how we raise our tilt." He added that he intended to include "a warning to the Argentines about Soviet intentions" in his public statement. In the subsequent weeks, Haig lent his public and private support to several additional peace initiatives, headed by Peru and the UN secretary-general, that followed the pattern of his earlier proposals and would have ceded significant ground to Argentina—reflecting essentially the same position he had held before the tilt. Weinberger, meanwhile, oversaw a significant acceleration of military aid to Britain that he had spearheaded quietly since the start of the crisis.[78]

For his part, Reagan continued to support Britain as his top priority, lending public and private backing to the international principles at stake, but he still sought ways to avoid war if possible, noting in his diary, "I don[']t think Margaret Thatcher should be asked to concede anymore." He went before the press on April 30 to explain his reasoning behind the tilt: "We must remember that the aggression was on the part of Argentina in this dispute over the sovereignty of that little ice-cold bunch of land down there, and they finally just resorted to armed aggression, and there was bloodshed. And I think the principle that all of us must abide by is, armed aggression of that kind must not be allowed to succeed." Yet he also reiterated that he was "still hopeful that before action takes place, that there still may be a diplomatic settlement."[79] One of the president's few comments during the April 30 NSC meeting that established the tilt toward Britain was to make the wry observation "that it would be nice if, after all these years, the U.N. could accomplish something as constructive as averting war between the U.K. and Argentina."[80]

The third key decision point for the Reagan administration came after the escalation of fighting at the start of May, when the Argentines and the British each lost ships to enemy attack and casualties began to mount. Reagan and his advisors put their weight behind a balanced resolution to the conflict, urging Thatcher at various points throughout May to rule out widening the war with direct attacks on the Argentine mainland and to accept a ceasefire short of total military victory. "That kind of victory," wrote a member of the NSC staff, "which will shatter the prestige of the Argentine armed forces . . . will come at great cost to us, the British, and the Western world over the long run."[81] Reagan asked in his diary on May 4, "Will they all now give peace a chance?" He repeated this sentiment throughout the month, revealing the genuineness and depth of his hopes to limit the bloodshed.[82]

In advancing this "balanced" position, US officials were attempting to protect as many interests of the United States as possible. The principles of reversing armed aggression and supporting self-determination factored as a genuine priority for the US government, but they counted for only one interest among several. The United States intended to support British victory in the war, but only to the minimum extent necessary to settle the dispute in a way that would keep Thatcher's government in power. Reagan and his team also hoped to keep the anticommunist government in Buenos Aires in power by forestalling the humiliation of a total military defeat for the junta, and they pressed Thatcher to continue negotiating with Argentina over the sovereignty of the Falklands even after the war was over.[83] Calling Thatcher on May 31, Reagan noted approvingly that "you've demonstrated to the whole world that unprovoked aggression does not pay." But then he pressed her to consider "an effort to show we're all still willing to seek a settlement . . . [that] would undercut the effort of . . . the leftists in South America who are actively seeking to exploit the crisis." Thatcher cut him off: "This is democracy and our island, and the very worst thing for democracy would be if we failed now." Reagan got the message, later writing in his memoirs that "she convinced me. I understood what she meant." Several days later, he refused to send Thatcher a message drafted by the State Department that called for a ceasefire short of complete military victory and curtailing the self-determination rights of the islanders.[84]

Principle won out in the end, but rather begrudgingly on the part of the US government. Margaret Thatcher's force of will and moral clarity carried the United

BACK TO THE FUTURE 35

FIGURE 3. A conflict of priorities: President Reagan visits Margaret Thatcher at the prime minister's residence in London, 10 Downing Street, near the end of the Falklands War, June 9, 1982. Haig stands on the threshold behind and between the two leaders.

States along and forced it to choose sides and order its international priorities in a way it was deeply reluctant to do. The Reagan administration offered its aid and support more hesitantly than Thatcher had desired, but this help was quite substantial all the same, particularly on the military front. Moreover, Thatcher pushed the United States, despite its misgivings, where it was already inclined to go. Speaking in the Palace of Westminster to a gathering of both houses of the British Parliament in the closing days of the Falklands War, Reagan embraced—more unequivocally than he ever had before—the principles that Thatcher had promoted so tirelessly throughout the conflict. In completely unambiguous terms, which the president wrote into the speech himself against the advice of the State Department, he praised the British cause:

> On distant islands in the South Atlantic young men are fighting for Britain. And, yes, voices have been raised protesting their sacrifice for lumps of rock and earth so far away. But those young men aren't fighting for mere real estate. They fight for a cause—for the belief that armed aggression must not be allowed to succeed, and the people must participate in the decisions of government . . . under the rule of law. If there had been firmer support for that principle some 45 years ago, perhaps our generation wouldn't have suffered the bloodletting of World War II.[85]

Margaret Thatcher, listening from the front row as Reagan delivered his remarks, could look with pleasure on her ally's adoption of her framing of the principles that lay at the heart of the Falklands crisis. Her own pithy summary of the stakes was less lofty but just as memorable, leaving no doubt of the lesson to be learned from the Falklands War: "We fought to show that aggression does not pay and that the robber cannot be allowed to get away with his swag."[86]

Setting Out a Strategy for the Nation's Security

While principle may have proved victorious in the US government by the end of the Falklands War, it did so within a wider Cold War context: President Reagan fit his tribute to the British cause into a speech devoted to laying out his views on confronting the global communist threat. As Richard Aldous notes, historians would later view his speech to the British Parliament as "perhaps the most complete statement of Reagan's foreign policy world-view that he ever gave."[87] He incorporated Britain's defense of international principle into his vision for the West's moral stand against Soviet aggression—"the march of freedom and democracy that will leave Marxism-Leninism on the ash-heap of history."[88] George Shultz, who took over as Reagan's secretary of state when Haig resigned shortly after the end of the Falklands War, likewise connected the ramifications of the Falklands War to the Cold War struggle, noting the jolt that Britain's stand against aggression gave to the international scene: it "was the first marker laid down by a democratic power in the post-Vietnam era to state unambiguously that a free world nation was willing to fight for a principle. The world paid attention to this—and not just the Third World either; it was noted by the Soviets too. Attitudes everywhere were significantly affected."[89]

The Soviets did indeed take note of the West's renewed sense of purpose and resolution on the world stage. Meanwhile, the United States continued to fret that "Moscow will try to use the Falklands conflict to stimulate hemispheric distrust of the United States and to expand its own influence in the region."[90] Indeed, despite Reagan and his advisors' deepened appreciation that the issues at the heart of the Falklands conflict spilled outside the bounds of the US-Soviet competition, they nevertheless persisted in doubling down on this binary framework in their creation of one of the most important strategy documents of the Reagan presidency, which the president signed only a few weeks before his Westminster address. This presidential statement of official US policy, National Security Decision Directive (NSDD) 32, codified the principles and goals that would guide the administration's overall approach to foreign policy.

While earlier NSDDs had addressed specific issues around the world, NSDD-32 was the first to lay out what Reagan's NSC staff called "an overall national strategy framework."[91] The document was appropriately crowned with the broad title "U.S. National Security Strategy" and brought together in one place the core tenets of the way Reagan and his chief advisors envisioned and intended to approach the world. William Clark, who began his new role as national security advisor in January 1982, took the reins of the NSC study that grew into NSDD-32. While Clark's own fervent anticommunist views certainly influenced the direction of the document, he and Reagan's other key advisors emphasized that the president was the true driving force behind the effort to lay out a central guiding strategy for the administration.[92] The directive was notable for its tight focus on countering the global threat posed by Soviet communism. This focus has led historians to view NSDD-32 primarily as a foundational document for the muscular approach that Reagan took toward the Soviets during his first term.[93] Yet its overwhelming emphasis on the Soviet threat also revealed much about the persistence of the Reagan administration's early mindset toward the world as a whole, and how deeply the president and his advisors believed disparate global issues to be tied to the Cold War struggle, even in the aftermath of the Osirak and Falklands crises.

There is no doubt about how high the Reagan national security team saw the stakes for their success on the world stage. The full report that gave rise to the more compact, eight-page NSDD-32, completed in April 1982, boldly asserted that "the decade of the eighties will pose the greatest challenge to the survival and well-being of the U.S. since World War II." There was also no doubt about the identity of the enemy: "The Soviet Union is and will remain for the foreseeable future the most formidable threat to the United States and to American interests globally."[94] The final NSDD was notable for the comprehensiveness of the strategy it set out, advocating the integration of "diplomatic, informational, economic/political, and military components" to accomplish a discreet set of "global objectives." Nearly half of these eleven objectives dealt explicitly with countering the Soviet Union, including five of the top six. Lower down the list was the need to "discourage" the proliferation of nuclear weapons, a concern that would rise to a level of greater urgency as the decade wore on.[95]

Among the top global objectives listed in NSDD-32 was the need to "contain and reverse the expansion of Soviet control and military presence throughout the world, and to increase the costs of Soviet support and use of proxy, terrorist, and subversive forces." This statement indicated the extent to which Reagan and his policymaking team continued to view Soviet influence as the backbone of the world's unrest—and therefore justification for addressing regional issues with Cold War priorities in mind. The directive emphasized the vulnerability of the developing world to Soviet exploitation, hence the greater likelihood of fighting "a war with a Soviet client arising from regional tensions" than a direct war with the Soviet Union itself.[96] The key Cold War battleground in the 1980s would therefore be the Third World, where "the USSR, in opportunistic fashion, exploits indigenous unrest in many regions to undermine U.S. influence."[97]

The study accompanying NSDD-32 revealed more specific fears of Soviet designs on particular regions of the developing world. In the Middle East, for example, "the most severe dangers" included increased Soviet influence or even "large-scale military intervention" in Iran and the toppling of friendly governments through insurrections "stimulated or exploited by the Soviets." Libya, Syria, and the Palestine Liberation Organization were labeled "surrogates for the USSR" that funneled Soviet-bloc arms into the region and fomented terrorism.[98]

By mid-1982, therefore, the Reagan administration had not yet incorporated the lessons it was beginning to learn that the key threats to global security were shifting in the direction of rogue actors operating outside the parameters of the Cold War. Complex regional problems, encompassing brazen armed aggression and attempts to acquire WMD, still did not find a place of their own—distinct from the US-Soviet confrontation—in the official strategic thinking of the top tier of the US government. Important as the Osirak and Falklands crises were to challenging its views, the Reagan administration's binary Cold War mindset was about to get a still greater shock as terrorism began to emerge as yet another new kind of global security threat in the middle of the decade.

Adapting to Emerging Threats

Ronald Reagan's determined focus in the early years of his presidency on reinvigorating the capacity of the United States to wage and win the Cold War was rooted in sound reasoning. His administration's stumbles and uncertainty in charting its response to the Osirak and Falklands crises should not necessarily be construed as proof of misplaced priorities in shaping the nation's foreign policy in the early 1980s. After all, the Cold War struggle against Soviet communism *was* the most pressing international concern for the incoming Reagan administration. Other important crises that lay at the very heart of the Cold War confrontation, such as the imposition of martial law in Poland in December 1981, erupted in between the Osirak raid in June 1981 and the Falklands War in the spring of 1982. Moreover, how Reagan infused a sense of moral purpose and confidence into the United States' role on the world stage—not to mention the investments he made in strengthening the nation's military defenses—would reap dividends in framing US global leadership in ways he could have hardly imagined when he entered office in 1981. Reagan could have scarcely predicted when he advocated for the modernization of the armed forces in 1981 and 1982 that, within a decade, these forces would be deployed with decisive result against terrorist bases in Libya and Iraqi invaders in Kuwait rather than against the Soviet Union.

While the Reagan administration's focus on the Cold War was not necessarily misplaced, the Osirak and Falklands crises did expose a lack of adaptability and flexibility in the mindset of many of the key members of the US national security team. In concentrating so single-mindedly on the threat of Soviet communism, Reagan and his chief advisors proved slow to recognize the urgency of new types of threats to international security that were only beginning to emerge on a global scale. While the US government was used to considering the need to counter the large-scale nuclear arsenals of major world powers such as the Soviet Union, US officials did not share Israeli prime minister Begin's sense of existential threat toward the nascent nuclear weapons program of an unpredictable and aggressive dictator such as Saddam Hussein. Meanwhile, the strategic insignificance of the remote Falkland Islands hardly seemed to warrant the abandonment of a promising new partnership with Argentina to roll back communist advances in South and Central America, however blatant the junta's breach of international law. In both cases, the Reagan administration was reluctant to adapt its anticommunist strategies to account for and meet the challenge of these new threats that did not fit neatly into the Cold War framework for the United States' approach to the world.

Even after the Osirak and Falklands crises had been resolved, the general mindset behind US foreign policy remained unchanged, as evidenced by the national security strategy laid out in NSDD-32. Nor did the change of one of the most critical members of the administration's foreign policy team alter its strategic priorities. As secretary of state, Haig had taken leading roles in framing the US response to both the Osirak raid and the Falklands War, seeking to preserve and balance his government's conflicting interests. His replacement in July 1982, George Shultz, was a man of deep experience in government who had held three cabinet-level posts in the Nixon administration. Recalling his and the administration's mindset upon assuming his position at the head of the State Department, Shultz made clear his overriding priority: "The U.S.-Soviet superpower contest was undeniably the central concern of our foreign policy."[99]

Nevertheless, both the Osirak raid and the Falklands War helped to jolt the Reagan administration's thinking, however tenuously, onto a more flexible path. Its overarching priorities may not have changed, but the president and his advisors increasingly recognized the need to incorporate these new types of threats into their approach to the world. In this shift, no one proved more influential than British prime minister Margaret Thatcher, whose unwavering advocacy of the need to safeguard the principles behind international norms eventually carried her US allies—and especially President Reagan himself—into her camp. The impact of these two early crises on US national security strategic thinking was limited but important, as they revealed in dramatic fashion two threats that would come to define the world that would replace the Cold War within a decade. In both cases, the Reagan administration lagged behind its allies in halting nuclear proliferation in Iraq and in turning back the aggression of the rogue dictatorship of Argentina. But in both cases the president himself revealed a sounder intuitive grasp of the importance of the issues at stake than did most of his advisors. Reagan's intuition did not decisively shape his administration's response to these crises, but it helped establish the more flexible approach to the world that would define the later years of his presidency.

2

ACT OF WAR
Libya and the Struggle to Confront Terrorism

"Only when he is made to pay an unacceptable price will he stop." Armed with this broadside against the Libyan dictator among his talking points, Vice Admiral John Poindexter, national security advisor to President Ronald Reagan, entered the meeting with leaders from Congress that would precede the impending airstrikes against Libya on April 14, 1986.[1] Over the previous year, a series of increasingly violent and costly terrorist attacks had escalated against US interests abroad, and the Reagan administration had searched in vain for an effective way to respond. Intelligence pointed to a common denominator tying the attacks to a single source: the sponsorship of the Libyan regime of Colonel Muammar Qadhafi. The bombing of La Belle discotheque in West Berlin, a hotspot for US servicemen, on April 5, at last provided the administration with an opportunity to mount a decisive response. Reagan and his advisors were determined not to let it pass.

Poindexter explained to the assembled senators and representatives that the United States had "tried every possible means short of military action to convince Colonel Qadhafi to stop his outlaw behavior." As he listed the elements of the administration's strategy for deterring terrorism, Poindexter did not linger on the lack of support that the United States' European allies, including British prime minister Margaret Thatcher, had mustered for successive US proposals, but his frustration on this point was palpable. "It is our unanimous opinion," he continued, "that a failure to respond by the world community has encouraged Qadhafi's aggression."[2] The proposed bombing of military and terrorist targets within Libya was designed to reverse this perception of passive inaction by warning friend and foe alike that the United States had entered a new era in how it would respond to the threat of terrorism.

The bombing of Libya in 1986 marked a seminal moment in the development of US counterterrorism strategy, establishing a clear precedent for the use of military force against states sponsoring terrorism. By focusing attention on the states that sponsored terrorist activities rather than on the loose terrorist networks themselves, the airstrikes against Libya allowed the Reagan administration to break free from the conventional means of countering terrorism as a matter of criminal law enforcement. In the eyes of Reagan and his advisors, this past approach had bred passivity and failed to address what they viewed as the root of the problem. Instead, by shifting the issue away from the hurdles and debates of international law enforcement and redefining terrorism as an act of war, the Reagan administration brought the terrorist threat into the geopolitical arena, where the United States could employ its decisive preponderance of military power.

Though President Reagan entered office in 1981 determined to bring a new sense of vigor to the fight against terrorism, disagreements within his administration over how best to confront that threat hampered the creation of a strategy to match Reagan's will. His first term witnessed a series of stumbles and deadlock in the face of the escalating challenge, as the president and his advisors grew increasingly frustrated at their inability to mount a decisive response.

It was the emergence of Qadhafi's Libya as the first rogue state—the first and most brazen poster child for what Reagan began to call "outlaw states" by the summer of 1985—that brought clarity and purpose to the United States' approach to combating terrorism. By the mid-1980s, Qadhafi's provocations had escalated from nuisances on the periphery of US interests to what Reagan and his advisors increasingly viewed as an urgent threat to international peace and stability. Critically, Qadhafi's repeated and unabashed sponsorship of terrorist attacks against the United States and its allies fused the emerging idea of rogue states with the related problem of international terrorism. These two challenges subsequently became intertwined and inseparable in the strategic thinking of US policymakers: terrorism became a key ingredient for how Reagan and his advisors began to define the rogue state paradigm, which they described as a "network of terrorist states" threatening the international order.[3] In turn, the Reagan administration used this new rogue state paradigm to help the US government frame and deploy a comprehensive strategy to combat terrorism. When focused on rogue states rather than elusive transnational terrorist organizations, the blueprint for US counterterrorism finally gained the direction and momentum it needed to achieve substantive results.

In the months leading up to the culmination of the Libyan terrorism crisis in April 1986, the measures that the US government developed, with significant input from Margaret Thatcher's government in Britain, marked the first coherent strategy in US history to combat state-sponsored terrorism. With an escalating series of steps to isolate such rogue regimes, the resulting strategy aimed to preempt imminent terrorist threats, build a strong deterrent against future attacks, and create conditions inside an offending country that would prove conducive to regime change. While the administration sought to enlist the cooperation of and instill a consensus among its European allies, who also suffered from the growing terrorist threat, it made clear its willingness to take the lead and act decisively on its own. The British, under the strong influence of Prime Minister Thatcher, provided crucial input to square US strategy with international law and set the precedent of backing US actions rather than face a split in the transatlantic alliance. For the British as well as the Americans, the bombing of Libya marked the point when terrorism was recognized as "a fundamental long-term security threat," laying the seeds for both countries' approach to the post–Cold War world.[4]

Stumbles, Deadlock, and Frustration, 1983–1985

Terrorism's rise to such an unparalleled level in Washington's hierarchy of priorities was a long time in the making. In fact, the United States saw little need for any counterterrorism strategy at all during the first half of the Cold War. A recurrent theme throughout the history of US counterterrorism was the jarring impact of particular attacks in altering the ways policymakers and the public viewed the threat of terrorism. In the absence of any especially horrific instances prior to 1972, the term "international terrorism" had not yet emerged in either the national consciousness or in high-level government circles. Rather, successive administrations through Lyndon Johnson's tended to view terrorist actions as "regional phenomena" connected to insurgency and guerilla warfare in the Third World.[5] The historian David Tucker notes that the US government insisted from the beginning that "trying to define terrorism is counterproductive and even harmful," since such debates would only diminish efforts to combat it. Though most observers agreed on the general definition of terrorism as 'politically motivated violence against noncombatants intended to influence an audience," the consensus largely ended there. Through the 1970s, the US government classified terrorist acts as criminal activity.[6]

The late 1960s and early 1970s witnessed a significant shift that, for the first time, made international terrorism a first-order concern for US foreign policymakers. The largest terrorist problem in these years—one that remains central to the public consciousness of the threat—was the issue of airplane hijackings.

Far from the horrific images that these words would later bring to mind, the hijackings of the late 1960s were more of a nuisance than an actual threat to national security. The historian Timothy Naftali explains that, until 1968, hijacking was "an almost entirely American problem" and "largely a victimless crime," whereby hijackers would demand that the plane in question reroute to Cuba. Indeed, the Federal Aviation Administration concluded that this was "an impossible problem," and the public came to view it as "a travel inconvenience more than a danger, something akin to bad weather in Chicago." This would change during the presidency of Richard Nixon, particularly after the Palestinian attack against Israeli athletes at the 1972 Munich Olympics. Following this attack, Nixon formed the first cabinet-level committee to address the problem of terrorism, but without wider support in his administration and with other challenges competing for his attention, counterterrorism remained a secondary problem at best. It stayed this way for most of the remainder of the decade, with presidents and their top advisors convinced that the threat had waned.[7]

The inauguration of Ronald Reagan in 1981 signaled a break with this trend and a rethinking of how the US government should define and approach the threat of terrorism. With the Iran hostage crisis ongoing, the 1980 presidential campaign had been the first in which terrorism had featured as an important part of the national debate, and Reagan vowed soon after taking office to enact "swift and effective retribution" for terrorist attacks against Americans.[8] From the start, Reagan made combating terrorism a higher priority than it had ever been under any previous administration. Initially, both Reagan and his first secretary of state, Alexander Haig, saw terrorism as inextricably linked to Soviet sponsorship. While experience would slowly move the president away from this stance and prompt him to view terrorism outside a traditional Cold War framework, he maintained his focus on the states that sponsored terrorist activities.[9]

A sense of mounting crisis had been building for some time prior to 1985, when Reagan and his national security team finally turned in earnest toward crafting and implementing a new counterterrorism strategy. Three of the most disastrous terrorist attacks against Americans all centered on the United States' involvement in a multinational peacekeeping force stationed in Beirut following the 1982 Israeli invasion of Lebanon amid that country's ongoing civil war. Bombings of the US embassy and the US embassy annex in Beirut in April 1983 and September 1984, respectively, bookended what amounted to the deadliest terrorist attack against Americans prior to 9/11: the bombing of the US Marine barracks at the Beirut airport on October 23, 1983, which resulted in the deaths of 241 US military personnel. These attacks, especially the bombing of the Marine barracks, shook Reagan and his advisors to their core. Reagan wrote later that the attack against the Marines amounted to "the lowest of the low" points of his eight years in the presidency.[10] George Shultz, Reagan's second secretary of state, who had served as a marine himself during World War II, called it "the worst day of my life."[11]

The attacks in Beirut had been orchestrated by a newly formed terrorist network that adopted the name "Hezbollah" in 1984. Drawn from several Lebanese militant groups, Hezbollah rapidly became the most destructive terrorist organization within the wider network sponsored by Iran. Beginning in the summer of 1982, Iran's radical Islamist regime sent members of its Revolutionary Guards to the city of Baalbek in Lebanon's Bekaa Valley, where they recruited followers and established a base of operations with the complicity of the Syrian military forces that controlled the area. Throughout 1983, Hezbollah fighters increased their role in the Lebanese civil war, receiving supplies from Iran with Syrian collusion and planning their attacks against Lebanese, Israeli, and eventually European and US targets through the Iranian ambassador in Damascus. As US intelligence reports disclosed throughout the rest of the decade, Iran sponsored terrorist organizations such as Hezbollah as an integral part of its foreign policy, seeking to spread its radical Islamist revolution throughout the region even while it dueled with Iraq in a war of massive proportions along the Persian Gulf. The United States' involvement in Lebanon drew it into the crosshairs of this Iranian-sponsored terrorist violence that exploded throughout the region in the first half of the 1980s.[12]

Although these terrorist attacks in Lebanon prompted Reagan and his national security team to appreciate the need for a more clearly defined approach toward the problem, divisions within the administration impeded the creation of a cohesive counterterrorism strategy. Moreover, the deliberations focused on how to *respond* to attacks that had already occurred rather than on how to *prevent* future strikes. The bombing of the US embassy in Beirut in April 1983 was the first major terrorist challenge for the Reagan administration, but there is no evidence that the president or any of his top advisors seriously considered using military force to respond. The situation was different following the much more destructive and deadly attack on the Marine barracks in October 1983. Reagan himself immediately indicated his determination to retaliate with military force against the terrorists responsible for the bombing. However, lacking a consensus for action within the administration and among key allies such as Britain, the United States did not mount any retaliatory response. Significant dispute persists over whether the president actually ordered airstrikes or if his secretary of defense, Caspar Weinberger, canceled them at the last minute. The evidence suggests that Reagan did not, in fact, issue an official order for military action, as he was uncertain about the available intelligence and hesitant because of the risk of escalation. He chose not to follow the matter up to iron out the disagreements among the members of his national security team. Shultz and the National Security Council

(NSC) staff favored mounting a military attack; Weinberger and the Joint Chiefs of Staff (JCS) were wary of using military force as a tool to counter terrorism. Still, the attacks prompted the first serious conversations over launching military action in the face of the terrorist challenge.[13]

One concrete outcome of the Beirut bombing was the articulation of a clearer policy toward terrorism, which eventually took official form as National Security Decision Directive (NSDD) 138, which the president signed in April 1984. NSDD-138 sought to improve coordination in the fight against terrorism among the various departments and agencies of the US government as well as with allies abroad. Most notably, the directive ordered the development of "a full range of military options" that would support "an active, preventive program to combat state-sponsored terrorism." NSDD-138 took aim at both terrorist organizations and the states that supported them, vowing that "the U.S. will hold sponsors accountable." This bold assertion of a proactive approach to counterterrorism meant little, however, without a consensus among Reagan's national security team to implement it. Indeed, deep divisions remained within the top ranks of the administration, leaving it mired in what the historian Hal Brands calls "a worst-of-both-worlds policy that involved tough talk and very little action."[14]

The schism within the administration centered on Weinberger and Shultz, who fought to win the president's support. As Weinberger later explained, "Successful terrorist activities always produce a reaction in which fury and frustration are combined, [which] ... makes it so very difficult to pursue a reasonable focus on the terrorists themselves, and not to yield to the temptation to launch an indiscriminate bombing in revenge." He favored mounting "an appropriate response" only "when and if we have the proof" to tie an attack clearly and unambiguously to a specific culprit.[15] Reagan shared this reservation and cited it in his memoirs as his central reason for forgoing the airstrikes after the bombing of the Marine barracks: "Our intelligence experts found it difficult to establish conclusively who was responsible for the attack on the barracks. . . . I didn't want to kill innocent people."[16]

Shultz, on the other hand, insisted that terrorism amounted to a form of warfare and ought to be countered as such, a conviction that deepened after the disaster of the Marine barracks bombing, which eventually precipitated the withdrawal of US peacekeeping forces from Lebanon. In a speech at the Park Avenue Synagogue in New York in October 1984, which he titled "Terrorism and the Modern World," Shultz argued that terrorism "is not just criminal activity but an unbridled form of warfare." In Shultz's view, which Reagan also shared, the defensive focus of the 1970s, which had defined terrorism as criminal and centered on bolstering security at embassies and airports, promoting international conventions for prosecuting terrorists, and eventually hostage rescue operations, was inadequate to addressing this growing threat. Shultz argued for the need to "reach a consensus in this country that our responses should go beyond passive defense to consider means of active prevention, preemption, and retaliation," including the use of military force, with the goal "to prevent and deter future terrorist acts." Responding directly to Weinberger's insistence on acting only with incontrovertible proof of culpability, Shultz countered that "we may never have the kind of evidence that can stand up in an American court of law. But we cannot allow ourselves to become the Hamlet of nations, worrying endlessly over whether and how to respond."[17]

The president increasingly came to share his secretary of state's convictions following the tragedies in Beirut. Speaking to the American Bar Association in July 1985, Reagan declared that terrorist attacks were "acts of war" and advocated for a new approach to counterterrorism that emphasized *offensive* as well as defensive measures to stave off the threat.[18] Reagan's growing willingness to use military force to retaliate against states that supported terrorism, as he would demonstrate in ordering the bombing of Libya in 1986, marked what Naftali calls "a dramatic shift in U.S. counterterrorism doctrine."[19]

"The Mad Clown" of Tripoli: Libya's Emergence as the First Rogue State

While Reagan and his national security team struggled to find an effective means of countering the escalation of terrorist violence, they also sought to curb the growing challenge to US interests from the dictator of Libya, Colonel Muammar Qadhafi. Qadhafi's aggressive behavior and support for international terrorism had set him squarely in the sights of the Reagan administration since it had come into office. Indeed, Qadhafi's support for international terrorism dovetailed with a conventional confrontation between the United States and Libya that had been growing since the former military officer had toppled the country's pro-Western king in a coup in 1969. Throughout the 1970s, Qadhafi's increasingly radical regime heightened tensions with the United States by appealing to pan-Arab nationalism, expressing hostility toward US and Western interests, vocally supporting the Palestinians and stoking anti-Israeli sentiment, and fostering commercial and military ties with the Soviet Union, all while crushing dissent within its own borders US leaders, however, decided to avoid confrontation throughout the 1970s, even when Libyans torched the US embassy in Tripoli in solidarity with the Iranian seizure of the US embassy in Tehran in 1979.[20]

Shortly after entering office, the Reagan administration determined to reverse course on US policy toward Libya and adopt a more confrontational stance. The US standoff with Libya reached its first flashpoint in August 1981, when US military

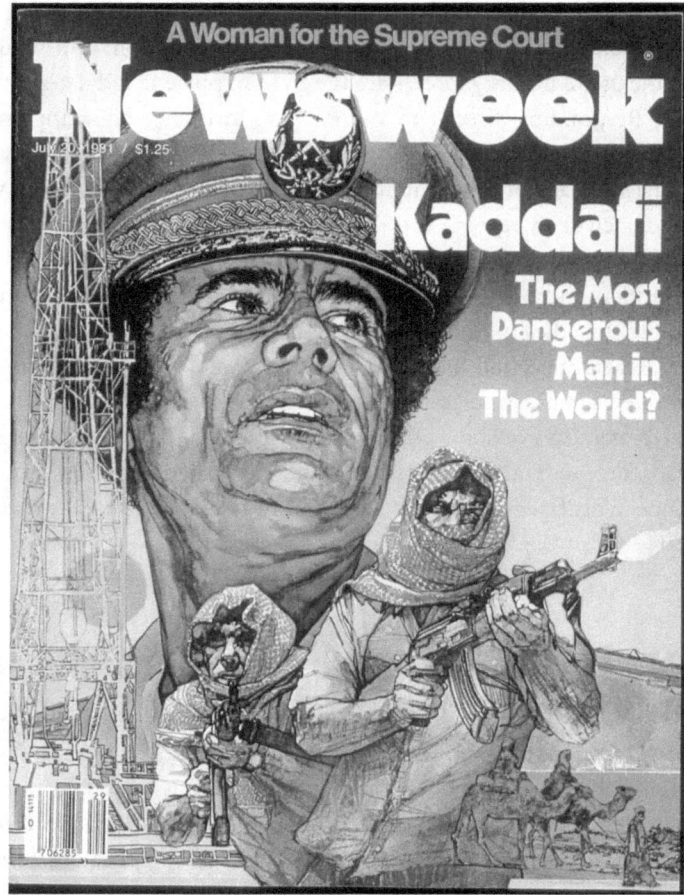

FIGURE 4. The first rogue state: Libyan dictator Muammar Qadhafi dominates the cover of *Newsweek* in an image that captures the growing public perception of the menacing features of his terrorist-supporting regime, July 1981.

aircraft shot down two Libyan air force jets that had fired on them during naval exercises in the Gulf of Sidra. Contrary to international law, Qadhafi laid claim to this region of the Mediterranean as part of Libya's territorial waters, dubbing its northern boundary the "Line of Death." Since the early 1970s, the US Navy and Air Force had conducted "freedom of navigation" (FON) exercises to challenge Qadhafi's claim to these international waters.[21] This burgeoning conventional confrontation merged with Qadhafi's increasingly brazen support for terrorist groups to make the Libyans the "boogeymen" of the 1980s, as such cinematic hits as *Back to the Future* (1985) memorably depicted.

As early as late 1981 and the beginning of 1982, Reagan and his national security team were forming and debating a comprehensive strategy toward Libya, which featured an initial discussion of the behavior and characteristics of rogue states, though they referenced only Libya at the time. Branding Libya an "international troublemaker," officials in the State Department and on the NSC staff outlined the various facets of the Libyan threat, from sponsoring terrorism by providing funds, weapons, and training camps to "sowing subversion, intimidation, [and] the overt use of military force" against vulnerable neighbors throughout the region.[22] Most alarming of all, noted administration officials, was Libya's "widely proclaimed" intention to produce or acquire nuclear weapons, perhaps with aid from the Soviet Union or the black market trade through Pakistan, which "would pose an intolerable threat to the security and well-being" of the United States and its allies.[23] Already the Reagan administration was referring to Qadhafi's as an outlaw regime, whose "lawless and aggressive behavior" was "antithetical to U.S. and western interests and to the norms of international order subscribed to by most civilized nations."[24]

The expanding scope and violence of Qadhafi's support for international terrorism, and the rising boldness of his anti-US and anti-Western targets, brought Libya even higher on the list of US and European concerns by the middle of the decade. British authorities uncovered Libyan support through money and weapons for the Provisional Irish Republican Army (IRA), the Irish nationalist terrorist organization that attempted to assassinate British prime minister Margaret Thatcher by bombing the Grand Hotel in Brighton in October 1984. Earlier that year, Libyan agents had murdered a policewoman in the streets of London when they fired into a crowd of protesters outside the Libyan embassy.[25]

In July 1985, Reagan's landmark speech to the American Bar Association tied together the twin threats of terrorism and the "outlaw states" that sponsored them. He made clear his intention to connect a more robust and proactive approach to counterterrorism with a strategy to combat the emerging menace of rogue states, naming Libya and Iran as the two prime culprits behind the escalation of terrorist violence directed against the United States and its allies. Rejecting the "temptation to see the terrorist act as simply the erratic work of a small group of fanatics," Reagan argued that "a confederation of terrorist states" had fostered a "pattern of state-approved assassination and terrorism" with the common goal to "expel America from the world." He emphasized the criminality of not only terrorist acts but of the regimes that supported them. Any successful strategy to counter terrorism, he insisted, had to target the "core group of radical and totalitarian governments" that "trained, financed, and directly or indirectly controlled" the terrorist organizations. Chief among the "outlaw states" in his sights was the dictatorship of Colonel Qadhafi of Libya. Reagan warned that "these terrorist states are now engaged in acts of war against the Government and people of the United States," and he vowed that America would defend itself.[26]

Forging a Strategy: Diplomacy, Sanctions, and Skeptical Allies, June 1985–March 1986

The year 1985 marked a turning point in the frequency, intensity, and violence of international terrorism. The escalating scale of the terrorist attacks during this year exacerbated the feeling within the Reagan administration that the existing approach to countering terrorism as a criminal offense was not adequate to curtail the ballooning threat. The attacks thus accelerated the shift in the administration's mentality from viewing terrorism as a crime to an act of war and spurred it to implement the more aggressive brand of counterterrorism that it had advocated rhetorically since 1981.

The string of attacks in 1985 finally brought the Reagan administration's frustration with the international hurdles of treating terrorism as a matter of criminal law enforcement to a boiling point. First, the hijacking of TWA Flight 847 in June created a spectacle for over two weeks in which numerous Americans were taken hostage and one was murdered, yet the Syrians and Lebanese allowed the Hezbollah hijackers to walk free. Then, in October, the Palestinian Liberation Front hijacked the cruise ship *Achille Lauro* in the Mediterranean, killing a handicapped American. When the hijackers surrendered to Egyptian authorities, they, too, were allowed to go free. With Israeli intelligence assistance and in the face of Egyptian deception, US military fighter jets dramatically intercepted the hijackers' escape plane and forced it to land at a NATO air base in Sicily. US commandos surrounded the plane to detain the hijackers and bring them to the United States to stand trial, only to be surrounded themselves by Italian authorities, who insisted that the hijackers remain in Italy for prosecution; the mastermind of the operation was allowed to go free. This operation, both a dramatic success and ultimately a disappointment, proved the final straw in the administration's growing frustration with the hurdles of international law enforcement. When operatives from the Abu Nidal terrorist organization opened fire on passengers in line at the departure desks for Israel's national airline El Al in simultaneous terrorist attacks at the Rome and Vienna airports on December 27, Reagan and his advisors swung into action in crafting and implementing a concerted strategy for countering future attacks.[27]

The United States quickly connected the Rome and Vienna airport attacks to the sponsorship of Qadhafi's regime in Libya. Having repeatedly run into dead ends attempting to craft decisive military responses to attacks perpetrated by individuals or transnational terrorist organizations, such as the bombings in Lebanon, Reagan and his advisors turned the focus of their thinking on counterterrorism toward the states sponsoring those organizations—Libya foremost among them. The hijacking of TWA Flight 847 in June 1985 triggered a process of recalibration for Reagan's approach to counterterrorism that culminated just after the Rome and Vienna airport attacks at the end of the year. Reagan made his speech to the American Bar Association declaring "terrorist states" to be "engaged in acts of war against the Government and people of the United States" just over a week after the conclusion of the TWA hijacking. Recognizing the ineffectiveness of attempting to merely react to terrorist incidents as they arose, Reagan argued for a more proactive approach, "taking a strategic, not just a tactical view of terrorism." The states that lent support to terrorist organizations, in Reagan's view, were the true power behind this threat.[28] By late July 1985, Reagan codified the ideas from his speech in a National Security Decision Directive, NSDD-179, establishing a task force under Vice President George Bush to examine and improve US counterterrorism policy and programs. Naftali writes that this task force amounted to "the most searching study of U.S. counterterrorism strategy attempted to date."[29] NSDD-179 confirmed as official government policy that terrorists were "waging a war" against the United States and that the country must therefore "develop a sustained program for combatting terrorism" in concert with other nations but also "be prepared to act unilaterally when necessary."[30]

The "sustained program" that Reagan had in mind came into clearer shape in the first days of 1986, in the immediate aftermath of the Rome and Vienna airport attacks. The work of the task force itself lifted the profile of terrorism in the administration's hierarchy of international priorities. Writing to Margaret Thatcher to seek her "personal views" on combating terrorism so the US government could "learn from [her] experience," Vice President Bush emphasized that "the problem is one of deep personal concern" and "occupies such a high priority in the concerns of President Reagan and myself."[31] Reporting its findings to the president in December 1985, the task force identified terrorism as a "threat to [US] national security" and "one of the most serious problems facing our government," evidence of its heightened place in the administration's ranking of threats. The report declared, "States that practice terrorism or actively support it will not do so without consequence," and laid out the broad outlines of the more proactive counterterrorism strategy that the administration had in mind, including preemptive action, deterrence, and long-term planning. The task force advocated political, economic, and military measures to "retaliate" against terrorist attacks and establish a "long-range deterrent effect," singling out military action as a means to "deter future terrorist acts" and "encourage other countries to take a harder line." Nevertheless, the report urged that such military

FIGURE 5. Under Churchill's watchful eye: President Reagan meets with Vice President George Bush and Secretary of State George Shultz in the Situation Room during the TWA Flight 847 hijacking crisis, June 16, 1985.

action "could be more effective if utilized in concert with diplomatic, political or economic sanctions."[32]

With the task force's recommendations as their rubric and the Rome and Vienna airport attacks as their catalyst, Reagan and his team wasted little time in the new year of 1986 to hone the president's and the task force's general guidance into a cohesive strategy ready to be put into action. The initial papers and press guidance that the president's staff produced following these latest attacks repeated the emerging theme that "states have a legitimate right to respond with appropriate force to repeated acts of terrorism" and that such acts "cannot go unanswered."[33] By the time the National Security Planning Group (NSPG), the administration's chief foreign policymaking body chaired by the president, met to discuss the issue on January 6, 1986, its focus was no longer on merely how to respond to this attack but rather on how to confront "the more general problem of Libyan support for international terrorism." The options on the table included enacting 1) economic and political sanctions, 2) simultaneous economic sanctions and limited military strikes, or 3) economic sanctions followed by limited military strikes after a two-week pause.[34] Already off the table was the fourth option that the deputies-level Crisis Pre-Planning Group had considered the previous week of taking "Decisive Action against Libya" rather than limited retaliation.[35]

Knowing that US allies in Europe were reluctant and had expressed "great nervousness to talk of U.S. economic and military actions," planners on the NSC staff emphasized the need to "generate momentum in Europe for firmer internal actions and closer cooperation with the United States." One of the most crucial benefits to the first option (economic and political sanctions) was therefore the greater chance to promote "international cooperation against terror," including increasing the prospects for parallel sanctions from the allies while reducing the chance of prompting "Allied criticism of precipitate U.S. action." One of the prime drawbacks that the NSPG discussed for the second and third options, with limited military strikes, was the possibility that they might "cause us to miss [an] opportunity to get Allies committed to [the] economic option."[36] Reagan accordingly chose to implement the first option, without any military action.

Had Reagan decided to launch immediate military strikes in response to this latest terrorist incident, it would have aligned with his inclination for more aggressive action, but it would not have fit within any wider strategy. The very reason that Reagan opted to hold off on military action at this juncture was to prevent any such response from being an isolated, one-off operation—ironically just what commentators and scholars would later claim the Libya bombing to be. Rather, Reagan wanted his new counterterrorism strategy to be a "sustained program," within which military action would be only one part. John Poindexter, his national security advisor, emphasized at the NSPG meeting that the present response should be part of an "integrated strategy" designed to "convince our Western allies to work with us to isolate Qadhafi economically and politically." Military strikes, he noted, were a "key component" of this strategy, but the immediate goal should be to "implement stringent, comprehensive economic and political sanctions against Libya." Far from a one-off response to an individual terrorist incident, these sanctions could be "ratcheted upward" in an escalating strategy of coercive diplomacy if Libyan support for terrorism continued unabated.[37]

The day after this NSPG meeting between the president and his chief advisors, Reagan issued an executive order declaring "a national emergency to deal with the unusual and extraordinary threat to the national security and foreign policy of the United States" posed by the Libyan government's support for international terrorism.[38] The president thus left no doubt as to the seriousness with which he viewed the problem. Noting the "indisputable" evidence that the "scope and tempo of Libyan-supported terrorist activity against western targets is widening and accelerating," Reagan laid out the general objectives for the first steps in his strategy to counter the threat: to reverse "the perception of U.S. passivity" in the face of terrorism and to isolate Libya economically and diplomatically. In addition to declaring a national emergency, Reagan announced a tightening of economic sanctions to "eliminate any U.S. contribution to the Libyan economy" and mandated that all US citizens and businesses leave Libya before the end of the month.[39] The need to evacuate US personnel from Libya prior to mounting any major military action weighed heavily on Reagan, who wrote in his diary, "We all feel we must do something yet there are problems including thousands of Americans living & working in the mad clown's country."[40]

With the first two steps underway in its "integrated strategy" against Libyan-supported terrorism—diplomatic isolation and economic isolation—the Reagan administration launched a diplomatic offensive to rally the support of European allied governments in implementing comparable sanctions or, at the very least, not replacing US business as it withdrew from Libya. It was here that the strategy the United States took hit its first major roadblock: the European allies refused to join the boycott of the Libyan economy. The biggest surprise and setback came from Reagan's closest ally of all: British prime minister Margaret Thatcher. Thatcher had every reason to share Reagan's disdain for the ruler he routinely referred to as "the mad clown" and "the crackpot in Tripoli."[41] In 1984, Britain had broken off diplomatic relations with Libya, banned arms exports, and put strict restrictions on investments and immigration following the killing of a policewoman at the hands of agents within the Libyan embassy in London and the revelation of Libyan efforts to fund and arm the Provisional IRA, responsible for the attempted assassination of Thatcher herself in October 1984. As Charles Powell, her private secretary for foreign affairs, explained, "Her resistance to terrorism was so powerful, so central to her being and existence, that there were no two ways about it."[42]

Nevertheless, Thatcher's resistance to the United States' plan for isolating Qadhafi sprang from two principal concerns, as she pointedly outlined in a press conference for US correspondents at her official residence at 10 Downing Street on January 10, 1986. First, she harbored a longstanding skepticism of the effectiveness of sanctions, particularly unilateral sanctions, which she believed caused more damage to the people who imposed them than the government they were imposed upon. "I do not, alas, think that sanctions against Libya would work," she told the US journalists. "The materials would be supplied by other countries." She worried that Reagan, who had supported her logic in relation to South Africa, was undermining her broader argument by making an exception for Libya. Pressed by the correspondents, Thatcher repeated time and again her message that "sanctions do not work."[43]

When one reporter asked whether she would support preemptive or retaliatory military action instead, Thatcher delivered an even more strident broadside against the United States' stance on counterterrorism, which revealed her second, weightier concern with the US plan: "I must warn you that I do not believe in retaliatory strikes which are against international law. . . . [O]nce you start to go across borders, then I do not see an end to it and I uphold international law very firmly." Thatcher sensed that the US plan included more than the initial moves toward Libya's diplomatic and economic isolation that Reagan had unveiled thus far, and she aimed to head off any shift in the direction of military action. Connecting the Libyan problem with Irish terrorism in the United Kingdom, she cautioned her US allies, "May I remind you that we have suffered over 2,000 deaths at the hands of terrorists, so we are well aware of the problems and at no stage has anyone in this country suggested that we make retaliatory strikes or go in hot pursuit or anything like that."[44]

This line about going in "hot pursuit" of terrorists ruffled more than a few feathers in Washington, as the Reagan administration began to see what an uphill battle it faced in enlisting European support for its newly developed strategy. Thatcher's private reply to Reagan's request for support concentrated on her case against sanctions but said little of her condemnation of retaliatory strikes, an omission that the Americans noticed: "The letter is perhaps more important for what it does not say." Rather, sensing that her comments would not dissuade the Americans from pursuing their plans, Thatcher tried to maintain her position of influence on US policy by asking that "we remain in close touch as our thinking develops." Despite her "nice noises about cooperating in the struggle against terrorism," the NSC staff expressed exasperation with the British response, with one staffer chafing, "It sounds to me as though the Brits have stiffed us completely."[45] As the analysis of the situation filtered up the chain of command, however, officials began to see the more positive sides to Thatcher's response, emphasizing a supportive public statement from the British and assurances that they "would not take any steps undercutting our measures." Reagan's reply to Thatcher's letter noted his disappointment that Britain "apparently is not prepared to take additional steps" but emphasized the importance of its willingness to play "an active role in energizing the EC [European Community] to take more severe measures against Qadhafi."[45]

The administration decided to regain the initiative by stepping up its diplomatic offensive, first by sending Deputy Secretary of State John Whitehead to European capitals to bolster allied cooperation and resolve against Libya—and to express in London the administration's disappointment and displeasure with Thatcher's remarks. Meanwhile, Secretary of State George Shultz gave a speech at the National Defense University in Washington on January 15 to "publicly challenge [Thatcher's] conjecture" that international law prohibited retaliatory or preemptive strikes against states that sponsor terrorism. Without naming Thatcher, Shultz argued that "there is substantial legal authority for the view that a state which supports terrorist or subversive attacks against another state . . . is responsible for such attacks. Such conduct can amount to an ongoing armed aggression against the other state under international law." Therefore, "a nation attacked by terrorists is permitted to use force to prevent or preempt future attacks, to seize terrorists or to rescue its citizens, when no other means is available." If this was not permitted under the United Nations Charter, he later commented, then the document was "nothing more than a suicide pact."[47]

While these high-level disputes played out, Anglo-American cooperation on counterterrorism continued unhindered at lower levels, a sign of the unique resiliency of the "special relationship" between the two countries. As the historian Richard Aldrich notes, the "fragmented structure" and "compartmentalized relationships" of the various aspects of the Anglo-American alliance, such as on matters of defense and intelligence, meant that close cooperation "could remain unshaken by high-level disagreements over Cold War policy, or by security failures."[48] Indeed, the British had set up an interdepartmental group on terrorism with representatives from its diplomatic, defense, and intelligence services following the Libyan embassy shooting in 1984. This group met regularly, approximately every four months, with its US counterpart under the national security advisor to consult and coordinate on counterterrorism policy, a process that became particularly close after the hijacking of the *Achille Lauro* in October 1985.[49]

These intergovernmental consultations on counterterrorism foreshadowed many of the areas of disagreement that boiled over into public view in the first months of 1986. The Americans noted, following a bilateral meeting in May 1984, that the recent Libyan embassy shooting had caused "a significant hardening of attitude" on the part of the British on which they hoped to capitalize to "develop a consensus that the international community needs to take steps to control Qadhafi's free-wheeling." Already, the British expressed concern that Shultz's public statements on US counterterrorism policy "sounded like they would be contrary to international law and that the US should be on notice that British cooperation would probably not be forthcoming. Moreover, the British thought that an active defense program would probably only make matters worse." The Americans left the meeting resigned to the probability that forging a consensus on economic sanctions was most likely a "non-starter."[50] The theme was essentially the same the following year, amid the TWA hijacking crisis, with the Americans trying to "press the British hard" on backing punitive sanctions against Libya and other states supporting terrorism. The US analysis of the meeting expressed frustration at the British concentration on merely keeping Middle Eastern terrorism "from spilling over" into Western Europe and the United Kingdom "rather than developing any strategy to combat Middle Eastern terrorism at its roots."[51]

By March 1986, with the implementation of the US "integrated strategy" underway, the Americans spoke more bluntly than ever to their British counterparts about their intentions in the unfolding fight against terrorism. Robert

Oakley, chairing the meeting as the State Department's coordinator for counterterrorism, declared that the US government had decided to move to a "more active, offensive policy" for combating terrorism. While Oakley and the rest of the US delegation repeatedly emphasized their preference for multilateral support from European allies, they stressed that they were "prepared to act bilaterally [i.e., in concert with only Britain], or alone, if need be." Oliver North of the NSC staff reminded the British that the US government was growing increasingly "frustrated by [the] futility of trying to get our allies to respond to what we see as a common threat." Questioned by the British delegation about the prospects for retaliatory strikes, Oakley explained that the "use of force could be only an element of [a] broader strategy," reflecting the administration's plans for an integrated approach to the problem. Toward the end of the meeting, however, the Americans left their British counterparts with little ambiguity of what was likely to come: North declared his "personal feeling" that the "next attack out of Libya will generate a military response."[52]

Accelerating the Strategy: Coercive Diplomacy, Confrontation, and Terror, March 14–April 5, 1986

On the morning of Friday, March 14, 1986, President Reagan chaired a meeting with all of his chief advisors on foreign affairs and national security in the Situation Room of the White House. The group was meeting to decide on the rules of engagement for the upcoming FON exercises that the US Navy would soon mount in the Gulf of Sidra, contesting Qadhafi's claim to the international waters below the "Line of Death." Though the navy had conducted such exercises regularly since the early 1970s, the timing in this case was no accident. Despite the resistance they had received from European allies, Reagan and his team were ready to set up the final chain of events that could lead to direct military confrontation with Libya. The naval exercises in disputed waters off the Libyan coast would comprise the third step in the administration's escalating formula for coercive deterrence: placing military pressure on Qadhafi's regime. "Our goal," explained the NSC staff, "is to reinforce other U.S. actions which deter Libya from worldwide terrorism and regional aggression," thereby clearly placing this step within the broader strategy to curtail Libyan-sponsored terrorism. The FON exercises were designed to complement the moves that the administration had already initiated to isolate Libya diplomatically and economically. "In conclusion," the NSC staff asserted, "we can now accelerate U.S. strategy toward Qadhafi" and "pursue a course which integrates current political and economic measures."⁵³ The strategy of escalation was reaching its penultimate stage.

The discussion between the president and his advisors at the NSPG meeting kept the wheels in motion on the administration's strategy to counter Qadhafi but also revealed disagreements over when it should implement the final stage of its new counterterrorism strategy: readying a military attack. Caspar Weinberger, the secretary of defense, left no doubt that the FON exercises were anything but routine: "We are going on the assumption that there will be a reaction." Reagan approved a loosening of the operation's rules of engagement, allowing US forces to attack Libyan air bases or missile sites "if hostile actions occur or appear imminent" and to attack nonmilitary targets "if there are losses to the U.S." However, he stopped short of permitting a wider military attack for fear of "crystaliz[ing] support" for Qadhafi. Where Weinberger and Admiral William Crowe, the chairman of the JCS, cautioned against "crossing a political line" by launching a nonproportional assault that would "end up leveling Tripoli," Shultz favored a more robust military response connected to the administration's goal to "undermine the confidence the Libyan people have in Qadhafi." "We should be ready to undertake action to hurt him, not just fire back," he urged. "Our forces should plaster him and the military targets." Shultz's point was that this confrontation would not be useful to the administration's wider, integrated counterterrorism strategy unless it were designed to further the strategy's overall goal to "put [Qadhafi] in a box."⁵⁴ For now, Reagan was not yet ready to implement this final step in his escalating plan of coercive diplomacy, but Shultz's preference for decisive action would not have long to wait.

The FON exercises in the Gulf of Sidra commenced on March 23, 1986, and came to a head the next day. A series of hostile maneuvers between the two countries' fighter jets did not result in any shots fired, but when the navy came under missile attack from the Libyan coast, it returned fire against the launch site and sank two Libyan patrol boats. Qadhafi responded by sending out a general order to all his European "People's Bureaux" (as he called his country's embassies) to organize terrorist attacks against US military and civilian targets. With the help of British intelligence, this message and other Libyan cable traffic were intercepted, including one especially ominous message to Qadhafi from the People's Bureau in East Berlin on April 4: "We have something planned that will make you happy.... It will happen soon, the bomb will blow, American soldiers must be hit." True to their word, a bomb went off in La Belle discotheque, a nightclub popular with US servicemen stationed in West Berlin, in the early morning hours of April 5, killing one US soldier and wounding eighty other US servicemen, one of whom would also later die from his injuries.⁵⁵

FIGURE 6. Preparing for confrontation: President Reagan meets in the Oval Office with (L–R) Chairman of the Joint Chiefs of Staff Adm. William Crowe, Secretary of Defense Caspar Weinberger, Vice President Bush, White House chief of staff Don Regan, and National Security Advisor John Poindexter to discuss the ongoing "freedom of navigation" exercises in the Gulf of Sidra during the escalating confrontation with Libya, March 24, 1986.

Reagan wrote in his diary that night, "Our intelligence is pretty final that this bombing was the work of Kadaffy." The president had finally found his smoking gun to launch the final stage of his strategy to counter Libyan-supported terrorism and hit back at long last against "the villain."[56]

Framing the Airstrikes: Retaliation Versus Self-Defense, April 5–15, 1986

The ten days between the terrorist attack in West Berlin and the US bombing campaign against Libya were a flurry of activity within the Reagan administration. The debates at this juncture no longer centered on forging a strategy for what to do—that was already in place—but rather on how to execute and explain to the world the final step in the escalating series of pressures on Qadhafi's regime to curb its support for terrorism: a military attack. The brazenness of the Berlin disco bombing and the clarity of the evidence tying it back to Libya lined up all the key members of the administration behind mounting the firm response that

Secretary of State Shultz had long advocated. Even Secretary of Defense Weinberger, usually wary of using the military for anything but the most decisive and clear-cut of actions, backed the attack when he learned how incontrovertible the evidence was of Qadhafi's involvement.[57]

While the administration busied itself selecting targets for the bombing raid, the most important debate during this crucial week and a half featured the input of the United States' closest ally, the government of British prime minister Margaret Thatcher. Thatcher and Reagan had nurtured a close personal and political bond since before either of them ascended to their respective countries' highest offices, and they worked hard to promote their image as "political soulmates" at the heart of a rejuvenated Anglo-American "special relationship," a term coined by Winston Churchill in the aftermath of World War II. Although the two leaders shared a common view of promoting free enterprise at home and combating communism abroad, their rapport was not without its hiccups—most notably over Thatcher's opposition to Reagan's decision to launch a military intervention on the Caribbean island of Grenada after a Marxist coup in 1983. Libya exemplified both the tensions and the closeness of the Anglo-American alliance in the 1980s and ultimately became, in the words of one of their joint biographers, "the supreme occasion when Thatcher delivered for Reagan."[58]

Yet as Thatcher's press conference in January 1986 opposing both sanctions and military strikes against Libya made clear, her support on the issue was far from a foregone conclusion. Her greatest concern was whether such military action could be squared with international law, and the thrust of the debate between the US and British governments in the days leading up to the attack centered on the question of how to frame the airstrikes against Libya and explain them to the world. Thatcher's influence on this question proved decisive and, in rooting the attack in the framework of self-defense rather than retaliation, helped cement a legally justifiable precedent for the use of military force against states sponsoring terrorism.

From the start of his recalibration of the United States' counterterrorism strategy in the summer of 1985, Reagan had not deemed the distinction between retaliatory strikes and military action in national self-defense to be an especially important one. On one hand, in his speech to the American Bar Association in July 1985, in which he declared terrorist attacks to be "acts of war," he also addressed the issue of the legal justification for a military response: "Under international law, any state which is the victim of acts of war has the right to defend itself."[59] However, Reagan twice wrote in his diary of selecting "targets for retaliation" in the days following the Berlin disco bombing, a clear indication that this was the way his administration originally envisioned the airstrike.[60] Indeed, Reagan's message to Thatcher on April 8, 1986, requesting her permission to use long-range precision bombers stationed on NATO bases in England, explained that he had "reluctantly taken the decision to use U.S. military forces to exact a response to these Libyan attacks" and expressed his hope that "this operation will be effective in deterring further Libyan terrorist actions."[61] Reagan thus outlined, without explicitly using either the words "retaliation" or "self-defense," the two sides of the debate over how to present the airstrike, as well as his own initial ambivalence to separating these two avenues for justification.

Thatcher, however, cared about this distinction greatly, and her previously stated belief that international law did not permit retaliatory strikes made her wary of acceding to the United States' request. While the Americans erroneously assumed that "British agreement would be pretty much automatic," Thatcher, in fact, had a series of reasons for distancing herself from the US action. British public opinion, as well as most of her cabinet ministers, opposed a US attack on Libya, and anti-American sentiment in Britain was running high following a recent unrelated political crisis regarding the proposed merger between the British helicopter manufacturer Westland and the American company Sikorsky. In her reply to Reagan's message, Thatcher urged the United States to avoid "precipitate action" that could boost Qadhafi's standing and cause a "cycle of revenge," including against British hostages held in Lebanon. Most of all, she "was concerned that there must be the right public justification for the action" and encouraged her counterparts in the United States to "think through precisely what their objectives were and how they were to justify them." Reagan's stated purpose to "exact a response" for the terrorist attack in West Berlin did not assuage Thatcher's belief that retaliatory strikes were counter to international law and that self-defense would make a much more effective legal justification than punitive action.[62]

Reagan, for his part, stood firm on his proposed course of action but incorporated Thatcher's advice on the legal and public justification for the attack into his administration's final stages of planning. Howard Teicher, a member of the NSC staff, later recalled, "We were conscious of her insistence that we frame the attacks in terms of self-defence . . . so definitely there would have been an impact on how things were framed as a result of her input."[63] Reagan's reply to Thatcher's concerns, however, did not mention the issue of self-defense that she considered so important, implying that her message had not yet sunken in. Instead, he merely asserted that there was "ample legal justification" for a "decisive blow against Qadhafi." On one hand, he admitted, "I have no illusions that these actions will eliminate entirely the terrorist threat." But he emphasized that the United States was "the only Western power in a position to act decisively. I do not feel I can shrink from this responsibility."[64]

Nevertheless, Thatcher found Reagan's "powerful, detailed" reply increasingly convincing as she pondered her decision through the night into April 10. As she later wrote, she progressively came to think of modern state-sponsored terrorism as a new, unprecedented phenomenon—"one which earlier generations never confronted"—and thus "the means required to crush this kind of threat to world order and peace are bound to be different too." Though there was no doubt that she had always despised terrorism, Thatcher was coming around to the conclusion that the Americans had recently reached themselves, that international terrorism had become "a fundamental long-term security threat" that needed to be countered with new strategies. Moreover, the realization that Reagan was determined to strike with or without British support led her to believe that "opposition to the attacks was a dead end," in the words of her biographer Charles Moore, for a few days of good headlines would not be worth the price of "gravely weaken[ing] the alliance and the relationship on which she had built so much." She did not want to repeat the transatlantic rift over Grenada and cited US support for Britain during the Falklands War as further justification in a meeting with members of her cabinet. As she later recalled, "Whatever the cost to me, I knew that the cost to Britain of not backing American action was unthinkable." Thus, early on the morning of April 10, Thatcher made her decision known to her private secretary Charles Powell: "We have to support the Americans on this. That's what allies are for."[65]

Once she had made this decision, however, she missed no opportunity to ensure that the United States reframed its justification for military action in terms of self-defense rather than retaliation. When General Vernon Walters, Reagan's ambassador to the United Nations, arrived in London to meet with Thatcher on April 12 to discuss the US plan in more detail, she repeated her insistence that the administration frame the attack in terms of self-defense; there must be no talk of "retaliation, revenge, or reprisal."[66] She seized on Walters' offer to share with the British in advance the president's public statement announcing and explaining the raid on Libya. This gave the British Foreign Office the chance to stress to their US counterparts that "the UK attached great importance to inclusion of explicit reference to Article 51 ('self-defense') of the UN Charter in the President's remarks." This point, Foreign Office officials believed, would be of "tremendous use" in bolstering wider European support for the operation.[67] As if she had not made her position clear enough already, Thatcher had her staff follow up with the NSC again on April 14, the day of the raid, to reiterate that she was "particularly concerned" that Reagan's speech reference self-defense.[68]

Reagan and his team did not let her down. If it took some time for the major theme of Thatcher's messages to sink in for the president and his staff, by the day of the airstrike, they had incorporated self-defense into all aspects of their public messaging. Most important was President Reagan's address to the nation on the evening of April 14 to announce the bombing raid against Libya. Speaking from the Oval Office, Reagan declared, "Self-defense is not only our right, it is our duty.

FIGURE 7. The bombing of Libya: President Reagan studies satellite imagery of the damage from the airstrikes on Libya in the Situation Room with (L–R) Secretary of State George Shultz, Director of Central Intelligence William Casey, and White House chief of staff Don Regan while Air Force Chief of Staff Gen. Charles Gabriel conducts the briefing, April 15, 1986.

It is the purpose behind the mission undertaken tonight, a mission fully consistent with Article 51 of the United Nations Charter."[69] The White House talking points for the press repeated the president's message that "the U.S. response was in self defense [sic] and was intended to pre-empt" Qadhafi's ongoing terrorist campaign.[70] Immediately following the president's speech, Secretary of State Shultz and Secretary of Defense Weinberger gave a press conference from the White House Briefing Room to explain the details of the operation. Shultz explicitly emphasized self-defense three times in his remarks, including in his opening line: "The President has just described an act of self-defense on the part of the United States."[71]

The airstrikes against Libya, codenamed "Operation El Dorado Canyon," occurred in two coordinated attacks. On the evening of April 14, 1986, eighteen US Air Force F-111 bombers left the Royal Air Force base at Lakenheath, England, to attack three targets near Tripoli. France's unwillingness to permit overflight rights required the bombers to fly on a circuitous route around Spain to enter the Mediterranean via the Strait of Gibraltar. Meanwhile, the navy launched an attack on two additional targets near Benghazi from aircraft carriers stationed in the central Mediterranean.[72] The administration selected targets "that play a key role both in maintaining Qadhafi in power and in directing terrorist operations abroad."[73] The two wings of the bombing raid reached their targets simultaneously in the early morning hours of April 15, about 7:00 p.m. on April 14 in Washington, DC. While one F-111 was shot down and Qadhafi narrowly escaped unscathed, the attack took the Libyans by surprise and caused significant damage to the intended targets. Reagan recorded in his diary that night, "One thing seems sure—ours was a success."[74]

The Aftermath: Keeping up the Pressure, Building International Consensus, and Regime Change, April 15–October 1986

President Reagan made clear in his Oval Office address that the airstrike against Libya would not be an isolated event but rather part of a wider effort. "Today we have done what we had to do," he declared. "If necessary, we shall do it again." He also explained that he had "no illusion that tonight's action will bring down the curtain on Qadhafi's reign of terror" and that the airstrike was therefore not intended as a one-time solution to the problem of international terrorism. Rather, he portrayed the bombing raid as a clear indicator of the new shift in the United States' active approach to countering terrorism as an act of war: "[Qadhafi] counted on America to be passive. He counted wrong. . . . I said that we would act with others, if possible, and alone if necessary to ensure that terrorists have no sanctuary anywhere. Tonight, we have."[75] Indeed, the bombing of Libya on April 14–15, 1986, was not the endpoint of the Reagan administration's new strategy to counter Libyan-supported terrorism. The months following the raid witnessed a series of intense discussions and analysis over how to continue to build international consensus for the administration's approach to counterterrorism and maintain pressure on Qadhafi's regime.

The job of building international support among the United States' European allies would prove an uphill battle, as the administration knew from before the time the strikes occurred. France's refusal to grant overflight permission for the F-111 bombers flying from Britain was the most glaring example of a general European feeling of condemnation for the United States' military action. Nevertheless, Shultz spoke for the administration in stressing the necessity to "fashion a collective approach to confronting the common enemy of terrorism." Otherwise, he predicted more accurately than he could have imagined, "terrorism will become the political determinant of our times."[76]

The difficulty of maintaining the momentum of international support for the approach the United States took regarding counterterrorism began where that support had been strongest, in Britain. Margaret Thatcher "stood up to the political heat with her usual tenacity and style," the US ambassador in London, Charles Price, wrote to Reagan, but "it looks like she will pay a price for her decision" to support the US action. While the airstrike on Libya was enormously popular in the United States, public opinion polls in the United Kingdom showed that two-thirds of the British public opposed Thatcher's support for it. Price wrote two weeks after the airstrike, "While she is with us, she is not with her own people despite every effort on her part to turn around public opinion."[77] Nevertheless, Thatcher remained resolute in her remarks to the House of Commons. "The United States is our greatest ally," she declared. "The time had come for action. The United States took it. Its decision was justified, and, as friends and allies, we support it." She also reasserted her conviction that the "growing threat of international terrorism" was now one of the greatest security challenges confronting Britain and its allies: "To overcome the threat is in the vital interests of all countries founded upon freedom and the rule of law."[78]

The Reagan administration sought to provide support for Thatcher's "effort to move terrorism higher up the national agenda" by mounting an all-out campaign to encourage the Senate to ratify a revised extradition treaty between the United States and Britain, which had been stuck in the Senate Foreign Relations Committee since the previous year. The revised treaty would close a loophole barring the extradition of those who had committed political crimes, such as members of the IRA.[79] Reagan took the unusual step of making a direct personal appeal to Senate leaders, emphasizing that Britain was "our staunchest Ally in the battle against international terrorism."[80] He repeated the same message in his weekly radio broadcast: "Rejection of this treaty would be an affront to British Prime Minister Margaret Thatcher—one European leader who, at great political risk, stood shoulder to shoulder with us during our operations against Qaddafi's terrorism."[81]

However, this initiative on the part of the Reagan administration was not merely a reward to Thatcher for her support of the Libya bombing, as it typically has been portrayed. Rather, the administration saw the treaty as "an important initiative in our overall counter-terrorism effort," an "anti-terrorist weapon" necessary to "put our own home in order in the international campaign against terrorism."[82] "The Treaty is important, both for US-UK relations and for its wider implications in the struggle against terrorism," Reagan told Thatcher when they met in May. Thatcher, in turn, asserted, "We cannot mount an active effort to fight terrorism in Libya, while ignoring it in Northern Ireland."[83] Thanks in significant part to Reagan's personal push, the Senate overwhelmingly ratified the treaty on July 17, 1986.

In the weeks following the bombing of Libya, the US government felt that the "time appears to be ripe to press allies" to take firmer measures against Qadhafi's regime, particularly at the G7 summit meeting in Tokyo in early May 1986.[84] The administration hoped to convince its European allies that "terrorism is a legitimate security concern of the NATO Alliance," and it received positive signs on this front in the days leading up to the summit.[85] French president François Mitterrand, whose support for the US airstrike on Libya had been conspicuously absent, "privately signaled" his sense that the differences between France and the United States were "resolvable" and "indicated [an] overall French desire to improve anti-terrorism cooperation with the United States."[86] A far more cooperative spirit on the issue of terrorism reigned between the allies at the summit meeting in Tokyo than might have been expected less than three weeks after the US bombing raid. Thatcher expressed her "sense that there was a certain coming together among the allies in the war against terrorism." She lent her support in drafting a joint communiqué that officially named Libya as a supporter of terrorism, and West German chancellor Helmut Kohl offered ideas about high-level intergovernmental cooperation on the issue.[87]

This diplomatic offensive to bolster international support was only one part of the Reagan administration's continuing strategy to keep the pressure on Libya following the airstrike in April. An intensive series of deliberations that continued through the summer revealed more clearly than ever that the ultimate goal behind the administration's strategy of escalating pressure on Libya was to create conditions favorable to regime change against Qadhafi. Even before the airstrike occurred, National Security Advisor Poindexter wrote to the president that "our most important objective over the long term" was "creating conditions for a regime change in Libya." He explained that the two immediate goals of the airstrike were to "weaken Qadhafi's ability to stay in power and damage his international terrorist activities."[88] In the days following the bombing raid, Reagan's team pondered ways to "use our action to help trigger a serious coup," convinced that the US airstrike had "created a vacuum" in Libya's political leadership that "presents an opportunity that we can exploit." Indeed, the NSC staff believed that "Qadhafi's vulnerability to a coup has never been greater" but that "this window will close rapidly." Further US airstrikes could catalyze a rebellion that was already simmering in parts of the Libyan armed forces.[89] The CIA undertook a series of studies on the likelihood of fomenting promising conditions to oust Qadhafi. While the resulting reports expressed concerns that Soviet influence could increase in a post-Qadhafi Libya, they also noted that popular discontent within Libya toward Qadhafi's regime "has become more open since the US strike." As late as July 1986, the CIA predicted that Qadhafi had "only a slightly better than even chance of staying in power through the end of this year" and recommended increased international pressure and even additional US military action to "further reduce his chances for survival."[90]

Reagan chaired an NSPG meeting in the White House Situation Room on August 14, 1986, to discuss the prospects of the strategy to counter Libyan terrorism that the administration had forged at the beginning of the year. The president and his top advisors and cabinet officials reiterated the major components of their "multi-faceted strategy designed to intensify the pressures on Qadhafi." Shultz stressed the need to "keep the diplomatic isolation on" and "turn up the heat on economic sanctions." The interdepartmental coordination that lay at the heart of the strategy was on full display as officials from the State, Defense, and Treasury Departments and the CIA outlined their various contributions to "tighten the screws" and "keep the pressure on." Poindexter noted that "a combination of economic and military pressure to deter terrorism . . . has been successful—even more successful than we had hoped." But the members of the NSPG also expressed concern that deterrence would only last for so long without additional action. President Reagan concluded unequivocally that "it is absolutely necessary that there be no delay in hitting Qadhafi again when the evidence links Libya to a terrorist act."[91]

Poindexter made a short-lived attempt following this NSPG meeting to generate the desired additional action against Libya. In August and September 1986, he directed the implementation of a disinformation campaign that combined "real and illusionary events" to exploit Qadhafi's insecurity and convince him that his rule was in jeopardy through further US attacks or an internal military coup. The crux of this plan was to plant news reports in foreign media outlets that the United States was preparing to strike Libya again. When the memo outlining the disinformation program was leaked in late September, it caused a firestorm in the US media. Though Reagan and his senior officials tried to put a positive spin on this deliberately misleading scheme, the damage to their credibility had been done and the plan was dropped. Concerns remained over Qadhafi's continued desire to harm US interests through terrorism, and the US government tapped his communications in May 1987 to keep tabs on his plotting. But by early 1988, as Qadhafi's support for terrorism appeared to wane while he maintained his hold on power, the United States' approach shifted to a less overtly confrontational track, focused instead on furthering the Libyan regime's diplomatic and economic isolation.[52] Moreover, by this time the Iran-Contra affair had engulfed the administration and discredited the NSC staff, prompting the resignations of many of the key architects and proponents of the proactive anti-Libya strategy, including Poindexter and his leading deputy on counterterrorism, Oliver North.

Although Libya faded from the headlines in the fall of 1986, the deliberations and planning of Reagan's national security team clearly revealed that this was not an administration that harbored any illusions that the airstrike in April had resolved the problem of state-sponsored terrorism. The bombing had been merely one act in a much broader counterterrorism strategy with the ultimate goal of regime change that the Reagan administration had begun executing well beforehand and planned to continue into the long-term future. As Reagan wrote in his diary after the August 14 NSPG meeting on the continuing prospects of his strategy against Qadhafi, "He's been pretty quiet but if he let's [*sic*] go with another terrorist act we're ready to respond immediately."[93]

Weapons of Mass Destruction, Terrorism, and Aggression: Crystallizing the Meaning of a Rogue

Qadhafi did not remain quiet for long. In the final months of Reagan's presidency, the Libyan regime leapt back into the administration's crosshairs in a new series of crises that underscored the defining elements of rogue state behavior that were beginning to crystallize in the minds of US officials. Libya was already the archetype for the "outlaw states" that Reagan had been denouncing regularly since 1985. This infamous status was, up to this point, primarily due to Qadhafi's brazen support for international terrorism and his unpredictable armed aggression against US forces in the Mediterranean and to destabilize governments in North Africa and the Middle East.

Reports picked up by US intelligence in the fall of 1988 added a new, and perhaps even more menacing, element to the Libyan threat: Qadhafi was completing construction of a chemical weapons factory and would soon possess stockpiles of weapons of mass destruction (WMD). The facility, known as Pharma 150, was located at Rabta, a sparsely populated and mountainous desert area approximately fifty miles south of Tripoli. Secretary of State Shultz explained in his memoirs that clear evidence came to light in September 1988 that revealed the true purpose of the large industrial complex: the production and storage of chemical weapons such as mustard gas and the nerve agent sarin. Despite Libyan claims that the plant was meant for the manufacture of pharmaceuticals, US intelligence considered Rabta the largest chemical weapons facility in the developing world.[94]

Reagan's advisors appear to have first brought the matter to the attention of the president in early November 1988, soon before the administration decided to release this revelation to the public to draw as much scrutiny and pressure to bear on Libya as possible. Reagan noted in his diary the high stakes with which he viewed the issue, arguing that the chemical weapons plant "threatens the entire Middle East."[95] Qadhafi's erratic behavior and close links with terrorist organizations made his potential use of such WMD, either directly or through terrorist surrogates, a distinct and frightening possibility. Indeed, he had already resorted to using chemical weapons in his war with Chad earlier in the decade: when Libya's military intervention there was near defeat in 1987 following a series of reversals against Chadian forces with French support, Qadhafi ordered his military to use Iranian-supplied mustard gas bombs against his adversaries.[96]

Though Qadhafi's desire to acquire nuclear weapons had been apparent to the international community since his rebuffed overtures to China in 1970, Libya remained without any substantial nuclear program through the 1980s. He turned instead to the "poor man's atomic bomb," purchasing chemical agents and weapons and beginning construction on his own production plant at Rabta in 1984. A host of Western European companies, most notably from West Germany but also from Belgium, France, and Italy as well as Japan, provided Libya with the technology and materials necessary for manufacturing chemical weapons and even assisted in the construction of the facilities. Most of these firms later claimed to have been unaware of the true nature of the enterprise in which they were engaged, under the false impression that their contributions were meant for a pharmaceutical plant—and in some cases one that would be located in Hong Kong rather than Libya.[97] However, through a combination of Libyan deception and the cooperation or willful denial of these companies, Qadhafi succeeded in launching "a crash program to develop chemical weapons to advance his revolution," in Reagan's words, "with all that meant to a world that had good reason to worry about the next move by this unpredictable clown."[98]

Alarmed by reports of the indispensable cooperation of firms from allied countries, Reagan and Shultz made personal overtures to the governments of Japan and especially West Germany. Both responded with decided coolness. Meeting with the West German chancellor, Helmut Kohl, and his foreign minister, Hans-Dietrich Genscher, Shultz and other top administration officials sought to impress upon their counterparts the seriousness and urgency of the matter through a thorough presentation of the evidence—of which, it later became clear, West German intelligence was already well aware. Noting Kohl's obvious discomfort, Shultz recalled that he felt the chancellor was merely "hearing me out, simply because he had been asked to listen." The West Germans "resisted taking any action," Shultz speculated, because of the political fallout that would result from public disclosure of West German involvement in poison gas production. He lamented, "I was deeply troubled by the willingness of these leaders to look the other way on a matter of such importance."[99]

The Reagan administration viewed the threat of Libyan chemical weapons so seriously that it took the extraordinary step of requesting the JCS to draw up top secret plans to destroy the Rabta plant "if we should decide to go that route," Reagan explained in his diary. The JCS presented these plans to the president and his NSC on December 21, 1988. Though Reagan opted not to launch a preventive attack, the threat of US military action was imminent enough for Reagan and his advisors to speculate that it impacted Qadhafi's decision to invite the international press corps to view the Rabta facility in a deceptive charade to disprove the United States' claims. As Reagan explained, the Libyans kept the press in the desert several miles from the plant until after dark, "then drove them past the plant whose lights were all out & took them back to town."[100]

In the final days of the administration, Shultz attended the Conference on Disarmament with other world leaders in Paris, hoping to curb and reverse the "erosion of international norms against CW [chemical weapons] use." Unsuccessful once again in enlisting meaningful West German cooperation, Shultz advocated the need for on-site inspections of suspected chemical weapons facilities without advance warning, which he called "the essence of any chemical weapons treaty," and urged deeper international cooperation "to restore respect for the international norms against chemical weapons use." Meanwhile, knowing of Soviet concerns over "implicit threats to use military options against Libya's CW facility" by the United States, he urged Soviet foreign minister Eduard Shevardnadze to join the US government in pursuing a "vigorous diplomatic campaign" to halt Libyan production of chemical weapons. As he had warned his colleagues in an NSPG meeting on arms control the previous spring, Shultz viewed the proliferation of chemical weapons as "totally out of control" and "one of the biggest problems we face."[101]

Concerns over the Rabta plant continued into the presidency of Reagan's successor and former vice president, George Bush. Asked while president-elect in December 1988 whether his administration would be "prepared to go beyond diplomatic means" to prevent Libya from developing a chemical warfare capability, Bush responded, "Not only should our administration be committed to that but in my view any civilized country around the world should be committed to that objective. . . . [T]his is a matter of real concern to us and, yes, we all ought to be committed to seeing that that plant not be permitted to spread further destruction."[102] Once in office, however, it became apparent that the matter was not among the new president's top priorities. Answering a question about the Libyan chemical plant from a high school student in March 1989, Bush noted that "it's a very important issue, but it's a peripheral issue."[103]

The issue came to an unexpected, if ambiguous, resolution on March 14, 1990, when reports came out of Libya that a fire had destroyed the chemical weapons facility at Rabta. Speculation from the world press—and accusations from Qadhafi—pointed fingers at US or Israeli involvement, particularly since White House press secretary Marlin Fitzwater had voiced the administration's renewed concerns over Rabta only the week before. Bush denied "absolutely" that the United States had played any role in attempting to sabotage the plant, and no evidence has come to light since that indicates otherwise. In fact, controversy still lingers over whether the fire was caused by an accident or was actually a Libyan hoax "to ward off the threat of another American attack" like the airstrikes of April 1986. Regardless, the Libyans most likely closed the plant until 1995, when they reopened it ostensibly to produce pharmaceuticals but likely to restart their chemical weapons program. In the aftermath of the fire, however, US officials were more than happy to see the threat neutralized. When asked about the plant's destruction, Secretary of Defense Dick Cheney commented, grinning, "It's a darned shame."[104]

The discovery of the chemical weapons plant was the most prominent—but far from the only—crisis involving Libya in the last days of the Reagan presidency. A far more immediately destructive tragedy occurred on the same day that the JCS presented Reagan with contingency plans for taking out the Rabta facility. In the evening sky over Lockerbie, Scotland, on December 21, 1988, Pan Am Flight 103 exploded in midair, killing all 259 passengers and crew (including 190 Americans) bound from London to New York, as well as eleven people on the ground. This shocking event was one of the world's most lethal acts of international terrorism prior to 9/11.[105]

It was far from clear at the time, however, that this crisis involved Libya at all. Initial evidence suggested that the bomb had been the handiwork of a Palestinian terrorist cell supported by Syria, though this preliminary finding was still far from definitive by the time Reagan turned over the keys to the Oval Office to Bush. The "Lockerbie bombing," as it became known, caught the US government in the transition between the two administrations. While Bush assured Reagan that he would support a retaliatory attack on Syria or Iran or any other state sponsor that turned out to be responsible, the CIA's Counterterrorism Center was not prepared to make a definitive call before Bush's inauguration on January 20, 1989.[106]

Indeed, it would take nearly another two years before the investigation—a remarkably complex feat of international cooperation between British, American, and West German intelligence authorities—began to point back to Qadhafi. Early indications of Syrian guilt gave way by mid-1989 to strong suspicions that Iran was to blame. Meanwhile, the global upheavals of 1989–1991 in Central and Eastern Europe, the Soviet Union, and the Gulf War in the Middle East monopolized the attention of the Bush administration's national security team. Finally, evidence began pointing definitively toward known Libyan agents in 1990 when British and American investigators recovered from the debris in Lockerbie a small fragment of a circuit board thought to belong to the bomb's timing device. Such devices have distinct characteristics unique and specific to their makers, and this timing device fragment bore the hallmarks of Libyan intelligence operatives with close links to Qadhafi.[107]

By the time these definitive links to the Libyan regime became known in 1990, enough time had passed since the December 1988 bombing that the Bush administration opted to treat the matter as one for criminal law enforcement rather than launch a retaliatory military strike. The United States and Britain charged two Libyans for the bombing in November 1991 and introduced a resolution that the United Nations Security Council passed in January 1992 directing the Qadhafi regime "to cooperate fully" with investigators "in establishing responsibility for the terrorist acts"—meaning to hand over the two prime suspects for trial. Qadhafi successfully stonewalled these demands in the face of UN sanctions for the next seven years, until he finally turned over the culprits in 1999 to be tried in a Scottish court temporarily established in the Netherlands, where one was acquitted and the other found guilty and sentenced to life in prison in 2001. Meanwhile, Qadhafi agreed to pay a modest sum in restitution to the families of the victims in a begrudging admission of ultimate responsibility as he sought to reenter the good graces of the international community at the start of the 2000s. Despite these modest results, Qadhafi's regime was able to evade the more severe punishment it had faced after the Berlin disco bombing in 1986.[108]

The Bush administration's intentional pivot away from the counterterrorism strategy developed under Reagan in 1985–1986, which had grown, in part, out of the recommendations of Vice President Bush's task force, and from the precedent of the April 1986 airstrikes on Libya, signaled a return to the earlier approach of treating terrorism as a crime rather than an act of war. Perhaps prudent, given the long time frame it took to uncover the responsible party for the Lockerbie bombing, this decision to break with the Reagan-Shultz counterterrorism strategy reintroduced the policy drift that had so plagued the issue of combating terrorism prior to 1986.

One final confrontation between the United States and Libya came just two weeks before the end of Reagan's term of office. As if to bookend the running conflict with Reagan that had begun in August 1981 with the downing of two Libyan fighter jets over the Gulf of Sidra, Qadhafi repeated the experience almost exactly with an air battle in the skies over the Mediterranean north of Tobruk on January 4, 1989. This time the engagement occurred much farther from Libyan airspace and was not prompted by US naval maneuvers to challenge Libyan claims to international waters. Rather, two Libyan jets engaged two US aircraft operating off of the USS *John F. Kennedy*, an aircraft carrier that was leading its battle group through the central Mediterranean toward Israel. Just as had happened seven and a half years before, the brief contest resulted in the destruction of both Libyan fighters.[109]

In Reagan's view, the timing of this unexpected encounter was no accident. Tensions between the United States and Libya had been extremely high since the US government had publicized its revelations about the chemical weapons plant at Rabta in November 1988. Since then, rumors had circulated that the Reagan administration was making plans to launch a military attack against the facility, which were in fact true, though it chose not to carry them out. Reagan noted upon hearing news of the air battle, "There have been signs that Quadafy is antsy about a possible attack on his chemical factory."[110] If he believed that US forces were preparing to attack the Rabta plant, Qadhafi may have been seeking to launch a preemptive attack—though this was more likely in an attempt to garner sympathy from the international community to undermine Reagan's efforts to isolate his regime over chemical weapons than an actual effort to gain military advantage, given the nature of the attack and the scorecard of the adversaries to date.[111]

This final flashpoint in the tumultuous contest between Libya and the United States over the course of the Reagan presidency pointed—not for the first time—to yet another central aspect of rogue state behavior: unpredictable armed aggression. With no rational hope of winning and no obvious objective, Qadhafi's final assault on US military forces underscored the unpredictable and erratic decision-making that had come to characterize his rule. The trio of crises involving Libya between the fall of 1988 and the first days of 1989 clearly confirmed the reputation of Qadhafi's regime, in the eyes of his US adversaries, as the poster child for the "outlaw states" that President Reagan had denounced since 1985. Perhaps even more importantly, these three crises highlighted with greater clarity than ever before the main features that were coming to define the rogue state phenomenon that Qadhafi's Libya represented: the pursuit of WMD, the sponsorship of terrorism, and regional armed aggression.

Derailed Strategy, Crystallizing Threat

The decisive year for crafting and deploying a US-engineered strategy to combat state-sponsored international terrorism was 1986. President Reagan told the American public a month after the Operation El Dorado Canyon airstrikes on Libya that "history is likely to record that 1986 was the year when the world, at long last, came to grips with the plague of terrorism."[112] After years of frustrating failure to mount an effective response to attacks from elusive transnational terrorist organizations, Reagan and his national security team refocused their efforts on the "outlaw states" that sponsored terrorism. They recalibrated US counterterrorism strategy in the wake of the alarming escalation of terrorist violence in the second half of 1985, devising a more proactive strategy that employed US military power alongside diplomatic and economic measures to deter and preempt attacks. Henceforward, the US government under Reagan would view terrorism as an act of war and would strike back against the "network of terrorist states" that waged it against the United States.

By the time of the airstrikes of April 1986, Libya had already become the first poster child for the rogue state phenomenon, the first "pariah in the world community," as Reagan labeled it.[113] The US confrontation with Libya escalated over the course of the 1980s at the same time that the threat of terrorism against the United States and its allies was on the rise, and Qadhafi's brazen sponsorship of terrorist attacks decisively fused the emerging rogue state paradigm with the related problem of international terrorism. As Washington increasingly turned its focus to the state sponsors of the nebulous networks of terrorist perpetrators, Libya became the prime target of and the test case for its counterterrorism strategy.

Reagan never assumed that 1986 would spell the end of terrorism altogether, and he sought to intensify pressure on Qadhafi following the airstrikes, with the ultimate goal of regime change. However, a combination of US success, Libyan deception, and unexpected distraction served to derail this newly robust strategy to fight terrorism in the final years of Reagan's presidency.

To begin, Libyan-backed terrorism appeared to largely fade away in the aftermath of the airstrikes. Despite a brief flurry of anti-American and anti-British violence, the few terrorist attacks in the months following the airstrikes were on a much smaller scale than the Berlin disco bombing and produced few US casualties. This was partly because of the success of Operation El Dorado Canyon in chastening Qadhafi and partly the result of Libyan deception. The CIA presciently predicted that Qadhafi would take increased precautions in the aftermath of the airstrikes to conceal the links between his regime and the terrorist organizations he supported.[114] Indeed, though the last major terrorist attack during Reagan's presidency—the bombing of Pan Am Flight 103 over Lockerbie, Scotland, in December 1988—eventually proved to have Libyan origins, Western intelligence agencies were not able to conclusively connect the dots back to Libya until the early 1990s.[115] In the absence of what Poindexter called another "spectacular" attack that could be linked to Qadhafi or the terrorist organizations he supported, the Reagan administration lacked sufficient domestic and allied support for intensified military action against the Libyan regime.[116]

Beginning in the fall of 1986, two unexpected distractions undercut the momentum behind Reagan's counterterrorism strategy. First, the Iran-Contra affair, which engulfed the administration and particularly the NSC staff from late 1986 through 1987, caused the ouster of two of the leading engineers of the counterterrorism strategy against Libya: National Security Advisor John Poindexter and his subordinate Oliver North. Poindexter's successor, Frank Carlucci, who had not been involved in the crafting of this strategy, sought to downgrade terrorism from the position of high prominence it had assumed in the administration's foreign policy concerns, arguing in an NSPG meeting in February 1987 that "terrorism is not our number one priority." He advocated a return to the mindset that terrorism should be viewed as "primarily a police and intelligence problem" more akin to "organized crime" than warfare, and he revived the fear that responding to terrorist attacks with military force could "play into the hands" of the terrorists. While the key tenets of the administration's counterterrorism strategy remained in effect, the growing consensus among Reagan's national security team behind their implementation had taken a serious blow.[117]

Second, a resurgence of Cold War concerns monopolized the administration's and US public's attention only months after the bombing of Libya. From the dramatic US-Soviet summit meeting in Reykjavik, Iceland, in October 1986 through the fall of communism in Eastern Europe in 1989 and the disintegration of the Soviet Union itself in 1991, these concerns crowded out other issues in the absence of a fresh terrorist crisis or provocation. Even the Lockerbie bombing, mired in an inconclusive investigation until 1990, did not refocus the energies of the US government on the fight against terrorism.

Nevertheless, in these same final years of the Reagan presidency, the threat of rogue states persisted and even expanded, with Libya once again at the forefront. Already synonymous with international terrorism, Qadhafi's regime returned after the April 1986 airstrikes to foment a series of crises in the final months of Reagan's presidency that underscored the three central features that would come to define rogue states: unpredictable military aggression, the pursuit of WMD, and the sponsorship of terrorism. It was the last of these—Libya's fusion of terrorism with the nascent rogue state paradigm—that ensured that these two threats to international security would remain intertwined in the thinking of US policymakers, with repercussions for US national security strategy that would reverberate for decades to come.

3

THE CRIMINAL ROGUE
Panama and the Question of Regime Change

Ronald Reagan left no doubt of the disdain with which he viewed the emerging threat of rogue states. In his July 1985 address to the American Bar Association advocating a more proactive strategy to combat state-sponsored terrorism, he vowed that the United States would not tolerate "attacks from outlaw states run by the strangest collection of misfits, loony tunes, and squalid criminals since the advent of the Third Reich."[1]

At first glance, Panama in the late 1980s appeared quite distinct from the threats and challenges posed by the poster child rogue state, Libya, and the quintessential rogue of the 1990s and early 2000s, Iraq. The Panamanian regime did not have a program to produce weapons of mass destruction (WMD); it did not invade its neighbors with conventional forces; it did not launch destructive acts of international terrorism. Hence, scholars rarely include Panama among lists of what would come to be known as "rogue states."[2] Indeed, Presidents Ronald Reagan and George H. W. Bush, in their most prominent speeches outlining the challenge of "outlaw states" and "renegade regimes," made no mention of Panama.[3]

This omission overlooks the significant role that Panama played, in a short two-year period from early 1988 through the first days of 1990, in expanding and deepening the emerging rogue state paradigm that was elbowing its way onto the international scene in the Cold War's final years. Not only did Panama and its dictator, General Manuel Noriega, in fact share important characteristics with Qadhafi's Libya and Saddam Hussein's Iraq, but the administrations of Ronald Reagan and George Bush viewed it as part and parcel of the same developing phenomenon. Their failure to include Panama in their key speeches—as well as the tendency of scholars to overlook it—was because of the unusually short time span when Noriega's regime factored highly on their threat radar. Between Reagan's address on "outlaw states" to the American Bar Association in 1985 and Bush's speech on "renegade regimes" at the Aspen Institute in 1990, the Panamanian problem had come to light and then been dispatched with remarkable speed.

Moreover, the ways in which Noriega's regime challenged and expanded the emerging rogue state paradigm, particularly through its explicit criminal dimension and its fusion with the parallel international issue of narcotics trafficking, account for its sidelining by historians whose attention has been more captivated by the larger crises of the post–Cold War era. Nevertheless, to an extent largely forgotten today, for a number of months in early 1988 and late 1989, the Panama crisis stood as one of the most acute international priorities for both the Reagan and Bush administrations. The ways they handled the challenge helped solidify the idea of rogue states as international outlaws led by criminal dictators and set precedents for how US administrations would deal with similar threats in the future. In particular, though they disagreed over the means to achieve it, both Reagan and Bush elevated regime change as a central strategic goal for dealing with rogue dictators like Noriega.

The confrontation between the United States and Panama occurred in two phases: the first under Reagan from February 1988 through May 1988 and the second under Bush from May 1989 through December 1989. Scholars have generally given this crisis cursory treatment in favor of the more momentous developments in 1989–1991 in Europe and the Middle East. When they do devote attention to the US-Panama standoff, it is typically with regard to only the second phase, which culminated in the largest US military action since the Vietnam War. The Reagan portion of the crisis usually features, if at all, as a brief prelude to the main event.[4]

However, the first phase of the crisis is at least as critical to understanding Panama's emergence as a rogue state and how top US officials grappled with how to respond to the threat. It was during this earlier phase that Reagan, Bush, and their advisors debated and disagreed—often vehemently, and more starkly and publicly than on almost any other foreign policy issue—over the nature of the threat and how to address it. These debates determined the menu of options available for a US response to Panama's provocations, and the decisions that Reagan and his team made limited the options available to the Bush administration the following year. Thus, some of the most critical decision points that eventually culminated in the US invasion of Panama in December 1989 actually occurred the previous year, when many of the senior members of Bush's administration (including Bush himself) held other central posts under his predecessor.[5]

By the culmination of the crisis in late 1989, Bush found himself left with only one viable option to achieve his central goal of regime change in Panama, and his decisive use of US military force to topple Noriega's dictatorship became a model for dealing with rogue states. As Reagan, Bush, and their national security teams grappled with how to confront Noriega's rogue regime, the strategies they fashioned to advance their goal of regime change—as well as their debates and disagreements over the merits of negotiations with and military intervention against outlaw dictators—laid the groundwork for a new approach to safeguarding US and global security that would transcend the end of the Cold War.

"A Bad Egg" in Central America

Panama's Noriega and Libya's Qadhafi shared many characteristics. Both were military officers who seized and consolidated their power against internal and external opponents by cracking down on dissent. To further this process of accumulating power, both turned to their regions' most lucrative trades to compound their wealth and thus their influence—the selling of oil for Qadhafi and the selling of drugs for Noriega. Neither regime was communist—indeed, both fought against communists at various points—but both were open to receiving aid from and forming alliances of convenience with communist powers. Both sought to bolster their legitimacy by appealing to their peoples' nationalism and inflaming their resentments over their historical exploitation at the hands of Western powers. And both actively courted confrontation with the United States.

Panama's history with the United States was, however, significantly longer and more fraught than was Libya's. Frequent US military interventions throughout the nineteenth and twentieth centuries created a deep-seated wariness of the "Yanquis" or the "colossus of the north" among the nations of Latin America. Panama gained its independence from Colombia in 1903 thanks in significant measure to US intervention on its behalf during the Panamanian Revolution. A treaty negotiated in the revolution's aftermath gave the United States control over the Panama Canal Zone, where the United States oversaw the canal's construction and thereafter controlled the operation of the highly important strategic waterway that connected the Atlantic and Pacific Oceans. Seeking to improve relations with the countries of Latin America, the Carter administration negotiated a set of treaties in 1977 that the Senate ratified the next year to transfer control of the canal to the Panamanians by the end of the century. By the late 1980s, approximately ten thousand US soldiers remained stationed at US bases in the Canal Zone, pending its return to Panama by the end of the 1990s.[6]

Manuel Noriega started his colorful career as an asset to rather than an enemy of the United States. As early as the late 1950s, he began providing intelligence to the United States as a paid informant of the CIA. As a close supporter of

Omar Torrijos, who took power in Panama at the head of a military junta following a coup in 1968, Noriega rose rapidly through the ranks of the Panamanian National Guard, which he later renamed the Panama Defense Forces (PDF) once he assumed command in 1983 following Torrijos's death in a mysterious plane crash. In 1970, Noriega became Panama's intelligence chief under Torrijos, a position from which he continued his work as a source of intelligence for the CIA, even meeting in 1976 with his US counterpart, George Bush, who was then serving as the director of central intelligence under President Gerald Ford.[7]

The trouble was that Noriega was also providing the same services to any other government that would pay, and his notoriously fickle loyalties earned him a reputation as the "rent-a-colonel" and the "Caribbean Prostitute." Indeed, Noriega was known to have close ties and give intelligence to Colombia while also helping the US Drug Enforcement Administration (DEA) to round up Colombian drug cartel leaders, and to Castro's communist government in Cuba while also informing the United States about Cuban subversion in Latin America. In some respects, it was this fickle nature that made Noriega such a useful—if unsavory—source of intelligence to all comers: because he worked for governments on all sides, he enjoyed a remarkable amount of access to sensitive information on all sides. Noting Noriega's "reputation as an unprincipled opportunist," State Department official Charles Hill cautioned, "He will work with us as long as it suits his interests, no longer." Both Secretary of State George Shultz and Colin Powell, who took over as President Reagan's sixth and final national security advisor in November 1987, claimed credit for the memorable quip about Noriega, "You can't buy him; you can only rent him." Clearly, the top members of the Reagan administration shared this assessment of Panama's strongman.[8]

Despite Noriega's opportunism and mercenary approach to alliances, US ties with him deepened once he became commander of the PDF and de facto ruler of Panama in 1983 after Torrijos's death. At the urging of Jeane Kirkpatrick, the US ambassador to the United Nations, the Reagan administration sought to distinguish between left-wing "totalitarian" regimes, with ties to the communist bloc, and right-wing "authoritarian" regimes, which could be helpful in the fight against communism. Nowhere did this approach affect US policy more than in Latin America, a top Cold War priority for the Reagan administration that Kirkpatrick called "the most important place in the world for us." Although Noriega and his regime might have been distasteful, his help in supplying and supporting the Contra rebels fighting against the communist government in Nicaragua made him more of an asset than a liability to the United States. Moreover, despite growing evidence of his own complicity in the international drug trade, Noriega also provided periodic help to the DEA with its efforts to police narcotics trafficking in Central America. For this assistance, Noriega remained on the payroll of the US government through 1987, receiving hundreds of thousands of dollars annually from the CIA, FBI, DEA, and other agencies.[9]

Beginning in 1986 and 1987, however, Noriega began to run increasingly afoul of US interests, and the Reagan administration started to shift its approach to the Panamanian general. First, as the 1980s wore on and Cold War tensions began to recede thanks to Reagan's growing partnership with Soviet leader Mikhail Gorbachev, the Cold War context in Latin America became decidedly less important than it had seemed to US officials in the first half of the decade. The single greatest reason to continue working with Noriega—his support for the Contras—had subsided with these global changes and the breaking of the Iran-Contra scandal in late 1986, which cast fresh controversy on any further US aid to the Contras. Moreover, evidence of Noriega's involvement in narcotics trafficking—an issue of growing importance to the US government and increasing concern to the US public—made his partnership with US authorities untenable.[10]

What finally pushed Noriega out of the United States' orbit was his increasingly brazen disdain for democracy. From the time he took command of the PDF in 1983, his standing as Panama's national ruler came not from an official political office but from his control of Panama's military, intelligence, and police forces. Throughout the 1980s, he oversaw rigged elections that placed his own handpicked puppets in the Panamanian presidency. The exposure by the *New York Times* in 1986 of Noriega's complicity in the brutal murder of Hugo Spadafora, the most prominent opposition leader against his regime, marked the dictator's breaking point with official and public opinion in the United States. Thereafter, his deepening ties to Cuba and Libya, from which he received funds and arms, exposed his increasing unreliability as an ally, especially one to whom the United States would have to turn over the Panama Canal by 2000. After more public revelations of rigged elections and corruption, Panama descended into a storm of rising unrest in 1987, as domestic opposition against the regime met with government crackdowns and violence. This breakdown of law and order put the large number of US soldiers and civilians in Panama at risk from the harassment that grew from Noriega's increasingly blatant and vitriolic anti-US rhetoric.[11]

Negotiating Regime Change: Reagan and Noriega, 1988

This downward cycle reached a crisis between the Noriega regime and the Reagan administration in the first days of 1988. It was a lack of coordination within the US government, rather than a coordinated strategy, that tipped the Reagan administration into active involvement in the mounting crisis with Noriega.

The deepening unrest in Panama in the summer of 1987 prompted calls in the US media for the administration to distance itself from its association with Noriega and take some kind of action against his regime. At the end of the summer, *Time* ran a story charging that Noriega had become "an embarrassment for Washington." Noting accusations that the Panamanian dictator was involved in "drug running, money laundering, election fraud and helping to steer restricted American technology to the Cubans and Soviets, not to mention repressing his own people," the article recounted sharp criticism in Congress for his previously close relationship with the US government. While Attorney General Edwin Meese remained generally supportive into 1987 of Noriega's usefulness to US narcotics investigators, his Justice Department—including the FBI, DEA, and Customs Service—opened a series of investigations of its own that same year into Noriega's complicity in the drug trade.[12]

These investigations reached a head on February 4, 1988, when two federal grand juries in Florida indicted Noriega and sixteen of his associates on charges of narcotics trafficking and racketeering, including assisting Colombia's notorious Medellin cartel. The cumulative sentences for Noriega, if convicted, amounted to 145 years in prison. The extent of Meese's personal involvement in ordering or overseeing the investigations and indictments remains murky. What is clear is that the indictments were not discussed among or directed from the senior levels of the Reagan administration, neither were they part of an overall plan across the government for concerted action against Noriega's regime. Indeed, Secretary of State Shultz later reported that the Justice Department handed down its indictments "without adequate consultation with the State Department or, as far as I could learn, with the White House." The president himself had not been consulted and had not signed off on the indictments. In response to complaints from the National Security Council (NSC) staff that the Justice Department was making foreign policy, US attorneys in Florida argued that they were merely indicting a criminal.[13]

The problem was that the United States did not have an extradition treaty with Panama, so US authorities had no legal jurisdiction or means to bring Noriega to Florida to stand trial. Noriega, for his part, dismissed the charges with scorn, calling them "a joke and an absurd political movement." The largely symbolic nature of the indictments immediately put the Reagan administration in a fix. Since the "war on drugs" had risen to become such a prominent national political issue in the late 1980s, the administration could not be seen as soft in its handling of drug traffickers; therefore, it could not backpedal and renounce the indictments against Noriega. That bridge had already been crossed. On the other hand, Reagan and his advisors had to scramble to figure out how to handle and follow up on this significant escalation in the their standoff with the Panamanian general.[14]

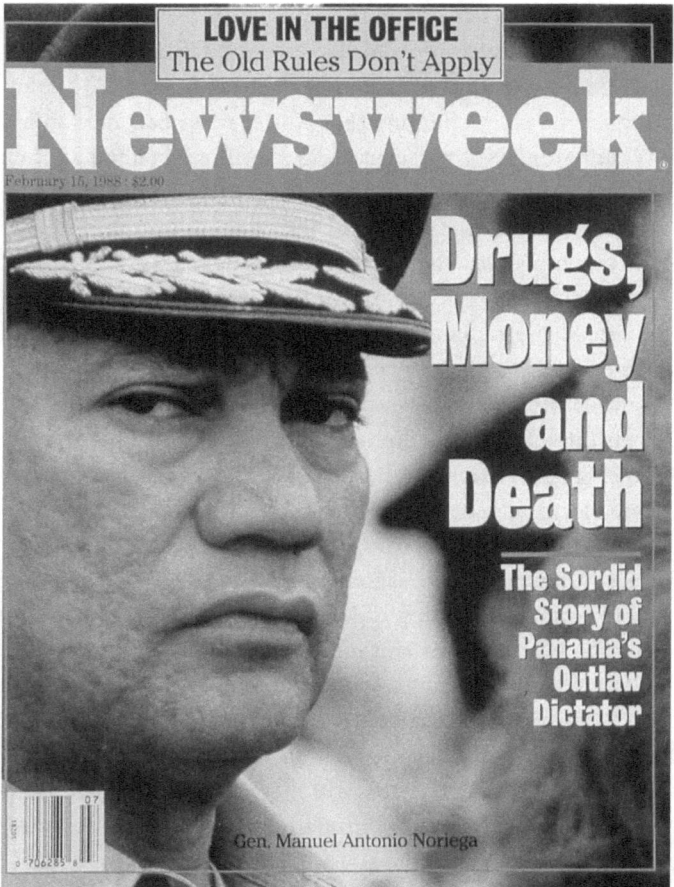

FIGURE 8. Outlaw dictator: This February 1988 *Newsweek* cover highlights the criminality of Manuel Noriega's Panamanian regime, following on the heels of the US grand jury indictments against him for drug trafficking.

News of the indictments had a galvanizing effect on popular demonstrations against Noriega's hold on power in Panama, with protesters filling the streets and workers declaring a general strike. As Shultz observed, "Panamanians assumed the United States meant business; they could now dare to express themselves." The administration's first step was private but direct, sending Assistant Secretary of State for Inter-American Affairs Elliott Abrams to meet with Panamanian president Eric Delvalle in Florida to urge him to fire Noriega. Before the end of February 1988, Delvalle did just that, dismissing Noriega from his post as commander of the PDF. Noriega, however, outmaneuvered Delvalle by convening the National Assembly and ousting him from the presidency instead. The United States responded by freezing Panamanian assets, consistent with its continued recognition of Delvalle as Panama's legitimate president, which immediately prompted a cash shortage and banking crisis in Panama, escalating the political crisis still further. "This was the moment," Shultz urged, "for the United States to move decisively."[15]

Reagan and his team faced their first major decision point in the showdown with Noriega. The president had been following developments in Panama with increasing concern over the course of the past year. As early as January 1987, Reagan was noting in his diary his growing disdain for "Noriega the mil[itary] dictator of Panama. Corruption there is rampant & he's too fond of Castro." Just as he had done with Qadhafi, Reagan bestowed a series of belittling monikers on Noriega: "a bad egg," "the bad boy of Panama," and, in short, "not our favorite person."[16] Prior to the indictments, the administration had sent Assistant Secretary of Defense Richard Armitage to Panama in January 1988 to urge Noriega to step down, an appeal that the dictator refused.[17] Once the Justice Department had issued its indictments, Reagan wrote that Noriega was "spouting lies all over the news" and expressed growing concern with the increased number of incidents of harassment and arrests of US soldiers and civilians on the part of the PDF. As the political crisis escalated and Noriega managed to foil his own ouster by replacing Delvalle, Reagan succinctly summed up the situation: "That really is a mixed up [sic] mess in Panama."[18]

Meeting with his top national security advisors on March 10, 1988, Reagan made his first major strategic decision to set the course for how his administration would respond to the deepening crisis in Panama. "We're agreed we must not let down or lose on this," the president recorded afterward. "We must get rid of him."[19] Shultz advocated most forcefully for taking decisive action to bring about Noriega's departure, insisting that the stakes were too high in terms of the credibility of US support for democracy in Latin America to allow for defeat: "Let's recognize that we are in a fight to the finish. . . . Let there be no doubt about it, Noriega has to go." For now, he urged tightening "the financial squeeze" as the principal tool to weaken Noriega's hold on power. Though Shultz's characterization of the crisis as a "fight to the finish" rankled colleagues such as Secretary of Defense Frank Carlucci, it resonated with the president, who agreed that "this is one we can't lose. . . . There is nothing worse than being defeated by this man."[20] Vice President Bush, though quiet during this National Security Planning Group (NSPG) meeting, had already publicly expressed his view that "Noriega should go and I think he will go."[21] Reagan, with the full support of his chief advisors, had drawn a line in the sand, declaring regime change in Panama to be his overall objective. But how he would accomplish this goal was less clear, and here the consensus among his advisors broke down. The NSC agreed on a series of preliminary "anti-Noriega actions" the next day, which included economic sanctions against his "illegitimate" regime and consideration of additional troop deployments to the Panama Canal Zone. Within days, Reagan approved a request to quietly send one hundred more marines to Panama to guard US facilities and aircraft.[22]

Shultz, however, soon urged bolder measures—"vigorous actions designed to exploit Panamanian developments." The secretary of state later wrote, "My strategy at this point, approved by President Reagan, was to generate as much pressure as possible on Noriega and couple that with a proposal that he seek asylum in a third country," such as Spain. With the United States agreeing not to seek extradition for Noriega—but with the indictments against him still in place—the general would be held firmly in exile and out of Panama. But Shultz did not feel that the economic measures against Noriega would be enough to force him to accept this proposal, for although the sanctions did substantial damage to Panama's economy, its dictator maintained his own sources of revenue through the drug trade and his connections with Libya and Cuba. In his memoirs, Shultz did not specify just what "vigorous actions" he and his deputy Elliott Abrams had in mind, but they likely centered on the threat or actual use of military force. Yet when Shultz and Abrams made their proposals for additional leverage against Noriega to the rest of the NSC, they were roundly shot down. Admiral William Crowe, the chairman of the Joint Chiefs of Staff (JCS), denounced Shultz's plan as "harebrained" and rejected any use of the military forces stationed in the Canal Zone. "That set the tone," Shultz recalled, and the others present voiced their agreement with Crowe. "The proposals went nowhere."[23]

By mid-March, therefore, the Reagan team had decided on an offensive strategic objective—to remove Noriega from power—but had settled on essentially modest and defensive means to accomplish it, through economic sanctions and a small boost to the security of US bases. Meanwhile, Noriega further consolidated his hold on power by imposing a "state of urgency" on March 18 following a failed coup attempt, and he rejected the State Department's overture offering him political asylum in Spain. Events were appearing to bear out Shultz's suspicion that the administration's approach was not enough to accomplish its overall goal, and the secretary of state already sensed that the momentum generated by the indictments and the cash and banking crisis had been squandered: "Through internal argument and inaction, our moment had passed: we had missed our chance to convert [the growing dissatisfaction with and isolation of the regime] into decisive pressure on Noriega."[24] Yet Shultz did not give up, sending the president a memo at the end of March outlining the "vital U.S. interests" that the crisis in Panama put "in great jeopardy," including the credibility of the US commitment to democracy in Central America and to the fight against international drug trafficking. He urged, "The time to act is now. . . . The longer we wait, the more we are faced with a stark choice between a Noriega victory and direct U.S. military action."[25]

Reagan himself was also losing faith in the likelihood of economic sanctions to produce the changes he desired in Panama. In early April, after approving another executive order imposing further economic restraints on Panama, he wrote ambivalently in his diary, "We're still no further with Noriega. I've O.K.'d further financial moves for whatever they are worth." Yet he also did not seem to favor any specific alternative to this course of action, noting that in an NSPG meeting on March 31 he "cleared up a few items that had been suggested but that would have been very counter productive [sic]."[26] He left unstated just what these counterproductive items were and who had proposed them—and whether they were Shultz's proposals for using military force, of which Reagan makes no mention in his diary. Nevertheless, with no breakthrough in sight, the administration had to devise a new plan of attack.

It was Shultz's State Department, pivoting to a new course after the rejection of its more "vigorous" proposals, that set in motion an alternative plan that could accomplish the administration's goal of removing Noriega without having to resort to military force. In mid-April, with Reagan's approval, Shultz sent Mike Kozak, a senior official in the State Department's Bureau of Inter-American Affairs, as a special envoy to Panama to deal with Noriega directly. Kozak had already met with the dictator at an earlier stage of the crisis, and he would remain the US government's chief negotiator with Noriega through the denouement of this phase of the standoff at the end of May. After meeting with Noriega in Panama on April 21, Kozak reported to Shultz that the broad outlines of a potential deal were already beginning to take shape. Most significantly, he revealed that pressure from the United States had succeeded in inducing the dictator to discuss his departure. Noriega expressed openness to stepping down if the United States lifted its sanctions; if the Panamanian legislature enacted a face-saving law setting a term limit for the PDF commander, which would allow him to relinquish power "with dignity"; and if he were not forced into exile after stepping down. However, Kozak did not feel that Noriega would agree to any final deal unless the United States agreed to lift the indictments against him, stressing to Shultz, "The indictment is our real leverage."[27]

The terms of this potential deal with Panama's strongman set off a debate within the administration over how to keep up the pressure on his regime—and especially whether to consider quashing the indictments as leverage to secure his removal from power. According to Shultz, the dividing lines on this question were initially reversed from what they would be at the climax of the crisis in the coming weeks. Kozak, the man on the ground in Panama, remained convinced that "there is no way Noriega will leave his job with that indictment hanging over his head." Treasury Secretary James Baker, along with most other members of the NSPG, expressed a willingness to terminate the indictments if necessary to secure a deal. At this point, it was Shultz, along with National Security Advisor Colin Powell, who rejected the notion of quashing the indictments, which, in Shultz's words, "stands for our commitment to fight drug trafficking" and amounted to the strongest leverage the United States had of ensuring that Noriega would keep his end of a possible deal.[28] As early as the NSPG meeting on March 10, Shultz had asserted his distaste for the idea of letting Noriega off the hook for the drug trafficking charges pending against him, while others such as Carlucci and Baker had advocated the need to "leave him a way out. We cannot corner Noriega."[29]

Meanwhile, Noriega's PDF and paramilitary forces increased their harassment of US personnel in Panama. The NSPG approved a series of measures, including demonstrations of military power, that US forces in Panama would undertake to put additional pressure on Panama's leader and reinforce his sense of urgency to reach a deal. Yet many of the planned actions, such as a jet fighter flyover of Noriega's headquarters, never took place. Moreover, public statements from some of Reagan's top advisors undermined the coercive diplomacy against Noriega before it could have its desired effect. Most damaging of all were comments that Baker made to the media "on background," in which he suggested that the United States was considering weakening its sanctions and ruled out the use of military force as an option, assuring reporters that "we're not going to do that."[30]

As April came to a close and Kozak continued his negotiations, he remained convinced that Noriega was serious about his willingness to step down, provided he got the right deal. As both sides edged closer to reaching an agreement, it became increasingly clear that the indictments were the prime sticking point; Noriega would agree to nothing with that threat hanging over his head. Back in Washington on April 29, Kozak pressed Shultz and Reagan hard to quash the indictments by framing it along the lines of a plea bargain, stressing, "It's the only way to get him out. . . . I can see no deal unless we get rid of the indictment." Still, Shultz held firm for the time being: "No quashing," he instructed Kozak.[31]

As negotiations languished, the administration faced its second major decision point in the crisis, and it was President Reagan himself who took the initiative to spur a breakthrough. His first key decision, on March 10, had set the removal of Noriega as the overall US strategic objective, and Shultz had followed this up by sending Kozak to Panama to test the waters for a potential deal. This time the decision centered on how to accomplish it—and specifically whether to put the indictments on the table as bargaining leverage. In two meetings with his national security team in the Oval Office on May 9 and 10, the president made what Shultz found a surprising decision: to drop the indictments if necessary to secure a deal for Noriega's removal from power in Panama. Up to this point, Reagan had been reluctant to take this step for the same reasons as Shultz. But as it became increasingly clear that Noriega would reject any deal that did not include dropping the indictments, both Reagan and Shultz had come around to the view that it was the only viable option short of using military force. The president first broached the topic with his NSC in the meeting on May 9. Present were Powell, Chief of Staff Howard Baker, their deputies, and Vice President Bush, joined later by Attorney General Meese. After Meese expressed his support for dropping the indictments on the grounds of national security, despite the likelihood that such a move would "kick up a fuss," Reagan gave his own approval. He returned to the issue the next day, this time with Shultz present in addition to Bush, Powell, Baker, and several of their deputies, to solicit the views of his top advisors and confirm that he had a consensus behind the move. Bush expressed some uneasiness about how it would be presented to the public and the need to ensure Latin American and congressional support, but he and the others all signed off on Reagan's decision to go ahead. The indictments were now in play.[32]

At this point the deal with Noriega came together rapidly. Kozak reported from Panama that he had reached an agreement on a detailed plan and timetable for Noriega to relinquish power. The general would leave Panama for a long "vacation" until at least after the Panamanian elections scheduled for May 1989. Several smaller points remained unresolved, but Kozak was convinced that the deal that would dismantle the Noriega regime was nearly closed. Noriega even tentatively agreed to announce the agreement on May 14.[33]

But in the meantime, a firestorm opened on the home front. On the morning of May 12, news of the arrangement for Noriega's departure leaked to the press. Shultz and his aides suspected that officials in the Justice Department were behind the leak to try to kill the deal, telling reporters that Meese had objected to it all along. Immediately, senators and commentators condemned the idea of dropping the indictments as part of the deal and distorted what few details they knew of the arrangements of the negotiation. Before the day was out, the president received a letter signed by seventy members of Congress declaring their "complete opposition" to the proposed deal with Noriega, which they protested was "both politically and morally . . . the wors[t] thing you could do at this time."[34]

Commenting on this "firestorm" in Congress in his diary and in a meeting with advisors the next day, Reagan explained the reasoning that lay behind his decision to use the cancellation of the drug indictments as leverage with Noriega. Still determined to remove Panama's dictator from power, Reagan reasoned that the US government had already used most of the tools in its belt. He could either strike a deal that would secure Noriega's voluntary relinquishing of power, or he could use military force to remove him directly. Referring to his critics in Congress, Reagan wrote, "They don[']t seem to realize the only alternative would be a military invasion of Panama . . . but again there is no alternative & we can[']t use the indictment anyway because Panama law does not allow extradition." Holding onto the indictments at this juncture would be merely symbolic, as the United States had no legal power to actually use them against Noriega while he remained in Panama. Reagan favored results over symbolism in this case, and he saw no other way, save military action, to accomplish his goal.[35]

Despite Reagan's determination to press ahead with the deal, the change in political headwinds was wearing on the support of his chief advisors. Opposition from Congress, the DEA, and the US Attorney's office was giving both Meese and Bush cold feet. The vice president sent Reagan a "sensitive memo" on May 14, marked "eyes only" with strict instructions to be hand delivered in a sealed envelope only to the president, Howard Baker, and Colin Powell. In this missive, Bush explained that he was "troubled" that the deal coming into shape would "undermin[e] our administration's position as tough on drug pushers." Though he sympathized with Reagan's "concern that there is no other choice" to oust Noriega from power, he argued that "we are not certain of that" and "continued pressure might just work." Nevertheless, Bush still expressed his support for a deal that would require Noriega to accept guilt for his drug trafficking crimes along the lines of a plea bargain, but he felt the administration would need more time to convince a skeptical Congress and public. He concluded by "strongly urg[ing] that the negotiators come home . . . no deal beats a bad deal." Meanwhile, James Baker joined Meese in warning the president that the Noriega deal would be "as big a problem for him as 'Irangate.'" Shaken by the reversals of three key members of his team, Reagan shelved the discussion pending his final decision the next week, delaying the tentative announcement of the deal in Panama.[36]

What ensued over the course of the next week was a battle royal among the members of Reagan's national security team over whether to move ahead with the proposed deal to remove Noriega from power in exchange for dropping the indictments against him. In a series of four key meetings between Reagan and his advisors, what started as internal dissention grew into heated and public divisions within the top level of the administration.

Battle lines hardened as the week began. The meeting on May 16 rehashed what the president and his team had discussed several days earlier, and Reagan reaffirmed his commitment to the deal with Noriega. Responding to reports of Noriega's prevaricating on some of the finer points, Reagan "interrupted the debate & told the negotiator to go back to Panama—lay down our terms & if Noriega doesn't go along tell him we'll send in our military. That ended the meet-

FIGURE 9. "We must get rid of him": President Reagan meets in the Oval Office on June 13, 1988 with Secretary of State George Shultz and National Security Advisor Colin Powell, the only two of his chief advisors to strongly support his approach to negotiating Noriega's removal from power in Panama.

ing." As Shultz recalled, Reagan "knew a negotiated outcome would be unpopular even if it succeeded, but he was firm."[37]

But for Bush the debate was not yet over. The vice president, who had recently secured that year's Republican presidential nomination, was away from Washington on a campaign swing through California, where he came under mounting pressure to take a public stance on the issue. On May 18, he met with the Los Angeles police chief, who warned him that the deal on the table with Noriega would be a slap in the face to the police officers on the front lines of the war on drugs. This warning, along with criticism from his Democratic opponent for his role in earlier US dealings with the Panamanian dictator, prompted Bush to publicly break with the president—an exceptionally rare occurrence in his nearly eight years of loyal service as vice president. Bush declared that "drug dealers are domestic terrorists. . . . I won't bargain with terrorists, and I won't bargain with drug dealers either, whether they're on U.S. or foreign soil." This public rebuke of Reagan's approach countered his assurance to the president several days earlier that he "will not leak [his judgment on the issue], never have, won't start now." At the same time, Bush sent Reagan a memo urging him once again to "bring the negotiators home." He explained that he was "more convinced than ever" that a deal that dropped the indictments against Noriega would be "a severe blow to those who are on the front line" of the war on drugs: "We have got to find another way to get Noriega out of there." Returning to Washington, Bush cornered Powell in the West Wing, completing his reversal from the approval he had given to Reagan's plan just a week earlier: "I have never been so sure of anything in my life, and I will do whatever I have to do to kill this deal."[38]

He was not the only one to express such sentiments, within as well as outside the administration. Public opposition to the proposed Panama deal was widespread, and the Senate overwhelmingly passed a resolution to block killing Noriega's indictments, prompting Reagan to lament that "they just don[']t know what they are talking about." By May 19, the day the *Washington Post* ran the headline "Bush Splits with Reagan on Handling of Noriega," opinion among Reagan's advisors continued to swing against the plan in what Shultz called a "wild" White House meeting. Despite the heated tone of the debate, Reagan put his foot down: "I stuck by my decision."[39]

This time it was Noriega who threw a wrench in the proceedings. His demand for money to ease the banking crisis that plagued Panama gave rise to concerns that the Colombian banks involved in the loans were connected to the drug trade. This gave just enough ammunition to the opponents of the deal for Reagan to request a final pair of meetings over the weekend of May 21–22 to resolve the crisis and finalize his government's position on the negotiations once and for all. He had reached his third and final major decision point in the standoff with Noriega—one that would determine the fate of the diplomatic track in resolving the dispute with Panama.[40]

On Saturday morning, May 21, Reagan gathered his full national security team in the Yellow Oval Room of the White House residence. As he recounted in his diary, a "division of ranks" formed among his advisors "supporting my position & the V.P.'s."[41] All who were present noted the unusually heated tone of the debate, particularly from Bush, who "fairly exploded over the issue" and "carried the fight to Reagan as he never had before. . . . He had never taken on the president so directly."[42] As Colin Powell recalled, "Bush did something none of us had ever seen him do before. He argued with the President directly in front of the rest of us."[43] James Baker remembered this as "one of the more contentious internal debates I recall during my twelve years of government service." In arguing against trading the indictments for Noriega's removal from power, Bush asked, "How can we make the argument we're getting tough on drug dealers if we let this guy off?" Baker firmly supported Bush "on both policy and political grounds." He explained, "As a nation, we couldn't be in the posture of cutting a deal with one of the worst drug dealers in the world. As a presidential candidate, the Vice President would also suffer politically from such a perception. It was bad policy—and bad politics."⁴⁴ Bush himself had admitted to Reagan a week earlier that "you have every reason to wonder if my judgement is based on pure political expediency." Rather than counter this notion, Bush explained that he no longer felt that the political storm "could be weathered," asserting plainly that "I will be severely damaged" if the proposed deal went forward.⁴⁵ However, Bush and Baker did not appear to offer any alternatives that would accomplish the tangible result that Reagan desired of regime change in Panama. Shultz noted with frustration their vague suggestions to "build up pressure on Noriega," which they had previously blocked when the secretary of state had earlier urged a more muscular approach.⁴⁶

It was President Reagan himself who displayed the clearest grasp of the alternatives. As he saw it, if he were to hold firm to his decision to oust the Noriega regime, his administration now had only two options left on the table: to broker a deal or to use military force. Otherwise, he would have to leave Noriega in place. Reagan understood the unpopularity of the optics of such an agreement, noting in his diary that Bush wanted "to refuse the deal because of the politics—how it will look giving in to a drug dealer." He countered this by asking, "What will it look like backing down & letting him continue as the absolute Dictator of Panama & still in the drug business[?]" Reagan remained determined that practical results should outweigh political optics. Bush took the opposite view, arguing that dropping the indictments was unwise "even if it does result in his stepping down & out of Panama." The president laid out his analysis: "My position is it's a good deal. The indictment is meaningless because the Panama Const[itution] prohibits our extraditing him," and "if we don[']t follow through N[oriega] can stay in Panama as mil[itary] dictator & we can[']t touch him." The only other option, as Reagan saw it, was military action, something he was determined to avoid if he had another way to achieve the same result.⁴⁷

Despite the president's clear and consistently held position, his advisors divided into opposing camps—and the camps were far from equal in numbers. By the meeting on May 21, James Baker, Howard Baker, and Meese, among others present, strenuously supported Bush's position, while only Shultz and Powell (as well as the negotiator, Kozak) came down on Reagan's side. Even Reagan's offer to publicly announce Bush and the others' opposition and take personal responsibility for the deal did not budge their views. Shultz sensed that Reagan "seemed to be waiting for the vice president and his other advisers to say, 'Mr. President, we feel your decision is wrong, but we will stand behind you and carry it out.' But they didn't say that." Finally, Reagan decided to think it over before making his final decision after one last meeting the next day.⁴⁸

This final showdown on Sunday evening, May 22, again took place in the Yellow Oval Room in the living quarters of the White House. The same group of

FIGURE 10. Negotiating regime change: President Reagan weighs the views of his divided national security team during the first of the "wild" and decisive weekend meetings in the Yellow Oval Room of the White House residence at the climax of the crisis with Panama, May 21, 1988. Vice President Bush makes a strenuous point to Reagan's left while Secretary of State Shultz leans forward to Reagan's right. Also pictured are Attorney General Ed Meese (next to Shultz), negotiator Mike Kozak (next to Bush), Secretary of the Treasury James Baker (next to Kozak with legs crossed), and National Security Advisor Colin Powell (across from Reagan with back turned).

Reagan's chief advisors argued the same points with the same intensity. As Reagan wrote later that night in his diary, "No one[']s minds had been changed so I made the decision." The US government would go ahead with the deal: Noriega would step down and leave Panama, at which time the United States would drop its indictments against him. Reagan keenly felt his isolation, "practically alone" with just Shultz and Powell's support: "Even Nancy is against me on this one but I'm absolutely convinced it's the only way to go." As Shultz commented at the time to one of his aides, "This is when you need a decisive president, and Reagan is."[49]

Once this final decision had been reached, Kozak returned immediately to Panama to close the deal with Noriega. Over the next three days, Reagan and his team anxiously awaited word from their envoy of Noriega's final agreement to the terms. After some wrangling over money to resolve the Panamanian banking crisis, Kozak reported to Shultz that the deal appeared to be set, pending a final handshake with Noriega, who would publicly announce the deal on the morning of May 25. But as the morning wore on and the general remained in his headquarters, it was clear that something had gone wrong. Finally, Kozak relayed word to Washington that Noriega's junior officers, vigorously opposing their commander's decision to relinquish power, had convinced him to delay once again. Shultz passed on this news to Reagan, who was aboard Air Force One en route to a summit with Gorbachev in Moscow, and they agreed to pull the plug. The deal had collapsed.[50]

In the months that followed, Reagan and his national security team considered a variety of alternative options to remove Noriega from power. Shultz renewed his push for a more muscular use of military pressure against Panama, including the possibility of using special forces in an operation to "snatch" Noriega to bring him to trial in the United States, which the Pentagon and JCS once again opposed.[51] In an effort to find another way to exert additional pressure on Noriega's regime, the CIA developed a set of plans for covert action to oust the Panamanian dictator, which they presented to the president in an NSPG meeting on July 6. The administration shelved these plans by the end of the month, however, when a leak to the *Washington Post* revealed them to the public, causing much consternation in Congress.[52] By the end of 1988, it did not appear likely that additional pressure, short of the actual use of military force, would compel Noriega to step down in the foreseeable future.

While Reagan's attempt to negotiate a change of regime in Panama came to naught, the episode revealed much about the emerging debates and priorities within the US government over how to deal with rogue dictators: whether to negotiate with or to coerce outlaw regimes; the political benefits of appearing tough against them; the disparities between political optics and practical results; the preference for regime change as a central goal; and the deep divisions within the top tier of a presidential administration, not to mention among the broader public and across the political spectrum. All these options and factors emerged over the course of this brief and quickly overshadowed crisis as important themes developing in the United States' outlook and approach toward this new type of security threat.

Noriega's rogue behavior was of a somewhat unique variety from that of his other rogue contemporaries, connected as it was to narcotics trafficking rather than terrorism or WMD. But the Reagan administration viewed it as part and parcel of the same phenomenon. As early as 1984, Shultz had pointed to "the growing link between drugs and terrorism." Emphasizing this "close connection between terrorism and international narcotics trafficking," he asserted that states in Latin America and the Caribbean "have used narcotics smugglers to funnel guns and money to terrorists and insurgents."[53] Where Reagan had resorted to limited military action against Libya, he displayed a determined willingness to negotiate a practical diplomatic solution with Panama. Many of his chief advisors, however, felt that the symbolic drawbacks of this approach toward such a distasteful regime outweighed any potential tangible results. By the time Reagan passed the keys of the White House to Bush, Noriega remained at the helm of Panama, to continue as an unresolved thorn in the new administration's side over the course of the next year. But the decisions that Reagan and his team made in 1988 had already limited the menu of options available to the new president, leaving essentially one tool left to remove the Panamanian leader: the US military.

Enforcing Regime Change: Bush and Noriega, 1989

When George Bush entered the presidency in January 1989, he found his administration caught between two unsatisfactory approaches to resolve the festering problem of Panama's rogue leader, General Manuel Noriega. From their experience during the previous year, US officials recognized that the chances of reaching a negotiated solution were remote so long as they held firm to the drug indictments. Meanwhile, Bush and his new foreign policy team remained hopeful that a significant military operation would not prove necessary. But the options between these two poles were meager and unpromising. Eventually, it was Noriega himself, through his increasingly provocative and belligerent actions, who overcame the administration's wariness to use force. In late December 1989, Bush unleashed the largest US military operation since the Vietnam War, providing a model for targeted armed interventions to depose rogue regimes to which he and his successors would turn on numerous future occasions.

The first question that faced the new administration was whether to reaffirm President Reagan's commitment to remove Noriega from power as the overall goal in its approach toward Panama. After all, since the May 1988 negotiations had collapsed, Noriega remained at the helm of the PDF and continued to consolidate his rule by cracking down on opposition and dissent. Reagan had seen only two options to accomplish his objective of regime change: to negotiate the dictator out in exchange for dropping the indictments, or to force him out using the military. But with a change in the overall objective—by deciding to leave Noriega in place and attempting to contain his provocations indefinitely—Bush could have introduced a third option. Reagan had rejected this more passive strategy in the first half of 1988, but this watch-and-wait approach had become de facto US policy in the months since then.

Several factors contributed to Bush's determination that eventually, one way or another, Noriega must go. For one, the controversial history of US ties to

Noriega was a long-running political issue of particularly personal salience for Bush. His opponents in the 1988 presidential election had criticized him heavily for his prior dealings with the Panamanian strongman while serving as CIA director and vice president. The rising prominence of drug-related crime and the drug trade as critical political issues to the US public made a tough stance against Noriega a necessity.[54] A White House official told the *Washington Post* in mid-1988 that "drugs are the No. 1 issue with voters and that it is an issue that cuts against the administration and the presidential candidacy of Vice President Bush. 'Whenever Noriega's name comes up, it is a negative for us and will be as long as he remains in power.'"[55]

These same political necessities, however, limited Bush's options. Just as he had done so vehemently during his debates with Reagan the year before, Bush as president made clear to his own administration that dropping the indictments against Noriega was out of the question, no matter how they impacted the spectrum of options or results regarding the Panamanian regime. James Baker, Bush's close friend who took over for Shultz as the new secretary of state, explained the tradeoffs that this policy caused: "While I agreed with the President's position, his principled refusal to drop the indictments substantially lessened any chance for a peaceful resolution to the matter." Baker "doubted that diplomacy alone would be enough" after the failure of Reagan's negotiations the year before and "feared ... that military action might prove necessary," despite his rejection of this possibility while serving as Reagan's treasury secretary. The new secretary of state concurred with his chief that "neither maintaining the status quo nor accommodating Noriega's continued presence in Panama was an acceptable alternative." He summed up the Bush administration's mindset, asserting that "the bottom line was clear: One way or another, Noriega's rule had to end."[56]

Regime change in Panama might have remained US policy under Bush, but the new administration initially found itself stuck in the same quandary as its predecessor, unsure of any means short of full-scale military action that would accomplish the desired result. "We had gotten ourselves into a box," recalled Colin Powell, soon to become chairman of the JCS.[57] The first months of 1989, therefore, saw a continuation of the de facto wait-and-see approach for which the divided Reagan team had had to settle. Baker noted that when the Bush administration took office, "the question of what to do about [Noriega] was one of our most pressing problems." At first, Bush and Baker sought to revive diplomatic efforts to persuade him to step down, but "despite some hopeful initial signs," these quickly stalled. "Since we knew the President would never drop the indictments," Baker admitted, "the negotiating track was at an impasse."[58] Trying to find ways to put additional pressure on Noriega short of military force, Bush approved a number of covert operations designed to further destabilize his regime, including transferring funds to opposition groups running against Noriega's handpicked candidates in the May 1989 elections and installing a radio transmitter in Panama to broadcast their message. The PDF discovered both of these initiatives, however, stymieing their effectiveness. Moreover, while the continuation of economic sanctions did considerable damage to the Panamanian economy, Noriega was able to maintain his own financial strength from the drug trade and aid from Cuba, Libya, and other nations. As the president wrote to the members of his NSC in early 1989, "We have come to a stalemate."[59]

In the lead-up to the May 1989 elections in Panama, several informed policymakers, especially Mike Kozak, who was serving in an acting capacity in Elliott Abrams's previous role as assistant secretary of state for inter-American affairs, pressed for firmer action. Kozak argued that "the status quo cannot be sustained. A fundamental policy choice can no longer be deferred," concluding, "If we want Noriega out, we must act ourselves." Arthur Davis, the US ambassador to Panama, concurred that "[our] policy has stagnated" and pressed for sterner measures. By this time, Baker himself had come to feel that the United States' failure to force Noriega's ouster had emboldened the dictator, who "had concluded that the United States would never intervene militarily and that his internal opponents were too weak to oust him on their own." But at this point, Baker was still wary of a military solution, admitting that "absent some action-forcing event, he was likely correct about the prospects of a U.S. invasion." Short of such an event, Kozak hoped that the "credible threat represented by our willingness to use force" would open additional options. Specifically, Kozak urged using the threat of US military action to "separate Noriega" from the PDF and incite a PDF coup against him.[60]

The urgency of the need to take stronger action against Noriega became even more blatantly evident after his handling of the much-anticipated Panamanian national elections in May 1989. Fearing that the general would rig or overturn the results of the election that was predicted to go in favor of his opponents, the US government arranged for teams of outside observers, including one led by former president Jimmy Carter, to monitor the polling. As Baker recalled, "If Noriega was going to steal the elections, we wanted the world to be a witness, in order to help prepare public opinion for a stronger U.S. and international response." Even before election day, it had become "apparent that a campaign of systematic fraud had turned the process into a sham," and Baker predicted to Bush that Noriega "will steal the election massively." True to form, Panama's strongman canceled the election results when even his own state-sponsored intimidation and fraud were not enough to overcome the estimated three-to-one margin in favor of the opposition's victorious presidential candidate, Guillermo Endara, who still took 55 percent of the doctored official vote tally. To make matters worse, television audiences around the world watched as Noriega's paramilitary "Dignity Battalions" brutally beat the opposition vice presidential candidate, Billy Ford, and murdered his bodyguard on the streets of Panama City, apparently flaunting their "naked theft of democracy" for all to see.[61]

In the wake of this flagrant disdain for the electoral process, Bush declared to reporters that "the days of the dictator are over," repeating a line from his inaugural address. Baker felt that the fraudulent election finally "presented us with a significant opportunity to increase pressure on [Noriega] and bring to an end the policy drift within our government." As Bush's staff explained, the US government would take "steps to increase political, military and other pressures against Noriega across the board." Indeed, the administration took a number of diplomatic and military actions aimed to further isolate Noriega's regime and to mount a campaign of psychological warfare against the dictator and his supporters. These steps included a resolution in the Organization of American States denouncing the Panamanian leader for stealing the election, recalling the US ambassador from Panama, withdrawing much of the embassy's staff and US military dependents, sending additional troops to the Canal Zone, and increasing US troop movements within Panama. These moves, especially the military demonstrations, were intended to send a stark and unmistakable message to Noriega to leave Panama or face the consequences. The Bush administration also sought to appeal to disgruntled officers in the PDF to encourage a coup against their leader. In a memorandum to the president, Baker cautioned, "We are setting out on a road that increases the possibility of confrontation." Hopefully, the momentum and pressure that these new steps would generate would finally convince Noriega to step aside, he continued, but if not, Bush had to be prepared to take "stronger steps" that could lead to military confrontation.[62]

A newly hardened and definitive mindset toward Noriega's regime took hold of the Bush administration following the May election fraud, along with a heightened sense of urgency. Within weeks of the election, Baker directed the US embassy in Panama to deliver a clear message directly to Noriega: "The crisis will not end until you give up power." Never had the president's decision for regime change in Panama—under Reagan or Bush—been so clearly or officially declared. The secretary of state also directed that the same message be delivered to PDF officers. He plainly admitted that "we were doing our best to foment a coup." Bush himself told congressional leaders, "I intend to start ratcheting up the pressure" until Noriega stepped down or someone forced him to do so. The explicit focus of the administration on encouraging a PDF coup put the United States on a collision course with Noriega more clearly than ever before.[63]

Meanwhile, Noriega had become the prime "outlaw" and "renegade regime" in the minds of Bush and his top advisors, taking the place of Libya's Qadhafi as the most vexing and dangerous rogue dictator in the United States' sights. Baker explained this line of thinking most clearly in his memoirs: Noriega had become "increasingly radicalized" as he engaged in subversion of neighboring governments and received financial help from Libya. "He was in effect becoming the Muammar Qaddafi of Latin America—a hostile, radical militant running drugs, allied with our enemies, and in absolute control of a country where American soldiers were stationed."[64]

Soon the coup for which Bush and his team were hoping materialized, but just as quickly the deficiencies of relying on this approach to solve the Panamanian rogue state problem became all too apparent in Washington. At the beginning of October 1989, a major in the PDF named Moises Giroldi approached US officials with his intention to depose Noriega. Giroldi had come to fear that his commander was courting war with the United States, particularly after the dictator gave orders to shoot down US aircraft in the vicinity of Panama City. Giroldi commanded Noriega's personal security detail at his headquarters, the Comandancia, where he planned to detain the general and convince him to resign and retire to the countryside. Given his key position, high level of access, and trusted status as a close confidant of Noriega, Giroldi expected to be able to catch his boss off guard at a vulnerable moment to carry out his plot. All he requested of US forces was to block several key access routes to prevent PDF reinforcements from coming to Noriega's rescue.[65]

With little information and fewer assurances, US officials in Panama and Washington were immediately skeptical of Giroldi and his coup plan. To begin, US military forces were adjusting to two important personnel changes less than forty-eight hours before Giroldi made his overture. General Maxwell Thurman, affectionately nicknamed "Mad Max" and "Maxatollah" for his toughness and compulsiveness, took charge of US Southern Command, based in Panama, on September 30 from the previous commander who had resisted the more aggressive policies the Bush administration had set in motion. The next day, General Colin Powell replaced Admiral Crowe as the newly appointed chairman of the JCS. Thurman and Powell shared a deep skepticism of Giroldi's motives and plan, fearing that it could be a ruse to embarrass the United States and its new commander in Panama by catching them in the act of supporting a coup that was not actually real. Moreover, all they knew of Giroldi was his status as one of Noriega's closest henchmen who had helped him put down a previous coup the year before. News of potential coup plots abounded in the months after the May elections, and all had turned out to be false alarms. Most importantly, Giroldi refused to disclose what he planned to do with Noriega once he had captured him, giving no indication that he intended to hand the dictator over to US forces, and he said nothing about the government that would replace Noriega's regime.

Without assurances that Panamanian democracy would be restored or that its military would fall under civilian control, Bush and his advisors found large-scale US support for this plot to be a hard sell. They did not wish to simply replace one military dictator with another. Nevertheless, Baker later lamented, "Instead of being so skeptical, we should have gone to Giroldi, demanded to know his plan in exchange for our help, assessed his scheme and quietly assisted in its execution."[66]

Despite the nearly universal skepticism of his advisors, Bush hesitated to reject all aid to the coup out of hand. He emphasized to his team that "you've had me out there for the last couple of months begging these guys to start a coup," so "if someone's actually willing to do one, we have to help them." US forces consequently blocked two critical roadways as Giroldi had requested once the plot began to unfold on October 3. But without a deeper knowledge of Giroldi and his plans, and without its own contingency plans in place to provide more robust assistance, the Bush administration held off from further involvement.[67]

What unfolded at the Comandancia was "a comic-opera coup," in Baker's words—"like amateur night," in Powell's. Giroldi successfully detained Noriega and held him captive, but when Noriega refused to simply step aside into retirement as his security chief had hoped, Giroldi did not seem to know what to do. Unwilling to simply kill his onetime friend and the godfather of his children or to turn him over to US authorities, Giroldi inexplicably allowed Noriega to use the phone to call in reinforcements, which craftily evaded the limited US roadblocks by commandeering airplanes to quickly reach the Comandancia. In short order these forces turned the tables on Giroldi, to whom Noriega did not show the same mercy, ordering him tortured and executed.[68]

The coup's aftermath left in tatters the Bush administration's approach of encouraging the PDF to oust Noriega. Though neither the president nor his advisors regretted their decision to hold off from more active participation in the failed venture, they admitted deficiencies in their decision-making process. Powell, the newest member of the national security team, noted the chaotic and "free-swinging" nature of policy deliberations and information gathering. Indeed, the administration came under withering criticism from all sides, particularly in Congress, for its hesitant and uncertain reaction to the very scenario that it had seemed to be actively promoting. Senators railed against Bush and his advisors as "a bunch of Keystone Kops, bumping into each other," while congressmen and the media revived the unfair but recurring criticism that Bush was a "wimp." Harsh as the criticism was, the Bush team agreed that the Giroldi coup had turned out to be a missed opportunity, even if not quite a golden one, to get rid of Noriega. Baker explained the renewed sense of determination that he and his colleagues shared: "All of us vowed never to let another such opportunity pass us by. If an opening ever presented itself again, the United States wouldn't be caught unprepared."[69]

As the dictator consolidated his hold on power in the following weeks by arresting and executing more PDF officers suspected of disloyalty, it became clear that the US policy of relying on an internal coup to topple the Noriega regime was no longer feasible. Bush and his team consequently accelerated plans for taking direct military action in Panama—the sole remaining alternative that Reagan and Bush had sought to avoid for the past year and a half. The military options fell into three main categories. The first, which Shultz had advocated the year before, called for a commando raid to "snatch" Noriega, kidnapping him individually to bring him to trial in the United States. Reflecting the opinion of much of Bush's team, Powell had come to believe that getting rid of Noriega would not be enough, worrying that another PDF commander would just take his place at the head of a similarly adversarial regime. Rather, he had become convinced that the United States needed to dismantle the PDF entirely, since its supremacy stood as the basic obstacle to democracy in Panama. The second military option involved using US forces already stationed in the Canal Zone to neutralize PDF units around the major cities and capture Noriega in his headquarters. Only the third option, a much more massive military invasion with troops from the US mainland as well as those already in Panama, promised to uproot Noriega's rogue regime entirely. By targeting the PDF as well as its commander, this course would offer the opportunity to restore democracy by turning the country over to the civilian leaders who had been democratically elected in May. The Pentagon initially dubbed this last plan Operation Blue Spoon but decided to rename it Operation Just Cause, a more rousing call to arms, as planning reached its final stages. Still, the military chiefs cautioned against launching any military action without direct provocation.[70]

They did not have long to wait. The deepening crisis gained momentum on December 15, 1989, when Noriega proclaimed himself "maximum leader" of Panama with new powers that ended any remaining illusion of constitutional government. He also declared before the Panamanian legislature, while wielding a machete, that a "state of war" now existed with the United States. US officials initially dismissed Noriega's declaration of war as mere theatrics, but an incident the next day changed the equation. On the evening of December 16, Panamanian soldiers shot and killed an off-duty marine lieutenant when he drove away from a roadblock; then they detained and beat a navy lieutenant who had witnessed the shooting and sexually harassed his wife. PDF troops had been harassing US military personnel and civilians in Panama in a stream of incidents for the past two years, but this was the first that involved the use of lethal force.[71]

When Bush received the news, he quickly determined that it was finally time to unleash the US military against Noriega and his regime. His senior advisors had all reached the same conclusion. While some members of Bush's team, such as National Security Advisor Brent Scowcroft, later expressed surprise at the modest nature of the actual grounds that prompted Bush's decision to launch the invasion of Panama, they all agreed with the president that Noriega had pushed the United States far enough. As Bush dictated to his diary, "We've had enough, and we cannot let a military officer be killed, and certainly not a lieutenant and his wife brutalized."[72]

Moreover, the president and his national security team had all come to view Noriega as the preeminent rogue dictator threatening US interests and security, and they used this criminal characterization to justify the use of military force to bring his regime to an end. Throughout the fall, Bush had declared that "the outlaw Noriega regime simply must be replaced." Powell, despite his discomfort with Bush's "demonizing" of Noriega in public out of concern that such rhetoric would focus too much attention on the dictator rather than his regime as a whole, shared his boss's views of the Panamanian leader. He argued to Secretary of Defense Dick Cheney that intervention in Panama was justified because "Noriega's not a legitimate leader. He's a criminal. He's under indictment."[73]

The many months of deliberations over the proper course of action to fulfill President Reagan's, and then President Bush's, decision to "get rid" of Noriega reached a climax on the afternoon of December 17, 1989, in the White House residence. Bush gathered all his top advisors in the same Yellow Oval Room where the weekend of "wild" and contentious meetings had occurred in May 1988 to decide the fate of the Reagan administration's negotiated deal with Noriega. This time, however, all of the senior members of the national security team were on the same page. Calling the meeting "anticlimactic," Baker wrote, "I recall very little if any debate over the merits of invading Panama." That said, the president had not yet made his final decision to go ahead with the military action—and just what form it would take. Powell strongly made the case for the large-scale invasion over a smaller commando raid to capture Noriega, arguing that the "prime objective" should be "to eliminate Noriega *and* the PDF," which would be necessary to resolve the fundamental problems in Panama. All those present agreed that the time for diplomacy had passed. Nevertheless, as the questions mounted and fears over US and Panamanian casualties, as well as the likelihood of capturing Noriega, caused the discussion to drift, Powell began to fear that the meeting would end without a clear resolution, as had many of those on Panama under Reagan the year before. But once everyone had voiced their views, Bush brought the meeting to a decisive close: "Let's do it. The hell with it."[74]

FIGURE 11. Enforcing regime change: With a Christmas party ongoing downstairs, President Bush meets with advisors in his Treaty Room study in the White House residence prior to making the decision to launch the invasion of Panama, December 17, 1989. Counterclockwise from Bush are Secretary of Defense Dick Cheney, National Security Advisor Brent Scowcroft, Deputy National Security Advisor Robert Gates, Chairman of the Joint Chiefs of Staff Gen. Colin Powell, and Lt. Gen. Thomas Kelly.

Once the president had issued the order to launch the invasion, the armed forces executed Operation Just Cause—the largest US military action since the Vietnam War—with remarkable efficiency and success, beginning just after midnight on December 20, 1989. The complexity of deploying troops stationed in the Canal Zone, while also ferrying troops from the US mainland for landing and parachuting into Panama, made this one of the most high-density air operations in the history of the US military, with little room for error. A combination of airstrikes, airborne and ground assaults, and special operations raids produced sharp but brief fighting that quickly persuaded most of Noriega's soldiers to surrender, with only pockets of fierce resistance.[75]

By 7:20 that morning, less than seven hours after the invasion had begun, President Bush was able to announce in his address to the nation from the Oval Office that "most organized resistance has been eliminated." Explaining the reasons why he ordered the invasion, Bush laid out the prime goals of the United States: "To safeguard the lives of Americans, to defend democracy in Panama, to combat drug trafficking, and to protect the integrity of the Panama Canal treaty."

Later in his speech he added one more fundamental goal: "To bring General Noriega to justice in the United States." It was this final goal that as yet remained unfulfilled. Emphasizing the dictator's criminality as "an indicted drug trafficker," the president declared that even though he remained at large, "yesterday a dictator ruled Panama, and today constitutionally elected leaders govern."[76]

Nevertheless, as more days passed with no sign of Noriega, the Bush administration's frustration grew. Asked by reporters whether the operation could be considered successful as long as Noriega was on the loose, Powell responded, "We have now decapitated him from the dictatorship of his country . . . we cut off the head of that government, and there is a new government that was elected by the Panamanian people." Indeed, just as the invasion was beginning on December 20, Guillermo Endara, Panama's rightfully elected president in the May elections, was sworn into office at the head of a civilian democratic government. Yet the dictator remained at large. US forces had had the foresight to destroy boats and airplanes that he might have used to escape Panama City, but they were not able to detain their prime target.[77]

In the days following the invasion, the US military launched a massive manhunt. US officials later learned that Noriega had evaded his pursuers on the first night of the invasion while hiding in a brothel. He remained barely a step ahead of them over the next several days, narrowly avoiding capture at a Dairy Queen in Panama City before seeking sanctuary in the Vatican embassy on Christmas Eve, walking in wearing a T-shirt, Bermuda shorts, and a baseball hat and carrying two AK-47 rifles slung over his shoulders. US soldiers could not follow him onto the Vatican's sovereign territory but instead surrounded the building once the papal nuncio informed them of the general's presence. While negotiations for Noriega's surrender ground on inconclusively over the next ten days, US troops blared rock music (which Noriega reputedly detested) into the embassy compound as a form of psychological warfare to convince the fallen dictator to give up—matching their selections to the situation at hand: "Voodoo Child," "Wanted Dead or Alive," "Nowhere to Run, Nowhere to Hide," and 'I Fought the Law and the Law Won." Eventually Noriega surrendered, but only once Vatican officials, who were unwilling to host the despot indefinitely, informed him of their intention to move their official embassy to the Catholic high school across the street and thereby shift their legal sovereignty to the new building; Noriega was not invited. On January 3, 1990, he emerged from the embassy in military fatigues, within sight of a massive demonstration of Panamanians chanting "Death to our Hitler," and US soldiers and DEA officers took him into custody. Moments later, he was whisked away in a US helicopter, bound for a prison cell in Florida to be tried and jailed as a "common criminal."[78]

Manuel Noriega was convicted of the charges of drug trafficking, racketeering, and money laundering for which he had been indicted nearly two years before his arrest, and he spent the rest of his life in prisons in the United States, France, and Panama, where he died in 2017. His fate reinforced the emerging image in the minds of the US government and public alike that the rulers of rogue states were criminals leading outlaw regimes that existed outside the bounds of accepted international behavior. The decisive end to his rule in the final days of 1989, overshadowed as it would become by dramatic events in Eastern Europe and the Middle East, set a model for how the United States could address the emerging threat of rogue states. President Bush and his team never wavered from the goal that the Reagan administration had set of seeking regime change in Panama. Limited as their options were in 1989, they slowly came to the realization that there was only one truly viable avenue that would achieve their desired result. The invasion of Panama was the first military operation conducted with a post–Cold War rationale, to overthrow a dictator whose behavior was unpredictably bellicose and unacceptably abhorrent and to restore democracy in his place. At its core, the effort of the Reagan and Bush administrations to resolve the crisis in Panama, which culminated in Operation Just Cause, was a defense of principle—in Baker's words "an exercise in supporting democracy and the rule of law" and a "determination that a naked assault on democracy wouldn't be tolerated."[79] This set a critical precedent for the new world emerging from the rubble of the Berlin Wall that had collapsed just a month and a half earlier.

The Emerging Rogue State Paradigm

By the end of the consequential decade of the 1980s, the phenomenon of rogue states—still called "outlaw states" and "renegade regimes"—had come into clear focus as an important, if not yet defining, security threat to the global order emerging from the ashes of the Cold War. Less than two months before General Noriega's capture on January 3, 1990, East German citizens had forced the peaceful fall of the Berlin Wall, the symbol of the divisions of Cold War Europe. Exactly one month before Noriega's surrender, President Bush had concluded his first summit meeting with Mikhail Gorbachev in Malta to discuss the revolutions occurring throughout Central and Eastern Europe that were bringing down communist regimes. With the world transforming so fundamentally as the 1990s dawned, the threats of the Cold War were receding. In their place, what had once seemed peripheral and disparate threats earlier in the decade—terrorism, WMD proliferation, regional armed aggression, and narcotics trafficking—were coalescing into the new phenomenon of rogue states.

The final years of the 1980s were decisive ones for US leaders to figure out the shape of this new phenomenon—to begin to understand what defined a rogue state. Libya and Panama each offered different elements but nevertheless shared important qualities that helped to solidify the essence of this new type of security threat in the minds of US policymakers. Where Qadhafi's Libya most visibly fused the emerging rogue state paradigm with the related problem of international terrorism, Noriega's Panamanian regime expanded the mold of rogue states in new ways. He, too, demonstrated an appetite for unpredictable belligerence and a desire to harm US citizens and interests, but he also introduced a new issue to the mix: international narcotics trafficking. Noriega's indictments and imprisonment for his role in drug trafficking gave an explicit criminal dimension to the public understanding of rogue dictators. Despite Noriega's differences from Qadhafi, both the Reagan and Bush administrations considered him as part of the same brand of security threats. Both of the influential secretaries of state in these years, George Shultz and James Baker, emphasized the connections between terrorism and the drug trade and between Qadhafi and Noriega, linking them together as variations of the same basic phenomenon. Baker even went so far as to label Noriega "the Muammar Qaddafi of Latin America."

These were also decisive years for US leaders to figure out what to do about this new phenomenon: how to handle rogue states. Both the Reagan and Bush administrations engaged in fierce debate and disagreement over the goals that the United States should pursue and the options that it should employ to achieve them. The most contentious debates among the top members of both national security teams (which included many of the same figures) centered on the wisdom of negotiating with such distasteful "criminal" leaders and whether the use of military force was justified to oust them from power. There was more agreement about the overall goal of seeking regime change, but less over how to achieve it. By the end of 1989, once all other approaches had failed, divided opinion gave way to the unified view that military action was necessary to depose Noriega's criminal regime. The invasion of Panama, however, was markedly distinct from the military action that Reagan had authorized against Libya in 1986. Where the latter included limited airstrikes against a handful of targets, Operation Just Cause became the largest US military action since the Vietnam War.

By the dawn of the 1990s, the United States had two clear and complementary models for the emerging phenomenon of rogue states. Just as critically, it had a model for how to deal with this new brand of security threat to the post–Cold War global order that Reagan, Bush, and Gorbachev were attempting to build. The sharp, short, and successful invasion of Panama set a precedent for how the United States could remove the threat of a rogue state through regime change. As such, it stood as a forerunner of the much more consequential standoff with Saddam Hussein's Iraq later that year.

4

NO GOOD DEMON

Iraq, Iran, and the Emergence
of the Quintessential Rogue

In the post–Cold War era, Saddam Hussein loomed larger over the United States' relations with the world than any other single figure. The Iraqi dictator, whose black mustache, black eyes, and military fatigues underscored the menace and brutality of his regime, quickly became—and remained—the arch nemesis of the United States after the Cold War ended—the archetypal rogue state in the eyes of America's leaders and public.

Saddam's malicious and destabilizing international record did not begin with his invasion of Kuwait in 1990, which triggered the Gulf War that, in turn, would set a defining precedent for enforcing global security against rogue states in the post–Cold War world. The dawn of the 1980s saw him launch a massively destructive war with Iran that consumed the Persian Gulf region in chaos for the rest of the decade, made worse by his exporting of terrorism and determined pursuit of weapons of mass destruction (WMD) as well as his repeated use of chemical weapons against his enemies on the battlefield and his own populace at home.

Ironically, given this long list of abuses of power, the United States sought to improve relations with the Iraqi regime throughout nearly the entire decade from 1980 to 1990. When viewed from the perspective of the years following 9/11 and the US invasion of Iraq in 2003 that toppled Saddam's regime, this attempted alliance of convenience stands out as one of the most critical puzzles of the transition from the Cold War to the post–Cold War world. How could the United States have sought friendly relations with such an evil despot?

The positive tilt of US policy toward Iraq during the Reagan presidency and the first year and a half of the Bush presidency did not originate from any lack of recognition of Saddam's menacing nature. Indeed, President Ronald Reagan and his secretary of state, George Shultz, displayed a clear-headed understanding of the malicious and disturbing features of Saddam's rule from the beginning of their time in office. Though they pushed their concerns aside in the mid-1980s, they left office with an increasingly clear assessment of the threat that the Iraqi strongman posed to US interests and the security of the emerging global order. Similarly, President George H. W. Bush and his national security team initially pursued a policy of seeking to moderate the Iraqi regime through "constructive engagement," but they built into this policy measures to reverse course if Saddam persisted in his litany of troubling actions.

Rather than from a lack of recognition or understanding, the US government's pursuit of positive relations with Iraq grew out of the broader strategic context of the final decade of the Cold War and the decision to prioritize other threats and goals that the Reagan and Bush administrations considered more pressing. The outbreak of the Iran-Iraq War in 1980 came on the heels of two shocks to US strategic interests in the Persian Gulf in 1979: the Soviet invasion of Afghanistan and the Islamic revolution in Iran. Both of these developments heightened the perceived threat of Soviet encroachment into the oil-rich Gulf—a concern of US policymakers since the final days of World War II—and the expansion of Iranian radicalism throughout the Middle East. While the Cold War persisted and the Iran-Iraq War dragged on, US leaders viewed Iraq, however unsavory its regime, as the lesser of evils—the "good demon" that could hold back even graver threats.

When this wider strategic context changed beginning in late 1988, so, too, did US perceptions of the Iraqi regime. The end of both the Cold War and the Iran-Iraq War removed the urgency behind curbing the threats from the Soviet Union and Iran. Moreover, the increasing brutality of Saddam's actions in the war's final phase and aftermath prompted a growing number of US officials, including Shultz, to align the Iraqi strongman with the patterns emerging from other regional outlaws such as Libya's Qadhafi and Panama's Noriega. The handover of power in the White House to a new administration in 1989 derailed any significant policy shift as the Bush team entered office focused on its own set of priorities—overseeing the Cold War endgame in Europe and hoping to enlist Iraqi support for reviving the Middle East peace process. Here, too, the changing strategic picture in 1989–1990 led to a slow policy shift away from trying to engage with Iraq. But it took a true shock to the international order—Saddam's brazen invasion of the neighboring sheikdom of Kuwait in August 1990—for US policymakers and the public to finally see Iraq as the quintessential rogue state.

FIGURE 12. The quintessential rogue: The menacing visage of Saddam Hussein on this *Newsweek* cover from shortly after Iraq's August 1990 invasion of Kuwait reflects his transformation from a "good demon" holding back Iran in the 1980s to the United States' arch nemesis in the post–Cold War world.

Jockeying with a "No Good Nut": Iraq during the Reagan Years

From the first months of his presidency, Ronald Reagan harbored no illusions about Saddam Hussein and his repugnant regime in Iraq. Amid the widespread international condemnation of Israel for launching its air attack on Iraq's Osirak nuclear reactor in June 1981, Reagan pushed back in his diary on the notion of Saddam as the victim of Israeli aggression: "The truth is the Arab indignation on behalf of Iraq is a waste. Saddam Hussein is a 'no good nut' and I think he was trying to build a nuclear weapon." Reagan continued, "He has called for the destruction of Israel & he wants to be the leader of the Arab world—that's why he invaded Iran." In this single diary entry of June 11, 1981, less than five months into his term of office, Reagan identified two of the most damning reasons why within a decade Iraq would become the most quintessential—and potentially dangerous—rogue state threatening the post–Cold War global order. Saddam's perennial military aggression to destabilize the Middle East and Persian Gulf region and his steadfast pursuit of a variety of WMD were clearly recognized and roundly disdained in the top ranks of Reagan's foreign policy team.

Then why, given its recognition of the menacing nature of the Iraqi regime, did the Reagan administration pursue a policy of engagement—and even a tacit alliance of convenience—with Iraq throughout much of the 1980s? Indeed, from 1982 to 1988, the United States provided significant levels of economic, material, intelligence, diplomatic, and even military support to Iraq. In the aftermath of the Gulf War shortly after Reagan left office, once Saddam Hussein had become the United States' greatest international foe, the friendly policies toward Iraq of the Reagan years came under greater scrutiny and criticism from commentators, scholars, and politicians.[2] These critiques, however, were formulated in a markedly different international context, after the tectonic transformations of the global order in 1989 and 1990 had profoundly reshaped and reordered security threats. For most of Reagan's time in office, his administration focused its policies toward the Middle East on countering what it considered two higher-priority threats than Iraq: that from the Soviet Union, whose war in Afghanistan had prompted fears in the US government since late in the Carter presidency of a Soviet drive to dominate the Gulf region; and that from Iran, whose Islamist regime had seized power in the 1979 revolution, held Americans hostage, and sought to spread its radical ideology throughout the Middle East through terrorism and subversion. In particular, Reagan and his team pursued policies that attempted to mitigate and contain the destabilizing effects of the Iran-Iraq War, the mammoth conflict that consumed the Gulf region from 1980 to 1988, nearly the entirety of Reagan's presidency. Facing a choice of enemies, the Reagan administration sought to bolster Iraq as a balance against the overriding threat from Iran.

Only once this conflict ended in 1988, and its threats dissipated, did the broader strategic context evolve. With Iraq no longer tethered down by the death struggle to its east, the threatening characteristics of Saddam's regime that Reagan had recognized as early as 1981 no longer had a productive outlet that could serve US interests. Rather than a source of stability as a counter to Iranian expansionist ambitions, Iraq emerged in the aftermath of the war as a pressing threat in its own right to the emerging global order. This shifting strategic calculus, combined with the Reagan administration's growing understanding of the new phenomenon of rogue states—and the threatening characteristics that Saddam shared with Qadhafi's regime in Libya—pushed the president and his advisors to consider reevaluating the US relationship with Iraq, a task that nevertheless remained unfulfilled when Reagan left office in January 1989.

Saddam Hussein rose to power through the ranks of the radical socialist Baath Party in the 1960s and 1970s, plotting coups and eliminating rivals until finally securing his position of supremacy in Iraq in 1979.[3] Shortly after assuming the Iraqi presidency, he launched a war of aggression against Iran, ordering Iraqi tanks across his eastern border on September 22, 1980. His reasons for invading Iran blended insecurity and opportunism. Hoping that a victorious war with a foreign foe would consolidate his position at the helm of Iraq, Saddam also sought to take advantage of the revolutionary tumult within Iran—and, he hoped, the disorder and weakness within its military ranks—to seize key oil fields in Iranian territory. However, what he expected to be an easy victory soon devolved into a bloody and protracted struggle for survival, as Iran began to draw on its superior manpower and resources to reverse the Iraqi army's initial gains and push into Iraq itself. As the tide of war turned, Iran's Ayatollah Khomeini vowed to end the fighting only once Iranian forces had toppled Saddam's regime.[4]

It was in this context that the Reagan administration began to develop its first proactive policies toward the Iran-Iraq War. Prior to 1982, the US government had adopted an official position of neutrality in the conflict and engaged little with either side. The Iran hostage crisis had consumed the final year of Carter's presidency, resulting in deep American enmity toward the revolutionary regime in Tehran. At the same time, the United States had not had formal diplomatic relations with Baghdad since 1967, when Iraq had severed ties during the Six-Day War between Israel and a coalition of Arab states.[5] As Secretary of State George Shultz later noted, "The temptation was to stand by and watch this dictatorial and threatening pair of countries pound each other to pulp." While this mindset became the de facto goal for many in the administration, Shultz argued that this was not in fact the US government's aim: "Such a posture by the United States would have been inhumane and unwise. We did have a major stake in the Gulf, and the horrors of the Iran-Iraq War fell on ordinary people, not on their leaders. U.S. policy, therefore, should be and was to try to stop the war."[6] He might have added, and surely would not have hesitated to admit, that US policy sought to end the war on terms favorable to US interests. As Charles Hill, one of Shultz's chief advisors, explained in a memo to National Security Advisor Robert McFarlane, "Current US policy attempts to ensure that neither Iran nor Iraq attain hegemony in the region because dominance by either country—particularly in view of [the] regimes now in power in Baghdad and Tehran—could be contrary to US interests."⁷

This blend of policies and objectives—to remain officially neutral, to bring the war to a close, and to do so on favorable terms for US interests in the Gulf region—resulted in what became known as Operation Staunch. As Shultz explained, "Our only tactic . . . was to work to dry up the sources of weaponry that enabled both Iran and Iraq to render death and destruction in this seemingly endless war." Operation Staunch, initiated in 1983, was designed to accomplish this purpose by denying weapons to both sides. While Shultz took pains to emphasize the even-handed intentions behind this policy, in practice it worked to Iraq's advantage, since it more effectively blocked arms sales to Iran while Iraq could continue to look to the Soviet bloc and Western European countries for arms. In their private discussions, Reagan and his team made explicit their intention to direct Operation Staunch against Iran: while Reagan saw it as a "crucial part of our general strategy" for bringing the war "to the earliest possible negotiated end," he and his advisors agreed that its chief aim was to "prohibit the export of weapons or spare parts to Iran."⁸

The United States' attempt to pursue policies that would support a balance of power in the Gulf eventually led to an increasingly substantial "tilt" toward Iraq. As Iraqi fortunes on the battlefield worsened in 1982, the United States undertook several initiatives to prevent an Iraqi defeat. Though the Reagan administration viewed both regimes as unsavory, it saw Iran as the bigger threat for its avowed ambitions to export its own radical Islamic revolution throughout the region. Iraq was, therefore, a useful counterweight to the greater Iranian menace.⁹ An intelligence assessment from the CIA noted the conviction of moderate Gulf states that "only the present Baghdad regime . . . stands between them and the spread of Iranian and radical Arab . . . influence in the Gulf."¹⁰ The administration's "principal objective," explained National Security Advisor William Clark in a memo to the president in the first half of 1982, was to bring the war to a close "before Iran can assume hegemony in the region and undermines our vital interests."¹¹

This sense of Iraq as the lesser of two evils was shared across Reagan's national security team throughout his presidency. Colin Powell, who served as Reagan's national security advisor during the climax of the United States' involvement in the conflict in 1987–1988, "thought Hussein was 'a good demon' whose draconian presence kept his potentially fractious country intact as a bulwark against Iran." Indeed, he "recommended that the Iran-Iraq War end with a cease-fire rather than a negotiated peace, commenting that it would be better if 'they stare at each other forever . . . and not turn their attention elsewhere.'"¹² Shultz summarized the administration's approach: "Our support for Iraq increased in rough proportion to Iran's military successes: plain and simple, the United States was engaged in a limited form of balance-of-power policy." He, too, felt that Iran posed the greater threat, admitting that the United States "simply could not stand idle and watch the Khomeini revolution sweep forward." With Iran poised to launch a massive series of attacks into Iraqi territory by early 1984, Shultz asserted that "a tilt toward Iraq was warranted to prevent Iranian dominance of the Persian Gulf and the countries around it."[13] Indeed, US concern spiked at various points during the conflict that an Iranian victory "could succeed in bringing down the regime of Sadaam Hussein," which in turn "could eventually result in an Islamic fundamentalist government in Baghdad."[14] Fears of this outcome made *preventing* regime change in Iraq one of the US government's utmost priorities throughout the decade.

Shultz found support for his assessment of the situation in a onetime and future secretary of defense who would later play a central role in destroying the Iraqi regime, Donald Rumsfeld. Rumsfeld had served with Shultz in the Nixon administration and then under President Ford, and with Shultz's endorsement Reagan appointed him special envoy to the Middle East in 1983. On a visit to Iraq that would draw much greater attention and scrutiny years later, Rumsfeld met with Saddam Hussein and his deputy prime minister and foreign minister, Tariq Aziz, in December 1983 to explore better relations between the two countries. Reagan's advisors felt that Rumsfeld's meeting with Saddam was "eminently worthwhile" for improving relations with Iraq, and in the following months the National Security Council (NSC) crafted a National Security Decision Directive (NSDD), a presidential statement of official US policy, linking the need to "avert an Iraqi collapse" with the defense of US interests in the Gulf.[15] Reinforcing Powell and Shultz's assessments, Rumsfeld later explained what he called the "clear logic in trying to cultivate warmer relations" with Iraq: "Whatever misgivings we had about reaching out to Saddam Hussein, the alternative of Iranian hegemony in the Middle East was decidedly worse."[16] The uniformity of these statements from top officials in the Reagan administration makes clear that although they appreciated the menacing nature of Saddam's regime, they prioritized the threat of Iranian expansion within the context of the Iran-Iraq War.

To support this view of Saddam's Iraq as the "good demon" that stood as the only effective counterweight to Iranian radicalism, the Reagan administration took a series of progressive steps starting in 1982 to prevent what Rumsfeld warned could become "a collapse" where the "Gulf could cave in to Iran."[17] First, the US government removed Iraq from the State Department's list of state sponsors of terrorism in 1982, following Saddam's expulsion of terrorist-for-hire Abu Nidal from Baghdad. This move allowed the United States to grant agricultural credits to Iraq for the purchase of American grain and food, which eventually amounted to over $2 billion by the end of Reagan's presidency. Even more significantly, the United States and Iraq restored official diplomatic relations in 1984 following Rumsfeld's visit to Baghdad, accompanied by hopes that a friendlier Iraq could help rekindle the Arab-Israeli peace process. In addition to agricultural credits, these developments resulted in substantial dividends for the Iraqi war effort. As Iranian offensives pushed deeper into Iraqi territory, the United States provided Saddam's military with intelligence drawn from satellite imagery of Iranian deployments to shore up its position on the battlefield.[18]

The increasing level of US involvement in stabilizing and tipping the scales of the Iran-Iraq War culminated in a major presidential decision in the spring of 1987 to deploy US naval forces to protect shipping in the Persian Gulf. As the fortunes of war seesawed back and forth in the mid-1980s, both Iraq and Iran sought to cripple the other nation's economy by attacking its oil tankers traversing the Gulf. While Saddam was the one who had initiated this venture in 1984, by 1986 it was the Iranians who had escalated what became known as the "Tanker War" by launching speedboat attacks against neutral as well as Iraqi shipping. In particular, Iran targeted oil tankers traveling to and from Kuwait, a key supporter and financer of Iraq in the ongoing war. When Kuwait approached both the Soviet Union and the United States with a request to protect its shipping, the Reagan administration decided that it could no longer remain aloof from active involvement in the war's hostilities.[19]

Recognizing that his attempts to contain the instability of the Iran-Iraq War had failed to prevent hostilities from spilling over into the Gulf, Reagan made the decision to agree to Kuwait's request by reflagging Kuwaiti tankers under the US flag and protecting this shipping directly with warships of the US Navy. While the decision caused an uproar in Congress over concerns that the naval deployment could draw the United States deeply into a protracted war, the deliberations leading up to it drew on an unusual level of agreement within the administration's ranks, especially between Shultz and Secretary of Defense Caspar Weinberger. Weinberger was typically far more conservative in his advice to the president on which missions warranted the use of military force than Shultz, who had long advocated pairing force with diplomacy. In this case, however, Weinberger led the charge in urging Reagan to agree to the Kuwaiti request. His reasoning, as he later outlined in his memoirs, rested on three pillars. The first was a matter of principle: the responsibility of the United States to protect freedom of navigation on the high seas, in this case in the Persian Gulf—an issue that had consistently held a place of high priority for the secretary of defense since the navy's "freedom of navigation" exercises in the Gulf of Sidra in 1981, which had prompted combat with the Libyan air force. His second, related reason was to maintain the flow of oil supplies from the Gulf to markets around the world, long a central strategic goal for the United States in the Middle East. Third, he feared that "if we did not respond positively to the Kuwaitis, the USSR would quickly fill the vacuum. . . . Then we would indeed see a large Soviet naval presence in the Gulf."[20]

The official record of US policy deliberations reflects Weinberger's reasoning. Seeking to build support for its Gulf policy among US allies, the Reagan administration enumerated what it saw as the "principal threats" to their shared interests in the region: "the possibility of an Iranian victory over Iraq," an expansion of the war that would result in "obstructing freedom of non-belligerent shipping and endangering the free flow of oil," and "skillful Soviet exploitation" of the situation that would cause "an expansion of Soviet influence in the area." "Our purpose," explained an NSC briefing memo for the president and his latest national security advisor, Frank Carlucci, was aimed at protecting freedom of navigation for shipping and the free flow of oil and against the expansion of Iranian and Soviet interests. "It is essential," Reagan's advisors concurred, "that the Soviets not be able to assume the posture of being the 'defender' of the Gulf."[21]

This last concern reflected the continuing importance of the broader strategic context to US actions in the Gulf region: with the Cold War ongoing, Soviet encroachment into the Middle East still trumped the unsavory Iraqi regime in the ranking of security threats. Indeed, it was not just Weinberger, a hardline anticommunist, who held such views; even Shultz, the leading proponent within the administration of engagement with the Soviet Union, noted "strong feelings throughout the administration that we should not be part of an effort by the Kuwaitis to draw the Soviets into the Gulf." Shultz also repeated the other dominant goal behind the reflagging operation, arguing that "it was critical that Iran not come to dominate the Gulf and therefore the Arabian Peninsula."[22] Indeed, while the United States promoted the venture as a neutral defense against attacks on commerce in the Gulf, it in fact favored the Iraqi cause, since it aided Kuwait, a key ally financing Iraq's war effort. Reagan and his team made this point explicitly in their discussions leading up to the decision to reflag Kuwaiti tankers. Opening a meeting with his chief advisors on February 17, 1987, the president "emphasized the need to help Iraq in order to block Iranian and radical Shia expansionism." Shultz reiterated this goal in a national security meeting later that spring, telling his colleagues that "it would be bad for [the] U.S. if Iran were to win the war." Most of the US Navy's engagements were with Iran, and direct US-Iranian hostilities escalated until US warships destroyed half of the Iranian navy in the largest US naval engagement since World War II on April 18, 1988.[23]

Despite the Reagan administration's clear intent to focus the reflagging operation against Iran, the first and most destructive blow against US naval forces deployed to the Gulf came from Iraq rather than Iran. On May 17, 1987, just as US forces in the Gulf were preparing to launch their escort mission, but before it had been officially announced, the USS *Stark* came under attack when two

FIGURE 13.   Escalation in the Gulf: President Reagan discusses the Iraqi attack on the USS *Stark* during the Iran-Iraq War with Secretary of Defense Caspar Weinberger and Vice Chairman of the Joint Chiefs of Staff Gen. Robert Herres in the Situation Room, May 18, 1987.

missiles from an Iraqi fighter jet struck the ship, causing substantial damage and killing thirty-seven crewmen. It quickly became apparent that the attack had been an accident. Saddam Hussein promptly issued an official apology expressing his "deepest regret for the painful incident," and the Iraqi government proposed a joint investigation when recordings showed that the pilot had erred, thinking he was attacking an oil tanker. Iraq even entered into discussions with the US government to pay compensation to the families of the crewmen killed on the *Stark*.[24]

Although most officials in the Reagan administration wanted to quickly accept the Iraqi explanation of the incident as an honest if unfortunate mistake, the longer aftermath of the attack on the *Stark* further clouded their desire to view Iraq as a friendly and reliable partner. Shultz explained that the "official Washington and public attitudes," shaped by the Iran hostage crisis less than a decade earlier, "had been conditioned to view Iran as the primary threat and Iraq as a fragile counterforce holding back the tide of Khomeini's human waves." The preference of many in the administration was therefore "to dismiss the attack: call it 'inadvertent,' an accident."[25] Indeed, Weinberger emphasized repeatedly in his memoirs the "mistaken" and "accidental" nature of the confrontation, which he believed should not deter the United States from its mission in the Gulf. Most of his colleagues agreed, noting "Iraq's genuine regret and interest in making amends." Weinberger even drew the contrast in a national security meeting immediately after the incident that "if an Iranian plane attacked a U.S. ship, he would recommend attacking Iran directly."[26]

Shultz's views on the incident were more conflicted and somewhat more skeptical toward Iraq, accepting the evidence that the attack on the *Stark* was in fact an accident but also coming to see it as part of a larger pattern of erratic and unpredictable behavior. On one hand, he sent official letters to Congress emphasizing the "tragic" nature of the accident and asserting that the incident "provides no reason for altering" US policy in the Gulf. Yet he and his advisors at the State Department also felt there was "some reason for skepticism" about the Iraqi explanations for the attack, and he initially "ordered all references to accident removed" from presidential statements on the incident until Iraq issued its formal apology. The negotiations with the Iraqi regime to obtain compensation for the victims on the *Stark* soon broke down into a difficult and protracted affair that eroded much of the goodwill and benefit of the doubt that Saddam's initial apology had engendered.[27]

Moreover, Iraqi aircraft continued to launch attacks on US naval ships in the months to follow, despite assurances to the contrary, causing much confusion among US officials over Iraqi intentions. Reagan noted in his diary in February 1988 that "Iraq[']s planes continue to harass our ships—we don[']t know whether they just don[']t know what they're doing or not. Some of our top military are in Bagdad trying to find out."[28] Meeting with Iraqi foreign minister Tariq Aziz in Washington, Colin Powell stressed that it was "absolutely essential that we avoid another accident" like the attack on the *Stark* and expressed concern over a "number of close calls recently." Aziz responded with a willingness to "improve procedures" and cooperation with US forces in the Gulf and listed a variety of factors including bad weather as reasons for the pilot's "mistake" in a recent near-miss incident. Excuses for later "close calls" included a "technical malfunction" and "confused" navigation.[29] This mixture of apologies and obfuscation managed to keep Iraq out of US crosshairs, but relations between the two countries had seriously deteriorated before the Iran-Iraq War drew to a close.

The issue more than any other that led Shultz and others in the administration to detect dangerous and menacing patterns in the behavior of the Iraqi regime was its use of chemical weapons. As Shultz later recounted, by late 1983 "something sinister seemed to be going on in Iraq."[30] US intelligence began receiving reports that confirmed Iranian accusations that Iraq was employing chemical warfare to repel the increasingly effective "human wave" assaults that Iranian forces were throwing against its defenses. Within the context of Iraq's dire military situation in holding off the Iranian advance, US officials opted to take a private approach to warn the Iraqi regime that further use of chemical weapons could jeopardize the improvement of US-Iraqi relations. While it first appeared that this démarche had done the trick, Iraqi desperation in the face of renewed Iranian offensives in early 1984 prompted more extensive use of and reliance on chemical weapons as a "regular and recurring" tactic and an "integral part" of Iraq's battlefield strategy for the rest of the war, according to US intelligence reports.[31]

Shultz led the charge in shaping the US government's efforts to curb the production and use of chemical weapons in the war, but he ran into stiff opposition both within the administration and among the United States' European allies. When Iraqi forces resumed their use of the internationally banned weapons in early 1984, the State Department publicly and formally denounced Iraq for its breach of international law, "condemning Iraq's use of chemical weapons and deploring the loss of life." In response, an internal administration memo lamented that "we have demolished a budding relationship [with Iraq] by taking a tough position in opposition to chemical weapons." While Shultz tried to press forward in introducing a new international treaty that would not only ban the production and use of chemical weapons but also monitor the transfer of chemicals that could be used to produce such agents, he ran into opposition from CIA director William Casey and others who feared the difficulties of verifying compliance with such a treaty. More significantly, US allies in Europe met Shultz's appeals with what the secretary of state called "a profound lack of enthusiasm." The West German government, for example, "seemed singularly indifferent and incurious" about reports that West German companies were providing crucial assistance to Iraq's efforts to develop its own production capacity for chemical weapons. After meeting with the West German ambassador to Iraq, the chief US diplomat in Baghdad, William Eagleton, reported to Shultz the West German government's skepticism that the problem was "immediate" and that it had "no intention to take any action" without "information definitely implicating" its companies in chemical weapons production. Meanwhile, Vice President George Bush introduced a draft of the treaty to the Geneva Disarmament Conference in the spring of 1984, where it remained mired for the rest of Reagan's presidency.[32]

In the face of this internal and international opposition to taking strong action against Iraq's use of chemical weapons, the Reagan administration faced limited options and competing priorities. On one hand, noted a US intelligence report, "If the use of chemicals continues or increases, it would be an indication to Third World states that chemical weapons have military utility, and a worldwide chemical protocol or treaty could become more difficult to obtain."[33] The use of such ghastly WMD could become regularized as a tool to feed the aggression of other unsavory regimes. Within the context of the continuing Iran-Iraq War, however, with the paramount danger of Iranian expansion looming as a real possibility in the middle of the decade, the Reagan administration sought to balance its condemnations of Iraqi behavior with its ongoing efforts to prevent an outright Iraqi military defeat. Iraqi officials such as Foreign Minister Tariq Aziz protested that his regime was fighting for its very survival: "They want to destroy our country, conquer us, of course we'll use every means at our disposal."[34] The Reagan administration concluded that it had to temper its confrontation with Iraq over the issue or risk undercutting the prospects of bolstering Iraqi defense. The United States, therefore, tried to contain the issue, with Shultz reassuring Iraqi officials later in 1984 that "our desires and our actions to prevent an Iranian victory and to continue the progress of our bilateral relations remain undiminished." The State Department repeated that the United States did "not want this issue to dominate our bilateral relationship."[35] As Shultz himself later admitted, "There had been a period of twelve to eighteen months in the mid-1980s when I, and American foreign policy, gave the benefit of the doubt to the Iraqi regime of Saddam Hussein."[36]

But just as it had in the aftermath of the attack on the *Stark*, this benefit of the doubt evaporated in the final years of the Iran-Iraq War. As reports of Iraq's use of chemical weapons persisted and multiplied in the second half of the decade, the United States' patience began to wear thin. Shultz continued to press allies to support the draft treaty to curb the spread of dangerous chemicals and to interdict the shipments of such materials to Iraq, though the administration kept its frustration and displeasure toward Iraq limited to verbal denunciations, both public and private, against particular incidents. By 1986, Iran was mounting its own chemical attacks against Iraqi forces, which in some respects heightened US alarm at the spread of such methods but also served to deflect blame from Saddam's regime and reinforce the prevailing notion of a war between two evils.[37] In his diary, Reagan noted with disgust several instances of Iraqi use of nerve gas in 1988 and the fact that "both sides are now using chemical warfare."[38] Nevertheless, Shultz observed that the United States remained "the only nation trying in a serious and systematic way to halt the traffic" in the materials necessary to produce chemical weapons.[39]

By August 1988, the need to balance the competing priorities of condemning Iraqi use of chemical weapons and preventing an Iranian victory disappeared with the end of the Iran-Iraq War. Just as Colin Powell had earlier urged, the enormously destructive conflict ended with a ceasefire that left neither side with a clear advantage, still insecure against the threat of its implacably hostile neighbor. By late 1987, Iranian offensives had petered out and the tide of the war began to turn toward Iraq. A combination of factors convinced Iran to accept a United Nations–mandated ceasefire to end the war in July 1988: Iraqi victories on the battlefield in the first half of 1988, which resulted in the recapture of lost territory and the threat of a thrust into Iran; a failing economy and ebbing morale at home; unified diplomatic pressure from the member states of the UN Security Council, which passed a resolution in July 1987 calling for a ceasefire; and the escalation of hostilities in the Gulf between US and Iranian naval forces, which the Iranian government interpreted as evidence of preparations by the United States to intervene decisively in the conflict. The ceasefire came into effect on August 20, 1988.[40]

Saddam Hussein wasted little time in presenting the world with evidence that his violent and destructive behavior would not come to an end with the close of his war against Iran. While his armies had driven back Iranian forces in the final months of the conflict, the war had ended with a ceasefire that merely restored the status quo from before the war, and eight years of brutal bloodshed had left the Iraqi economy and society—and Saddam's regime—in tatters. Seeking to repress the rebellious Kurdish population in northern Iraq that was pushing for autonomy from his rule even before the war's end, Saddam unleashed a devastating attack on the Kurdish city of Halabja on March 16, 1988. Using rockets, napalm, and eventually mustard gas and nerve agents in what amounted to the largest chemical weapons attack on civilians in history, Saddam's forces killed up to five thousand Kurds and injured as many as ten thousand more. This brutal attack was part of the final campaigns of the war, and the harsh details of the scale and nature of the devastation and the responsibility behind it emerged only slowly. The worldwide response was, therefore, muted until Saddam followed up with a new round of violent repression against his Kurdish population just days after the ceasefire with Iran. From August 25 to September 3, 1988, his forces used conventional and chemical weapons to crush the remaining Kurdish resistance.[41]

No longer under the cover of holding back Iranian radicalism, Saddam's regime came under heavy criticism from the US government. When reports reached Washington, Shultz directed the State Department to denounce the attacks as "abhorrent" and "a grave threat to regional stability" and to lodge a formal protest with the Iraqi government. The administration shared with members of Congress a statement of its official policy asserting that halting the use of chemical weapons was "of transcendant [sic] importance" and "overrides other bilateral considerations" with Iraq. Without strong support for these public charges from the United States' European allies, Reagan authorized, in an attempt to build international consensus behind the US accusation, the disclosure of US intercepts of Iraqi military communications proving that Iraq had used poison gas against the Kurds. But beyond approving a fact-finding mission whose representatives Iraq blocked from entering the country, the United Nations did little in response to Saddam's gassing of the Kurds. Even the Reagan administration would only go so far, resisting a bill in Congress to impose unilateral sanctions against Iraq on the grounds that such actions would not be effective without broader international support. Moreover, some ranks within the US government still held out hope that Saddam's regime would stabilize his country and moderate its behavior with the end of hostilities with Iran. As Iraq emerged from the war "as a major regional power aligned with many of our friends," argued one high-ranking official in the State Department, it had "more to gain from conforming to international standards than flouting them" and should therefore be open to US overtures to moderate its excesses.[42]

Nevertheless, opposition to the policy of accommodating Iraq as a buffer against Iran was growing within the Reagan administration. With the war over and Iran gravely weakened from the eight-year struggle, the need to protect against what Rumsfeld had called a "collapse" of the Persian Gulf to Iranian domination, which had justified the US tilt toward Iraq over the course of the 1980s, was no longer nearly as pressing. A State Department intelligence report predicted in September 1988 that Iranian foreign policy would follow a more moderate course in the war's aftermath, and the regime's Islamist radicalism would likely decline following the expected imminent death of Ayatollah Khomeini. Moreover, the report declared that already the "export of revolution and fundamentalist Islam has greatly diminished as an interest of the regime."[43]

This changed international context, combined with the significant deterioration in US-Iraqi relations and the escalating Iraqi use of chemical weapons, prompted officials in the State Department to consider a reevaluation of US policy toward Iraq. At the end of December 1988, Shultz received a memo from several State Department officials that noted, "The regime of Saddam Hussein has long been known as one of the most brutal and repressive in the world. But its actions in 1988 outdid its previous performance."[44] Shultz himself explained that the end of the Iran-Iraq War "greatly diminished" the United States' interest in maintaining a balance of power in the Gulf to curb the threat from Iran. Surveying the recent behavior of Saddam's regime, Shultz enumerated the issues on which the Reagan administration was "at sword's point" with Iraq: "over chemical weapons, the difficulty of obtaining compensation from Iraq for the victims of the attack on the U.S.S. *Stark*, and signs of Iraq's support for terrorists." Moreover, the United States regarded with growing concern Iraqi efforts "to construct a regionally dominant military machine that could not be explained by his fear of Iran alone." Recognizing the defining features that were coalescing into the new rogue state paradigm, Shultz concluded in the fall of 1988 that Saddam Hussein's Iraq had become "one of the enemy states of the responsible world community."[45]

By the end of the Reagan presidency, therefore, the US government was seriously considering reorienting its stance toward Iraq from one of accommodation to one of containment. Shultz explained that "it was clear to me that no further reason existed for the United States to give Iraq the benefit of the doubt for balance-of-power purposes against Iran." The trouble was that the Reagan administration's time at the helm of US foreign policy was drawing to a close. Shultz himself admitted to his advisors that any official reappraisal of Persian Gulf policy was "properly something which we should not decide one way or the other, leaving a free field to the incoming Administration," a decision with which James Baker, Shultz's successor as secretary of state, concurred. But this did not keep Shultz and his team from offering their suggestions to the incoming Bush administration that "a new and tougher policy toward Saddam Hussein's Iraq was now appropriate."[46]

Most notable was a paper written by State Department official Zalmay Khalilzad for one of the transition books that the Reagan team prepared for the new administration. Khalilzad argued for the need to contain Iraq as well as Iran. With the war over, he wrote, Iraq had replaced Iran as the regional hegemon that was poised to dominate the Gulf and therefore represented the more dangerous threat. The United States should selectively strengthen Iran as a counterbalance to Iraq, reversing the "tilt" of the mid-1980s in the other direction. It was only a matter of time, he warned, before Iraq turned to confront the other regional power, the United States, possibly by targeting its allies in the Gulf, including Saudi Arabia or Kuwait. Controversy lingers over how much weight Khalilzad's arguments held among his superiors. While most accounts present his as a "dissenting voice" that "found no takers" in Washington, Shultz called it "our recommended new policy to contain Iraq" in his memoirs. Regardless of its intentions, the Reagan administration did not make meaningful changes to its Gulf policy before leaving office in January 1989. The Bush transition team, meanwhile, either overlooked or rejected the Reagan State Department's recommendations for a change of course, instead predicting that Iraq would function in the future as "a more responsible, status-quo state working within the system." The existing policy of engagement with Iraq in the hopes of moderating its behavior remained in place.[47]

The legacy that Reagan left on Iraq was a mix of finished and unfinished business. Through most of his presidency, Reagan, along with Shultz, had to temper his recognition of the dangerous qualities of Saddam Hussein's regime with the necessity of combating what he considered higher-priority threats to the security of US interests in the Middle East: Soviet and particularly Iranian expansion. The US government accordingly provided an increasing level of aid to Iraq to prevent its collapse and thereby maintain a delicate balance of power against two unsavory and threatening regimes. As the destructiveness of the Iran-Iraq War threatened to spill over into the Persian Gulf and menace the global economy by disrupting oil supplies, US involvement culminated in the deployment of the US Navy in what became the largest US naval operation since the Second World War. Meanwhile,

Saddam's regime in Iraq, while providing a useful counterweight to Iranian ambitions in the Gulf, grew ever more disdainful of the norms governing international behavior, sowing chaos in the strategically important region through clearly demonstrated military aggression and the pursuit—and repeated use—of WMD.

By the time it left office in early 1989, the Reagan team faced a markedly changed international context as it related to policy toward Iraq. With the Cold War nearly over, fears of Soviet expansion into the region were greatly diminished. Even more significantly, the close of the Iran-Iraq War had left both belligerents—but particularly Iran, which had suffered repeated defeats on the battlefield in the final months of the war—gravely weakened, with the need to stem the tide of Iranian domination no longer the pressing strategic imperative that it once was. This sense of finished business came too late for Reagan and his team to follow through on reorienting its policies in the region, for just as they began to seriously consider an adjustment to their stance toward Iraq, a new administration took office.

Nevertheless, even before the end of the Iran-Iraq War, relations between Saddam's regime and the Reagan administration had deteriorated to the point that a growing tide of opinion in the US government felt that the end of hostilities should warrant a change toward a firmer and more confrontational approach toward Iraq. With Iranian power on the wane and Saddam's brazen disdain for international norms on the rise, Iraq had come to eclipse Iran as the more dangerous of the two regimes in the eyes of some US officials. Shultz and many of his advisors at the State Department recognized that Saddam's unpredictable behavior, his proven military aggression, his continued support for terrorist organizations, and his increasingly brazen use of WMD placed him squarely in the camp of "enemy states of the responsible world community," alongside other rogue foes such as Qadhafi of Libya and Noriega of Panama. But they did not communicate these changing views clearly or forcefully enough to their successors for the new Bush administration to alter the course of US policy. This sense of unfinished business toward lingering dangers in the region left Reagan with a feeling of regret, admitting in his memoirs that at the end of his presidency "the Middle East was as much a snake pit of problems as it was when I unpacked my bags in Washington in 1981."[48]

The Rise and Fall of "Constructive Engagement": Bush and Iraq before the Gulf Crisis

Few, if any, of the senior officials in the incoming Bush administration appeared to have an awareness of their predecessors' inclination to take a firmer line

FIGURE 14. The Bush national security team: President Bush speaks to reporters in the Rose Garden outside the Oval Office during the Gulf War, February 11, 1991, flanked by the key members of his national security team known as the "Gang of Eight": (L–R) National Security Advisor Brent Scowcroft, Deputy National Security Advisor Robert Gates, Secretary of Defense Dick Cheney, Vice President Dan Quayle, White House chief of staff John Sununu, Secretary of State James Baker, and Chairman of the Joint Chiefs of Staff Gen. Colin Powell.

toward Iraq. At first glance this would seem surprising, given the high level of personnel crossover between the two administrations. Yet by the time the Iran-Iraq War ended and opinions on the United States' approach toward Saddam Hussein began to shift in the fall of 1988, much of this crossover in the top ranks had already left the decision-making circles of the outgoing national security team. Most notably, James Baker, soon to become Bush's secretary of state, had resigned his post as Reagan's secretary of the treasury to take charge of managing Bush's campaign days before the ceasefire in the Gulf took effect. Vice President Bush himself, meanwhile, was then at the peak of his efforts on the campaign trail for the upcoming presidential election. Colin Powell, still serving in the White House as Reagan's national security advisor during the campaign and transition, would not join Bush's team as chairman of the Joint Chiefs of Staff (JCS) until the following fall. None were therefore in a position to carry the new direction of the Reagan team's thinking on Iraq policy into the new administration. In fact, Bush was under the impression that his predecessor's position was just the opposite, writing in his memoirs that "the Reagan Administration set out to institutionalize this somewhat improved relationship with Iraq" after the war's end.[49]

President Bush, therefore, determined to continue the policy of accommodation toward Iraq that the Reagan team had developed to meet the challenges of the Iran-Iraq War, pending a fuller policy review for the Persian Gulf region. With higher priorities on his foreign policy agenda—and even on his agenda in the Middle East—Bush adopted a policy of "constructive engagement" in an attempt to moderate Saddam's behavior and corral as much support from his regime as possible toward the goal of furthering the stagnated Arab-Israeli peace process. As Saddam's behavior grew more bellicose and antagonistic in the spring of 1990, dashing Bush and his advisors' hopes to enlist him as a stabilizing partner in the region, they shifted away from engagement and eventually dropped the economic incentives that lay at the heart of their push to moderate his regime, instead shifting toward a policy of containment. Until the moment Saddam's army crossed the border into Kuwait, however, the Bush team was not yet willing to fully pivot toward a position of confrontation with Iraq. As it was, such a position had little support among allies in Europe or the Middle East and would likely have had a minimal effect on Saddam's actions beyond exacerbating the growing paranoia that drove his aggression.

Across the board, the senior members of Bush's national security team later admitted that the monumental transformations to the international order that dominated their attention during their first year in office gave them little opportunity to focus on policy toward Iraq. President Bush and his national security advisor, Brent Scowcroft, later wrote in their joint memoir that the Persian Gulf "had not been among our major concerns early in the Administration." Despite Iraq's often "exasperating" behavior, they explained, they felt that the region "had begun to return to normal" following the end of the Iran-Iraq War and therefore "occupied the attention of our specialists rather than the policy-making team."[50] Secretary of State Baker agreed, noting that right up to the Iraqi invasion of Kuwait in August 1990, the administration was preoccupied in "grappling with one of the most revolutionary periods in world history," juggling the revolutions in Eastern Europe, the fall of the Berlin Wall and the unification of Germany, upheaval in the Soviet Union, and democratic unrest in China that ended in the bloody Tiananmen Square crackdown—not to mention the escalating standoff with and eventual military action against Noriega's regime in Panama. Even within the Middle East region, relations with Iraq did not rank as a top priority, with much greater attention focused on reviving the stalled peace process between Israel and the Arab states. Against this backdrop of international crisis and transformation, Iraq was "hardly even in the second tier among their concerns," according to one study. It remained "on the back burner," wrote Baker. No senior administration officials considered it an urgent priority, so "it was simply not prominent on my radar screen, or the President's."[51]

Meanwhile, military planners at the Department of Defense also sought to deprioritize the Middle East from the increasingly prominent place it had achieved among US security concerns by the end of the Reagan presidency. With the Iran-Iraq War over, the peril to shipping and oil supplies in the Persian Gulf had dissipated and the Iranian expansionist threat appeared subdued. With the Cold War winding down, the even greater threat to the region's security in the eyes of generations of defense officials going back to the Truman administration—a Soviet move to dominate the Arabian Peninsula—was also greatly diminished. In 1989, therefore, Admiral William Crowe, the chairman of the JCS for the first months of Bush's term, issued guidance to the US military "that made the Gulf into an afterthought as far as America's strategic priorities were concerned." The new secretary of defense, Dick Cheney, strongly disagreed with this assessment, and in January 1990 he reversed Crowe's guidance to make clear that the Persian Gulf should still rank as a high priority for US defense planners and that "we should plan for a crisis in the Gulf," as he later recounted in his memoirs. Yet even Cheney's belief that the Gulf region still posed dangers to US security interests was not driven primarily by fears of an imminent threat from Iraq. Rather, he felt it was "too early to discount the Soviets entirely" and a mistake not to prepare for the possibility of "a threat arising from within" the notoriously unstable region.[52] Responding to media reports in February 1990 of a downgrading of the Persian Gulf region in US defense priorities, Lawrence Eagleburger, the deputy secretary of state, sent an overview of Cheney's revised guidance to US embassies across the Middle East and Europe. He asserted that US defense planning for the region would "concentrate on contingencies on the Arabian Peninsula and defense of the Persian Gulf Arab states," including against potential threats from the Soviet Union, whose "military capabilities remain impressive." The United States remained committed to stability in the Gulf "irrespective of the source of instability."[53]

Cheney's elevation of the Gulf region among the priorities of US military planners notwithstanding, the Bush administration devoted only sporadic attention to Iraq policy during its first year in office. The preliminary strategic review of Persian Gulf policy concluded in April 1989 with discussion and approval of a draft presidential National Security Directive (NSD) in the Deputies Committee of the NSC, chaired by Deputy National Security Advisor Robert Gates. The NSC staff member in charge of the Middle East, Richard Haass, who led the policy review, had long been a strong opponent of closer relations with Iran and thus wished to explore the possibility of warmer ties with Iraq. Even among this lower-level group of officials, however, Iraq was no more than a "distant concern" amid a range of global unrest and developing crises. The matter did not reach the full NSC for Bush's final approval until October 1989, not out of controversy or disagreement within the administration but rather as a sign of "the low priority the administration as a whole accorded Persian Gulf affairs in the summer of 1989."[54]

What resulted from this belated strategic review was NSD-26, a presidential policy directive covering the entire Persian Gulf region, with Iraq as one element among several. NSD-26 codified the policy of "constructive engagement" toward Iraq that the administration had been following on a preliminary basis since entering office. Regarding Iraq, the directive's central assertion held that "normal relations between the United States and Iraq would serve our longer-term interests and promote stability in both the Gulf and the Middle East." To achieve these normalized relations and to "increase our influence with Iraq," the United States would offer "economic and political incentives" to encourage Iraq to "moderate its behavior." At the same time, the directive warned that "any illegal use of chemical and/or biological weapons," as well as any "breach by Iraq of IAEA [International Atomic Energy Agency] safeguards in its nuclear program," would lead to economic and political sanctions, "for which we would seek the broadest possible support from our allies and friends." NSD-26 went on to note that human rights and the need for the Iraqi regime to "cease its meddling in external affairs" should also factor prominently into US relations with Iraq.[55]

While the bottom line of the Bush administration's policy toward Iraq, as outlined in NSD-26, was to seek "normal relations" and offer "economic and political incentives," most of the directive's section on Iraq in fact focused on the dangers emanating from Saddam Hussein's regime. This reflected the two conflicting sides to the Bush national security team's assessment of Iraq during its first year in office. On one hand, Saddam's regime had shown some signs of moderating its behavior toward its neighbors and curtailing its radicalism in the immediate aftermath of the Iran-Iraq War ceasefire, most notably in starting to support negotiations between the Palestine Liberation Organization and Israel. Baker, therefore, "saw Iraq as a potentially helpful Arab ally in moving the moribund Middle East peace process forward," the top priority on the administration's initial agenda for the region. US officials also assumed that with its economy and infrastructure in ruins in the aftermath of its war with Iran, the Iraqi government would seek friendly relations with the West to attract the foreign capital it needed for the physical and economic reconstruction of the country, and that the desire for productive relations would therefore flow in both directions.[56]

On the other hand, as Baker explains, "We were under no illusions about Saddam's brutality toward his own people or his capacity for escalating tensions with his neighbors." Bush and Scowcroft recounted the litany of concerns they held toward this "tough, ruthless, and even paranoid dictator" and his regime in Baghdad, including his "abysmal" human rights record, which showed no signs of improvement; his continued support for and harboring of terrorists, which had persisted in a tempered fashion even after the State Department had removed Iraq from its list of state sponsors in 1982; his substantial chemical and biological weapons programs and actual use of such weapons against Iran and the Kurds; his development of ballistic missiles that could threaten ever-greater portions of the Middle East; and, most ominous of all, his efforts to build a nuclear weapons capability, though US intelligence estimates on the extent of his progress varied widely. Given this long list of potential dangers, Baker explained that NSD-26 "explicitly envisioned a policy of disincentives if our overtures proved unsuccessful," as the administration knew they very well might. This second half of the policy toward Iraq set forth in NSD-26 has been largely overlooked. The flexibility and readiness to shift from incentives to sanctions was in fact "a central component of the strategy."[57]

The Iraq policy set out in NSD-26, therefore, represented a compromise consensus view among Bush's advisors, balancing those who hoped to enlist Iraqi support in furthering the Middle East peace process, as well as securing a significant role for American business in Iraq's postwar reconstruction effort, and those whose fears of the pace and scope of Saddam's WMD programs pointed toward a more adversarial relationship with his regime. "The problem," admitted Bush and Scowcroft, "was how to encourage Saddam Hussein to be at least a minimally responsible member of the international community and yet not accept or ignore his depredations." What swung the scales in favor of seeking constructive engagement rather than confrontation with Iraq was the US assessment that in the aftermath of the massively destructive war with Iran, this "battered and demoralized nation" would not be able to "muster the capacity" to launch further wars. Baker explained that the notion that the United States would soon go to war with Iraq was simply "inconceivable" in 1989. Moreover, Iraq's Arab neighbors, particularly Egypt, believing that Saddam would focus on domestic reconstruction, encouraged the United States to seek a constructive relationship with his regime. Meanwhile, the United States' European allies, especially France and Germany, as well as the Soviet Union, strongly favored deepening rather than curtailing economic ties with Iraq. In this regional and international context, Baker recognized that the United States "could have pursued a policy of dual containment against Iran *and* Iraq only by going it alone," an approach that "would not have worked." Bush and his advisors, therefore, decided that making "a good-faith effort toward better relations" with Iraq was worth a try.[58]

The primary economic incentive behind the policy of constructive engagement—and thus the administration's main piece of leverage to moderate Iraqi behavior—was providing agricultural credits to Iraq for the purchase of American grain and food. This program, run through the Department of Agriculture's Commodity Credit Corporation (CCC), represented a continuation of a practice that had begun during the Reagan administration. In late 1989, the US government allocated $1 billion in CCC credit guarantees to Iraq, with $500 million available immediately and the rest subject to further review before its release. Contrary to public and media perceptions at the time and since, the CCC credit program did not involve the transfer of these funds to Iraq but rather to American businesses, providing a degree of insurance to facilitate US agricultural exports to Iraq: American banks, insured by the US government, advanced money to American exporters, who then sent wheat and rice—not cash—to Iraq; then Iraq paid cash to the American banks in fulfillment of the CCC credit guarantees. Despite Iraq's precarious financial state in the aftermath of the Iran-Iraq War, its record of repayment of these loans was "spotless," according to Baker. The program, unsurprisingly, was enormously popular in farm states across the country and among their congressional representatives on Capitol Hill. More controversial in Congress was an additional program providing short-term credit insurance from the Export-Import Bank of approximately $200 million per year.[59]

Just as Bush approved NSD-26, the implementation of his constructive engagement policy hit a major roadblock in Congress. The cause was a federal investigation into the Atlanta branch of the Italian-owned Banca Nazionale del Lavoro (BNL). The Justice Department discovered that BNL-Atlanta had made unauthorized loans of over $2 billion to Iraq, which in turn had used the funds to purchase military equipment, prohibited under US law. Because BNL-Atlanta had been a leading participant in the CCC program, investigators initially suspected that the bank had diverted CCC credits to fund the illicit Iraqi arms purchases. The public outcry over what the media soon dubbed "Iraqgate"—a nod to "Irangate" (now better known as the Iran-Contra affair) during the Reagan presidency, and of course to the Watergate scandal before that—grew through the fall of 1989. It later became clear that BNL-Atlanta's inadequately secured loans of cash to Iraq were entirely separate from the CCC credit guarantees—which, after all, provided only foodstuffs, not cash, directly to Iraq.[60]

However, the BNL scandal greatly complicated the Bush administration's efforts to facilitate approval for the first tranche of the total $1 billion in CCC guarantees that lay at the heart of its constructive engagement policy. In addition, Congress passed a bill to deny loans to Iraq from the Export-Import Bank. In keeping with the just-approved NSD-26, and without clear evidence of the complicity of Iraqi government officials in the BNL scheme, Baker personally advocated allowing the full CCC program to proceed. Bush and his team worried that the "loss of the CCC program would have nearly erased what little leverage we had with Iraq." Baker's State Department still judged that the prospects of

Iraqi cooperation with the Middle East peace process outweighed any symbolic benefits of jettisoning the economic programs. Accordingly, in January 1990 Bush overrode congressional opposition and signed a directive authorizing the Export-Import Bank line of credit, and Congress dropped CCC sanctions from pending bills. This decision, Baker later noted, "turned out to be the high-water mark of our efforts to moderate Iraqi behavior."[61]

As it later became clear, the relatively optimistic assessment of Iraqi intentions that undergirded the Bush administration's constructive engagement policy was rooted in a fundamental misreading of Saddam Hussein's state of mind in the aftermath of the Iran-Iraq War. This was less a matter of overlooking the dangerous capabilities of the Iraqi regime, as the focus of NSD-26 on his WMD programs, human rights abuses, and aggressive "meddling" in the affairs of his neighbors made clear. Bush and his team even appreciated the low chances that Saddam would moderate his behavior or "change his spots." Rather, they based their assessment that he would be open to partnership and cooperation with the West—and therefore behave responsibly—on the assumption that he would focus his attention on the reconstruction of his war-torn and devastated country. His tendency to bluster aside, Saddam was in no state to launch further acts of aggression, a point that his Arab neighbors emphasized to US officials. In this context, notes one historian, "Bush resolved to treat Saddam as a friend in hopes of making it so."[62]

Iraqi records captured after the 2003 US invasion reveal all too plainly that the cooperation and friendship that the Bush administration hoped for in the fall of 1989 was simply not in the cards. The historian Hal Brands, who has worked extensively with these records documenting the deliberations of Saddam's regime, explains that the Iraqi dictator's mindset in the aftermath of the Iran-Iraq War amounted to "an explosive cocktail of strength and weakness." On one hand, Iraq had emerged from the war as a major regional military power, with the largest and best equipped armed forces in the Arab world, and with its perennial enemy Iran greatly weakened. However, his regime also faced crippling foreign debts and grave economic problems that were fueling domestic instability and discontent with his rule. The Iraqi leader therefore came out of the war as "a well-armed but increasingly desperate actor ... confident in his martial prowess but also feeling aggrieved and cornered," especially as his problems deepened in 1989 and 1990. "For Saddam Hussein to survive," warned one Pakistani official, "he needed a state of confrontation, if not with Iran then with somebody else."[63]

Fueling Saddam's sense of desperation was his own assessment of the United States. Far from seeing a potential partner for reconstruction, Saddam viewed the United States by the close of the Iran-Iraq War as "a deeply malevolent power that was determined to thwart Iraqi ambitions and break the Baathist government." Brands explains that the Baathist ideology of his political movement and his own conspiracy-minded personality, combined with the United States' history of intervention in the Middle East, had long provoked Saddam's suspicions of US intentions. He interpreted the Iran-Contra revelations that the Reagan administration had supplied arms to Iran as evidence that the United States had become "a dangerous enemy that was implacably opposed to his regime." Despite US economic assistance and Bush's attempts at engagement, these suspicions only deepened, and Saddam saw Washington's hand in all manner of intrigues against his regime. Meeting with Baker in October 1989, Iraqi foreign minister Tariq Aziz accused the US government of mounting covert operations to destabilize Iraq and subvert its government. In private, Saddam alleged that the United States was seeking to topple his regime, ruin Iraq's economy, and perhaps even assassinate him, asking his advisors, "Did they not conspire against us during the war? Their conspiracy was obvious." With his erstwhile ally the Soviet Union in decline, Saddam feared that unchecked US power would allow it to dominate the Middle East and undermine his own claim to primacy in the region. He warned, "If the Gulf people, along with all Arabs, are not careful, the Arab Gulf region will be governed by the U.S. will." His half-brother argued that "we are the only obstacle in front of them." Fueled by his paranoia, Saddam increasingly came to perceive a US-led plot to encircle Iraq and destroy his regime. Throughout the spring and summer of 1990, Saddam shared this accusation with US officials, arguing that he had to act against what he called an "Imperialist-Zionist conspiracy" and a "U.S.-British-Israeli conspiracy to discredit Iraq and undermine his leadership." Rather than focusing his attention on domestic reconstruction, therefore, he began looking for ways to lash out against this plot of encirclement that threatened his rule.[64]

As Saddam's problems worsened in the first half of 1990, his deep-seated paranoia drove his behavior in a more erratic and bellicose direction. Scowcroft later recalled that he recognized "an abrupt change" in Iraq's relations with the United States in early 1990, launching what one State Department official called Saddam's "spring of bad behavior." The first unmistakable sign of this shift toward unpredictability and confrontation came with an escalation in Saddam's rhetoric, which grew more inflammatory and threatening toward both the United States and his neighbors. At a February 1990 meeting in Jordan, he pressed his fellow Arab leaders to cancel the debts that Iraq had amassed during the Iran-Iraq War, arguing that his country had protected the whole Arab world from Iranian aggression. Sensing resistance to his demands, he made a vague but ominous threat: "Let the Gulf regimes know that if they do not give this money to me, I will know how to get it." At the same meeting, he declared that the US military presence in the Gulf was no longer necessary, and that its only purpose could be to aid

Israel. Earlier that month, Saddam had taken offense to a Voice of America radio broadcast asserting that in the wake of the anticommunist revolutions in Eastern Europe in 1989, "the tide of history is against" rulers of police states, listing Iraq among seven others. Despite reassurances that the broadcast did not represent official US policy, it fed Saddam's growing sense of paranoia.[65]

March and April 1990 became the turning point in the evolving American perception of Saddam Hussein, both within the US government and in public circles. On March 15, Saddam ordered the execution of Iranian-born British journalist Farzad Bazoft, who had published stories on Iraq's nuclear weapons program, on charges of espionage. The Iraqi leader rejected appeals for his clemency from Western governments. Over the next month, US and British authorities uncovered evidence that Saddam had accelerated his efforts to obtain sophisticated technology to advance his WMD programs, as they blocked shipments of triggering devices for nuclear weapons and parts for a long-range "supergun" artillery piece. Finally, the event more than any other that set off alarm bells in Washington was a speech that Saddam gave to the General Command of his armed forces on April 2. He confirmed publicly for the first time that Iraq possessed chemical weapons and then explicitly threatened Israel, vowing that if he were attacked, perhaps fearing a repeat of the Osirak raid of 1981, "By God, we will make fire eat up half of Israel." Baker later wrote that these remarks "set off alarms throughout the Western world and in Middle East capitals," and that as a result "our strategic calculation changed irrevocably."[66]

The question that faced Bush and his advisors was how irrevocably to change their policy toward Iraq in response to this string of provocations. The NSC staff and the State Department shared similar assessments of the situation but were of two minds on how the administration should proceed. In the White House, Scowcroft felt that the marked shift in Saddam's behavior indicated that "our current policy was no longer appropriate," but the very unpredictability of the Iraqi leader that prompted this assessment also pointed to the wisdom of "wait[ing] for further evidence before changing direction ourselves."[67] NSC staffer Peter Rodman wrote Scowcroft a lengthy memo sharing his agreement with the administration's "growing concern that Iraq, deliberately or inadvertently, is moving toward a position of strategic confrontation with the U.S." Rather than badgering Iraq on its recent string of transgressions, Rodman argued that the United States should impress upon Saddam the "convergence of *strategic* interest" between the two countries through a mix of reassurance and verbal warning in an effort to not let "our relationship . . . be torn apart if at all avoidable." In pressing for dialogue rather than confrontation, Rodman reflected the wing of the administration, which included Richard Haass, that was "not yet ready to forsake the Iraqi relationship, which was one of our strategic gains of the mid-80's."[68] In the

State Department, by contrast, Baker and his chief aides felt that by April "it had become clear that our policy had not produced the results we had hoped for," and therefore a "more confrontational stance toward Baghdad was now necessary." Baker's top advisors argued that Saddam's "Burn Israel" speech had revealed the fallacy behind the "illusion that we can moderate this guy," which had underpinned the policy of constructive engagement. Now that economic incentives had not worked on the Iraqi regime, "it's time to go to disincentives."[69]

The problem, both Scowcroft and Baker appreciated, was a question of flexibility: "How to respond aggressively to Iraq's unacceptable behavior and Saddam's threats while also preserving an ability to rebuild the relationship gradually if Baghdad's behavior improved," as Baker later summarized their dilemma. Even Baker thought it would be unwise at this juncture to take "irrevocable actions" toward confrontation, and he accordingly argued before a Senate Foreign Relations subcommittee on May 1 that it was "a little bit premature" to discuss sanctions against Iraq. Adding to his hesitancy toward taking bolder action were the pleas of Arab allies such as Egypt and Saudi Arabia, concerned that US relations with Iraq had already grown too confrontational, for the United States to take a middle-ground approach. Bush assured Egyptian president Hosni Mubarak in mid-May that he did "not want this problem to get out of hand" and believed that US relations with Iraq had "suffered a setback, but not, from my view, an irreparable one." A week later, Scowcroft wrote Senate Minority Leader Bob Dole that Iraq remained "a country that we are better off doing business with rather than isolating in order to influence its behavior."[70]

Despite this continued defense of the logic behind the policy of constructive engagement, the administration made the decision on May 29 to halt the second tranche of $500 million in CCC credits but hold off from further action that could inflame the situation. This decision came only after extended debate within the NSC Deputies Committee between the NSC staff, where Haass argued emphatically to allow the credits to go forward, and Baker's chief advisors from the State Department, who argued that the time had come to cancel all aid programs for Iraq. Scowcroft reasoned that the wait-and-see approach that the administration adopted after halting the CCC credits carried "minimal risk" because "there was little remaining of our positive policy" anyway. Still under the auspices of the incentives/disincentives approach of NSD-26, the US government had shifted to a policy of containment but not yet one of confrontation.[71]

While it is easy in retrospect to criticize Bush and his team for not taking firmer action against Iraq earlier, there were in fact few options for additional steps that promised substantive results. The May 29 decision to halt the remaining tranche of CCC credits removed the last positive incentive toward Iraq and thus effectively ended the policy of constructive engagement. Without a more blatant provocation from Saddam than his menacing rhetoric, neither the United States' European allies nor the moderate Arab states supported any form of sanctions and certainly not a buildup or demonstration of US military force. Moreover, the lack of reliable intelligence sources within Iraq, mixed with Saddam's increasing unpredictability, left the inner workings of the Iraqi regime and its intentions opaque to the US government. While there was general consensus within the administration of the need to move away from constructive engagement, Bush and his team did not yet want to alienate the Iraqi regime entirely or close off the possibility—however remote—that relations could turn in a more positive direction. Reasonable as they were, however, the mixed signals that the Bush administration sent in parting with constructive engagement but not adopting a clearly firmer policy to replace it did little to dissuade Saddam from taking an increasingly reckless path over the course of the summer of 1990.[72]

By the late spring and early summer of 1990, meanwhile, congressional and public perceptions of Saddam Hussein and his regime had swung in a decisively confrontational direction. Calls in Congress and the media intensified for enacting unilateral sanctions against Iraq as his provocations mounted. Critics began to label Bush's constructive engagement policy as appeasement, challenging the core assumption that the United States could moderate this dictatorial regime.[73] In early June, *U.S. News and World Report* ran a cover story declaring Saddam Hussein to be "the most dangerous man in the world." The article focused attention on his accelerating quest to produce WMD capabilities, including chemical and especially nuclear weapons, and to acquire powerful and long-range missiles to deliver them across the Middle East. The report warned that Iraq could be as close as two to five years to developing a nuclear weapons capability, despite the official US government estimate of five to ten years. These trends were all the more frightening given the "ample indications" that Saddam had "few qualms about using" his arsenal of WMD. The article also emphasized Iraqi support for terrorists and his proven military aggression against his neighbors, targets which could soon include Kuwait and Saudi Arabia in addition to Israel. Capping off the list of factors that made Saddam's regime in Iraq "the most dangerous and destabilizing member" of the international community was his sheer unpredictability: "He is so isolated, both from his own people and from the international community, that no one knows for sure what he might do."[74] Saddam Hussein was already becoming the defining poster child in the public eye of the as-yet-unnamed rogue state paradigm, bringing together all of the central features of the phenomenon that US officials had been slowly but surely recognizing over the past several years.

The downward spiral of Saddam's recklessness culminated in an escalating crisis with Kuwait from May to July 1990. Iraq's financial position was deteriorating at an alarming rate, with its debts to fellow Arab states mounting and foreign lines of credit drying up. He focused his resentment and anger on Kuwait, the small but oil-rich and wealthy kingdom on his southern border to which he owed over $10 billion from loans during the Iran-Iraq War. Beginning in late May, he launched accusations at the Kuwaitis of overproducing oil and thereby driving down oil prices, robbing Iraq of funds that it desperately needed. Moreover, he charged the Kuwaitis of "slant-drilling" across the two countries' disputed border to steal oil from the shared Rumaila oil field. Declaring these offenses to be "direct aggression" against Iraq that was "not less effective than military aggression," Saddam and his foreign minister, Tariq Aziz, demanded that Kuwait cancel Iraq's war debts and repay the country for the "stolen" oil from the Rumaila oil field. When the Kuwaitis rejected all of his demands, Saddam ordered several divisions of his elite Republican Guards to mass on the Iraq-Kuwait border on July 15.[75]

As Iraq's military buildup grew in scale, the Bush administration followed the lead of the Arab states, particularly Egypt, Saudi Arabia, and Jordan, whose leaders insisted that Saddam was only attempting to intimidate concessions from his smaller neighbor and that no attack was imminent. US officials were inclined to agree: Haass advised Scowcroft on July 25 that "things may have cooled," explaining that Iraq "seems to be engaging in a form of gunboat diplomacy that should pass peacefully." If it did use force, he predicted, "the most likely scenario" would be a limited incursion to seize the disputed territory with Kuwait; "a full-scale invasion of Kuwait" was "least likely (though by no means out of the question)." As a show of solidarity against the Iraqi threats, the United States agreed to a request from the United Arab Emirates, whose oil production had also drawn the ire of Saddam, to take part in a joint military exercise in the Gulf on July 24.[76]

Otherwise, the Bush administration sought to walk the fine line of pushing Iraq toward a negotiated solution to its dispute with Kuwait while not taking a stance on the substance of the contested issues. Accordingly, in a meeting with Saddam on July 25, the US ambassador in Baghdad, April Glaspie, emphasized to the Iraqi leader that while "we don't take a stand on territorial disputes," "we can never excuse settlement of disputes by other than peaceful means." As late as July 28, taking the unusual step of a direct message from the president to Saddam Hussein, the US government insisted that it "continues to desire better relations with Iraq" even while "we still have fundamental concerns about certain Iraqi policies and activities." Bush reiterated that "we believe that differences are best resolved by peaceful means and not by threats involving military force or conflict." Fearing that US rhetoric and actions toward Iraq had grown too confrontational and might provoke rather than deter an attack, Arab leaders urged Washington to allow them to handle Saddam and find an "Arab solution" to the crisis.[77]

Both the United States and its Arab allies underestimated the extent to which Saddam viewed Kuwait as both the cause of and the solution to his economic crisis. They based their assumption that he did not want conflict on the belief that Iraq was too exhausted from the Iran-Iraq War to fight another major conflict and that, in Baker's words, "no realistic calculation of his interests could have foreseen a full-scale invasion of Kuwait." However, Saddam's desperation and economic weakness, instead of making him less likely to attack, in fact emboldened him to "rob a bank like Kuwait" as the catch-all solution to his problems, as Baker later reflected. Paranoid that the "Imperialist and Zionist" noose was tightening around his neck and threatening the very survival of his regime, Saddam explained, "Our only choice was to go after the . . . circle of conspirators tasked with this mission." With this mindset, a lightning attack against Kuwait promised to both solve Iraq's economic crisis *and* disrupt a US-led conspiracy to destroy his regime. A controversy later arose that the statements from Glaspie and Bush to Saddam prior to the invasion were insufficiently strong to prevent Iraqi aggression and hence gave him a "green light" to seize Kuwait. But far more likely than trying to secure US approval for his attack is the probability that Saddam geared his diplomacy toward offering the United States enough reassurances to prevent any chance of US intervention that would spoil his plans. His gambit was successful: only days after the US embassy in Baghdad reported to Washington that "Saddam has blinked," Iraqi tanks swarmed across the border to overrun Kuwait.[78]

Adjusting to a New Context

President Reagan recognized the key elements of Saddam Hussein's threatening regime as early as the summer of 1981, less than half a year into his first term Similarly, President Bush and his team of advisors laid out the menacing trends in Saddam's behavior within their policy of constructive engagement with Iraq during their first year in office. However, faced with a wider strategic scene with a host of urgent threats to national security and international order, both administrations sought to develop positive relations with the Iraqi regime.

Within the broader context of the Cold War and the Iran-Iraq War, the threat of Saddam's regime appeared peripheral and secondary to US policymakers, distasteful but tolerable as the lesser of evils in a region with nothing but imperfect allies. Iraq did not seem as pressing of a concern to US interests as did the more immediate possibility of Soviet and especially Iranian expansion to dominate the Persian Gulf with its vital supplies of oil. When stripped away from this broader context, however, Saddam Hussein's Iraq loomed far more threatening in its own right.

During two brief windows of time, the transformation of the strategic landscape allowed the Reagan and Bush administrations to begin to fit the threatening features of Saddam's regime into a broader pattern that was then still in the process of emerging: the rogue state paradigm of international outlaws challenging the global order. The first window came at the close of Reagan's presidency, after the August 1988 Iran-Iraq ceasefire and revelations of Saddam's widespread use of chemical weapons to suppress his Kurdish population. George Shultz and others in the administration identified Iraq as a growing danger to the international community, but they failed to press their reassessment clearly or forcefully enough before leaving office to leave an impression with their successors. By mid-1989, with the rush of transformative events leading to the dismantling of the communist empire in Europe, Cold War concerns again monopolized the attention of the US government. A second window opened in the spring of 1990, as the dust of communism was still settling, for the Bush administration to reassess the Iraqi regime as a pressing threat to international order. It is clear in retrospect that Bush and his team should have responded more quickly to Saddam's provocations by shifting away from their policy of engagement and toward one of containment and confrontation. But the United States was not acting in a vacuum, and the opinions and actions of its allies limited the range of options available to Bush, who would have had little international support for a more confrontational stance toward Iraq before August 1990. Therefore, such a policy, however wise it might appear in hindsight, would likely have proven ineffective—and might even have exacerbated the warped and paranoid worldview that prompted Saddam to lash out in the first place.

Despite the gradual American reassessment of Saddam Hussein and his threatening qualities, and despite the shift in US policy toward his regime by the summer of 1990, the Iraqi invasion of Kuwait on August 2, 1990, still took the US government by surprise. This lack of preparation was a sign that while the rogue state paradigm was coming into clearer shape in US thinking, it had not yet become the defining threat to global security in the post–Cold War era. Strategies for dealing with international outlaws such as Iraq were still in flux.

Saddam Hussein's blitzkrieg into Kuwait threw the international community on its heels. The situation would demand improvisation on the part of the Bush administration and its allies to define the stakes of the crisis and devise a response to it. How they chose to confront the quintessential rogue state of Iraq would set a formative precedent for global security after the Cold War.

5

THE FORMATIVE PRECEDENT
The Gulf War and the Future of Global Security

President George H. W. Bush strode onto the stage to applause and cheering so loud that the band's rendition of "Hail to the Chief" could barely be heard. With British prime minister Margaret Thatcher seated alongside his podium, Bush was set to deliver the keynote address at the Aspen Institute's annual symposium on foreign affairs on August 2, 1990. The long-planned presidential speech, titled "Renewal," was going to lay out a new military strategy and force structure that would adapt to the changed international environment brought on by the subsiding Cold War.

Noting that the "decades-old division of Europe is ending, and the era of democracy-building has begun," thanks in large part to the newly "open and honest" relationship with Mikhail Gorbachev's Soviet Union, President Bush emphasized the need to "seize this historic opportunity to help create lasting peace." He cautioned that although these changes had "transformed our security environment," the United States needed to remain engaged in Europe and around the world to meet the "emerging challenges" of this new era taking shape.

In the most important lines of his address, Bush outlined what he viewed as the central threats to global security in the post–Cold War era: "Even in a world where democracy and freedom have made great gains, threats remain. Terrorism, hostagetaking [sic], renegade regimes and unpredictable rulers, new sources of instability—all require a strong and an engaged America." He went on to warn of the dangers posed by the growing number of states seeking chemical and nuclear weapons, to which he referred with the as-yet infrequently used phrase "weapons of mass destruction." Bush emphasized that even with the Cold War over, "the world remains a dangerous place with serious threats to important U.S. interests wholly unrelated to the earlier patterns of the U.S.-Soviet relationship."[1]

The timing of Bush's address could not have come at a moment more perfectly suited to his message. Only two weeks earlier, Gorbachev had officially agreed to support German unification within NATO, thereby eradicating the most glaring symbol of the Cold War division of Europe. The final treaty had yet to be signed, but it was clear that the Cold War had run its course and that the world was on the cusp of a new era of international relations. Just what this era would hold and how the United States should prepare to meet its emerging challenges were the questions that Bush was seeking to answer in Aspen, Colorado, on August 2, 1990.

The timing of the speech was fortuitous for another, far more remarkable and urgent reason as well: just the evening before, as he was sitting in the White House Medical Office receiving deep-heat treatment for his sore shoulders after hitting a bucket of golf balls, Bush had received the news from Brent Scowcroft, his national security advisor, that Iraqi forces had invaded Kuwait.[2] As the president delivered his remarks at Aspen, he stood at a watershed moment for defining the future of global security, caught quite immediately between the visible ending of the Cold War and the first test of the new global order that was in the process of rising from its ashes.

With the threat of Soviet aggression and communist expansion diminished, what dangers would define this new era of international affairs? Bush defined three in his Aspen speech: 1) terrorism; 2) hostage taking (really a subset of terrorism that had stymied the Carter administration in Iran and the Reagan administration in Lebanon); and 3) "renegade regimes and unpredictable rulers" (which Reagan had termed "outlaw states"), to which he added the troubling efforts of such regimes to acquire weapons of mass destruction (WMD). While the shocking news of Iraq's invasion of Kuwait prompted Scowcroft to "frantically" draft a number of revisions to the speech on the flight from Washington to Colorado to make explicit reference to the Iraqi regime's "brutal aggression," the passage listing the principal security threats of the new era was not among the last-minute additions.[3]

It was not the Iraqi invasion, therefore, that sparked the Bush administration's intention to reorient US foreign policy toward confronting the emerging national security threats of rogue states, terrorism, and WMD. Rather, the experiences of the past decade had prompted a growing recognition of the issues that would come to define national and international security in the post–Cold War world. As the 1990s dawned, this troika of threats loomed large enough in the thinking of the nation's top policymakers to warrant a central place in President Bush's speech outlining the US approach to national security for a new era.

However, it was not until Saddam Hussein ordered his tanks across the Kuwaiti border that these threats truly crystallized in the thinking of US officials. Though the rogue state paradigm had been taking clearer shape over the course of the confrontations with Libya and Panama and during the period of rising tensions with Iraq, it was still only one potential threat among many—not yet the *defining* threat to global security in the post–Cold War era.

Moreover, the crisis took the Bush team by surprise and necessitated an improvised rather than preplanned response. Strategies for how to deal with rogue states were still in flux. The experiences with Libya, Panama, and Iraq from 1986 to 1990 had not yielded any clear plan for how to deal with such threats in the future. Rather, the objectives and means of confronting such regimes had become sources of heated debate, particularly within the Reagan administration during its negotiations with Manuel Noriega of Panama.

The Iraqi conquest of Kuwait became a test case for how the emerging global system that President Bush and his foreign policy team were trying to forge would handle outlaws. Alongside its allies, the Bush administration had to define the norms of global safety that it thought essential, decide who or what posed the gravest threats to those norms, and then decide how the norms could be enforced. What had seemed like abstractions while Bush and his speechwriters were drafting his Aspen address were now clear-cut, tangible, and pressing concerns. As Philip Zelikow and Condoleezza Rice note in their study of the end of the Cold War and the construction of the new world order that followed, "How the world responded to this case would offer a blazing example of how such questions would be answered."[4]

From August 1990 through the end of the ground war in February 1991, the improvised US response to this crisis evolved into a clear sense of the critical principles at stake for the emerging post–Cold War order and the United States' role in defending it. This evolution did not come about without significant debate, disagreement, and dissent within the Bush administration and among allies such as the British government under Margaret Thatcher as they deliberated the three key questions at the heart of the crisis: how to understand and explain the *nature of the threat*; what the *stakes* of the crisis were; and *what to do* about it. From quite early on, President Bush and his team sought to frame their response to the crisis as a model for how the international community should react to similar threats in the future, setting a defining precedent for enforcing global security against rogue states in the post–Cold War world.

The improvised nature of the response to the crisis in the Gulf, however, resulted in the Bush administration answering the three key questions in reverse order: only after the means and objectives of containing and reversing the Iraqi conquest were set in motion did Bush and his team fully lay out the stakes of the crisis for the emerging global order. And only when the dust of war had settled to reveal a far more menacing and advanced nuclear program in Iraq than anyone had expected—along with the rogue dictator still in power in Baghdad—did the full and lasting scope of the threat become clear. Ironically, the enormity of the victory and the success of the diplomatic and military efforts to liberate Kuwait clouded the central failure of US policy during the war's endgame: leaving the rogue dictator in power to continue to menace the international community and seek to build WMD. Indeed, the decision of Bush and his team to focus on the problem of the Iraqi occupation of Kuwait rather than on Saddam Hussein himself, though made for sound strategic reasons, would carry consequences that would reverberate throughout the dawning era of international relations. By the aftermath of the Gulf War, both the successes and the shortcomings of the precedent that the Bush administration had set in responding to the aggression of Saddam Hussein's "renegade regime"—decisively resolving the crisis at hand while leaving its root cause in place—shaped the twin features defining global security in the post–Cold War world: the central threat of international outlaws challenging the global order and the enforcement role of the United States to confront them.

Improvising the Initial Response: August 2–8, 1990

The Bush administration's response to the Iraqi invasion of Kuwait evolved over the course of the crisis, the war, and its aftermath from one of improvisation to the conscious setting of a precedent for enforcing global security in the dawning era of international relations. Three key decision points from August 1990 to March 1991 shaped this precedent for the post–Cold War world, as President Bush and his team decided how to *define their mission* through the *objectives and means* with which they responded to Iraqi aggression, how to *frame the stakes* of the crisis, and how to understand and explain the *nature of the threat* to the security of the new world order.

The first of these decision points came during the first week of the crisis, a time marked above all by the improvised nature of the Bush administration's response. After brief but significant disagreement and debate, Bush and his team opted to deploy US military forces to the region and forge a broad international coalition to contain Iraqi aggression and defend Saudi Arabia from attack. With these essential means and objectives in place, there was much initial dissent within the US government over the stakes of the crisis, which the administration framed at the outset in relatively conservative terms—that the international community could not allow aggression and must restore Kuwaiti sovereignty.

Confusion over the stakes of the situation in the Persian Gulf reigned over the first National Security Council (NSC) meeting that Bush convened following the invasion on the morning of August 2, 1990. The president himself contributed to this atmosphere of uncertainty. Speaking to reporters lined along the back wall of the Cabinet Room in the West Wing, Bush stated that he was not considering military intervention among his options: "We're not discussing intervention. I would not discuss any military options even if we'd agreed upon them.... I'm not contemplating such action."[5] Bush's confusing remarks left the impression that the United States had already limited its options and thus its resolution to reverse the Iraqi invasion. The opposite was in fact the case, as Bush later admitted: "The truth is, at that moment I had no idea what our options were.... What I hoped to convey was an open mind about how we might handle the situation."[6]

The president's contradictory remarks set the tone for the long, rambling NSC discussion that followed. Most participants left with the same impression—that the meeting was "a bit chaotic," "disjointed and unfocused," and "did not come to grips with the issues." Part of this unwieldiness came from the large number of participants—twenty-nine from across eleven different executive departments and agencies—and part from continuing uncertainty about the situation on the ground in Kuwait. Most of the discussion revolved around the economic impact of the invasion and potential sanctions against Iraq, as well as Saddam's next moves. As General Colin Powell, the chairman of the Joint Chiefs of Staff (JCS), recalled, "As much time was spent discussing the impact of the invasion on the price of oil as on how we should respond to Saddam's aggression."[7]

The first reactions of Bush's advisors were marked more by resignation and calculated national interest than by principle—far from a clear-cut determination to do whatever it would take to counter and reverse Saddam's brazen aggression. During this first NSC meeting, officials openly mused about whether it really mattered, from a purely strategic perspective, who controlled Kuwaiti oil fields, so long as the oil kept flowing into the global economy, as Saddam had every reason to ensure. Indeed, his depleted treasury, which lay at the heart of his reasons for grabbing Kuwait, made it likely that he would actually pump more oil than the Kuwaitis had and thereby cause the price per barrel to plummet—not a bad outcome for Western markets. Moreover, the Kuwaiti regime was "generally unloved" in the Arab world for its "insufferable arrogance," and its antidemocratic nature made its rescue a tough sell in the West. Although a US ally, Kuwait had also developed close ties with the Soviets, as reflected in its 1987 request to both superpowers to protect its oil tankers from Iranian attacks in the Persian Gulf. Although the US government had already frozen Iraqi and Kuwaiti assets by the time of this first gathering of the NSC, the Bush administration's initial response, as the historian Jeffrey Engel notes, was "disjointed, unclear, and largely devoid of any high-minded principle of salvation or defense of the Kuwaiti regime."[8]

The defense of Saudi Arabia was another matter entirely. If Saddam captured the oil fields of the Saudi kingdom, concentrated along the Gulf coast and within striking distance of Kuwait, he would have control of approximately 70 percent of the oil reserves in the Persian Gulf—amounting to as much as 40–50 percent of the world's known oil reserves. This would give him a "dominance over Gulf oil supplies," noted Under Secretary of Defense for Policy Paul Wolfowitz in a memo just before the invasion, that would "enable [him] to dictate oil prices and production, placing the economies of the US and its allies in an extremely vulnerable position."[9] With no military forces standing in Saddam's way, US officials worried that an Iraqi drive across the Saudi border could be imminent. Those present at the NSC meeting agreed that this was a line that the United States could not permit Saddam to cross. As Bush's budget director, Richard Darman, explained to his colleagues, "There is a distinction between what to do to defend Saudi Arabia and to liberate Kuwait. . . . There is a chance to defend Saudi Arabia if we do all that's possible. On liberating Kuwait, I sense it's not viable. Therefore we would need an intermediate option if we can't liberate Kuwait, one to limit Iraqi power with an annexed Kuwait." Even General Powell pointed to the distinction between defending Saudi Arabia and liberating Kuwait, asking the group whether they should declare ("put out a strong redline on") Saudi Arabia to be a "vital interest" of the United States, offering his own view that "there is no choice," with which the president agreed. Powell reasoned that while securing the Saudi oil fields—the world's largest—seemed clearly worth the risk, he doubted that the United States should "go to war over Kuwait." As Secretary of Defense Dick Cheney later recalled, Powell had earlier dismissed the idea of rescuing Kuwait to Cheney and others at the Pentagon with the question, "Does anybody really care about Kuwait?" That the top general in the US military was asking this question indicated the widespread wariness within the US government of becoming too deeply involved in reversing the damage that Saddam had already done.[10]

This confusion and dissent over the stakes of the crisis was a sign of the extent to which the Iraqi invasion had caught the US government by surprise. Richard Haass, the senior director for Near East and South Asian affairs on the NSC staff, later noted that the enormity of the unexpected development took time to sink in for US officials: "The people who were in the room hadn't quite realized that this was not business as usual."[11] Scowcroft was even blunter in his reaction to the meeting, recalling that he was "frankly appalled" by the tone of the discussion that seemed to assume that Iraq's takeover of Kuwait was a "fait accompli." He told one of his NSC staff members that he felt a "very instinctive" and "visceral reaction" that Saddam would likely get away with his gambit. In his recorded diary, Bush summarized the initial prevailing view of passivity that emerged from this meeting that emphasized the difficulties of finding an effective solution:

"It's halfway around the world; U.S. options are limited; and all in all it is a highly complicated situation." Scowcroft's recollection was the same: "The tone implied that the crisis was halfway around the world and doing anything serious about it would just be too difficult." At a time when the great tectonic shifts in international affairs were centered on Europe, the first response of many of Bush's advisors was to treat the situation in the Gulf, however troubling, as a peripheral issue and simply the "crisis du jour" rather than the linchpin around which to build the foundations of post–Cold War global security.[12]

Scowcroft and Haass were two of the first to recognize the developing situation as "the major crisis of our time," one in which the United States had an "enormous stake" and that would have lasting "ramifications . . . on the emerging post–Cold War world." Scowcroft alone attempted to broaden the scope of the initial NSC discussion from one of oil and economics to the larger signal that the United States' response to the crisis would give to the rest of the world: "It would be a significant event if the US were to say that this small fracas is of little concern." He warned the gathered officials, "That signal would send shock waves throughout the Middle East" and beyond, emphasizing that "we don't have the option to be inactive in reversing this." Bush replied that "no one here would disagree," but no one else spoke up in support of Scowcroft's appeal. The national security advisor saw the issue with a starkness and clarity that his senior colleagues would only gradually come to adopt, arguing privately to the president following the NSC meeting that "this was a case of naked aggression, as clear as you could find."[13]

Before the day was out, the momentum began to shift in favor of Scowcroft's view of the crisis as one with grave stakes for the United States and the international community at large. Immediately after the initial NSC meeting on the morning of August 2, Scowcroft asked Haass to write a memo that he could give to the president outlining "why we have to act." By "accepting this new status quo" and allowing Saddam to benefit from his aggression, Haass wrote, "We would be setting a terrible precedent—one that would only accelerate violent centrifugal tendencies—in this emerging 'post Cold War' era. We would be encouraging a dangerous adversary in the Gulf at a time when the United States has provided a de facto commitment to Gulf stability . . . that also raises the issue of US reliability in a most serious way."[14]

Back at the Pentagon, Secretary of Defense Dick Cheney was reaching similar conclusions over the need for bolder action in pursuit of a more expansive objective than merely defending Saudi Arabia. Cheney had worked in the White House under Presidents Nixon and Ford, eventually rising to become Ford's chief of staff for roughly the second half of his tenure. Like Scowcroft, but unlike many of the other top members of Bush's national security team, he did not serve in the Reagan administration, instead rising through the ranks of the Republican leadership in Congress. Cheney had shared the Bush team's skepticism toward the direction of Reagan's Cold War policy at the end of his term, particularly the president's warm relationship with Soviet leader Mikhail Gorbachev, though he maintained his harder-line views even when Bush and most of his top advisors pivoted to adopt their predecessors' growing partnership with Gorbachev later in 1989. Cheney, too, was unsettled by the tenor of the first NSC meeting of the Gulf crisis, and he sought to work through his thoughts by writing notes to himself on a yellow legal pad. He questioned the prevailing idea that the United States should draw its red line at the Saudi border but leave Kuwait to its fate. "Shouldn't our objective be to get him [Saddam] out of Kuwait?" he wrote. "Isn't that the best short and long term strategy?" He instinctively felt that Saddam was unlikely to budge with anything less than the use of force: "No non-military option is likely to produce any positive result." "The key to our success," he believed, was "U.S. military power—the only thing Hussein fears" and a "determination to use whatever force is necessary."[15]

President Bush's views likewise began to evolve and harden as he flew from Washington to Colorado to deliver his address at the Aspen Institute. Two important factors contributed to Bush's growing determination to take a more robust stance toward undoing Iraq's aggression against Kuwait. First, as he worked the phones to consult with world leaders, he detected a potential willingness on the part of several Arab leaders to reach some sort of accommodation with Saddam that would leave him in control of part or all of Kuwait. Saudi King Fahd likened the Iraqi strongman to "Hitler in creating world problems," with "one difference": though Hitler was "conceited," Saddam was "both conceited and crazy." Fahd doubted that anything could compel him to retreat "but [the] use of force." Yet even he demurred in accepting Bush's offer of military assistance. Troubled by this vacillation in the face of clear-cut aggression, Bush explained the next day, "My fear is of handwringing by offering a payoff to Saddam Hussein."[16]

He confided this fear to Margaret Thatcher, whose timely presence in Aspen served as the second factor in buttressing Bush's hardening views. By the time he reached the Aspen ranch home of the US ambassador to Britain, where he met with Thatcher, Bush already saw the crisis in a distinctly firmer light than he had that morning. Scowcroft later noted that "it became obvious to me" on the plane ride across the country "that the President was prepared to use force to evict Saddam from Kuwait if it became necessary."[17] But it took Thatcher's quintessential clarity of expression to confirm in Bush's mind the sense of what stakes lay at the heart of the crisis for the international community.

While awaiting Bush's arrival in Aspen, Thatcher met with her closest foreign policy advisor, Charles Powell, and Britain's ambassador to the United States, Sir

Antony Acland, "to sort things out in my own mind." "As is my wont," she later wrote, "I set about arguing through the whole problem with them and by the end had defined the two main points. By the time I was due to meet [with Bush] . . . I was quite clear what we must do." Displaying her characteristic impatience to make her points, Thatcher noted, "Fortunately, the President began by asking me what I thought." She then laid out, "in the most straightforward terms," the two issues that would animate the response of the US-led coalition for the remainder of the crisis: "First, aggressors must never be appeased. Second, if Saddam Hussein were to cross the border into Saudi Arabia he could go right down the Gulf in a matter of days. . . . Not only did we have to move to stop the aggression, therefore, we had to stop it quickly." Cutting to the core of the matter, Thatcher viewed principle as the chief matter in jeopardy, one that the international community must move rapidly to defend. In reaching this conclusion, she drew on her generation's lesson of the outbreak of World War II that "we should have stopped Hitler when he went into the Rhineland," arguing that "British foreign policy is at its worst when it is giving away other people's territory, as in the Sudetenland and Czechoslovakia." She also drew a direct line between the developing crisis in the Gulf and her own experience leading Britain through the Falklands War nearly a decade earlier. Though the underlying context of the two conflicts was different, she saw the matters of principle at stake as identical in the need to clearly demonstrate for the global order that armed aggression could not be permitted to trump international law as a means of resolving disputes.[18]

Thatcher had been buttressed in her strident views by a memo from Charles Powell on the morning of August 2, prior to her meeting with Bush. Powell argued forcefully for the deep significance of Iraq's attack on Kuwait: "This is no ordinary territorial dispute. A major issue of principle is at stake: the need for the international community to prevent large, bullying countries from simply marching in and taking over small ones. We cannot just let this go by." Thatcher underlined "cannot" four times and made sure to drive the point home with Bush.[19]

It turned out that Thatcher's arguments reflected the hardening direction of Bush's evolving views of the crisis. As Powell noted after their meeting, the two allies "were in very close agreement in their assessment of the situation and what should be done. . . . The President seemed reassured." Following their meeting, the two leaders spoke to the press against the backdrop of the Rocky Mountains. Bush stressed his unity of purpose with the British prime minister, declaring them to be "on exactly the same wavelength: concerned about this naked aggression, condemning it and hoping that a peaceful solution will be found." Yet Bush still took a restrained and cautious public approach to the situation, repeating his assertion from earlier that morning that he was not at that point contemplating

FIGURE 15. Unity of purpose: Against the backdrop of the Rocky Mountains, President Bush and British prime minister Margaret Thatcher speak to reporters in Aspen, Colorado, where they begin coordinating the initial allied response to the Gulf crisis, August 2, 1990.

military intervention, though this time he emphasized that "we're not ruling any options in, but we're not ruling any options out." Thatcher, by contrast, spoke much more forcefully, declaring that the Iraqi invasion was "totally unacceptable, and if it were allowed to endure, then there would be many other small countries that could never feel safe." She argued emphatically that "what has happened is a total violation of international law. You cannot have a situation where one country marches in and takes over another country which is a member of the United Nations."[20]

Thatcher's remarks at the press conference in Aspen also drew attention to another key aspect of the allied response to the invasion: the centrality of collective action through the United Nations. "The fundamental question is this," she argued: "whether the nations of the world have the collective will effectively to see [that] the Security Council resolution is upheld; whether they have the collective will effectively to do anything . . . to see that Iraq withdraws and that the government of Kuwait is restored. . . . None of us can do it separately. We need a collective and effective will of the nations belonging to the United Nations." Thatcher framed the crisis as a test of the collective will of the international community to enforce norms of global security in the dawning era.[21]

Indeed, the Bush administration had been thinking along the same lines from the outset of the crisis, taking the lead in the UN Security Council to present a resolution condemning Iraq's invasion of Kuwait on behalf of the community of nations. Immediately upon receiving word on the evening of August 1 that Iraqi tanks had crossed the border into Kuwait, even before the first chaotic NSC meeting the next morning, President Bush had instructed his UN ambassador, Thomas Pickering, to organize a vote on a resolution in the Security Council denouncing the Iraqi aggression. Bush later explained his reasoning in placing collective action through the United Nations at the heart of his administration's response, noting the importance of "decisive UN action" to the success of whatever course he chose for "rallying international opposition" to counter Saddam's actions. While he insisted that he was "prepared to deal with this crisis unilaterally if necessary," he also instinctively saw it as a potential opportunity for building the "commonwealth of free nations" for which he had been advocating since even before the dramatic changes in Eastern Europe in 1989 had brought down the curtain on the Cold War. As he explained, "I was keenly aware that this would be the first post–Cold War test of the Security Council in crisis." Though he "was not yet sure what to expect from the UN," he suspected and hoped that the dissipation of Cold War tensions that had stalemated the Security Council since its founding now "offered the possibility that we could get [Soviet and Chinese] cooperation in forging international unity to oppose Iraq." Indeed, in the early morning of August 2 the Security Council voted 14–0 in favor of the resolution condemning Iraq's actions; both the Soviet Union and China supported the measure.[22]

As Bush would tell a joint session of Congress later in the crisis, the effort to forge a broad-based international coalition under the auspices of the United Nations, drawing on traditional allies in Europe as well as Arab nations, former Cold War foes, and even erstwhile enemies such as Syria, transformed the conflict from one that pitted Iraq against the United States to one of "Iraq against the world." This collective international action proved, Bush insisted, that a "new partnership of nations has begun."²³ While Bush might have been able to rely on US power alone to resolve this particular crisis, his coalition-building efforts were aimed at leaving a durable and widely supported precedent for how the international community as a whole should handle outlaw states in the new global era.

Returning from Aspen to the White House, President Bush had turned a corner in viewing the broader significance of the Gulf crisis with greater clarity and resolution. This was not so much a change in his views as a solidification and confirmation of the direction in which he had already been inclined to go. Walking into the Oval Office on the morning of August 3 after only a few hours' sleep, Bush recorded his more definitive view of the stakes of the crisis in his diary: "The enormity of Iraq is upon me now. The status quo is intolerable." Scowcroft also recounted that it was during their discussion with Thatcher that the full significance of the Iraqi invasion had hit them.²⁴

The tone of the NSC meeting that morning marked a turning point in the administration's response to the takeover of Kuwait. One day removed from the initial confused session, the tone of this second meeting could not have been more different. Scowcroft decided to take the lead in making clear to Bush's national security team the grave stakes of the crisis. He proposed a plan to the president that he open the meeting with a clear statement "outlining the absolute intolerability of this invasion to US interests." Bush readily agreed and offered to make the opening statement himself, but the two decided that that approach would stifle discussion. In what Haass later called Scowcroft's "Churchill speech" rousing his colleagues to action, the national security advisor stated that he "detected a note in the end [of the previous NSC meeting] that we may have to acquiesce to an accommodation of the situation. My personal judgment is that the stakes in this for the United States are such that to accommodate Iraq should not be a policy option. There is too much at stake."²⁵ In a memo to Scowcroft, NSC staffer Peter Rodman elaborated on his boss's growing appreciation of the stakes of what he called "the first Third World crisis of the post–cold war period." "The stakes are high," Rodman declared: the crisis with Iraq amounted to nothing less than "a test of whether the industrial democracies together can dominate events in the new era . . . or are helpless in the face of Third World bullying," a situation that he noted "reminds me of the Falklands" with its test of Western principles and resilience. Most critically, Rodman argued, "U.S. leadership is also being put to a make-or-break test" that will determine whether the vindication of democratic values that the "Revolution of 1989" appeared to represent "will give way to the perception of an anarchic world governed by no agreed concept of order or equilibrium or mechanism of discipline."²⁶

As agreed prior to the NSC meeting, several of Bush's advisors jumped in to reinforce Scowcroft's call for a determined US response. Lawrence Eagleburger, the deputy secretary of state filling in for the overseas James Baker, was the first to back up Scowcroft's position. "I couldn't agree more," he declared, pounding the table for effect. "This is the first test of the post[-Cold] war system.... If he [Saddam] succeeds others may try the same thing. It would be a bad lesson." Hinting at the desirability of regime change, Eagleburger emphasized the strategic dangers that Saddam would pose to the Gulf region and US interests "unless he leaves the scene. We need to think of this as a very, very critical time." Cheney spoke next about how he saw the "stakes and consequences" of the Iraqi invasion, soberly anticipating the need for US military action while cautioning against underestimating the scale of the forces that would be required to undertake such a "major conflict." The secretary of defense also warned his colleagues that Saddam's newly seized oil wealth would allow him to "acquire new weapons, including nuclear weapons. The problem will get worse, not better." This marked the first official discussion since the invasion of Saddam's WMD programs as a unique part of the threat he posed, and the pressing need for the United States to counter this danger forcefully.[27]

Colin Powell, concerned at the more bellicose direction the NSC was taking from the day before, offered cautionary remarks regarding the forces that would be required for any military options. He asked the president and his advisors "if it was worth going to war to liberate Kuwait." As he later explained, his question was not so much out of opposition as out of a desire to test the determination of the president and his team and press them to give the military clear objectives backed with the political will to see them through. Nevertheless, Powell recalled that a chill came over the room. Not only had the question been "premature," he later admitted, but it was also not the place of the chairman of the JCS to weigh in on the political choices that his civilian superiors had to make. Still, he felt the question was necessary.[28] If the United States were to deploy the forces that would be required to defend against an Iraqi attack on Saudi Arabia or to eject Saddam's forces from Kuwait, he warned that "this is harder than Panama and Libya [the last two major US military actions in 1989 and 1986, respectively]. This would be the NFL, not a scrimmage." Powell, too, mused over the advisability of seeking regime change. He asked his colleagues, "How individualized is this aggression?" and wondered whether there would be "a more reasonable replacement" for Saddam "if he is gone." The NSC did not pursue this line of thinking far enough to reach consensus, but Scowcroft expressed his concern that without Saddam "Iraq could fall apart."[29]

Bush himself brought the discussion of this second NSC meeting to a close, laying out clearly the administration's growing recognition of the broader importance of the crisis. The Cold War was over, he told his advisors. "At stake is the shape of the world to come."[30] Haass reflected in his memoir that it was far from a foregone conclusion that the United States or the international community at large would deploy large-scale military forces to counter and eventually reverse the Iraqi aggression. "A different president and set of advisors," Haass wrote, "might have tolerated Iraqi control of Kuwait and limited the U.S. response to sanctions so long as Saddam did not go on to attack Saudi Arabia." Scowcroft pointed out that it might not have even taken different personnel to reach this outcome, since the prevailing view in the Bush administration itself had initially been "vastly different" from the ultimate course it chose, focused "on controlling the damage rather than reversing it." The stark difference in tone between the first and second NSC meetings—and the marked change in the Bush team's approach to the crisis between August 2 and 3—"highlights a fundamental truth," Haass concluded: "People matter."[31] The convergence of the views of Bush, Scowcroft, and Thatcher—supported by Cheney, Eagleburger, and others—during the first thirty-six hours of the crisis reinforced their deepening resolution to counter Iraq's aggression decisively and forcefully.

Convening the NSC at Camp David for its third meeting on August 4, the president received a fuller briefing of the military options and set the narrow initial objective of protecting Saudi Arabia. General Powell distinguished between three different military goals, each of which would require a progressively larger buildup of forces: to deter Saddam from further aggressive moves against Saudi Arabia with a baseline force, to defend Saudi Arabia from a full-scale Iraqi attack with a larger force, and finally to roll back the Iraqi takeover of Kuwait with an overwhelming offensive force. For the time being, Bush and his advisors decided to limit US objectives to the immediate imperatives of deterring an Iraqi strike into Saudi Arabia and beginning to build a defensive force sufficient to contain Saddam's ambitions in the longer term. Bush recognized, however, that this approach would not resolve the situation: "We have a problem if Saddam does not invade Saudi Arabia but holds on to Kuwait."[32]

While Bush's attitude toward the situation in the Gulf had evolved significantly in private over the first few days of the crisis, his public remarks remained restrained. This changed dramatically on the afternoon of August 5. As he flew aboard Marine One from Camp David to the White House, Bush reflected on the clarity of the stakes of the crisis in his own mind. He felt he now had a clear understanding of "the military situation on the ground and the strategic implications of the invasion." Dictating to his diary, he said, "This is a terribly serious problem, it's perhaps the most serious problem that I have faced as President because the downside is so enormous." If the Iraqis conquered Saudi Arabia, he feared, "we would really be involved in something that could have the magnitude of a new world war." Concerned that failing to confront Saddam now over Kuwait could lead to a wider and bloodier struggle later on, Bush strode across the White

House South Lawn toward the waiting press. With what would become the most famous words of his presidency, President Bush expanded his overall objective from what the NSC had decided the previous morning, the need to defend Saudi Arabia, to a definitive vow to reverse the Iraqi invasion altogether: "This will not stand. This will not stand, this aggression against Kuwait."³³

Bush's declaration that "this will not stand" and his avowed "determination to reverse out this aggression" startled his team of advisors who had so recently discussed the more limited, defensive objectives that the administration had set down. Across the board, they recognized that Bush had gone well beyond any commitments the administration had made in public or private up to this point. Vice President Dan Quayle, who was with Scowcroft in the Oval Office when the president walked in after speaking with the press, recalled that Bush's bold statement had "caught everybody off guard a little bit because it was so definite and so dramatic." When Bush asked them what they thought of his statement, Scowcroft replied, "Where'd you get that 'this will not stand'?" "That's mine," the president answered. "that's what I feel."³⁴ Most notable was the reaction of General Powell, who was watching Bush's remarks from his study at home before leaving for that afternoon's NSC meeting. Hearing Bush's famous line, Powell jolted upright, recognizing that the president had made "a giant step." It appeared that the commander in chief had "just committed the United States to liberating Kuwait." As he prepared to leave for the White House, the JCS chairman thought, "I might have just received a new mission."³⁵

The same day that President Bush declared his resolve to reverse Iraq's invasion of Kuwait, Margaret Thatcher delivered her own speech to close out the Aspen Institute Symposium. The prime minister's strident remarks homed in on the principles that Iraq's aggression and breach of international law had put in jeopardy, just as she had over Argentina's seizure of the Falkland Islands in 1982: "Iraq's invasion of Kuwait defies every principle for which the United Nations stands. If we let it succeed, no small country can ever feel safe again." Using words that Bush would adopt in his own public addresses throughout the crisis, Thatcher warned that failing to turn back such aggression would mean "the law of the jungle would take over from the rule of law." She advocated the need for the world community to determine and "agree on certain basic standards" to govern international behavior that would "resolve disputes and keep the peace." The crisis in the Gulf, she argued, proved the necessity of enforcing one critical norm: "A vital principle is at stake: an aggressor must never be allowed to get his way."³⁶

Thatcher's words, her biographer Charles Moore notes, were "amplifying and fortifying" Bush's own public messages. En route home to London the next day, she was able to stop off in Washington for another round of consultations with Bush at the White House that would allow her to reinforce the stance that her US counterparts were taking. Never before, marveled Thatcher's advisor Charles

Powell that day, had the Anglo-American "special relationship" operated "with this degree of closeness and trust." In their two-hour meeting in the Oval Office, Bush demonstrated to Thatcher "total frankness and confidence" and drew her "directly into the US Administration's decision-making . . . being made privy to every aspect of their thinking." When Cheney called from Riyadh to report the Saudi king's acceptance of US military forces on his soil, Bush confided in Thatcher the details of US plans for deploying troops to the Gulf. The prime minister immediately pledged British support and participation in the deployment. Thatcher herself was deeply impressed, writing in her memoirs, "For all the friendship and co-operation I had had from President Reagan, I was never taken into the Americans' confidence more than I was during the two hours or so I spent that afternoon at the White House."[37]

Thatcher's return to Washington and meeting with Bush at the White House on August 6 helped to solidify, both in private and in the public eye, the backbone of international support that would buttress US power and resolve to confront Iraq. Her discussions with Bush also helped to clarify the unique characteristics of the threat that Saddam's regime posed. She raised the question of what he might do with his chemical weapons, which he had repeatedly displayed a willingness to use in past conflicts. This appears to have been the first meaningful discussion at the top levels of the US administration of this aspect of Saddam's WMD capabilities, as Charles Powell noted that Bush did not seem to have considered this question before. But the idea that Saddam Hussein embodied the qualities that were coming to define the essence of a rogue state was one that the Americans and British shared. During the NSC meeting the day before, Bush commented that he was not sure that anyone could predict what the Iraqi leader would do: "Saddam is irrational. . . . We are dealing with a mad-man [sic] who has shown he will kill." British officials shared this anxiety over Saddam's unpredictability on the battlefield and beyond, even fearing that he might try to drop bombs on London from a Boeing 707. Thatcher, echoing Bush's reference at Aspen to "renegade regimes and unpredictable rulers," referred to Saddam as "an international brigand" later that month. On both sides of the Atlantic, the Iraqi dictator was becoming the exemplar of the rogue state threat.[38]

The fortuitous and visible presence of the British prime minister throughout this first crucial phase of planning for the US and allied response to the Gulf crisis begs the question of how significant Margaret Thatcher's role was in shaping the course that the Bush administration would ultimately follow. The contrast in the demeanor and language the two leaders employed in this first showing of allied solidarity, particularly during their joint appearance in Aspen, contributed to the impression, which has lingered in the decades since, that Thatcher was the dominant partner in pushing the US president toward a more resolute stance against the Iraqi aggression. Thatcher's famous warning to Bush "not to go wobbly," a comment actually offered in support rather than criticism of Bush's actions several weeks later and taken significantly out of context in later accounts, added to the sense that Thatcher had "stiffened George Bush's spine" at Aspen. Those who were present at Aspen, however, stress a meeting of minds between the two leaders rather than any vacillation or weakness on Bush's part. Thatcher played an important part in the evolution of the president's thinking toward a determination to reverse Saddam's aggression, but her role was more to confirm the approach he was already instinctively inclined to take than to push him in a direction in which he was hesitant to go. Thatcher's biographer Charles Moore sums up his assessment of the impact of the prime minister in these first days of the Gulf crisis with a nuanced appraisal: "Perhaps the best way to put it is not that George Bush was weak, but that Margaret Thatcher was strong. Both from instinct and from experience she believed passionately that aggressive adventurers had to be denied all gains from conquest. . . . In a word, she was confident—more so than Bush—and she helped impart to him the confidence that he needed."[39]

Thatcher's meetings with Bush at Aspen and the White House during the first week of the Gulf crisis held critical importance for the broader significance of this moment in shaping global security in the post–Cold War world. It was not that Thatcher's meetings with Bush in the first days of the crisis "pushed," "stiffened," or reshaped the president's stance toward the situation in the Gulf. Rather, it was her innate sense of the *stakes* of the crisis and her instinctive grasp of the key elements of the nature of this new "rogue state" type of threat that clarified, bolstered, and articulated why the Western allies and the international community at large had no choice but to confront and turn back this challenge to the global order. Her experience as Britain's leader during the Falklands War—when her arguments for the defense of international law and principle found limited resonance among the international community, including a reluctant United States—proved decisive in shaping her more advanced grasp of the idea of rogue states than that of many of her peers. She, therefore, appreciated more instinctively than most world leaders the danger that rogues such as the Argentine junta or Saddam Hussein posed to the values of the international order beyond the bounds of the remote islands or the tiny sheikhdom they seized.

On the morning of August 8, with US military forces already beginning their deployment to Saudi Arabia, President Bush spoke to the nation from the Oval Office in his first formal address outlining his administration's response to the crisis in the Persian Gulf. Laying out what would become Operation Desert Shield, Bush stressed the "wholly defensive" nature of the mission of US forces. He explained the strategy of containment that stood at the heart of US actions, beginning with the rapid deployment of a deterrent force against further Iraqi attack, then building up to a defensive force to keep Saddam's forces at bay—all to complement and to help enforce the broad international sanctions set down by the United Nations. Most crucially, Bush began to articulate his understanding of the stakes and the nature of the threat that the United States and the world faced. Emphasizing that this was "not an American problem or a European problem or a Middle East problem" but rather "the world's problem," he explained that the United States' purpose was "driven by principle"—one that it had learned to defend from the experience of earlier conflicts and that was especially critical now that "we're beginning a new era" with the potential to be "full of promise, an age of freedom, a time of peace for all peoples." Iraq's invasion of Kuwait put all this at risk. The president asserted that "if history teaches us anything, it is that we must resist aggression or it will destroy our freedoms." Likening Saddam's actions to those of Hitler, which brought on World War II, he told his listeners, "Appeasement does not work. As was the case in the 1930's, we see in Saddam Hussein an aggressive dictator threatening his neighbors."[40] This analogy of the Iraqi invasion and "the situation in the Rhineland in the 1930s, when Hitler simply defied the Treaty of Versailles and marched in," was especially important to Bush's understanding of the broader meaning of the Gulf crisis, and he would employ it frequently in the months to come.[41]

By the end of the first week following the Iraqi invasion of Kuwait, what had begun as a chaotic and improvised reaction within the US government had evolved to take clearer shape in the form of tangible diplomatic and military measures to confront Saddam's aggression. The Bush administration's initial uncertainty and disagreement over the importance of the fate of Kuwait and the necessity of taking firm action had given way to a determined stance to confront international aggression and restore the legitimate Kuwaiti government. To accomplish these objectives, the United States was leading the way in building and coordinating not one but three coalitions simultaneously: political, economic, and military. Despite some prominent statements to the contrary, the goals of these US-led coalitions were still focused on containment and defensive measures against Iraq rather than rolling back its conquest. As its understanding and articulation of the stakes and the nature of the threat became clearer as summer shifted into fall, the Bush administration would expand these initial goals as it sought to set a lasting precedent for the new global era.

Forging a Lasting Precedent: Mid-August 1990–Mid-January 1991

As summer gave way to fall and the crowded days of the first week of the Gulf crisis began to fade, a sense that the administration's policy was beginning to drift set in among the top members of Bush's team. With the essential elements of their initial response set in motion, President Bush and his key advisors gave great thought and consideration to the broader meaning and implications not only of Saddam Hussein's actions against Kuwait but also—and far more significantly—of their own actions in confronting the aggression. While the president and his team had already shown a cognizance of the stakes of the crisis for the emerging post–Cold War world, it was not until the rush of events had slowed by the end of August and into the fall that they thought systematically about the lasting significance of each element of their strategy for handling the situation in the Persian Gulf. In each of their actions throughout the fall of 1990, Bush and his team sought to develop a precedent upon which the international community could draw in similar situations in the future, thereby heralding a new, more peaceful and cooperative era governed by broadly accepted norms of international behavior. The coalition's handling of Iraq's aggression would establish the expectation of collective enforcement of those norms, with the United States' role standing central.

The evolution of the Bush administration's thinking and determination to forge a durable precedent resulted in major shifts in the means it employed and the objectives it pursued—from a defensive deployment to the development of an offensive military option, and from the containment to the rollback of Iraqi aggression. This evolving mindset also prompted the president and his advisors to shift from a relatively conservative framing of the stakes of the crisis—to halt aggression and restore Kuwait—to a far more creative articulation of the stakes: not just preserving and restoring stability and international law but also building a new world order for an entirely different era of global affairs.

This idea of a "new world order" grew out of a particularly important conversation between Bush and Scowcroft on August 23 aboard the president's speedboat *Fidelity* while fishing off Walker's Point, the president's summer home in Kennebunkport, Maine. More than three weeks removed from the beginning of the crisis, Bush was growing impatient. He was coming to believe that the use of force would eventually become necessary to remove Saddam from Kuwait, but he was uncertain of the path forward. Like several of his top advisors, he felt that after the initial set of decisions framing the US and coalition response, policy was beginning to drift, and he did not want the initiative to slip out of his hands. "I wanted to find a path out of the stalemate," Bush recalled, and he "asked impatiently when we could strike." The president revealed himself to be ahead of other top US officials in this line of thinking.[42]

With the waves lapping against the boat's hull and the fish refusing to bite, the conversation turned into what Bush called "a long, philosophical chat" that absorbed the two men during this "first opportunity" since the hectic rush of events over the previous weeks "for the two of us to unwind and talk." Stepping back from the developments of the moment, Bush and Scowcroft considered the ongoing crisis, more explicitly and deliberately than they had ever done before, within the context of the seismic changes that had taken hold of the international system over the past year. Perhaps this unexpected emergency in a region of the world that had not been a major focus truly marked "a watershed of history," they mused. If it did, they agreed on the vital importance of "being sure we handled the crisis in a way which reflected the nature of the transformed world we would face in the future." A new era of international relations was at hand, they recognized, and it would be a mistake not to seize on the opportunity to shape that era into a more peaceful and cooperative one than the Cold War era that was ending. With the United States and the Soviet Union joining to condemn Iraq's actions, Bush and Scowcroft hoped that the original vision of the framers of the United Nations for the Security Council to play an effective peacekeeping role might finally be realized. It was this idea—that the United States and the Soviet Union could "stand together against unprovoked interstate aggression"—that animated the sense of building a new world order, an order with safeguards in place for "dealing successfully with aggression between states." Bush and Scowcroft were determined to use the Gulf crisis as a means of establishing norms for global security to stand as the backbone for this new world order.[43]

With this time to reason through the broader implications of the events unfolding in the Gulf, President Bush prepared to deliver his first major address on the crisis since his announcement of his decision to deploy troops to Saudi Arabia. This time he would give his speech before a joint session of Congress rather than from the Oval Office, choosing a dramatic setting to underscore the bold message he prepared to deliver. In this critical address on September 11, 1990, which would become known as his "New World Order" speech, the president articulated more clearly and fully than he ever had before his vision of the new global system taking shape in the wake of the Cold War, and where he viewed the Gulf crisis fitting into the creation of this new order. In laying out his ideas for the United States' role in constructing a new era of international relations, Bush's landmark speech contained echoes of the 1918 "Fourteen Points" address of President Woodrow Wilson, who had transformed America's role on the world stage and sought to fashion a more cooperative and peaceful international system based on principle rather than national interest.[44]

President Bush lost no time in highlighting his view of the broader significance of US actions in the Persian Gulf "to check [Iraqi] aggression," devoting far less emphasis to the tangible national interests and objectives of the military deployment than to "our concern for principle." "We stand today at a unique and extraordinary moment" in history, he declared. "The crisis in the Persian Gulf, as grave as it is, also offers a rare opportunity to move toward an historic period of cooperation." Bush stressed his administration's efforts "to fashion the broadest possible international response" to the crisis, which resulted in a "level of world cooperation and condemnation of Iraq" and "concerted United Nations action against aggression" that was nothing short of "unprecedented." Finally, after more than four decades of Cold War stalemate, he noted, "We're now in sight of a United Nations that performs as envisioned by its founders" by "backing up its words with actions."

This unique moment of international cooperation, Bush argued, offered the United States and its allies the chance to forge "a new world order" that could be "freer from the threat of terror, stronger in the pursuit of justice, and more secure in the quest for peace." That "new world" was "struggling to be born," Bush told his listeners, and its success or failure rested on the United States' and the world's willingness to take decisive action in defense of principle—"to defend civilized values around the world." The Iraqi invasion of Kuwait marked a test case—"the first assault on the new world that we seek," and its implications would stretch forward to define the new era for good or for ill: "How we manage this crisis today could shape the future for generations to come."

Most poignantly and critically, Bush declared. "Vital issues of principle are at stake." A new world order was in reach, one "where the rule of law supplants the rule of the jungle" and "where the strong respect the rights of the weak." The stakes, Bush repeated, were great. If the United States and the world did not stand determined and united in "shared resolve to counter Iraq's threat to peace," he argued, then such inaction would reverberate beyond the Gulf as "a signal to actual and potential despots around the world" that they could also benefit from flouting international law. On the other hand, if the United States and the world came together to "support the rule of law" and "stand up to aggression," then they would be able to cement in place a set of norms governing acceptable international behavior and ensuring global security. These norms, alongside a proven willingness of the world community to join together in "collective effort" to enforce them, would underpin the new world order that Bush hoped to build.

As he concluded his remarks before Congress on the Gulf crisis, President Bush outlined the United States' "lasting role" in the Persian Gulf region long after the end of the present emergency. This role would be focused on the enforcement, alongside allies, of some of the central norms that would stand at the heart of the new world order: namely, "to deter future aggression" and "to curb the proliferation of chemical, biological, ballistic missile and, above all, nuclear technologies," the various forms of WMD. Though he did not explicitly connect these norms to the idea of "renegade regimes" of which he had spoken at Aspen, Bush was framing the United States' future international role around combating the central features that had come to define rogue states over the past decade. Saddam Hussein's regime had unquestionably become the poster child of this phenomenon—one that was no longer a peripheral concern but rather, in Bush's calculation, the primary threat to global security in the emerging post–Cold War era. Saddam's invasion of Kuwait might have come to define this new type of threat, but Bush made clear that the United States should remain poised and ready to confront similar challenges in the future if it wanted to protect the new world order.

In his remarks to Congress, Bush individualized and personified the rogue state threat in the form of Saddam Hussein, noting that the United States' "quarrel" was not with the Iraqi people but rather "with Iraq's dictator and with his aggression."[45] Throughout the fall he continued this trend of demonizing Saddam by increasingly drawing on historical comparisons to Adolf Hitler. The frequency of Bush's use of this Saddam-Hitler analogy, imperfect and problematic though it might have been—along with the fact that he used it just as often in private conversations and even in his personal recorded diary as with public audiences—underscores its salience for his own deepening understanding of the nature and importance of this new kind of security threat to the as-yet-undefined global landscape emerging from the dust of the Cold War.

The "lesson of history" from the outbreak of World War II drove Bush's thinking and actions as early as the first week of the crisis, when he took the time to personally edit his address announcing troop deployments to Saudi Arabia by "tighten[ing] up the language to strengthen the similarity I saw" with the failure of the world community to act when Hitler's forces occupied the Rhineland in 1936. Bush's life experience predisposed him to look to the Second World War for historical analogies, having served as a naval aviator in the Pacific theater as a young man. The British historian Martin Gilbert's history of World War II, which Bush happened to be reading while the crisis was unfolding, also strengthened his growing conviction that the confrontation with Saddam was one between good and evil. As he told a crowd in October while campaigning for the midterm elections, "I'm reading a book . . . great, big, thick history about World War II. And there's a parallel between what Hitler did to Poland and what Saddam Hussein has done to Kuwait." He was horrified in reading reports of atrocities committed by Iraqi troops, pillaging Kuwait and brutalizing its citizens. "This just hardens my resolve," he dictated to his diary in late September, "and I am wondering if we need to speed up the timetable" to oust Iraqi forces from Kuwait. On another occasion, he added to his diary, "The more I think of this . . . I can't see how we can get out of it without punishing Iraq. What they are doing is unprincipled."[46]

It was around this time in late September when he was learning of the shocking extent of Iraqi atrocities in Kuwait that he shifted, in his words, "from viewing

Saddam's aggression exclusively as a dangerous strategic threat and an injustice to its reversal as a moral crusade." He declared categorically to staffers in the White House, "It's black and white, good vs. evil. The man has to be stopped." "He is the epitome of evil," he asserted to his diary. "It has been personalized." Some of his advisors worried that the president was becoming too emotionally invested in the treatment of Kuwait, but Bush felt that the emotional horrors only deepened the urgency to respond vigorously to turn back the Iraqi conquest and "strengthened my determination not to let the invasion stand and encouraged me to contemplate the use of force to reverse it." He insisted that US policy was "based on principle, not personalities," and that he was driven not by a "personal grudge" against Saddam but rather by "a deep moral objection" to his "unprincipled" actions.[47]

Just as it helped him in private to make sense of the nature of the threat he faced in the Gulf, Bush deployed the analogy between Saddam and Hitler in closed-door conversations with other world leaders as he built a global coalition of support for confronting Iraq. Meeting with Mikhail Gorbachev in Helsinki, Finland, on September 9, Bush became frustrated with the Soviet leader's push for a solution to the crisis that would allow Saddam to save face, demanding of his counterpart, "Do you think one could reach a compromise with Hitler?" Gorbachev protested that the two were "disparate phenomena" and "there is no analogy." Bush insisted, however, that they were, in fact, "comparable in terms of personal cruelty" and that he had no intention of repeating the crucial mistake of the 1930s by appeasing Saddam and letting the dictator get away with his aggression.[48]

As the crisis continued into the fall and the midterm campaign season got in full swing, Bush faced the question of how to educate the public on what he and his advisors recognized as "a totally new threat" to security in the post–Cold War world. The challenge of explaining the gravity of the danger was all the more acute because of the difficulty of fitting Saddam—a dictator who was hitherto little known to most Americans and whose attack was against a country that few Americans could find on a map—into the well-known, well-worn shoes of the Soviet Union as the United States' prime adversary for over the past four decades. To fill the void that the receding Soviet danger left in the minds of Americans and to impress upon them the gravity with which he saw the stakes of the crisis in the Gulf, Bush turned repeatedly to the Saddam-Hitler analogy in his public addresses throughout the fall. Saddam Hussein was "Hitler revisited, a totalitarianism and a brutality that is naked and unprecedented in modern times," he proclaimed, and 'America will not stand aside."[49] Bush overlooked the irony of drawing on a historical analogy to explain what he saw as a new and unprecedented threat. What was new, to Bush's mind, was the context: Saddam's regime had launched its aggression at a moment of unprecedented opportunity to forge a peaceful global order in the Cold War's wake, and the brutality and brazenness of his aggression, mixed with the destructive potential of his ambitions to acquire WMD, made his attack on Kuwait a uniquely critical challenge to overcome.

Bush himself noted that his constant linking of Saddam and Hitler got him into "hot water" with the press and critics who wondered whether the president might be overpersonalizing the problem or misinterpreting history. As one prominent columnist wrote, "Saddam Hussein is pretty bad," but "I don't think he's in Hitler's class." Even Bush's own top advisors expressed their discomfort with how passionately he was pushing the analogy in his public justifications for confronting Iraq. James Baker, Bush's secretary of state and close personal friend, worried that the quickness of the administration's shift, "practically overnight," from trying to work with Saddam's regime to likening him to Hitler might in fact prove counterproductive to convincing a skeptical public of the significance of the new threat. Scowcroft sought to tamp down Bush's rhetoric by traveling with him on campaign trips in an effort to head off the public charge that the president was "turning the crisis into a personal vendetta against Saddam." Colin Powell, too, feared that Bush's demonizing of Saddam, "just as he had Manuel Noriega," was excessive and "unwise," and he urged Scowcroft and Cheney to persuade the president "to cool the rhetoric." While he agreed with the essence of Bush's charges against the Iraqi despot, he was concerned that "elevat[ing] public expectations by making the man out to be the devil incarnate and then leaving him in place" was the wrong way to justify a mission that called for "only ejecting Iraq from Kuwait," not regime change.[50]

Nevertheless, Bush persisted in making the comparison. Though he "caught hell" from the press, he believed too deeply in the link between the present moment and the lost chance to avert world war in the 1930s to abandon it. The analogy helped to clarify his own understanding of the momentousness of the situation in the Gulf and the possible ramifications of failing to stand up to Saddam's aggression. "My mind goes back to history," he wrote in a letter to his children on New Year's Eve in 1990. "How many lives might have been saved if appeasement had given way to force earlier on in the late '30's or earliest '40's? How many Jews might have been spared the gas chambers, or how many Polish patriots might be alive today? I look at today's crisis as 'good' vs. 'evil'—Yes, it is that clear." Noting the importance of the lessons he drew from World War II in shaping his thinking on the Gulf crisis and propelling the urgency he felt to take action, he explained to his diary on the eve of war, "I have Saddam Hussein now as clearly bad and evil as Hitler and as the Japanese war machine that attacked Pearl Harbor. And I say, check him now, check him now."[51]

As the nature and significance of the threat he faced from Saddam sank in for Bush throughout the fall, he sought ways to break out from what he and his advisors considered a deepening stalemate in the situation in the Gulf. Broad international sanctions were in place with effective means of enforcing them, but the president was growing more and more skeptical that they would have the desired effect "in an acceptable time frame." His sense of urgency for bringing the crisis to a decisive conclusion was becoming more acute as he learned of the atrocities and devastation that Iraqi forces were inflicting on Kuwait. He was also gravely concerned that his ability to hold together the fractious international coalition he had forged and to maintain the support of the American public for his policies was beginning to wane. He vented this frustration to his diary in mid-September: "I worry, worry, worry about eroded support." A month later, he again recorded in his diary his pained observation that "our support is eroding in the Middle East" and talked with Scowcroft about "how we get things off center in the Middle East."[52]

As he looked for a way to retake the initiative from Saddam Hussein, Bush was increasingly coming around to the view that the use of force might be necessary if he were to accomplish his stated goal to not let Iraq's aggression against Kuwait stand. Scowcroft observed that Bush left him with the impression that he had come to this conclusion—"that he had to do whatever was necessary to liberate Kuwait and the reality was that that meant using force"—"somewhere in early to mid-October," amid fears that "time was not on our side" and they would not be able to "keep the coalition together indefinitely." Bush later reflected that his national security advisor was likely correct. By October 17, he was growing impatient to take the next steps toward resolving the crisis, asserting to his diary, "We must get this over with. The longer it goes, the longer the erosion [of support]."[53]

Not all of his top advisors agreed with him, however. For a national security team that worked in tandem as well as Bush's did, and for one that presented such a unified front to the public, the months of September and October marked a significant period of dissent within the administration's top ranks over the proper course to chart for the next stage of the crisis. One of the most persistent voices of caution came from Bush's closest friend, Secretary of State Baker. Baker argued consistently and forcefully, from the opening of the crisis in August 1990 until the eve of war in January 1991, that the administration and coalition should give diplomacy and sanctions every opportunity to compel Iraqi forces to withdraw from Kuwait. He was not opposed to planning for the possibility of using military force as a last resort, but he did not completely share his boss's urgency and impatience to abandon sanctions. As Bush later reflected, Baker "remained hopeful longer than the rest of us that we could induce Saddam to give up without resorting to force." As early as mid-August, Baker raised his profound concerns with the president, "worried that we will get bogged down in another Vietnam and lose the support of the people, and have the Bush presidency destroyed," as Bush recorded in his diary. Baker privately warned his friend, "I know you're aware of the fact that this has all the ingredients that brought down three of the last five presidents," including the distinct possibilities of "a hostage crisis, body bags, and a full-fledged recession caused by forty-dollar oil."[54]

Another voice of caution was the president's top military advisor, JCS chairman Colin Powell. Like Baker, Powell never expressed opposition to the deployment and potential use of US military might, but he at times felt that Bush was too impatient to give up on sanctions and turn toward force as the necessary solution. Powell had been skeptical from the first days of the crisis that Kuwait was worth going to war, though he had fully backed and implemented the president's decision to deploy a deterrent and then a defensive force to Saudi Arabia to contain Iraqi aggression. In his meetings with Bush once Operation Desert Shield was underway, Powell stressed to the president that he would not need to make any major decisions to alter the military force structure or mission until later in October, and that in the meantime he had several months "to assess the impact of sanctions." By late September, Powell had grown more concerned with Bush's scarcely concealed impatience to take military action. "I think we owe him a more complete description of how long-term sanctions and strangulation would work" as an "alternative to going to war," he told Cheney, who promptly set up a meeting in the Oval Office. The general did not advocate for the sanctions route over the use of force but laid out in detail how it would work, with both its advantages and disadvantages, feeling that "both options had to be considered fully and fairly." Bush heard him out but once again expressed his deepening view that "I really don't think we have time for sanctions to work."[55]

Powell's fellow military leaders shared his concerns of the risks of resorting to force before they had given other avenues enough time to do the job. General Norman Schwarzkopf, the commander of US Central Command who would lead any potential military campaign against Iraq, also hoped to temper Bush's enthusiasm for a military response, arguing publicly in early September that "the next move right now" was to wait for sanctions to take their effect. Presenting their first war plan for ousting Iraqi forces from Kuwait to the president and his national security team on October 11, Pentagon planners called for a frontal assault against Iraqi positions, emphasizing the likelihood of high casualties in any conflict with Saddam's forces.[56]

Two of Bush's advisors who shared his skepticism that sanctions would have the desired effect and "recognized early that sooner or later it would come to force" were Scowcroft and Cheney, who sent the Pentagon's planners back to the drawing board. Bush understood that his secretary of defense was "ahead of his military on this," but he also appreciated Powell's desire "to be sure that if we had to fight, we would do it right and not take half measures."[57]

FIGURE 16. "Defend or eject?": President Bush meets with his chief advisors in the Situation Room for the decisive meeting on October 30, 1990, when he approves a dramatic military buildup to drive Iraqi forces from Kuwait. Counterclockwise from Bush are Secretary of State James Baker, National Security Advisor Brent Scowcroft, Deputy National Security Advisor Robert Gates, Chairman of the Joint Chiefs of Staff Gen. Colin Powell, and Secretary of Defense Dick Cheney.

The decisive meeting to determine the administration's next steps in the Gulf crisis came on the afternoon of October 30 in the Situation Room of the White House. As he had for the past several months, Powell laid out the options available to the president. Though his advisors had refined and revised the details of the alternatives based on a variety of contingencies, the options essentially boiled down to two: whether to wait on (or ratchet up) sanctions while remaining on the defensive, perhaps indefinitely, or perhaps until an Iraqi provocation would justify a US military response; or whether to generate an "offensive option" that would allow coalition forces to launch their own military strike to oust Saddam's forces from Kuwait at a time and in a manner of their own choosing. The president opened the meeting by summarizing the choice they faced: "The time has arrived to determine whether we continue to place most of our eggs in the sanctions basket, which would take a good deal more time as things now stand but would possibly avoid the risks and costs of war, or whether we raise the pressure on Saddam by pressing ahead on both the military and diplomatic tracks." Powell summarized the options more concisely: "Defend or eject?"[58]

Creating an offensive option would require enormous changes to both the objectives the administration would pursue and the means it would employ to achieve them. Powell outlined for the president how the forces available to the coalition as well as their mission had evolved since Bush's initial decision to send troops to Saudi Arabia in early August. The initial phase of Operation Desert Shield was intended only as a deterrent force "to discourage Saddam from attacking" beyond the borders of Kuwait. By early September, the US military deployment had grown to substantial enough levels to shift to "the defensive phase," the buildup for which would be complete by early December, when the coalition could feel confident in its ability to defend Saudi Arabia from any kind of Iraqi assault. If Bush wished to maintain this strong defensive posture while relying on sanctions to force Saddam out of Kuwait, the first option under consideration at the October 30 meeting, then he would need to give the order to cap off the buildup and begin the rotation of military units to allow for a long-term deployment in the Gulf. This option, Powell conceded, had the serious disadvantage of leaving the initiative with Saddam and the Iraqis "to decide when they had had enough."[59]

On the other hand, if Bush wanted to bring the crisis to an end on his own terms, he could pair an expanded military buildup with a renewed diplomatic initiative in a strategy of "coercive diplomacy" to force Saddam out of Kuwait. This approach would combine the potential use of force with an ultimatum for Iraqi forces to withdraw from Kuwait by a certain deadline. The creation of an offensive military capability would make such an ultimatum seem credible. If Saddam saw the United States and its allies preparing for war with overwhelming force, perhaps he would reason that retreat was his wisest option. If he opted to stay put, the coalition would be prepared to take the offensive to push him out. Either way, he would leave Kuwait.[60] Bush admitted the danger of this course of action in the meeting in the Situation Room, noting that by giving Saddam an ultimatum "we are in effect committing ourselves to going to war." But making such a credible threat "may also increase the odds that Saddam agrees to a peaceful solution." The only way to convince him to compromise, Bush argued, might well be "to push matters to the brink of war."[61]

The resources that would be necessary to make such a bold move, however, were staggering. The Pentagon's military planners had redrawn their proposal to include a large-scale air campaign to be followed by a feint attack into Kuwait to hold the occupying Iraqi army in place, while a massive armored attack swept in a "left hook" into Iraq itself to wrap around the Iraqi flank and cut off their retreating forces. But to execute this plan would require a much larger force than that which the president had authorized for Operation Desert Shield. When Powell explained that he would need a force twice the size of the nearly

250,000-man-strong defensive deployment, bringing the total number of US troops in the Gulf to almost half a million, participants in the meeting remember an audible gasp around the room. "We are at a fork in the road," the chairman said. "We either have to rotate or build up." Robert Gates, the deputy national security advisor, was so stunned at the scale of the military's requests that he felt the Pentagon intentionally "put together a package that was so daunting he [the president] would say, 'Well, let's stand pat,'" and back off from plans to eject Saddam from Kuwait with force. But the president was unfazed. "You've got it," Bush replied as he pushed back his chair and stood up, "let me know if you need more." Then he walked out of the room, leaving behind a group of startled advisors.[62]

Bush's decision on October 30 to move forward with the strategy of coercive diplomacy against Iraq by creating an offensive option contended for the most significant decision he made during the entire course of the Gulf crisis and war. Not only would the means he would put to use expand dramatically—to the largest deployment of military forces that any president had authorized since Lyndon Johnson during the Vietnam War, and any Republican president since Abraham Lincoln—but their mission had also undergone a major change.[63] When Bush doubled down on creating an offensive rather than a defensive force in the Gulf, he decisively altered its prime objective from the containment of Saddam's aggression and the protection of Saudi Arabia to the rollback of Iraq's conquest of Kuwait. Bush's instincts had pushed him in this direction since his declaration on the White House lawn that Iraqi aggression against Kuwait "will not stand." But up to this point the actions he had undertaken had had the conservative mission of preventing further damage. Now Bush unequivocally shifted to rolling back Saddam's seizure of his smaller neighbor, matching his increasingly creative and deliberate framing of the broader stakes of the crisis for building a new world order that he had been outlining for the public since his September 11 speech to Congress.

Once the president had made his decision, his full national security team moved to implement it, the period of disagreement and debate over the next steps to take behind them. Baker, writing on the back of an envelope, summarized the administration's thinking at this stage of the crisis, linking the expanded objective of forcing Saddam from Kuwait with the goal of creating a precedent for the post–Cold War world based on the defense of principles and norms of international behavior: "New world order—Have to be principled & stand up to aggression. Don't make same mistake we did in 30s; *nor* same as in Vietnam—uncertain, tentative, etc.—if we go in we have to have *massive* force. At the same time, we should go to the Congress and the U.N. to ask their support for possible use of force."[64] Baker's words and reasoning encapsulated the president's own evolving thinking on the broader implications and lasting importance of how the US government and the world community as a whole handled this crisis, as well as the historical analogies he used to make sense of the threat that Saddam's rogue regime posed.

Baker's summary also pointed to another critical element of the Bush administration's efforts to retake the initiative in the late fall of 1990: seeking the support of the United Nations and of the US Congress for the possible use of military force to oust Iraqi forces from Kuwait. The president's decision to develop an offensive military capability in the Gulf was a unilateral American one, but the administration wasted no time in seeking the endorsement of the international community by returning to the UN Security Council for a new resolution authorizing the use of force and setting the deadline for Saddam to withdraw his forces from Kuwait. In the immediate terms of the current crisis, such a resolution would enhance the weight of an ultimatum against him and lend clear international legitimacy to the potential conflict to follow. Margaret Thatcher disagreed with Bush's decision to return to the United Nations for an additional resolution, arguing strongly that the existing UN resolutions against Iraq, alongside Article 51 of the UN Charter, which permitted the use of force in self-defense, were sufficient justifications for launching military action. She also feared that further resolutions could put restraints or reservations on the coalition's freedom of action.[65]

Bush, however, was looking beyond the imperatives of the current crisis to the pattern he wished to set for the new world order he hoped to bring to life in its wake. Remaining conscious that the manner in which he handled each aspect of the Gulf crisis would impact the likelihood that it would stand as a precedent for the new global system he was creating, Bush highly valued the need to maintain the steadfast support of his diverse coalition of nations that spanned the globe. Taking unilateral action beyond the mandate of the United Nations, he explained in his memoirs, "would have destroyed the precedent of international response to aggression that we hoped to establish." Instead, he sought to align the expanded objectives and means he had set in motion on October 30 with the multilateral framework for cooperative action that he had established at the outset of the crisis. From the first week after Iraq's invasion of Kuwait, he later wrote, "We had been self-consciously trying to set a pattern for handling aggression in the post–Cold War world."[66]

Baker drew on the notion of the Gulf crisis as an opportunity to set a precedent for the future as he circled the globe to consult with allies and build support for a new resolution among members of the UN Security Council. In Moscow, Gorbachev offered some of the stiffest skepticism that Baker faced toward the necessity of using force against Iraq, still hoping to find a diplomatic solution that would convince Saddam to withdraw his forces from Kuwait. Baker reported to Bush that he answered the Soviet leader by arguing for the need to defend broadly supported principles governing international behavior: "It's hard to establish recognized norms of civilized and peaceful behavior if a brutal aggressor who quite simply rejects these norms is allowed to succeed because the will to use force is absent."[67] He reiterated this case at the United Nations as the Security Council voted on the proposed resolution authorizing the coalition to use "all necessary means" to enforce Iraq's withdrawal from Kuwait. Declaring that "we meet at the hinge of history," the secretary of state set out a challenge for the international community: "We can use the end of the Cold War to get beyond the whole pattern of settling conflicts by force, or we can slip back into ever more savage regional conflicts in which might alone makes right." The choice was between "peace and the rule of law" or "aggression and the law of the jungle." The Security Council approved the resolution by a vote of 12–2 with one abstention, calling for unconditional Iraqi withdrawal from Kuwait by midnight on January 15, 1991. Not since the Korean War in 1950 had the United Nations granted such clear authorization to wage war.[68]

The success of securing the endorsement of the United Nations for the use of force in the Gulf helped the Bush administration make its case to a skeptical Congress that was wary of getting bogged down in another Vietnam. In fact, the effort to win passage of the UN resolution turned out to be easier than the fight for a congressional resolution supporting the use of force, which eventually passed with a particularly narrow margin in the Senate on January 12, 1991. While members of Congress broadly shared Bush's indignation at Saddam's actions and supported the president's initial measures to check his aggression, they remained reluctant to adopt his view of the stakes for the post–Cold War world and the necessity for the United States to take the lead through military action. Bush himself was of two minds with respect to securing Congress's support before committing to war. On one hand, he later wrote, "I was confident I did not need a resolution. . . . Even had Congress not passed the resolutions I would have acted and ordered our troops into combat." On January 4, he explained to his diary that he was "more determined than ever to do what I have to do," even at the risk of impeachment. "I don't care if I have one vote in the Congress," he commented on November 28. On the other hand, just as he had with the international community, Bush yearned for the full backing of the US government not just for his actions regarding the Gulf but for the principles he was seeking to establish and protect. "For the country's sake, and to show Saddam we were speaking as one voice," he explained, "I wanted Congress on record, and before the deadline passed." Official congressional approval would help to cement the idea that the developments in the Gulf would form the basis for a precedent to extend beyond the current crisis.[69]

Over the course of the fall, President Bush and his team of advisors devoted much time and attention to considering the long-term consequences of the actions they took in response to the crisis in the Gulf. Having stemmed the tide of Iraqi aggression through the initial US deployment of troops to Saudi Arabia in August, the Bush administration had the space to hone its understanding and framing of the stakes of the crisis to deliberately set patterns for future instances of international aggression. Recognizing that the establishment of norms governing international behavior and the willingness to enforce them could not endure as unilateral US efforts, Bush and his advisors fashioned their actions within a framework of global cooperation and endorsement. Bush's own understanding of the nature of the threat posed by Saddam Hussein's rogue regime deepened during these months as Iraqi atrocities and contempt for international law drew him to compare the Iraqi strongman to Hitler during the lead-up to World War II. Bush was determined not to repeat the failure of the 1930s to turn back acts of aggression before they could escalate into global conflict, particularly as Saddam's brazen invasion stood to spoil the unique opportunity to forge a more peaceful and cooperative international system. If necessary, Bush would inaugurate his new world order through war.

Rapid Victory, Unsettled Questions: January–March 1991

With the world community and the military might of a vast coalition of nations arrayed against him, Saddam Hussein chose war. Once the UN-mandated deadline had passed and the fighting began, the Bush administration's months of methodical planning to set a precedent for preventing international aggression in the post–Cold War era paid off with dramatic success on the battlefield. In keeping with the disciplined and carefully choreographed approach he had taken toward the crisis from its start, President Bush unleashed US and coalition forces for over a month of aerial assaults on Iraqi targets prior to launching a devastating ground attack that ejected Saddam's army from Kuwait in exactly one hundred hours. The stunning success of the combined air and ground components of Operation Desert Storm helped to solidify the US-led effort against Iraq as the defining model for how the international community should handle such crises in the future.

However, as the dust of combat began to settle, it soon became clear that the war's endgame left a number of critical questions unresolved regarding the threat that rogue states such as Iraq would continue to pose to the emerging global order. The rapid coalition victory in the Gulf decisively settled the dispute over Kuwait, but in certain key respects the decisions that Bush and his team made at the end of the war ironically hampered the setting of a foolproof precedent for dealing with rogue states. By allowing Saddam to remain in power with the potential to restart his unexpectedly advanced WMD programs, the Bush administration allowed the problem of Iraq and similar rogues to fester beyond the current crisis, throughout the next decade and beyond, with grave consequences for the United States and the world. The actions that Bush and his advisors took to preserve their coalition against Iraq prevented them from inflicting the decisive end to Saddam's rogue regime that they had accomplished in Panama the year before. The remarkable success of the diplomatic and military efforts to reverse Iraqi aggression drew wide acclaim for the model they had set, but their incomplete ending also helped to cement rogue states as the defining and lasting threat to international security in the new era.

Waiting for the deadline for Iraq to withdraw from Kuwait to expire at midnight on January 15, 1991, President Bush went for a solitary walk on the South Lawn of the White House, just as his son would do a dozen years later prior to launching another war against Iraq. Returning to a meeting with his national security team in the Oval Office that morning, Bush signed the National Security Directive authorizing the execution of Operation Desert Storm, which would begin the following evening if Saddam refused to comply. The president addressed the nation from the Oval Office two hours after the first bombs fell on Baghdad in the early morning hours of January 17, still January 16 in Washington. "Tonight, the battle has been joined," Bush told the largest US television audience on record. He had written much of the address himself and reiterated the defense of principle and norms for international behavior that lay at the heart of his framing of the stakes of the crisis: "I am convinced not only that we will prevail but that out of the horror of combat will come the recognition that no nation can stand against a world united, no nation will be permitted to brutally assault its neighbor." The aggression and atrocities that Saddam and his forces had committed were "an affront to mankind."[70]

The air war against military targets in Iraq and Kuwait, the first phase of Operation Desert Storm, met with immediate success. "We own the skies," Bush dictated to his diary less than three days into the fighting. During the opening weeks of combat, US and coalition air forces achieved unchallenged air supremacy over the Persian Gulf and Kuwait and "virtually paralyzed" the Iraqi command and control network. By early February, Bush and his team were contemplating when to unleash the ground forces that would complete the mission. The ground war began in the early morning of February 24, still the evening of February 23 in Washington. Contrary to fears among the American public of another Vietnam, this phase, too, went "quicker than anyone ever thought," Bush dictated on the first day of fighting. While a force of US Marines pinned down Iraqi forces in Kuwait, the coalition mounted a massive armored assault through the Iraqi des-

FIGURE 17. The decision to end the Gulf War: President Bush, working the phones with Gen. Colin Powell to confer with allies and commanders, makes the decision to end the war against Iraq, February 27, 1991. Seated around Bush in the Oval Office are (L–R) White House chief of staff John Sununu, Deputy National Security Advisor Robert Gates, and Secretary of Defense Dick Cheney.

ert around the flank of the Iraqi positions to cut off their retreat. By February 27, though this gate of retreat was not yet as fully closed as the US commanders thought, the completeness of the rout of Iraqi forces and the growing bloodiness of their desperate retreat along the "highway of death" from Kuwait City back into Iraq prompted Bush to ask whether the time to end hostilities had come. With the mission to liberate Kuwait accomplished, coalition forces declared a ceasefire at midnight on February 27 (the morning of February 28 in the Gulf), only one hundred hours after what Saddam had threatened would be "the mother of all battles" had begun. Iraqi forces lost nearly 90 percent of their tanks and over 20,000 dead, while US forces lost only 148 soldiers killed in action.[71]

In the National Security Directive (NSD-54) authorizing the execution of Operation Desert Storm if Saddam did not withdraw his forces before the deadline on January 15, Bush mapped out the war aims that would guide the military campaign. These central objectives included the "immediate, complete and unconditional withdrawal of all Iraqi forces from Kuwait" and the restoration of the Kuwaiti government, as well as ensuring "the security and the stability" of the Persian Gulf region. To accomplish this overarching mission, the president directed his military forces to degrade and destroy Iraq's offensive capability by "targeting Saddam's vast military arsenal," as he explained in his address announcing the start of the war. Destroying Saddam's war-making potential, particularly his elite Republican Guards—a task that would require a ground campaign, not just air power—would eliminate the danger of future military aggression that had come to define the rogue state threat.[72]

Another critical factor that had become central to the rogue state paradigm loomed large in the minds of the president and his key advisors as they prepared for war in January 1991: the potentially catastrophic danger posed by Iraq's WMD programs. Included prominently in the set of military goals listed in NSD-54 was the imperative to "destroy Iraq's chemical, biological, and nuclear capabilities" and to discourage the use of such weapons on the battlefield against coalition forces.[73] Speaking from the Oval Office, Bush emphasized to the nation his determination "to knock out Saddam Hussein's nuclear bomb potential" and his chemical weapons facilities. He warned of the urgency of taking action to head off Iraq's efforts to bolster its WMD capabilities with the most terrifying weapon of all: "While the world waited, Saddam sought to add to the chemical weapons arsenal he now possesses, an infinitely more dangerous weapon of mass destruction—a nuclear weapon."[74]

Indeed, Bush and his team of advisors fully expected the likelihood that Saddam would unleash a chemical weapons attack to stem the advance of coalition forces that his own military could not possibly match. He had a well-known history of deploying chemical agents such as nerve and mustard gas on the battlefield in Iraq's war with Iran throughout the 1980s, and most notoriously against Kurdish civilians to suppress an uprising in 1988. As the United States prepared for war, the CIA estimated that Iraq possessed at least a thousand tons of chemical agents. Powell reported to Bush on the eve of the start of the ground war that there was "a high probability of chemical attack." Nevertheless, the chairman of the JCS felt that such an attack would be "manageable": US and coalition forces were supplied with the necessary protective equipment as well as detection and alarm systems that would keep a chemical attack from becoming a "battlefield disaster." Despite such thorough preparation, Bush still agonized over Saddam's potential use of WMD, confiding to his diary his worries about chemical weapons or "some surprise weapon" for which his forces were not prepared.[75]

What concerned Bush and his advisors more than Iraq's chemical arsenal was Saddam's capability for launching a biological weapons attack against coalition ground forces. US intelligence considered Iraq's biological weapons program far enough advanced to potentially include stockpiles that it could release or deploy on the battlefield. While US preparations against chemical weapons, including the fact that the ground campaign would involve fast-moving, shielded vehicles advancing through the open desert, would limit the damage they could do, the unleashing of germ warfare could be far more destructive and terrifying, not least in terms of public morale. Just before the start of the air campaign, Powell discussed with his British counterpart the risks of bombing Iraq's biological weapons production sites, which were important targets for the aerial bombardment phase of Operation Desert Storm. Powell assured his ally, as he had the president, that the bombing would likely destroy any disease agents present, though there was still the possibility that it would release them instead. "It was a gamble," he argued, "but one we had to take."[76]

In keeping with the military objectives that Bush and his team had set down in NSD-54, Iraq's WMD installations became central targets for destruction during the air war. Just hours into the first night of the air campaign, General Schwarzkopf reported to Powell that Iraqi WMD facilities—particularly its biological and nuclear weapons sites—had been "clobbered."[77] Bush recalled that the need to destroy Saddam's nuclear and biological weapons capabilities weighed heavily on his mind in the lead-up to and start of the conflict. The high priority that the president and his chief advisors placed on this goal had been evident throughout the preceding months of war planning. In a memo prepared for the NSC meeting in late October in which Bush decided to build up an offensive military capability against Saddam, Scowcroft had argued in favor of setting an early ultimatum for Iraqi forces to leave Kuwait in order to "bring matters to a head before Iraq had much more time to work on its biological and nuclear weapons capability."[78]

An especially pressing question plagued Bush and his national security team as they planned for the outbreak of hostilities on the ground: how to respond if Saddam did decide to launch WMD attacks against US and coalition forces. At a meeting at Camp David on Christmas Eve 1990, with the deadline for Iraq to withdraw from Kuwait only three weeks away, Bush and his advisors briefly considered retaliating in kind by using their own chemical weapons, but they just as quickly rejected this option.[79] Scowcroft later insisted that "no one advanced the notion of using nuclear weapons" against Iraq, a course of action that Bush rejected "even in retaliation for chemical or biological attacks."[80] However, this did not mean that the president's top advisors did not privately contemplate what such a scenario would look like. Cheney, in particular, felt it was his duty as secretary of defense to be ready in the disastrous event that Saddam did use his WMD. He quietly asked Powell and the Pentagon's military planners "how many tactical nukes are we going to have to use to take out an Iraqi Republican Guard division" if circumstances required it. The answer took some time to figure out, and Powell eventually responded to Cheney's persistent questioning that seventeen tactical nuclear bombs would be needed to guarantee its destruction, perhaps less if the division were more densely positioned. Cheney held back from briefing the president on this nuclear planning but wanted to be prepared in case "we have to follow through on our threat."[81]

Though Bush ultimately decided to rule out any use or explicit threat to use US nuclear or chemical weapons and stated clearly in NSD-54 that Operation Desert Storm would be carried out only by "conventional military forces," his administration relied on ambiguity to maximize its deterrence against Iraqi use of WMD in battle. Cheney summarized the public position of the US government that "were Saddam Hussein foolish enough to use weapons of mass destruction, the U.S. response would be absolutely overwhelming and it would be devastating." The Iraqis interpreted this to mean that the United States was prepared to use nuclear weapons. Indeed, the head of Iraqi military intelligence later called this warning "quite severe and quite effective" in convincing the Iraqi government that coalition forces were "certain to use nuclear arms" in response to a WMD attack. Though this was not the case, Bush and his team felt there was "no point in undermining the deterrence it might be offering" by publicly denying Iraqi fears. Powell prepared his own warning to Saddam in mid-January outlining a series of drastic, conventional (non-WMD) measures that coalition forces would employ in retaliation for a WMD attack, including destroying Iraq's merchant fleet, its port and oil facilities, and its infrastructure systems—and perhaps even the dams on the Tigris and Euphrates Rivers, thereby flooding Baghdad. These threats were not officially cleared in time to make this warning public, but the message Powell intended to send was clear: "We would fight a conventional war, unless Saddam drove us to other means, which would be swift and crushing."[82]

NSD-54 introduced the severest warning yet against a WMD attack from Iraq, vowing to alter the entire mission of US forces in the war from the UN-authorized goal of ejecting Iraqi forces from Kuwait to forcing regime change in Baghdad. "Should Iraq resort to using chemical, biological, or nuclear weapons" or sponsor a terrorist attack against the United States or its allies, the official statement of US war aims asserted, "it shall become an explicit objective of the United States to replace the current leadership of Iraq." Folded into a top-secret US government document, this vow to seek regime change in Iraq in the event of a WMD attack was a statement of policy, not mere bluster, bluff, or public warning—particularly for an administration that was so careful and judicious with the explicit threats it was willing to make.[83]

Barring the use of Iraq's WMD arsenal, however, regime change against Saddam Hussein was not a war aim of the US government. As the president and his advisors deliberated on how to define the war aims of the US military effort, they briefly considered making regime change an explicit objective of the conflict. However, no senior member of Bush's national security team considered such a course as a serious possibility, and they quickly rejected the idea. The main reason was a straightforward one: Bush had been able to garner such broad support and build such a vast coalition, backed by a host of UN resolutions, by limiting his mission in the Gulf to the clearly defined goal of removing Saddam's forces from Kuwait and restoring the legitimate Kuwaiti government, thereby reversing the Iraqi aggression that had created the crisis. To march on to Baghdad, topple Saddam's regime, and then occupy Iraq, Bush and his advisors feared, would "instantly shatter our coalition" that they had worked so hard to build.[84]

The danger of upending the coalition and exceeding the legal mandate of the United Nations was both immediate and long term. In terms of the crisis at hand, Bush and his advisors feared that deposing Saddam would be far harder in practice than in principle. The US military was barred by law from explicitly targeting Saddam for assassination, though it might get lucky with airstrikes against his command posts. The Iraqi despot was known to be "far more elusive and better protected" than Manuel Noriega had been in Panama, where US forces had been forced to undertake a long and difficult manhunt even in a country they knew well. Moreover, Bush feared, it was likely that toppling Saddam would necessitate "an indefinite occupation of a hostile state" that could degenerate into "an unwinnable urban guerrilla war" and consequently "plunge that part of the world into even greater instability." A shattered Iraq would not be able to serve as a counterbalance to Iran, still an important strategic consideration for US policymakers and their coalition partners. Even more importantly, Bush felt that going "way beyond the imprimatur of international law" bestowed by the UN resolutions would "destroy the credibility we were working so hard to reestablish." This was a concern not just for the present crisis but one that went to the heart of the broader precedent and pattern that the Bush administration was trying to establish for how the international community, led by US power, should respond to future instances of aggression. Leaving Saddam in place, however unsatisfactory for the present crisis, was worth the price, Bush felt, to preserve the international consensus behind the model that his actions were creating for the new global order taking shape.[85]

A significant factor buttressing Bush and his advisors' willingness to limit their war aims was their high level of confidence that Saddam would fall from power without their help. Supported by the optimistic predictions of Arab leaders in the coalition, Bush and his team fully expected that the Iraqi people or the Iraqi military would take matters into their own hands to overthrow the tyrant who had so recently led their country to a disastrous and humiliating defeat. The president expressed this wish on numerous occasions in meetings with his coalition partners: "I hope that the Iraqi army or the Iraqi people just take matters into their own hands and put him out," he told the German foreign minister at the end of the war. Hoping to encourage such a development, Bush did go so far as to codify as a military objective in NSD-54 the goal of "weaken[ing] Iraqi popular support for the current government" while stopping short of making regime change a US responsibility.[86]

Bush may have presented to his advisors and the public a consistently restrained stance in keeping regime change separate from his administration's stated war aims, but his views in private were far more conflicted. From the opening days of the crisis, he had expressed his conviction that the danger to the international order would not be fully resolved until Saddam was removed from power: "All will not be tranquil until Saddam Hussein is history," he declared in an NSC meeting on August 6, 1990. This opinion did not change over the ensuing months of diplomacy and war, as he asserted to the German foreign minister on March 1, 1991, that Saddam "is like a cancer . . . it will be impossible for us to do anything constructive with Iraq as long as he is there." On January 20, as bombs fell on Baghdad, Bush recorded in his diary his desire to remove Saddam: "As I think about it, it would be very good if we didn't leave him intact. . . . But it would be far simpler if his military did what they ought to do and take him out." Homegrown regime change at the hands of "his own people" would be "the best thing," Bush thought, rather than anything that the coalition imposed on Iraq. Still, the president's conflicted views on the issue of regime change festered as the air campaign continued. "I just keep thinking the Iraqi people ought to take care of [him] with the Iraqi military," he dictated on January 31. They needed to "stand up and do that which should have been done a long time ago—take the guy out of there—either kick him out of the country or do something where he is no longer running things." This was Bush's polite way of referring to assassination, something for which he was loath to explicitly advocate even to himself, though this was clearly where his preferences lay. He insisted that "they've got to do something about it. I wish like hell that *we* could."[87]

Part of Bush's determination to see Saddam fall from power as the ultimate consequence of his aggression was rooted in the parallels he continued to see between the crisis in the Gulf and the confrontation with Hitler during World War II. Meeting with his advisors in the Yellow Oval Room of the White House residence to decide on the date for launching the ground war, the president learned from Powell that the coalition's offensive would be triple the size of the Allied invasion of Normandy to liberate Nazi-occupied Europe. Bush noted that FDR had learned of the attack on Pearl Harbor in that very room, and that it was also the place where FDR and Churchill had signed their charter of alliance alongside representatives of the Soviet Union and China on New Year's Day 1942.[88] History's echoes also loomed over Bush's thoughts in the war's immediate aftermath. He regretted the war's murky ending with Saddam still clinging to power and claiming victory to his people. The end of the war "hasn't been clean,"

Bush recorded in his diary, lamenting that "there is no Battleship *Missouri* surrender" that would "make this akin to World War II, to separate it from Korea, and Vietnam." Ruminating on his depressed rather than euphoric mood in the wake of victory, he again harkened back to the Second World War: "Hitler is alive, indeed, Hitler is still in office, and that's the problem."[89] Bush might have stood by his decision to stop the fighting short of regime change as a matter of sound diplomatic and military policy, but he sensed that leaving the rogue dictator in place only perpetuated the danger and risked allowing it to resurface another day.

Margaret Thatcher agreed with the essence of US policy toward Saddam Hussein's regime but not its execution during the war's endgame. By this time, she was no longer in power herself, unseated as Britain's prime minister in November 1990 prior to the outbreak of hostilities. In her memoirs, she noted her agreement with the position of the Bush administration that bringing about Saddam's downfall "would not be a specific objective" of the coalition's war effort but rather "a desirable side-effect of our actions." However, she believed that Bush had called a halt to the ground offensive too soon, allowing Saddam to escape from the coalition's clutches with too much of his war machine left intact. She argued that the "failure to disarm" Saddam and to "follow through the victory so that he was publicly humiliated" in the eyes of his people and throughout the Middle East was a mistake that grew from Bush and his advisors' "excessive emphasis" on maintaining the consensus of the international community. Such an opinion might have been easier to hold for a former statesman like Thatcher who no longer made policy, and she did not elaborate on the steps she would have taken to accomplish a fuller disarmament and humiliation of Saddam. Nevertheless, the former British leader clearly foresaw that the failure to neutralize or replace the Iraqi regime would allow Saddam to continue as a threat to the international norms that the Gulf campaign was seeking to establish.[90]

The stunning speed and success of the war prompted some discussion within and outside government over whether to "move the goalposts" and redefine the mission to seek regime change in Iraq by marching on to Baghdad. The top ranks of the Bush administration never gave serious consideration to this possibility, however much they hoped to see Saddam's downfall, and instead maintained their disciplined focus on limiting their mission to achieving the clearly defined and broadly supported strategic objectives of ejecting Iraqi forces from Kuwait and restoring the Kuwaiti government. Bush and Scowcroft later wrote that they were determined to avoid "mission creep" that could turn a clear-cut victory into a bloody and costly stalemate, like the one that had followed President Truman's decision to try to reunify Korea following the rout of North Korea's invading army in the fall of 1950. While reviewing a memo from Scowcroft on plans for a liberated Kuwait in early February 1991, the president noted his enthusiastic agreement with the argument that the United States should not "follow up Iraq's occupation with one of our own," but rather base its "model" for the war's aftermath on "post–World War II France, not Germany." Moreover, even while he expressed in his diary his hope for Saddam's ouster, Bush insisted to his advisors on the need to maintain the territorial integrity of the Iraqi state after the war to avoid instability and preserve a balance of power against Iran. His determination to avoid the dismemberment of Iraq also contributed to Bush's decision not to provide any direct support to the popular uprisings that sprouted up in the north and south of Iraq in the war's immediate aftermath. The president's verbal encouragement of such rebellions against Saddam's rule opened him to criticism that he was turning his back on the rebels by not providing aid, but he again decided to keep the coalition's mission within its internationally endorsed bounds.[91]

The rapidness of the coalition's victory on the battlefield was not the only development that stunned the Bush administration and its allies at the end of the Gulf War. As the dust of combat settled and US and allied forces took stock of their defeated adversary, they discovered that Iraq's WMD programs—particularly its program to develop nuclear weapons—were far more advanced and better concealed than US intelligence had believed at the war's outset. Following Israel's successful raid against Iraq's Osirak nuclear reactor in 1981, the US government did not consider the Iraqi nuclear program to be a serious threat and adopted a "blasé approach" toward the issue that kept it from noticing the progress of Saddam's restarted and far more covert nuclear effort over the rest of the decade. A 1986 State Department memorandum stated that a majority of officials in the Reagan administration at the time believed that Iraq did "not have the resources for a weapon-program development and will not have in a foreseeable future." This view remained largely unchanged during the rest of the Reagan presidency and the beginning of Bush's term in office. Indeed, one detailed study notes that at the beginning of the Gulf War in early 1991, "the international community was largely oblivious to the size and scope of Iraq's nuclear weapons program." What US intelligence failed to uncover was the Iraqi regime's creation of an even more extensive program that placed much greater emphasis on shielding its progress from the outside world. After Saddam's invasion of Kuwait in August 1990, the clandestine nuclear effort took on "a new sense of purpose" as his lieutenants ordered the acceleration of a "crash program" to develop a crude nuclear explosive, though numerous technical obstacles still stood in the way. Estimates vary as to how close Iraq came to achieving the nuclear weapons threshold, but most sources concur that "Iraq was not far away from a major breakthrough in 1990–1991." By the time the coalition launched its air campaign, Iraq was far closer to possessing a nuclear weapons capability—both in terms of a single crude device and a fully operational arsenal—than Western intelligence sources expected. Prior to the war, US and British intelligence estimated that Iraq was at least five to ten years away from the nuclear weapons threshold. The unexpected discovery that it was in fact much closer to producing a nuclear warhead—possibly in as little as a year or two or even less—was shocking to the allies arrayed against the Iraqi regime.[92]

Of all the facets of Iraq's WMD programs, the threat of nuclear weapons was the one that US war planners had worried about least in the lead-up to the war, so the discovery of how unexpectedly close Saddam had been to possessing a nuclear weapons capability came as a particular shock to the senior members of the Bush administration. US and coalition forces expected and were fully prepared for a chemical weapons attack. As they launched the ground campaign, their most acute WMD concern was the possibility that Iraq would employ biological weapons against the coalition. The Bush administration recognized that Saddam's efforts to acquire nuclear weapons were ongoing and needed to be halted, but they did not think that the threat was immediate. As Scowcroft had written in a memo responding to Bush's questions on the status of the Iraqi nuclear program in March 1990, "Iraq is nowhere near capable of possessing a nuclear weapon."[93] The realization that Saddam would likely have wielded nuclear weapons within a matter of years or less, had the military confrontation over Kuwait not provided the opportunity to discover and dismantle Iraq's advanced nuclear program, magnified the level of danger his regime posed in the eyes of Bush and his advisors.

In the aftermath of the war, Bush and his team sought to turn back this danger by building international consensus behind a system of inspections to uproot Iraq's nuclear program and ensure that Saddam would never acquire such devastating weapons. As Baker recalled, "We were determined to use our victory in Desert Storm to put the Iraqi regime under the intense glare of the most intrusive weapons-inspections regime ever developed, to root out every last bit of that program."[94] UN Security Council Resolution 687, adopted in April 1991, mandated the destruction of any stockpiles of and production facilities for Iraqi WMD that had survived the aerial bombardment of the Gulf War and established the United Nations Special Commission (UNSCOM) to oversee Iraq's lasting compliance with such measures.[95] Within days of the official signing of the ceasefire ending the war, the Bush administration issued a statement announcing new measures to curb the spread of WMD and "enhance our ability to head off these dangers so that in the future we will not be forced to confront them militarily as we have in Iraq." The statement made clear that the US government viewed the proliferation of WMD as a defining threat to national and international security for the new era—and one that was decisively fused with the danger of rogue states such as Iraq.[96]

The end of the Gulf War left a number of questions unsettled, even while its remarkably rapid success on the battlefield helped to solidify the Bush administration's diplomatic and military efforts as a lasting model against international aggression for the post–Cold War world. Bush's decision to halt the military campaign short of regime change preserved the unprecedentedly broad coalition against Iraq and strengthened the international consensus behind the coalition's actions. But Saddam's unexpected tenacity in clinging to power even after his defeat pointed to the durability of the rogue state threat to the "new world order" that Bush was attempting to build. Moreover, the chilling specter of Saddam's startlingly advanced WMD—and particularly nuclear weapons—programs elevated the potential danger of such unpredictable and aggressive regimes. Perhaps the most glaring unresolved question in the Gulf War's wake was whether regime change was necessary for one as bad and untrustworthy—and with as dangerous ambitions—as Saddam Hussein's. The victory of the United States and its allies in the Gulf War left Saddam in a cage of sanctions and weapons inspections—a defanged rogue, but one still in power.

What Kind of Precedent?

The Gulf War and the five-and-a-half-month crisis that preceded it became the formative precedent for defining global security in the post–Cold War world. The moment that Saddam Hussein launched his unprovoked invasion across his southern border into Kuwait was a turning point for international relations. The Cold War was coming to a symbolic close with Soviet agreement to German unification, and what would take the place of anticommunism and containment of Soviet power as the driving force for the United States' role in the world was not yet clear. Into this vacuum came the most glaring act of international aggression since World War II. Despite the unexpected nature of the crisis and initial uncertainty over its importance to US interests, the US government improvised a response in concert with its allies and an unprecedentedly broad international coalition to halt and eventually reverse the Iraqi aggression against Kuwait.

Over the course of the late summer and fall of 1990, President George Bush and his national security team consciously framed their actions to set a pattern for the future. What began as an improvised reaction to an unexpected crisis soon evolved into a creative framing of the stakes to establish rules and norms governing international behavior for a new global era. Bush's instinctive determination that the Iraqi conquest "will not stand" grew into a defense of principle and the rule of law for a "new world order" that offered the hope of international cooperation to prevent aggression and ensure peace. Bush and his team therefore built the elements of their strategy to combat the Iraqi invasion around developing national and international consensus behind a model for concerted international action and the use of force against aggressive states. The remarkably successful execution and outcome of the air and ground war that drove Iraqi forces back into their own country helped to cement the multilateral effort that Bush led as the defining precedent he hoped to construct for the post–Cold War world.

As the crisis continued through the fall and erupted into war in early 1991, President Bush's understanding of the nature of the threat posed by Saddam's regime deepened. He had warned of "renegade regimes and unpredictable rulers" as early as his August 2, 1990, address in Aspen, Colorado, but the parallels he saw between the Iraqi despot and the militaristic aggression and brutality of Hitler prior to and during World War II grew starker in the following months. The idea of rogue states had been present in the minds of US policymakers before Iraq's invasion of Kuwait, but no clear strategy yet existed for how to address this threat—nor was it yet viewed as such a prominent danger to the global order. Saddam's brazen aggression confirmed his regime as the quintessential rogue state, one that starkly brought together the characteristics of armed aggression, support for terrorism, and pursuit of WMD into a single phenomenon. Speaking to the press in November 1990, Bush linked his defense of principle and norms of international safety with the features of Saddam's rogue regime that threatened them: "We're in the Gulf because the world must not and cannot reward aggression. . . . And we're in the Gulf because of the brutality of Saddam Hussein . . . a dangerous dictator all too willing to use force who has weapons of mass destruction and is seeking new ones and who desires to control one of the world's key resources—all at a time in history when the rules of the post–Cold War world are being written."[97] For Bush, the stakes of defeating this central challenge to the new global order could not be clearer.

Ironically, it was also the questions that the Gulf War left unresolved that helped to establish rogue states as the defining security threat of the new era. Bush's decision not to include regime change among his war aims preserved his vast coalition but allowed the dangerous and unpredictable dictator to remain in power to fight another day, weakening the usefulness of the precedent that the successful war had set. Moreover, while Saddam's unexpectedly advanced WMD programs came under an intensive United Nations inspection regime after the war, his ambitions to acquire and potentially even use chemical, biological, and nuclear weapons appeared untamed. As Margaret Thatcher wrote presciently after the war, "There will be no peace and security in the region until Saddam is toppled."[98] With Saddam still ruling in Baghdad, Israeli prime minister Yitzhak Shamir likewise warned Baker soon after the end of the war that "everything in the region will be temporary until this fact changes."[99] Thus, it was the uncertainties as well as the successes that the Gulf War left in its wake that established the two defining features of global security in the post–Cold War world: the central threat of rogue states challenging the international order while seeking WMD, and the role of the United States in enforcing essential global norms of international safety against these outlaws. In both respects, the Gulf War set a formative precedent that would guide US national security strategy through the crises of the coming decades.

Conclusion

NEW WORLD DISORDER

The window from 1988 to 1990 at the end of the Cold War was a brief period full of possibilities for the shape of the world to come. The United States' role in the world and the focus of its national security strategy in this promising but uncertain new era were not yet settled. The waning need to base US foreign relations around the once-central threat of Soviet communism left a vacuum that former government officials and public intellectuals sought to fill with their own prescriptions for the future. Indeed, these years witnessed a robust public debate over the range of competing issues around which US national security could be oriented in the post–Cold War world. Why did rogue states emerge from this milieu as the preeminent concern for US policymakers after the Cold War?

Shortly after relinquishing his office as secretary of state to James Baker, George Shultz penned an article outlining his assessment of the United States' role in this "turning-point in world affairs." Rejecting the rosy view that the new era would be one of "total peace," Shultz warned of "a spectrum of often-ambiguous challenges, of uncertain possibilities, of fresh developments that overflow traditional lines of control." He drew specific attention to "the novel threats to world security that have already begun to emerge." In particular, he pointed to the rising danger of the spread of weapons of mass destruction (WMD), especially chemical weapons, and the missile technologies needed to deploy them. Their demonstrated use in the Iran-Iraq War, he feared, had accelerated "the erosion of respect for the norms" that had prohibited belligerents from resorting to them since World War I. "The worst nightmare of all," Shultz presciently argued, "would be the eventual combination of ballistic missiles and chemical warheads in the hands of governments with terrorist histories"—"parties with little regard for traditional inhibiting controls." What the former secretary of state was pointing to was the emerging threat of rogue states, combining unpredictable aggression, support for terrorism, and the pursuit of WMD. He also added narcotics trafficking to this list, linking "the war against drugs and terror" by noting the cooperation between terrorists and drug traffickers, "whose immense funds provide them money to finance the muscle of terror." To address this gathering threat, Shultz urged his successors in the US government to enlist broad international cooperation behind the United States taking on a leadership role in enforcing essential norms of global security.[1]

Another former government official who had served in the Carter administration, Jessica Tuchman Mathews, offered a competing proposal for how to frame "a redefinition of what constitutes national security" in the 1990s. Mathews had directed the Office of Global Issues on the National Security Council (NSC) staff from 1977 to 1979 and played a central role in crafting President Carter's early attempt to pivot US foreign relations toward a "post–Cold War" agenda of issues such as economic and energy interdependence. Now she made the case for broadening the definition of national security to include "resource, environmental and demographic issues." Noting the explosion of population growth that would put unprecedented strains on natural resources, particularly in the developing world, Mathews argued for "multilateral diplomacy" to build "new institutions and regulatory regimes to cope with the world's growing environmental interdependence" and head off the worst effects of climate change, deforestation, and ozone depletion. She, too, pressed for the need for the enforcement of norms governing international behavior, in this case regarding environmental protection, which could become "the driving force of the coming decades."[2]

Shultz and Mathews' competing perspectives on the issues that should dominate the national security agenda of the United States in the post–Cold War world illustrate the range of possibilities for the direction that US policy might have taken. Different combinations of leaders and policymakers might have chosen to pursue different options, and rogue states and their accompanying threats of terrorism and WMD were by no means foreordained to emerge as the driving force behind the United States' conception of national security in the new era of global affairs.

But a particular set of policymakers at the helm of US foreign policy in the 1980s and early 1990s, led by Presidents Ronald Reagan and George H. W. Bush and Secretary of State George Shultz, reshaped US national security strategy in response to a series of unplanned and unexpected crises that culminated in the Gulf War of 1991. Saddam Hussein's invasion of Kuwait closed the window of open-ended debate over the possibilities for the future direction of US national security to which Shultz and Mathews' essays contributed. Prior to the Gulf crisis, US policy might have conceivably taken a different course based on a different set of global issues. After the war to eject Iraqi forces from Kuwait, rogue states became the defining threat to global security in the post–Cold War world.

This book is therefore the story of the birth and establishment of a new geopolitical framework around which to orient US national security for the post–Cold War era. It seeks to historicize the contemporary concept of rogue states and trace the process through which it came to define the United States' role in the world following the demise of the Cold War order, with particularly acute consequences in the aftermath of 9/11. The 1980s were as much a *beginning* as an ending of an era of global history, one marked by efforts to *build* a new world order, not just to wind down an old one. The strategic influence of the Reagan and Bush presidencies extended well beyond the Cold War, despite the focus of contemporaneous headlines and the bulk of historical scholarship in the years since. Indeed, the 1980s were a period of *learning* and *adaptation* to newly emerging security threats—terrorism, WMD, and rogue states—that had seemed peripheral and disparate at the start of the decade. Over a series of important crises from 1981 to 1991, both Reagan and Bush, alongside their national security teams, increasingly recognized the nature and urgency of these new dangers to global security. They aired sharp disagreements and made significant stumbles but also critical progress toward forging strategies and determining priorities to guide the United States into a new era. Their experience navigating this period of strategic flux provides a telling example of how policymakers have historically made US grand strategy "in reverse," first improvising to address unexpected crises and then building a "grand strategy" framework to make sense of these improvisations after the fact.

This book argues that in redefining US national security around the threat of rogue states, the Reagan and Bush administrations set precedents that conditioned their successors to view future crises through the lens of this central menace to global security. Though Reagan and Bush did not leave a single clear-cut approach for how to deal with rogues, their responses to a series of formative crises elevated the concepts of regime change and preemptive military action in US strategic thinking. Their evolving strategies toward rogue states established a lasting US enforcement role against such outlaw regimes in the new global era that followed the Cold War.

The legacy Ronald Reagan left regarding the emerging challenge of rogue states was his ability to learn and adapt on the job. He entered the presidency with a single-minded focus on the Cold War standoff with Soviet communism, a rigid mindset that made him and his team of advisors slow to appreciate the non–Cold War dangers and principles at stake in the Osirak and Falklands crises in their first years in office. British prime minister Margaret Thatcher was quicker to grasp the necessity of defending the principles of nonaggression and self-determination that the Falklands War imperiled, pushing Reagan toward her viewpoint just as she would bolster Bush's resolve to take a firm stand against Iraq's aggression in 1990. Thanks to her tenacious prodding, Reagan eventually began his shift toward the more flexible mindset that allowed him to view emerging international dangers in their own right, separate from the menace of Soviet communism. With the critical influence of Secretary of State Shultz and spurred by a series of formative crises, Reagan increasingly recognized over the course of his eight years in the White House the convergence of the essential components of the rogue state paradigm, bringing the phenomenon into clearer focus: Libya, the first poster child for rogue states, linked the idea of outlaw regimes with the sponsorship of terrorism; Panama highlighted the connection between rogues and narcotics trafficking; and Iraq, even during the Reagan years, fused the rogue state concept with the pursuit of (and willingness to use) WMD.

Growing recognition of these threats did not translate, however, into clearcut strategies for combating them. Indeed, Reagan and his team—particularly Shultz and Secretary of Defense Caspar Weinberger but also the typically loyal and even-keeled Vice President Bush—engaged in acrimonious debates and disagreements over when to use military force against or to negotiate with such nefarious regimes. Where Reagan saw more success was in his openness to reimagining national security to account for a reordering of priorities, elevating the importance of rogue states, terrorism, and WMD while testing new strategies based on the concepts of preemption and regime change. The tensions and disagreements among his team were never resolved, and their strategies toward rogue states were not definitively set in place by the time they left office. However, the Reagan administration established precedents, set the parameters of debate, and laid the groundwork for the strategies that would guide their successors through the crises of the coming decades, particularly after 9/11.

George H. W. Bush's legacy on rogue states both furthered and constrained the strategic advances made by his predecessor. Though Bush played a major role as vice president in shaping the Reagan administration's policies on terrorism, Panama, and many other sensitive national security issues, he was slow to continue on Reagan's trajectory when he assumed the presidency himself, for example in allowing the momentum behind Reagan's proactive approach to counterterrorism and toward Libya to further dissipate. Bush's attention was understandably directed elsewhere as the Berlin Wall fell and democratic revolutions overtook the former Soviet empire. The end of the Cold War held a particular salience for the Gulf crisis that followed quickly on its heels, offering Bush the unique opportunity to establish a new world order based around a set of norms and rules governing international behavior. The crisis crystallized the rogue state paradigm and allowed Bush to add his own stamp to the redefinition of US national security that had begun under Reagan.

In a letter to the nation published in newspapers across the United States in November 1990, prior to the outbreak of war, Bush elaborated on the broader issues at stake in the Gulf beyond the plight of tiny Kuwait, issues that would carry far-reaching implications for the United States' role in the new era taking shape. Calling this the "first crisis of the Post Cold War era," he declared that the United States and the world "stand now at a singular moment" when the international community was "in the process of fashioning the rules that will govern the new world order beginning to emerge in the aftermath of the Cold War." "Lasting and meaningful peace must be founded upon principle," he insisted, and "Iraq cannot be rewarded for its blatant aggression." Bush emphasized Saddam Hussein's active pursuit of "the most sophisticated weapons of mass destruction known to man"—chemical, biological, and nuclear—as especially ominous threats to US national security. By demonstrating that "aggression will not be tolerated," Bush vowed, "we will have established principles for acceptable international conduct and the means to enforce them."[3]

The remarkably short and successful war that Bush oversaw accomplished both of these goals, but in so doing it set a double-edged precedent for the post–Cold War world. On one hand, the swiftness of the victory of Operation Desert Storm became a model for reversing aggression through collective international action and consensus. However, Saddam Hussein had established himself as the paragon of the rogue phenomenon, the epitome of a rogue state in the eyes of the public, the Bush administration, and the international community alike, cementing this new menace to global security into the public consciousness. Yet he remained in power, defeated but unrepentant. Bush's rejection of regime change, though made for sound strategic reasons, contradicted the earlier model he had set in removing the rogue regime of Noriega in Panama and allowed the rogue state menace to persist indefinitely. Moreover, the shock of the discovery that Saddam's WMD programs—particularly his effort to build a nuclear weapons capability—were far more advanced than Western intelligence had believed possible left the threat he posed to the world sharper in the minds of his recent adversaries than ever before. The aftermath of the Gulf War, therefore, left twin precedents to define the future of global security: the central and lasting threat of rogue states challenging the international order while seeking WMD, and the enforcement role of the United States against them.

The durability of Reagan and Bush's combined legacy in redefining US national security around the framework of rogue states became apparent when their successor, a Democrat who had campaigned against Bush's record, further cemented the concept as the central threat to the new global order. In fact, Bill Clinton was the first president to bring the term "rogue states" into the lexicon of US foreign policy, completing the evolution of the terms his predecessors had used to describe the small, notorious, eccentric band of villains who had taken the place of the Soviets as the United States' prime adversary. In 1985, Reagan had bestowed the first memorable label of "outlaw states" on what he ridiculed as "the strangest collection of misfits, loony tunes, and squalid criminals since the advent of the Third Reich."[4] Bush had warned of the unpredictable dangers posed by "renegade regimes" in his Aspen speech on the day that Saddam Hussein's tanks rolled into Kuwait in August 1990.[5] Finally, in a speech in Brussels in January 1994 to "define a new security at a time of historic change," Clinton completed the process by giving the phenomenon the name that would stick for the coming decades: "rogue states."[6] Indeed, the term became so iconic that even the Clinton administration itself could not replace it with the more benign "states of concern" when it sought to downgrade the issue at the end of President Clinton's time in office.[7]

In early 1994, around the same time as the president's "rogue states" address, the Clinton administration offered the additional option of "backlash states" in a speech and an article written by Clinton's national security advisor, Anthony Lake. Though the term did not have the staying power of its alternative, Lake's words articulated the US government's understanding of the rogue state threat more explicitly and clearly than it had ever been before. Lake focused primarily on three culprits: Iraq, Iran, and North Korea; he also included Libya and Cuba in his list of "recalcitrant and outlaw states that not only choose to remain outside the family but also assault its basic values." These "backlash states" defined their place in the world in opposition to the rules and norms of the global order that was still taking shape in the Cold War's aftermath. Their "aggressive and defiant" behavior, Lake continued, gave them a shared "siege mentality" that prompted them to seek WMD "in a misguided quest for a great equalizer to protect their regimes or advance their purposes abroad." Echoing and building upon the work of Reagan, Shultz, and Bush, Lake urged a unique enforcement role for the United States, whose status as "the sole superpower" gave it "a special responsibility for developing a strategy to neutralize, contain and, through selective pressure, perhaps eventually transform these backlash states into constructive members of the international community." While stopping short of calling for regime change, Lake drew a connection between the "containment of an outlaw empire" of the Soviet Union, which had defined US foreign relations during the Cold War, and "containing the band of outlaws we refer to as 'the backlash states,'" which would define US national security in the new era.[8] The rogue state paradigm had taken root and was here to stay.

188   CONCLUSION

What did all this mean for the future of the United States' role in the world? The euphoria in the aftermath of the Gulf War victory led many current and former government officials to advocate using this experience of coalition building and overwhelming military power as the model for future actions, just as President Bush and his team had hoped and intended. For example, Richard Haass, who had served in both the Reagan and Bush administrations, proposed in his 1997 book *The Reluctant Sheriff* that the United States should act as an "international sheriff" that would round up "posses" of other states to regulate international behavior on the model of the Gulf War coalition of 1990–1991.[9] The United States' position as the lone superpower after the Soviet Union's dissolution in 1991 made it "the indispensable nation" for solving global problems, in the memorable words of Clinton's secretary of state, Madeleine Albright, in this "unipolar moment" that gave it unprecedented freedom of action on the world stage.[10] But the shackles of the Gulf War model soon became all too apparent in the face of a host of international crises and challenges that were far less clear-cut than Saddam Hussein's blatant aggression against Kuwait—and hence less conducive to the approach of rallying broad international consensus behind overwhelming military force that the Bush administration had pioneered in the Gulf.

Had the Reagan and Bush administrations misread the future of global security by latching on to an invented or overblown threat? The experience of the 1980s and the lead-up to the Gulf crisis in 1990 reveals that Reagan, Bush, and their advisors were, in fact, reluctant and even resistant to making rogue states the United States' central enemy after the Cold War. Crises from Libyan-sponsored terrorist attacks to Noriega's escalating provocations to Saddam's unexpected invasion of his neighbor forced their hands and necessitated the crafting of new strategies to address this developing threat. Reagan and Bush proved adaptable enough to increasingly incorporate rogue regimes into their strategic calculus, but their transition from the Cold War framework to the rogue state framework for guiding US national security was an act of improvisation rather than design—and only later translated into a cohesive post–Cold War grand strategy.

Coercive diplomacy was the central strategic legacy of the Reagan and Bush years for confronting rogue states. This concept brought together the full spectrum of sources of US power to pressure rogue regimes to change their behavior and to enforce the rules governing global security that they put in jeopardy. Diplomatic initiatives—rallying allies into a coalition of multilateral support, increasing the political isolation of rogues, establishing economic sanctions and WMD inspections against their regimes, and perhaps engaging in negotiations with them—would be combined with the credible threat of military force to maximize pressure. Though not a new concept, coercive diplomacy became inextricably linked over the course of the 1980s and early 1990s with the challenge of confronting rogue states. It was the British who first demonstrated its usefulness during the Falklands War in 1982, sending a naval task force to the South Atlantic while engaging with US mediation efforts. Then, after years of stumbles, Reagan and his team developed a multifaceted, escalating counterterrorism strategy of coercive diplomacy against Libya in 1986 that incorporated political, economic, and eventually limited military means to disrupt the Qadhafi regime's sponsorship of terrorist attacks. Coercive diplomacy failed to secure a negotiated settlement with the Noriega regime in Panama in 1988 but resulted in his ouster from power when carried through the next year. Finally, the most elaborately orchestrated use of coercive diplomacy came during the Gulf crisis of 1990–1991 to reverse Iraq's invasion of Kuwait. These experiences did not leave a clear prescription for how to balance military force, negotiations, and economic sanctions when confronting rogue states. But they did elevate the concept of coercive diplomacy to the forefront of US national security strategy in dealing with this challenge.

The George W. Bush administration would draw on this legacy of coercive diplomacy as a centerpiece of its Global War on Terror following the terrorist attacks of September 11, 2001, most notably in the lead-up to the US invasion of Iraq in March 2003.[11] In this context, as in the 1980s and early 1990s, the strategy suffered from several limitations. First, for coercive diplomacy to work, the United States would need someone to negotiate with and someone to coerce. Its focus, therefore, would have to be on *states* and *regimes* rather than more nebulous non-state actors such as terrorist networks. This necessity forced Reagan to equate the international terrorist challenge in the mid-1980s with Libya, just as George W. Bush would center his attention on Iraq following the successful toppling of the Taliban regime in Afghanistan. Moreover, the demonization that accompanied the United States' approach to rogue states from the start increased the political difficulty of negotiating with such unsavory regimes, as Reagan discovered amid the uproar within and outside his administration over his negotiations to remove Noriega from power in Panama. Perhaps most critically, the coercive diplomacy strategy that the Reagan and the first Bush administrations established typically resulted in the need to resort to force, leaving open the question of whether the diplomatic side was worth undertaking. The failure of US measures short of war against rogue states during the 1980s and early 1990s contrasted sharply with the broader story of the Cold War that was unfolding at the same time, where measures short of war between the United States and the Soviet Union ultimately succeeded in bringing about a generally peaceful resolution. This contrast would become even more stark following the tragedy of 9/11.

A principal reason for the failure of the diplomatic track, in addition to the intractably bellicose behavior of the rogues themselves, was the objective of regime change that stood at the heart of the Reagan and Bush teams' approach toward rogue states. The 1989 invasion of Panama offered a clean and clear solution in bringing what both Reagan and Bush had insisted was a criminal dictator to justice. Meanwhile, the persistence of the menace posed by Saddam Hussein following the Gulf War—and the sense that he would continue his quest for WMD—helped swing a growing consensus in the US government and public behind the desirability of seeking regime change that could secure the same fate for Saddam as that faced by Noriega.[12]

The Gulf War helped to establish the new world order that Bush championed for the post–Cold War world. But already in the war's messy aftermath, with the rogue dictator clinging to power in Baghdad, hopes for clarity in the United States' mission in the new global era were beginning to dissolve in the face of a range of murkier, less clear-cut problems. With the sheer diversity of the threats of the 1990s—from nuclear proliferation and political instability to famine and civil war to ethnic cleansing—the new world order of 1990–1991 soon gave way to a new world disorder where the United States' purpose was far less certain.

A new framework for US national security was set in place, with strategies at the ready to enforce global security against outlaws, but the US government was growing increasingly unsure when and against whom to apply them in the absence of such brazen challenges to the global order as the Gulf War. US policymakers would need a new context to fully apply the strategies and principles—coercive diplomacy, preemptive action, regime change—that the Reagan and Bush administrations had pioneered.

The traumatic shock of the 9/11 terrorist attacks finally presented the context in which the United States could fully implement the strategies toward rogue states that had been taking shape since the Reagan and the first Bush presidencies. The aftermath of 9/11 offered the George W. Bush administration the opportunity to reach back to the ideas and precedents that had been forged and tested during the 1980s and early 1990s. By explicitly incorporating the definition of terrorism as an act of war, the link between terrorist attacks and rogue states, the goal of regime change, and the necessity for preemptive military action as cornerstones of their response to 9/11, George W. Bush and his national security team established the Global War on Terror, and particularly the Iraq War, as the true test case of the rogue state strategy that had been born in the final decade of the Cold War.[13]

September 11, 2001, was not a breaking point between eras in global history for which new national security strategies had to be invented from scratch, as many of the architects of the Global War on Terror have since argued. Rather, the threats that would define the post–9/11 world had already emerged over a decade earlier, and US policymakers in the 1980s and early 1990s had already crafted the outlines and the key principles of the strategies on which George W.

Bush and his team would draw. What was different about the post-9/11 world was the dramatically altered perception in the top echelons of the US government of the severity of the danger that these security threats posed—and the unprecedentedly broad alignment of support and consensus among US officials and the public behind the proactive and ambitious strategy to confront rogue states that Reagan and the first Bush had not had the chance to fully implement.

Where George H. W. Bush's decision during the Gulf War in 1991 not to seek regime change in Iraq had cemented the creation of the rogue state paradigm by leaving Saddam Hussein in place, George W. Bush's approach to the Iraq War in 2003 led to the dismantling of the rogue state paradigm by decisively toppling Saddam's regime. The first Bush's actions during the successful Gulf War cured the symptom but not the underlying disease, reversing Iraq's invasion of Kuwait while leaving the rogue dictator in place to continue menacing the global order. The second Bush, by contrast, utterly eradicated the disease itself, decapitating Saddam's rogue regime so swiftly and effectively that it left a vacuum into which tumbled the chaos and violence that the tyrant's rule had ironically held in check. In making his decision for war in 2002–2003, George W. Bush had not been willing to rely on measures such as inspections and sanctions that merely contained what he viewed as the symptom, Iraq's WMD programs. Instead, he chose to remove the source of the problem in the form of Saddam himself. The aftermath of 9/11 created the context where a major preemptive action with the explicit goal of regime change found broad currency among government officials in the administration and Congress, as well as among the public and key allies.

The legacy of the Reagan and the first Bush administrations in redefining national security around rogue states during the transition to the post–Cold War world did not make the later Bush's decision to invade Iraq inevitable. However, the strategies they established for the post-9/11 generation to draw upon encouraged George W. Bush and his team to define the United States' new challenge in terms of a familiar foe, focusing not just on non-state terrorist networks such as al Qaeda but also on state sponsors of terrorism such as Iraq. The "Global War on Terror" therefore became in many ways a "War on Rogue States." In this respect, the strategies that George W. Bush put to the test, originally conceived under Reagan and the first Bush, proved stunningly successful against Saddam Hussein's Iraq. But this success also gave rise to a host of unexpected problems that followed in the wake of regime change in Baghdad—problems of occupation and insurgency that did not fit into the rogue state framework that had driven the United States to invade Iraq in the first place. As was the case under Reagan over two decades before, what initially seemed peripheral nuisances grew into fundamental threats as the situation in Iraq deteriorated from the summer of 2003 through 2006. The security threats that emerged during the US occupation of Iraq required another period of adjustment, stumbles,

192 CONCLUSION

FIGURE 18. Between two eras: The World Trade Center's Twin Towers loom on the horizon as President-elect George Bush, President Ronald Reagan, and Soviet general secretary Mikhail Gorbachev gaze across New York Harbor during the waning days of the Cold War, December 7, 1988.

and recalibration. They forced the George W. Bush administration to develop a new framework for understanding US national security that would replace the rogue state paradigm that Reagan and the first Bush had established. The process of learning and adaptation had to begin once again.

All this lay in the future. When Ronald Reagan, George Bush, and Mikhail Gorbachev met for their summit meeting on Governors Island in New York Harbor on December 7, 1988, their rapport and partnership captured the dawning era of hope for the world emerging from the Cold War's ashes. Pictures of the three leaders along the waterfront standing in front of the Statue of Liberty symbolized this unique window of opportunity to build a new global order of freedom and peace. But when photographers asked the trio to turn to face the city skyline, they captured images with a more foreboding symbolism that would not become apparent for more than a decade. Still smiling, Reagan, Bush, and Gorbachev stood before the World Trade Center's iconic Twin Towers, ominous symbols of what lay ahead for the post–Cold War world. Standing between two eras, the three leaders had no way of knowing the tragedy that loomed on the horizon—a trauma that would put to the test the strategic foundations that Reagan and Bush had laid for this new chapter in global history.

Acknowledgments

The research and writing of this book have been the centerpiece of my formative years as a historian. Over the course of its evolution from the first seed of an idea in graduate school to a fully formed book, this project has marked the culmination of my training as a historian and the starting point for what I hope will be a full and productive career of historical inquiry and investigation. I have been enormously fortunate to have received the help and support of so many fellow scholars—mentors and colleagues alike—who have shaped the evolution of this book and my thinking as a historian.

First and foremost, I would like to give my heartfelt thanks to Will Hitchcock, who has guided my work since I first set foot on Grounds at the University of Virginia to begin my doctoral studies. His encouragement and advice have pushed me to broaden my skills as a historian, and he has played an indispensable role in helping me develop my topic, hone my arguments, and draw out the wider importance of my scholarly contributions. His belief in my abilities as a historian has driven me to do my best work and will continue to inspire me as I move on to the next stages of my career.

I am also immensely grateful to Philip Zelikow, who has sharpened my thinking as an investigator of history. From my first week at UVA, his probing questions and intellectual generosity have meant a great deal to my development as a scholar. Moreover, his unique approach to examining historical questions by identifying and reconstructing key choices has greatly influenced the trajectory of my work and the way I seek to unpack historical problems.

Special thanks also go to Brian Balogh, who has offered his generous guidance and support since the beginning of my time at UVA, going out of his way to provide helpful advice and broadening my approach to historical inquiry.

I am grateful to my academic home, the Salmon P. Chase Center for Civics, Culture, and Society at the Ohio State University, for its support as this book reached the final stages of the publication process and prepared to enter the world. Special thanks to Lee Strang, Brian Schoen, Chris Green, and the Chase Center's cohort of founding faculty for their embrace of my research and belief in its value to advance the center's mission of developing citizen leaders.

The America in the World Consortium (AWC) and the Henry A. Kissinger Center for Global Affairs at Johns Hopkins University's School of Advanced International Studies sponsored my postdoctoral fellowship that provided the time and resources to allow me to complete the book manuscript. I am grateful for the input and support for the project from Hal Brands and the interdisciplinary network of scholars that AWC and the Kissinger Center bring together. I also benefited from the support of the Ronald Reagan Institute, which organized a book workshop that provided helpful feedback to fine-tune the manuscript in its later stages.

I am deeply appreciative of my graduate alma mater, the University of Virginia, for its generous funding of my archival research through a number of fellowships and grants. Most notable were the Jefferson Fellowship through the Jefferson Scholars Foundation, which became my home base for writing throughout the COVID-19 pandemic; the Corcoran Department of History, which funded the research trips that kickstarted the project; and the National Security Policy Center in UVA's Frank Batten School of Leadership and Public Policy, which provided support to help me complete it.

At the University of Virginia, where this book truly took shape and substance, I owe a debt of thanks to many mentors, colleagues, and friends who influenced my development as a historian: Mel Leffler, whose courses, feedback, and example improved my skills as a scholar; John Owen, who served on my dissertation committee and offered valuable suggestions for refining my work's arguments and contributions; and Barbara Perry, along with the scholars and staff at the Miller Center, who always expressed enthusiasm for my work and my keen interest in studying the presidency; as well as Vivien Chang, Ian Iverson, Audrius Rickus, and the fellow members of my graduate cohort. At Columbia University and the London School of Economics, where my graduate studies began, I greatly benefited from the guidance and mentorship of Steven Casey, Anders Stephanson, and Line Lillevik. My academic journey began at Princeton University, where Sir David Cannadine and Paul Miles guided me through my initial forays into deep historical research and have continued to provide guidance in the years since.

My visits to archives including the Ronald Reagan Presidential Library, the George H. W. Bush Presidential Library, and the Hoover Institution Library and Archives were all exceptionally valuable for the research that makes up the foundation of this book. I appreciate the help of the staff at each of these archives, with special thanks to Jennifer Mandel at the Reagan Library for her thoughtful advice and guidance on each of my visits to Simi Valley.

My editor at Cornell University Press, Sarah Grossman, has expressed steady enthusiasm for the value of my research while guiding the book through the process of revision and publication. I am grateful to her and to the editorial team at Cornell for their assistance at each stage of bringing the book from manuscript to finished product. I also appreciate the generosity of Paul Gero for going above and beyond in tracking down his particularly resonant photograph of Reagan, Bush, and Gorbachev in front of the World Trade Center's Twin Towers.

Finally, I could not have completed this rewarding but arduous undertaking without the support and encouragement of my family. My parents have recognized and stoked my passion for history for as long as I can remember, and their interest in my research and my book project from its very beginning to its very end has meant the world to me. My Nana has been by my side at each step of my education, and it is such a joy to share this accomplishment with her.

Most especially, the one person who is always my bedrock of support is my wife, Brianna. From the time we met on the first day of graduate school at UVA, her patient, listening ear, loving encouragement, and shared passion for history have inspired me throughout each phase of researching and writing this book, as I know they will throughout our future together.

Notes

INTRODUCTION

1. Svetlana Savranskaya and Thomas Blanton, eds., *The Last Superpower Summits: Conversations That Ended the Cold War*, vol. 1, *Gorbachev and Reagan* (Budapest: Central European University Press, 2020), 453–461.

2. "President Reagan's Luncheon Meeting with Mikhail Gorbachev on December 7, 1988," White House Television Office (WHTV): Records, Ronald Reagan Presidential Library (RRPL), 19 min., 18 sec., https://www.youtube.com/watch?v=i7x6FtTQ4Mg.

3. Memo, John Poindexter to Ronald Reagan, "Next Steps: Libya," April 9, 1986, folder "Libya–El Dorado Canyon [6 of 10]," Box 91747, James Stark Files, RRPL.

4. The historian Hal Brands defines grand strategy as "the intellectual architecture that gives form and structure to foreign policy." Hal Brands, *What Good Is Grand Strategy? Power and Purpose in American Statecraft from Harry S. Truman to George W. Bush* (Ithaca, NY: Cornell University Press, 2014), 3. For general discussion of whether and how leaders in US and world history have framed and deployed grand strategies, see Hal Brands, ed., *The New Makers of Modern Strategy: From the Ancient World to the Digital Age* (Princeton, NJ: Princeton University Press, 2023); Brands, *What Good Is Grand Strategy?*; John Lewis Gaddis, *Strategies of Containment: A Critical Appraisal of American National Security Policy during the Cold War*, rev. ed. (New York: Oxford University Press, 2005). For a sampling of scholarship that specifically debates whether Ronald Reagan's approach to the Cold War constituted a grand strategy or improvisation, see Archie Brown, *The Human Factor: Gorbachev, Reagan, and Thatcher, and the End of the Cold War* (New York: Oxford University Press, 2020); William Inboden, *The Peacemaker: Ronald Reagan, the Cold War, and the World on the Brink* (New York: Dutton, 2022); Melvyn P. Leffler, "Ronald Reagan and the Cold War: What Mattered Most," *Texas National Security Review* 1, no. 3 (May 2018): 76–89; James Graham Wilson, "How Grand Was Reagan's Strategy, 1976–1984?" *Diplomacy and Statecraft* 18, no. 4 (December 2007): 773–803; James Graham Wilson, *The Triumph of Improvisation: Gorbachev's Adaptability, Reagan's Engagement, and the End of the Cold War* (Ithaca, NY: Cornell University Press, 2014); among other works cited in this introduction.

5. The scholar Thomas Henriksen provides a complementary definition to frame a general understanding of rogue states: "Rather than joining international society, the rogues menaced it by exporting terrorism, seeking nuclear weapons, and disrupting the peace in their respective regions." It was the nuclear threat, he continues, that "set them apart from their historical predecessors." Thomas H. Henriksen, *America and the Rogue States* (New York: Palgrave Macmillan, 2012), 21.

6. Henriksen, *America and the Rogue States*, 5–10.

7. For examples of the limited historical literature on US policy toward rogue states, see Henriksen, *America and the Rogue States*; Michael Klare, *Rogue States and Nuclear Outlaws: America's Search for a New Foreign Policy* (New York: Hill and Wang, 1995); Robert S. Litwak, *Rogue States and U.S. Foreign Policy: Containment after the Cold War* (Washington, DC: Woodrow Wilson Center Press, 2000).

For examples of historical works on terrorism and US and international counterterrorism policy over the course of the twentieth century, see Mary S. Barton, *Counterter-

ism between the Wars: An International History, 1919–1937 (New York: Oxford University Press, 2020); Christopher J. Fuller, *See It/Shoot It: The Secret History of the CIA's Lethal Drone Program* (New Haven, CT: Yale University Press, 2017); Adrian Hänni, Thomas Riegler, and Przemyslaw Gasztold, eds., *Terrorism in the Cold War: State Support in Eastern Europe and the Soviet Sphere of Influence* (London: I. B. Tauris, 2021); Adrian Hänni, Thomas Riegler, and Przemyslaw Gasztold, eds., *Terrorism in the Cold War: State Support in the West, Middle East, and Latin America* (London: I. B. Tauris, 2021); David C. Martin and John L. Walcott, *Best Laid Plans: The Inside Story of America's War against Terrorism* (New York: Harper and Row, 1988); Timothy Naftali, *Blind Spot: The Secret History of American Counterterrorism* (New York: Basic Books, 2005); National Commission on Terrorist Attacks upon the United States, *The 9/11 Commission Report: The Attack from Planning to Aftermath*, 2nd ed. (New York: W. W. Norton, 2011); David Tucker, *Skirmishes at the Edge of Empire: The United States and International Terrorism* (Westport, CT: Praeger, 1997); Silke Zoller, *To Deter and Punish: Global Collaboration against Terrorism in the 1970s* (New York: Columbia University Press, 2021).

For works specifically on the counterterrorism policies of the Reagan administration, see John Arquilla, *The Reagan Imprint: Ideas in American Foreign Policy from the Collapse of Communism to the War on Terror* (Chicago: Ivan R. Dee, 2006), 179–210; Christopher J. Fuller, "Reagan and the Evolution of US Counterterrorism," in *The Reagan Moment: America and the World in the 1980s*, ed. Jonathan R. Hunt and Simon Miles (Ithaca, NY: Cornell University Press, 2021), 64–83; Kiron K. Skinner, "The Beginning of a New U.S. Grand Strategy: Policy on Terror during the Reagan Era," in *Reagan's Legacy in a World Transformed*, ed. Jeffrey L. Chidester and Paul Kengor (Cambridge, MA: Harvard University Press, 2015), 101–123; Joseph T. Stanik, *El Dorado Canyon: Reagan's Undeclared War with Qaddafi* (Annapolis, MD: Naval Institute Press, 2003); Mattia Toaldo, *The Origins of the US War on Terror: Lebanon, Libya, and American Intervention in the Middle East* (New York: Routledge, 2013); David C. Wills, *The First War on Terrorism: Counter-Terrorism Policy during the Reagan Administration* (Lanham, MD: Rowman and Littlefield, 2003).

For works on WMD (especially nuclear) proliferation, see Arquilla, *The Reagan Imprint*, 88–111; Målfrid Braut-Hegghammer, *Unclear Physics: Why Iraq and Libya Failed to Build Nuclear Weapons* (Ithaca, NY: Cornell University Press, 2016); Francis J. Gavin, *Nuclear Statecraft: History and Strategy in America's Atomic Age* (Ithaca, NY: Cornell University Press, 2012); Jonathan R. Hunt, *The Nuclear Club: How America and the World Policed the Atom from Hiroshima to Vietnam* (Stanford, CA: Stanford University Press, 2022); Nicholas L. Miller, *Stopping the Bomb: The Sources and Effectiveness of US Nonproliferation Policy* (Ithaca, NY: Cornell University Press, 2018); Vipin Narang, *Seeking the Bomb: Strategies of Nuclear Proliferation* (Princeton, NJ: Princeton University Press, 2022); Rachel Elizabeth Whitlark, *All Options on the Table: Leaders, Preventive War, and Nuclear Proliferation* (Ithaca, NY: Cornell University Press, 2021). Gavin and Hunt argue that the communist regime in China in the 1960s can be considered the first rogue state, particularly for its successful pursuit of nuclear weapons.

8. Likewise, this book is less interested in theoretical debates over how terms related to rogue states, particularly *terrorism* and *weapons of mass destruction*, should be defined in the abstract than in examining how US policymakers and strategists viewed them at the time. Nevertheless, it is worth noting basic definitions for these two terms to help guide the reader's understanding. While defining terrorism has long posed a challenge to scholars and policymakers alike, a useful and concise definition is "the unlawful use of violence and intimidation, especially against civilians, in the pursuit of political aims" (Oxford Languages). The term "weapons of mass destruction," while used in policy circles throughout the period under examination, did not come into widespread popular usage until the early to mid-1990s. The phrase refers to three types of unconventional, high-

casualty weapons that are regulated or banned by long-standing international agreements: chemical, biological, and nuclear.

9. The three rogue states that have featured most prominently and consistently in speeches, articles, and books on the subject in the years following the end of the Cold War are Iraq, Iran, and North Korea. These three rogues most famously comprised the "axis of evil" of which President George W. Bush warned in his 2002 State of the Union address. A rotating cast of "lesser rogues," including Libya, Syria, and Cuba, among others, has shifted depending on the circumstances of the moment. See Ronald Reagan, "Remarks at the Annual Convention of the American Bar Association," July 8, 1985, American Presidency Project digital archive (APP), https://www.presidency.ucsb.edu/documents/remarks-the-annual-convention-the-american-bar-association; George W. Bush, "Address before a Joint Session of the Congress on the State of the Union," January 29, 2002, APP, https://www.presidency.ucsb.edu/documents/address-before-joint-session-the-congress-the-state-the-union-22; Henriksen, *America and the Rogue States*; Anthony Lake, "Confronting Backlash States," *Foreign Affairs* 73, no. 2 (March/April 1994): 45–55; Litwak, *Rogue States and U.S. Foreign Policy*.

10. George P. Shultz, *Turmoil and Triumph: My Years as Secretary of State* (New York: Charles Scribner's Sons, 1993), 243.

11. For works examining US policy toward Iran during the 1980s and the Iran-Iraq War, see Nigel Ashton and Bryan Gibson, eds., *The Iran-Iraq War: New International Perspectives* (London: Routledge, 2013); Paul Thomas Chamberlin, *The Cold War's Killing Fields: Rethinking the Long Peace* (New York: HarperCollins, 2018); David Crist, *The Twilight War: The Secret History of America's Thirty-Year Conflict with Iran* (New York: Penguin Press, 2012).

12. For examples of prominent works that take a "traditional" Cold War focus on US-Soviet relations as the defining feature of international affairs in the decades after World War II, see Gaddis, *Strategies of Containment*; Melvyn P. Leffler, *For the Soul of Mankind: The United States, the Soviet Union, and the Cold War* (New York: Hill and Wang, 2007); among many others.

13. See Chamberlin, *The Cold War's Killing Fields*; Niall Ferguson, Charles S. Maier, Erez Manela, and Daniel J. Sargent, eds., *The Shock of the Global: The 1970s in Perspective* (Cambridge, MA: Belknap Press of Harvard University Press, 2010); Lorenz M. Lüthi, *Cold Wars: Asia, the Middle East, Europe* (New York: Cambridge University Press, 2020); Odd Arne Westad, *The Cold War: A World History* (New York: Basic Books, 2017); Odd Arne Westad, *The Global Cold War: Third World Interventions and the Making of Our Times* (New York: Cambridge University Press, 2005).

14. George H. W. Bush, "Remarks at the Aspen Institute Symposium in Aspen, Colorado," August 2, 1990, APP, https://www.presidency.ucsb.edu/documents/remarks-the-aspen-institute-symposium-aspen-colorado.

15. Jussi M. Hanhimäki, Introduction to H-Diplo Roundtable XXIII-4 on *Engaging the Evil Empire: Washington, Moscow, and the Beginning of the End of the Cold War*, by Simon Miles (September 27, 2021), https://hdiplo.org/to/RT23-4.

16. Most books and articles on Ronald Reagan's foreign policy focus on his approach to waging the Cold War, debating whether Reagan developed a coherent Cold War strategy, what the goals of that strategy were, and which aspects of it contributed most to the transformation of US-Soviet relations in the 1980s. For examples of works arguing that Reagan maintained a consistently robust anticommunist strategy to win the Cold War based on strong defense policies, see Steven F. Hayward, *The Age of Reagan: The Conservative Counterrevolution, 1980–1989* (New York: Crown Forum, 2009); Paul Kengor, *The Crusader: Ronald Reagan and the Fall of Communism* (New York: Harper Perennial, 2006).

For works that emphasize Reagan's willingness to change course away from his hawkish policies toward engagement and negotiation with the Soviets as the more critical factor for ending the Cold War, see Beth A. Fischer, *The Reagan Reversal: Foreign Policy and the End of the Cold War* (Columbia: University of Missouri Press, 1997); Leffler, "Ronald Reagan and the Cold War"; Jack F. Matlock Jr., *Reagan and Gorbachev: How the Cold War Ended* (New York: Random House, 2004); Wilson, *The Triumph of Improvisation*.

For works that present a particularly nuanced analysis of both the confrontational and conciliatory elements of Reagan's Cold War "grand strategy," see Hal Brands, *Making the Unipolar Moment: U.S. Foreign Policy and the Rise of the Post–Cold War Order* (Ithaca, NY: Cornell University Press, 2016); Inboden, *The Peacemaker*.

Three edited volumes take a broad view of US relations with the world during the Reagan years, examining issues and regions both within and beyond the scope of the Cold War, but they do not draw out the collective impact of these emerging challenges on the approach that the United States took to the post–Cold War world. See Chidester and Kengor, *Reagan's Legacy in a World Transformed*; Bradley Lynn Coleman and Kyle Longley, eds., *Reagan and the World: Leadership and National Security, 1981–1989* (Lexington: University Press of Kentucky, 2017); Hunt and Miles, *The Reagan Moment*.

17. See Spencer D. Bakich, *The Gulf War: George H. W. Bush and American Grand Strategy in the Post–Cold War Era* (Lawrence: University Press of Kansas, 2024); Brands, *Making the Unipolar Moment*; Jeffrey A. Engel, *When the World Seemed New: George H. W. Bush and the End of the Cold War* (Boston: Houghton Mifflin Harcourt, 2017); Nuno P. Monteiro and Fritz Bartel, eds., *Before and After the Fall: World Politics and the End of the Cold War* (New York: Cambridge University Press, 2021); Daniel J. Sargent, *A Superpower Transformed: The Remaking of American Foreign Relations in the 1970s* (New York: Oxford University Press, 2015); Mary Elise Sarotte, *1989: The Struggle to Create Post–Cold War Europe* (Princeton, NJ: Princeton University Press, 2009); Kristina Spohr, *Post Wall, Post Square: Rebuilding the World after 1989* (London: William Collins, 2019); Philip Zelikow and Condoleezza Rice, *To Build a Better World: Choices to End the Cold War and Create a Global Commonwealth* (New York: Twelve, 2019).

1. BACK TO THE FUTURE

1. Warren Bass, *A Surprise Out of Zion? Case Studies in Israel's Decisions on Whether to Alert the United States to Preemptive and Preventive Strikes, from Suez to the Syrian Nuclear Reactor* (Santa Monica, CA: RAND Corporation, 2015), 27; Shlomo Nakdimon, *First Strike: The Exclusive Story of How Israel Foiled Iraq's Attempt to Get the Bomb*, trans. Peretz Kidron (New York: Summit Books, 1987), 211–212, 216–221.

2. Nakdimon, *First Strike*, 232, 235.

3. George H. W. Bush, "Remarks and an Exchange with Reporters on the Iraqi Invasion of Kuwait," August 5, 1990, American Presidency Project digital archive (APP), https://www.presidency.ucsb.edu/documents/remarks-and-exchange-with-reporters-the-iraqi-invasion-kuwait-0.

4. James Graham Wilson, *The Triumph of Improvisation: Gorbachev's Adaptability, Reagan's Engagement, and the End of the Cold War* (Ithaca, NY: Cornell University Press, 2014), 9.

5. Ronald Reagan, "Remarks at the Annual Convention of the National Association of Evangelicals in Orlando, Florida," March 8, 1983, APP, https://www.presidency.ucsb.edu/documents/remarks-the-annual-convention-the-national-association-evangelicals-orlando-florida.

6. Ronald Reagan, "The President's News Conference," January 29, 1981, APP, https://www.presidency.ucsb.edu/ documents/the-presidents-news-conference-992.

7. George C. Herring, *From Colony to Superpower: U.S. Foreign Relations since 1776*, 2nd ed., vol. 2, *The American Century and Beyond: U.S. Foreign Relations, 1893-2015* (New York: Oxford University Press, 2017), 511, 532, 561; Melvyn P. Leffler, *For the Soul of Mankind: The United States, the Soviet Union, and the Cold War* (New York: Hill and Wang, 2007), 281; Daniel J. Sargent, *A Superpower Transformed: The Remaking of American Foreign Relations in the 1970s* (New York: Oxford University Press, 2015), 11, 263, 295, 309.

8. Jimmy Carter, *Keeping Faith: Memoirs of a President* (New York: Bantam Books, 1982), 471-472; Herring, *From Colony to Superpower* (vol. 2), 557; Sargent, *A Superpower Transformed*, 288.

9. Leffler, *For the Soul of Mankind*, 334.

10. Herring, *From Colony to Superpower* (vol. 2), 553, 557, 561; Leffler, *For the Soul of Mankind*, 336; Sargent, *A Superpower Transformed*, 11, 261-262, 285, 288, 291-293.

11. Colin Dueck, *Hard Line: The Republican Party and U.S. Foreign Policy since World War II* (Princeton, NJ: Princeton University Press, 2010), 189; John Lewis Gaddis, *Strategies of Containment: A Critical Appraisal of American National Security Policy during the Cold War*, rev. ed. (New York: Oxford University Press, 2005), 349-350.

12. H. W. Brands, *Reagan: The Life* (New York: Doubleday, 2015), 246-247; Lou Cannon, *President Reagan: The Role of a Lifetime*, rev. ed. (New York: PublicAffairs, 2000), 52-59.

13. Alexander M. Haig Jr., *Caveat: Realism, Reagan, and Foreign Policy* (New York: Macmillan, 1984), 14, 26, 32, 95; Alexander M. Haig Jr. with Charles McCarry, *Inner Circles: How America Changed the World: A Memoir* (New York: Warner Books, 1992), 549-550, 553, 555; Roger Morris, *Haig: The General's Progress* (New York: Playboy Press, 1982), 373.

14. Caspar W. Weinberger with Gretchen Roberts, *In the Arena: A Memoir of the 20th Century* (Washington, DC: Regnery, 2001), 273, 275, 278, 281.

15. Stephen F. Knott and Jeffrey L. Chidester, *Presidential Profiles: The Reagan Years* (New York: Facts on File, 2005), 107.

16. Cannon, *President Reagan*, 157-158, 280, 665.

17. Brands, *Reagan*, 250-251; Cannon, *President Reagan*, 304-305; Robert M. Gates, *From the Shadows: The Ultimate Insider's Story of Five Presidents and How They Won the Cold War* (New York: Simon and Schuster, 1996), 199; Knott and Chidester, *Presidential Profiles*, 134-135; David C. Wills, *The First War on Terrorism: Counter-Terrorism Policy during the Reagan Administration* (Lanham, MD: Rowman and Littlefield, 2003), 32.

18. Philip Zelikow, "Offensive Military Options," in *New Nuclear Nations: Consequences for U.S. Policy*, ed. Robert D. Blackwill and Albert Carnesale (New York: Council on Foreign Relations Press, 1993), 169.

19. Richard V. Allen, "Reagan's Secure Line," *New York Times*, June 6, 2010.

20. Haig, *Caveat*, 182-183; Nakdimon, *First Strike*, 186.

21. Haig, *Caveat*, 184; Nakdimon, *First Strike*, 235.

22. Bass, *A Surprise Out of Zion?*, 36.

23. Letter, Menachem Begin to Ronald Reagan, transmitted within letter, Ephraim Evron to Ronald Reagan, June 8, 1981, folder "Israel [06/06/1981-06/09/1981]," RAC Box 2, Geoffrey Kemp Files, Ronald Reagan Presidential Library (RRPL).

24. Public Statement, "A Special Statement by the Government of Israel," June 8, 1981, folder "Israel [06/06/1981-06/09/1981]," RAC Box 2, Geoffrey Kemp Files, RRPL; Moshe Fuksman-Sha'al, ed., *Israel's Strike against the Iraqi Nuclear Reactor, 7 June 1981: A Collection of Articles and Lectures* (Jerusalem: Menachem Begin Heritage Center, 2003), 7, 73; Nakdimon, *First Strike*, 82, 214-215; Rachel Elizabeth Whitlark, *All Options on the Table: Leaders, Preventive War, and Nuclear Proliferation* (Ithaca, NY: Cornell University Press, 2021), 168-171.

25. Allen, "Reagan's Secure Line"; Bass, *A Surprise Out of Zion?*, 36–41; Haig, *Caveat*, 184; Nakdimon, *First Strike*, 236–237, 244–245.

26. Allen, "Reagan's Secure Line"; Bass, *A Surprise Out of Zion?*, 36–41; Haig, *Caveat*, 183–184; Nakdimon, *First Strike*, 236–237, 244–245.

27. Allen, "Reagan's Secure Line."

28. Memo, "Situation Room Checklist," June 10, 1981, folder "Iraq (Israeli Strike on Iraqi Nuclear Facility 6/8/81) [3 of 6]," Box 37, Executive Secretariat, NSC: Country File, RRPL; Fuksman-Sha'al, *Israel's Strike against the Iraqi Nuclear Reactor*, 20, 54. Shortly after the raid, former Supreme Court justice Arthur Goldberg sent Reagan a letter arguing that the Israeli action was justified as self-defense under international law because Iraq remained in a state of war with Israel. Letter, Arthur Goldberg to Ronald Reagan, June 17, 1981, folder "Israel [07/01/1981–07/23/1981]," RAC Box 2, Geoffrey Kemp Files, RRPL.

29. Fuksman-Sha'al, *Israel's Strike against the Iraqi Nuclear Reactor*, 55–56; Zelikow, "Offensive Military Options," 167.

30. Memo, Richard Allen to Ronald Reagan, "Political Strategy for Responding to Israeli Attack," June 15, 1981, folder "Israel [06/10/1981–06/30/1981]," RAC Box 2, Geoffrey Kemp Files, RRPL; Memo, Walter Stoessel to Ronald Reagan, "Political Strategy for Responding to Israeli Attack," June 15, 1981, folder "Israel [06/10/1981–06/30/1981]," RAC Box 2, Geoffrey Kemp Files, RRPL.

31. Margaret Thatcher, "House of Commons PQs," June 9, 1981, Margaret Thatcher Foundation digital archive (MTF), https://www.margaretthatcher.org/document/104661.

32. Haig, *Caveat*, 167–193; Ronald Reagan, *An American Life* (New York: Simon and Schuster, 1990), 410–416.

33. Shai Feldman, "The Bombing of Osiraq—Revisited," *International Security* 7, no. 2 (Fall 1982): 128–129; Haig, *Caveat*, 168–170; Reagan, *An American Life*, 409–411.

34. Talking Points, "Effects on U.S. Regional Policy," attached to memo, Walter Stoessel to Ronald Reagan, "Political Strategy for Responding to Israeli Attack," June 15, 1981, folder "Iraq (Israeli Strike on Iraqi Nuclear Facility 6/8/81) [2 of 6]," Box 37, Executive Secretariat, NSC: Country File, RRPL; Memo, Douglas Feith to Richard Allen, "Acting Secretary Stoessel's Memo to the President on 'Political Strategy for Responding to Israeli Attack,'" June 15, 1981, folder "Israel [06/10/1981–06/30/1981]," RAC Box 2, Geoffrey Kemp Files, RRPL; Feldman, "The Bombing of Osiraq," 128–129.

35. Cable, William Eagleton to Alexander Haig, "Meeting with Tariq Aziz," May 28, 1981, folder "Iraq 1/20/81–12/31/83 [2 of 4]," Box 37, Executive Secretariat, NSC: Country File, RRPL; Cable, William Eagleton to Alexander Haig, "Conversation with Saddam Hussain's Interpreter, Maxen Zahawi," June 11, 1981, folder "Iraq 1/20/81–12/31/83 [2 of 4]," Box 37, Executive Secretariat, NSC: Country File, RRPL; Feldman, "The Bombing of Osiraq," 129. William Eagleton, the career foreign service officer and diplomat who headed the US "interests section" in Iraq from 1980 to 1984, was the principal advocate for restoring diplomatic relations between the two countries, which had been suspended since the 1967 Six-Day War. After the raid, Eagleton went so far as to suggest that Reagan send a personal letter to Saddam Hussein to "help establish [a] rapport at the highest level." Cable, William Eagleton to Alexander Haig, "Iraqi Reaction to the UNSC Resolution and Next Steps," June 21, 1981, folder "Iraq 1/20/81–12/31/83 [2 of 4]," Box 37, Executive Secretariat, NSC: Country File, RRPL.

36. Fuksman-Sha'al, *Israel's Strike against the Iraqi Nuclear Reactor*, 15, 54.

37. Memo, Richard Allen to Ronald Reagan, "Your Meeting with the Five Arab Ambassadors," June 11, 1981, folder "Israel/Iraq—Book II (4)," Box 37, Executive Secretariat, NSC: Country File, RRPL.

38. For example, when asked at a press conference about Israel's decision not to sign the NPT or submit to IAEA inspections, Reagan admitted, "I haven't given very much thought to that particular question." Ronald Reagan, "The President's News Conference," June 16,

1981, APP, https://www.presidency.ucsb.edu/documents/the-presidents-news-conference-993.

39. Ronald Reagan Diary, June 7, 9, 10, and 11, 1981, *The Reagan Diaries*, unabridged ed., vol. 1, *January 1981–October 1985*, ed. Douglas Brinkley (New York: HarperCollins, 2009), 46–47; Memo, Richard Allen to Ronald Reagan, "Your Meeting with Israel's Ambassador Evron at 3:30 p.m. Today," June 11, 1981, folder "Israel/Iraq—Book II (4)," Box 37, Executive Secretariat, NSC: Country File, RRPL; Nakdimon, *First Strike*, 289; Reagan, *An American Life*, 410, 413.

40. Ronald Reagan Diary, June 9, 1981, *Reagan Diaries* (vol. 1), 46; Reagan, "President's News Conference," June 16, 1981, APP; Nakdimon, *First Strike*, 260.

41. Memo, Richard Allen to Ronald Reagan, "Diplomatic Background to Israeli Raid on Iraq's Nuclear Reactor," June 15, 1981, folder "Iraq (Israeli Strike on Iraqi Nuclear Facility 6/8/81) [2 of 6]," Box 37, Executive Secretariat, NSC: Country File, RRPL; Memcon, Eugene Rostow and Ephraim Evron, "Israeli Strike on Iraqi Nuclear Reactor," June 19, 1981, folder "Israel/Iraq—Book I (1)," Box 37, Executive Secretariat, NSC: Country File, RRPL; Bass, *A Surprise Out of Zion?*, 28, 33; Fuksman-Sha'al, *Israel's Strike against the Iraqi Nuclear Reactor*, 15; Nakdimon, *First Strike*, 125, 131–132, 173–175, 186–187, 263–264.

42. Cable, Samuel Lewis to Alexander Haig, "Israeli Strike on Iraqi Nuclear Facility: Background for the Decision," June 9, 1981, folder "Iraq (Israeli Strike on Iraqi Nuclear Facility 6/8/81) [1 of 6]," Box 37, Executive Secretariat, NSC: Country File, RRPL. See also the attached backlog of Lewis's reports on his dialogue with Begin on the Iraqi nuclear program from July to December 1980, as well as Nakdimon, *First Strike*, 173–174.

43. As noted previously, Haig's memoirs implicitly dispute Nakdimon's assertion in *First Strike* (186–187) that he ever discussed the Iraqi nuclear program with Begin. He states that the issue "was never discussed with the Reagan Administration." Haig, *Caveat*, 183. No written record of this meeting exists to confirm either of these accounts.

44. Ronald Reagan Diary, June 16, 1981, *Reagan Diaries* (vol. 1), 49; Cable, Alexander Haig to Samuel Lewis, "Aide Memoire on Israeli Raid," July 4, 1981, folder "Israel [06/06/1981–06/09/1981]," RAC Box 2, Geoffrey Kemp Files, RRPL; Feldman, "The Bombing of Osiraq," 131; Nakdimon, *First Strike*, 289.

45. United Nations Security Council (UNSC) Resolution 487, June 19, 1981, United Nations Digital Library (UNDL), https://digitallibrary.un.org/record/22225.

46. Memo, Walter Stoessel to Ronald Reagan, "U.S. Strategy for UN Security Council Meeting on the Israeli Raid on the Iraqi Nuclear Facility," June 12, 1981, folder "Israel/Iraq—Book I (1)," Box 37, Executive Secretariat, NSC: Country File, RRPL; Letter, Ronald Reagan to Jon Kaufman, July 15, 1981, folder "Israel [07/01/1981–07/23/1981]," RAC Box 2, Geoffrey Kemp Files, RRPL.

47. Charles Moore, *Margaret Thatcher: The Authorized Biography*, vol. 1, *Not for Turning* (London: Penguin Books, 2013), 656–662.

48. The Argentine nuclear program did not factor highly into US discussions and deliberations over how to approach the Falklands crisis. Nevertheless, several US officials did take note of the inherently dangerous combination of an aggressive state willing to flout international law and a nuclear weapons capability.

The first to express this concern was Deputy DCI Admiral Bobby Ray Inman, who fervently argued for supporting Britain on April 7, 1982, during the first senior-level meeting to discuss the crisis: "If we let the Argentines get away with aggression now using purely conventional stuff, who is to say that in ten or fifteen years down the road they won't be tempted to try it again with nukes?" *Foreign Relations of the United States, 1981–1988 (FRUS)*, vol. 13, *Conflict in the South Atlantic, 1981–1984*, ed. Alexander R. Wieland (Washington, DC: US Government Publishing Office, 2015), Document 76.

In his memoirs, Haig also expressed concern over Argentina's efforts to develop nuclear weapons: "To place such devices in the hands of a country that was willing to resort to aggression, and suffer a crushing humiliation as a result, is to change strategic perceptions in Latin America in a serious way." Haig, *Caveat*, 295.

49. As Lawrence Freedman explains in the second volume of his *Official History of the Falklands Campaign*, many other countries shared this attitude of indifference toward the Falklands crisis: "Few other governments, even amongst the most friendly, were quite sure why Britain was putting in such an effort and accepting such high risks to retake an asset with so little real value, and less sure why they should put themselves out to help." Lawrence Freedman, *The Official History of the Falklands Campaign*, vol. 2, *War and Diplomacy* (London: Routledge, 2005), 40.

50. The best succinct summary of the differences between UK and US perspectives on the stakes involved in the Falklands War is Patrick J. Garrity, "The Falklands Factor," *Claremont Review of Books* (April 24, 2013), https://claremontreviewofbooks.com/digital/the-falklands-factor.

51. Freedman, *The Official History of the Falklands Campaign* (vol. 2), 18–19; Moore, *Margaret Thatcher* (vol. 1), 687–688; Margaret Thatcher, *Margaret Thatcher: The Autobiography* (New York: Harper Perennial, 2010), 339–340. In Thatcher's own words, recounting the Falklands War in her memoirs, "Much was at stake: what we were fighting for eight thousand miles away in the South Atlantic was not only the territory and the people of the Falklands, important though they were. We were defending our honour as a nation, and principles of fundamental importance to the whole world—above all that aggressors should never succeed and that international law should prevail over the use of force." Thatcher, *Margaret Thatcher*, 339.

52. Margaret Thatcher, House of Commons Speech on the Falkland Islands, April 14, 1982, MTF, https://www.margaretthatcher.org/document/104918.

53. Moore, *Margaret Thatcher* (vol. 1), 667.

54. Margaret Thatcher, House of Commons Speech on the Falkland Islands, April 3, 1982, MTF, https://www.margaretthatcher.org/document/104910.

55. Thatcher, *Margaret Thatcher*, 353.

56. Richard Aldous, *Reagan and Thatcher: The Difficult Relationship* (London: Hutchinson, 2012), 78–80; Brands, *Reagan*, 368–369; Andrea Chiampan, "Running with the Hare, Hunting with the Hounds: The Special Relationship, Reagan's Cold War, and the Falklands Conflict," *Diplomacy and Statecraft* 24, no. 4 (December 2013): 640–660; James Cooper, "For Better and for Worse: Ronald Reagan's Relationship with Margaret Thatcher, 1981–1983," in *Reagan and the World: Leadership and National Security, 1981–1989*, ed. Bradley Lynn Coleman and Kyle Longley (Lexington: University Press of Kentucky, 2017), 134–135; Lawrence Freedman, *The Official History of the Falklands Campaign*, vol. 1, *The Origins of the Falklands War* (London: Routledge, 2005), 190–191; Jeane Kirkpatrick, "Dictatorships and Double Standards," *Commentary* 68, no. 5 (November 1979): 34–45; Louise Richardson, *When Allies Differ: Anglo-American Relations during the Suez and Falklands Crises* (New York: St. Martin's Press, 1996), 113–114.

57. Haig, *Caveat*, 266. Haig also outlined these endangered US interests in greater detail in a memo to Reagan on April 5, 1982. *FRUS* (vol. 13), Document 64.

58. Freedman, *The Official History of the Falklands Campaign* (vol. 2), 129; Haig, *Caveat*, 267–268, 271, 274; Moore, *Margaret Thatcher* (vol. 1), 689; Geoffrey Smith, *Reagan and Thatcher* (New York: W. W. Norton, 1991), 80, 85–86.

59. Moore, *Margaret Thatcher* (vol. 1), 689.

60. NSC Meeting Minutes, April 30, 1982, folder "NSC 00048 04/30/1982 [Falkland Islands]," Executive Secretariat, NSC: Meeting File, NSC 48, RRPL; *FRUS* (vol. 13), Document 195; Smith, *Reagan and Thatcher*, 92; Thatcher, *Margaret Thatcher*, 349. As recorded

in the NSC meeting minutes: "Our proposal, the Secretary [Haig] affirmed, gave Argentina a great deal." Haig "then described the elements of the American plan which in effect would give ultimate sovereignty to Argentina but under evolutionary conditions which the Islanders could ultimately accept.... Our proposals, in fact, are a camouflaged transfer of sovereignty." The self-determination of the Falkland Islanders would clearly not have been binding and sacrosanct under Haig's proposed plan.

61. Freedman, *The Official History of the Falklands Campaign* (vol. 2), 124.

62. Aldous, *Reagan and Thatcher*, 79; Richardson, *When Allies Differ*, 121–122; Smith, *Reagan and Thatcher*, 84.

63. Weinberger with Roberts, *In the Arena*, 375.

64. Aldous, *Reagan and Thatcher*, 92; Smith, *Reagan and Thatcher*, 84; Caspar W. Weinberger, *Fighting for Peace: Seven Critical Years in the Pentagon* (New York: Warner Books, 1990), 217.

65. Aldous, *Reagan and Thatcher*, 92–93; Freedman, *The Official History of the Falklands Campaign* (vol. 2), 379–380; Edward C. Keefer, *Caspar Weinberger and the U.S. Military Buildup, 1981–1985* (Washington, DC: Historical Office, Office of the Secretary of Defense, 2023), 357–367; Richardson, *When Allies Differ*, 127; Smith, *Reagan and Thatcher*, 87–88.

66. Smith, *Reagan and Thatcher*, 87, 94.

67. The Falklands Roundtable, May 15–16, 2003, Ronald Reagan Oral History Project, Presidential Oral History Program, Miller Center, University of Virginia, https://millercenter.org/the-presidency/presidential-oral-histories/ falklands-war-roundtable.

68. *FRUS* (vol. 13), Document 42.

69. Moore, *Margaret Thatcher* (vol. 1), 668.

70. Ronald Reagan, "Remarks and a Question-and-Answer Session on the Program for Economic Recovery with Editors and Broadcasters from Midwestern States," April 30, 1982, APP, https://www.presidency.ucsb.edu/ documents/remarks-and-question-and-answer-session-the-program-for-economic-recovery-with-editors-and.

71. Ronald Reagan Diary, April 6, 1982, *Reagan Diaries* (vol. 1), 122.

72. Ronald Reagan, "Question-and-Answer Session with Reporters on Domestic and Foreign Policy Issues," April 5, 1982, APP, https://www.presidency.ucsb.edu/documents/question-and-answer-session-with-reporters-domestic-and-foreign-policy-issues-5.

73. Ronald Reagan Diary, April 12, 1982, *Reagan Diaries* (vol. 1), 122; Telcon, Ronald Reagan and Leopoldo Galtieri, April 15, 1982, transmitted within cable, William Clark to Alexander Haig, April 16, 1982, folder "Falklands Crisis 1982," RAC Box 5, Dennis Blair Files, RRPL; Reagan, *An American Life*, 359.

74. Aldous, *Reagan and Thatcher*, 77; Moore, *Margaret Thatcher* (vol. 1), 689–690.

75. Memo, "Critical Issues," undated, folder "Falkland/Malvinas: NSC and State Memos, 1982 (3)," RAC Box SUB 4, Latin American Affairs Directorate, NSC: Records, RRPL. Haig's deputies at the State Department outlined the competing interests for the US government in terms that made clear their overwhelming focus on Cold War priorities: "Preserving our relationship with the UK and its role in the defense of the West; maintaining the Thatcher Government in power; nurturing our new relationship with Argentina; insulating our hemispheric policy, particularly in the Caribbean, from this crisis; and minimizing opportunities for increased Soviet influence in the region." *FRUS* (vol. 13), Document 143.

76. According to a Special National Intelligence Estimate issued on April 9, 1982, "Only a negotiated settlement achieved before hostilities, or following an extremely limited military engagement, however, is likely to leave US interests relatively unscathed. In the event of extensive armed conflict, the United States will be increasingly pressured to 'choose' between Britain and Argentina, and by extension between Latin America and the US-European alliance." *FRUS* (vol. 13), Document 87.

77. *FRUS* (vol. 13), Document 196.
78. NSC Meeting Minutes, April 30, 1982, RRPL; *FRUS* (vol. 13), Document 195.
79. Ronald Reagan Diary, April 19, 1982, *Reagan Diaries* (vol. 1), 125; Reagan, "Program for Economic Recovery," APP; Moore, *Margaret Thatcher* (vol. 1), 717–718, 724–725.
80. NSC Meeting Minutes, April 30, 1982, RRPL; *FRUS* (vol. 13), Document 195.
81. *FRUS* (vol. 13), Document 309.
82. Ronald Reagan Diary, May 3, 4, and 5–7, 1982, *Reagan Diaries* (vol. 1), 129–130.
83. Brands, *Reagan*, 374–375.
84. Ian Glover-James, "Reagan Asked Thatcher to Stop Falklands War," *Sunday Times*, March 8, 1992, MTF, https://www.margaretthatcher.org/document/110526; Moore, *Margaret Thatcher* (vol. 1), 737–738, 743; Reagan, *An American Life*, 360.
85. Ronald Reagan, "Address to Members of the British Parliament," June 8, 1982, APP, https://www.presidency.ucsb.edu/documents/address-members-the-british-parliament; Moore, *Margaret Thatcher* (vol. 1), 746–747.
86. Margaret Thatcher, "Speech to Conservative Rally at Cheltenham," July 3, 1982, MTF, https://www.margaretthatcher.org/document/104989.
87. Aldous, *Reagan and Thatcher*, 113.
88. Reagan, "Address to Parliament," APP.
89. George P. Shultz, *Turmoil and Triumph: My Years as Secretary of State* (New York: Charles Scribner's Sons, 1993), 152.
90. *FRUS* (vol. 13), Document 382.
91. Memo, Allan Myer to William Clark, "Basic Differences between Reagan Administration's National Security Strategy (NSDD-32) and Carter Administration's Strategy (PD-18 and PD-62)," October 5, 1982, folder "NSDD-32 [3 of 4]," Executive Secretariat, NSC: Records, NSDD-32, RRPL.
92. Paul Kengor, *The Crusader: Ronald Reagan and the Fall of Communism* (New York: Harper Perennial, 2006), 125–126.
93. Hal Brands, *Making the Unipolar Moment: U.S. Foreign Policy and the Rise of the Post–Cold War Order* (Ithaca, NY: Cornell University Press, 2016), 85; Hal Brands, *What Good Is Grand Strategy? Power and Purpose in American Statecraft from Harry S. Truman to George W. Bush* (Ithaca, NY: Cornell University Press, 2014), 118–119; Kengor, *The Crusader*, 125–132.
94. National Security Study Directive (NSSD) 1-82 Study, "U.S. National Security Strategy," April 1982, folder "NSDD-32 [1 of 4]," Executive Secretariat, NSC: Records, NSDD-32, RRPL.
95. National Security Decision Directive (NSDD) 32, "U.S. National Security Strategy," May 20, 1982, folder "NSDD-32 [1 of 4]," Executive Secretariat, NSC: Records, NSDD-32, RRPL.
96. NSDD-32, May 20, 1982, RRPL.
97. NSSD 1-82 Study, April 1982, RRPL.
98. NSSD 1-82 Study, April 1982, RRPL.
99. Shultz, *Turmoil and Triumph*, 155.

2. ACT OF WAR

1. Memo, Oliver North et al. to John Poindexter, "National Security Advisor: Talking Points for Congressional Leadership," April 12, 1986, folder "Libya Sensitive 1986 [1 of 7]," Box 91668, Howard Teicher Files, Ronald Reagan Presidential Library (RRPL).
2. Memo, North et al. to Poindexter, "National Security Advisor," April 12, 1986, RRPL. The name of the Libyan dictator admits of numerous spellings. "Qadhafi" was the most popular version within the Reagan administration and is thus what will be used here, except in direct quotations from written sources.

3. Ronald Reagan, "Remarks at the Annual Convention of the American Bar Association," July 8, 1985, American Presidency Project digital archive (APP), https://www.presidency.ucsb.edu/documents/remarks-the-annual-convention-the-american-bar-association.

4. Memo, John Poindexter to Ronald Reagan, "Next Steps: Libya," April 9, 1986, folder "Libya–El Dorado Canyon [6 of 10]," Box 91747, James Stark Files, RRPL.

5. Timothy Naftali, *Blind Spot: The Secret History of American Counterterrorism* (New York: Basic Books, 2005), 13, 23–24, 26, 52.

6. David Tucker, *Skirmishes at the Edge of Empire: The United States and International Terrorism* (Westport, CT: Praeger, 1997), 4, 24–25.

7. Naftali, *Blind Spot*, 19, 22–24, 37, 59, 77, 79, 107; Silke Zoller, *To Deter and Punish: Global Collaboration against Terrorism in the 1970s* (New York: Columbia University Press, 2021), 25–35, 71–74, 86–92.

8. Ronald Reagan, "Remarks at the Welcoming Ceremony for the Freed American Hostages," January 27, 1981, APP, https://www.presidency.ucsb.edu/documents/remarks-the-welcoming-ceremony-for-the-freed-american-hostages; Christopher J. Fuller, *See It/Shoot It: The Secret History of the CIA's Lethal Drone Program* (New Haven, CT: Yale University Press, 2017), 23–25; David C. Wills, *The First War on Terrorism: Counter-Terrorism Policy during the Reagan Administration* (Lanham, MD: Rowman and Littlefield, 2003), 2.

9. Fuller, *See It/Shoot It*, 25–28; Naftali, *Blind Spot*, 118–122, 166; Tucker, *Skirmishes at the Edge of Empire*, 24.

10. Ronald Reagan, *An American Life* (New York: Simon and Schuster, 1990), 458.

11. George P. Shultz, *Learning from Experience* (Stanford, CA: Hoover Institution Press, 2016), 7.

12. Report, CIA Directorate of Intelligence, "State Support for International Terrorism, 1985: An Intelligence Assessment," May 1986, folder "Terrorism [State Support for International Terrorism] 1985," RAC Box 17, Near East and South Asia Directorate, NSC: Records, RRPL; Jack Carr and James M. Scott, *Targeted: Beirut: The 1983 Marine Barracks Bombing and the Untold Origin Story of the War on Terror* (New York: Emily Bestler, 2024), 131–133; David Crist, *The Twilight War: The Secret History of America's Thirty-Year Conflict with Iran* (New York: Penguin Press, 2012), 122–138.

13. Carr and Scott, *Targeted: Beirut*, 223–224, 286–290; Crist, *The Twilight War*, 139–151; William Inboden, *The Peacemaker: Ronald Reagan, the Cold War, and the World on the Brink* (New York: Dutton, 2022), 253–256; Edward C. Keefer, *Caspar Weinberger and the U.S. Military Buildup, 1981–1985* (Washington, DC: Historical Office, Office of the Secretary of Defense, 2023), 298–305; Naftali, *Blind Spot*, 128–135, 140–141; Wills, *The First War on Terrorism*, 62–75, 82–83.

14. National Security Decision Directive (NSDD) 138, "Combatting Terrorism," April 3, 1984, The Reagan Files digital archive, https://www.thereaganfiles.com/nsdd-138.pdf; Hal Brands, *Making the Unipolar Moment: U.S. Foreign Policy and the Rise of the Post–Cold War Order* (Ithaca, NY: Cornell University Press, 2016), 250–251; Inboden, *The Peacemaker*, 273–276.

15. Caspar W. Weinberger, *Fighting for Peace: Seven Critical Years in the Pentagon* (New York: Warner Books, 1990), 154–155.

16. Reagan, *An American Life*, 463–464.

17. George P. Shultz, "Terrorism and the Modern World," October 25, 1984, folder "'Terrorism and the Modern World,' 10-25-84," Box 1969, George P. Shultz Papers, Hoover Institution Library and Archives (HILA); Philip Taubman, *In the Nation's Service: The Life and Times of George P. Shultz* (Stanford, CA: Stanford University Press, 2023), 237–250; Tucker, *Skirmishes at the Edge of Empire*, 3–4, 10, 33, 52; Wills, *The First War on Terrorism*, 27–28.

18. Reagan, "American Bar Association," APP.

19. Naftali, *Blind Spot*, 121.

20. Thomas H. Henriksen, *America and the Rogue States* (New York: Palgrave Macmillan, 2012), 147–150; Mattia Toaldo, *The Origins of the US War on Terror: Lebanon, Libya, and American Intervention in the Middle East* (New York: Routledge, 2013), 125–126, 130–131; Wills, *The First War on Terrorism*, 163–166.

21. Henriksen, *America and the Rogue States*, 150; Joseph T. Stanik, *El Dorado Canyon: Reagan's Undeclared War with Qaddafi* (Annapolis, MD: Naval Institute Press, 2003), 38–56; Toaldo, *The Origins of the US War on Terror*, 125–126, 130–131; Wills, *The First War on Terrorism*, 163–166.

22. Memo, Michael Ledeen to Robert McFarlane, "Material to Be Used in an Information Program Concerning Libya," October 27, 1981, folder "Libya 1981 [1/4]," Box 5, Geoffrey Kemp Files, RRPL; Memo, Robert Blackwill to Raymond Tanter et al., "Libyan Contingencies and U.S. Options," November 17, 1981, folder "IG on Libya, November 13, 1981," RAC Box 19, Near East and South Asia Directorate, NSC: Records, RRPL; Memo, Raymond Tanter to William Clark, "Talking Points for White House Backgrounder on Libya," March 9, 1982, folder "NSDD-27 Libya (1 of 2)," Executive Secretariat, NSC: Records, NSDD-27, RRPL.

23. Memo, "U.S. Policy toward Libya," undated, folder "NSC Meeting on Libya/Caribbean, May 15, 1981," RAC Box 19, Near East and South Asia Directorate, NSC: Records, RRPL; Memo, Ledeen to McFarlane, "Material to Be Used," October 27, 1981, RRPL; Memo, Elaine Morton, "A Public Affairs Strategy for Actions against Libya," November 13, 1981, folder "IG on Libya, November 17, 1981," RAC Box 19, Near East and South Asia Directorate, NSC: Records, RRPL.

24. Memo, Morton, "Public Affairs Strategy," November 13, 1981, RRPL; Memo, Robert McFarlane to Paul Wolfowitz et al., "Integrating Paper: Economic and Security Policy toward Libya," November 16, 1981, folder "IG on Libya, November 17, 1981," RAC Box 19, Near East and South Asia Directorate, NSC: Records, RRPL.

25. Charles Moore, *Margaret Thatcher: The Authorized Biography*, vol. 2, *Everything She Wants* (London: Penguin Books, 2015), 172–173, 504–505.

26. Reagan, "American Bar Association," APP.

27. Naftali, *Blind Spot*, 162–165, 171–174, 180; Tucker, *Skirmishes at the Edge of Empire*, 36–37.

28. Reagan, "American Bar Association," APP.

29. Naftali, *Blind Spot*, 177.

30. NSDD-179, "Task Force on Combatting Terrorism," July 20, 1985, folder "VP Task Force on Combatting Terrorism 1st Meeting with Senior Review Group—09/11/1985," Box 32, Oliver North Files, RRPL.

31. Letter, George Bush to Margaret Thatcher, September 17, 1985, folder "London Trip, 09/30/1985–10/01/1985 (1 of 3)," Box 32, Oliver North Files, RRPL.

32. Report, "Public Report of the Vice President's Task Force on Combatting Terrorism," February 1986, folder "NSDD on Vice President's Task Force (13 of 13)," Box 34, Oliver North Files, RRPL.

33. Memo, Michael Kraft and Ryan Crocker, "Terrorism: Theme Paper," December 28, 1985, folder "Terrorist Attacks—Rome/Vienna 12/27/1985 (1 of 4)," Box 48, Oliver North Files, RRPL; Memo, "Press Guidance," December 29, 1985, folder "Terrorist Attacks—Rome/Vienna 12/27/1985 (3 of 4)," Box 48, Oliver North Files, RRPL.

34. Memos, James Stark et al. to John Poindexter, "NSPG Meeting, January 6, 1986," and "Summary of Options," January 4, 1986, folder "Terrorist Targets: Libya (9)," Box 48, Oliver North Files, RRPL.

35. Agenda, "Crisis Pre-Planning Group: U.S. Response to Terrorist Attacks in Rome and Vienna," December 27, 1985, folder "Terrorist Attacks—Rome/Vienna 12/27/1985 (1 of 4)," Box 48, Oliver North Files, RRPL.

36. Memos, James Stark et al. to John Poindexter, "Background Paper on Approaches to European Governments" and "Summary of Options," January 4, 1986, folder "Terrorist Targets: Libya (9)," Box 48, Oliver North Files, RRPL.

37. Memo, "Non-Military Alternatives," December 28, 1985, folder "Terrorist Targets: Libya (6)," Box 48, Oliver North Files, RRPL; Memo, James Stark et al. to John Poindexter, "Talking Points," January 4, 1986, folder "Terrorist Targets: Libya (9)," Box 48, Oliver North Files, RRPL.

38. Public Notice, Ronald Reagan, "Continuation of Libyan Emergency [from January 7, 1986]," December 23, 1986, folder "Libya Financial (12/09/1987–09/19/1988)," RAC Box 6, Office of Counterterrorism and Narcotics, NSC: Records, RRPL.

39. Memo, John Poindexter to Ronald Reagan, "Acting against Libyan Support of International Terrorism," January 6, 1986, folder "Libya Sensitive 1986 [1 of 7]," Box 91668, Howard Teicher Files, RRPL; Memo, "Fact Sheet: Significance of U.S. Sanctions," undated, folder "Libya Sensitive 1986 [6 of 7]," Box 91668, Howard Teicher Files, RRPL; Memo, Tom Gibson to David Chew, "A Chronology of Terrorist Attacks; U.S.-Libya Relations," April 24, 1986, folder "Libya Sensitive 1986 [1 of 7]," Box 91668, Howard Teicher Files, RRPL.

40. Ronald Reagan Diary, December 29, 1985–January 3, 1986, *The Reagan Diaries*, unabridged ed., vol. 2, *November 1985–January 1989*, ed. Douglas Brinkley (New York: HarperCollins, 2009), 557.

41. Ronald Reagan Diary, December 29, 1985–January 3, 1986, *Reagan Diaries* (vol. 2), 557; Reagan, *An American Life*, 518.

42. Moore, *Margaret Thatcher* (vol. 2), 172–173, 504–505, 509.

43. Margaret Thatcher, "Press Conference for American Correspondents in London," January 10, 1986, Margaret Thatcher Foundation digital archive (MTF), https://www.margaretthatcher.org/document/106300; Richard Aldous, *Reagan and Thatcher: The Difficult Relationship* (London: Hutchinson, 2012), 206–207; Moore, *Margaret Thatcher* (vol. 2), 505.

44. Thatcher, "Press Conference," MTF; Aldous, *Reagan and Thatcher*, 206–207; Moore, *Margaret Thatcher* (vol. 2), 505.

45. Memo, Peter Sommer to John Poindexter, "Presidential Reply to Mrs. Thatcher: Libyan Sanctions," January 16, 1986, Case File 8600439, Executive Secretariat, NSC: System File, Series I: System I, RRPL; Note, unknown author to John Poindexter, January 21, 1986, Case File 8600439, Executive Secretariat, NSC: System File, Series I: System I, RRPL. Emphasis in original source.

46. Memo, John Poindexter to Ronald Reagan, "Presidential Reply to Mrs. Thatcher's Letter on Libyan Sanctions," January 16, 1986, Case File 8600439, Executive Secretariat, NSC: System File, Series I: System I, RRPL; Letter, Ronald Reagan to Margaret Thatcher, undated, Case File 8600439, Executive Secretariat, NSC: System File, Series I: System I, RRPL.

47. George P. Shultz, "Low-Intensity Warfare: The Challenge of Ambiguity," January 15, 1986, folder "'Low-Intensity Warfare,' Jan. 15, 1986," Box 1969, George P. Shultz Papers, HILA; Aldous, *Reagan and Thatcher*, 207–208; Moore, *Margaret Thatcher* (vol. 2), 506; George P. Shultz, *Turmoil and Triumph: My Years as Secretary of State* (New York: Charles Scribner's Sons, 1993), 678.

48. Richard J. Aldrich, "British Intelligence and the Anglo-American 'Special Relationship' during the Cold War," *Review of International Studies* 24, no. 3 (July 1998): 337.

49. Geoffrey Smith, *Reagan and Thatcher* (New York: W. W. Norton, 1991), 190.

50. Memo, Robert Sayre to Ronald Spiers, "Meeting with British on Terrorism," May 9, 1984, folder "Terrorism: US-British (05/01/1984–05/14/1984)," Box 14, Oliver North Files, RRPL; Memo, Oliver North to John Poindexter, "Meeting with British Representa-

tives re Combatting Terrorism," May 14, 1984, folder "Terrorism: US-British (05/01/1984–05/14/1984)," Box 14, Oliver North Files, RRPL.

51. Memo, Oliver North to John Poindexter, "Follow-on Talks with the British, June 27, 1985," June 26, 1985, folder "Terrorism: US-British (05/16/1985–06/26/1985)," Box 14, Oliver North Files, RRPL.

52. Memcon, "US-UK Bilateral Meeting on Terrorism, March 5, 1986, Washington, D.C.," March 10, 1986, folder "US-UK Meeting [March 5, 1986]," RAC Box 2, Craig Coy Files, RRPL.

53. Memo, Howard Teicher and James Stark to John Poindexter, "Meeting with the National Security Planning Group," March 12, 1986, folder "Libya Sensitive 1986 [3 of 7]," Box 91668, Howard Teicher Files, RRPL.

54. NSPG Meeting Minutes, March 14, 1986, folder "NSPG 129, 14 Mar. 1986 [Libyan Oil Strategy]," Executive Secretariat, NSC: Records, NSPG 129, RRPL.

55. Moore, *Margaret Thatcher* (vol. 2), 506–507. The attack also killed a Turkish woman and injured 150 other civilians, for a total of 232 casualties.

56. Ronald Reagan Diary, March 28–April 6, 1986, and April 7, 1986, *Reagan Diaries* (vol. 2), 586.

57. Wills, *The First War on Terrorism*, 196–197.

58. Smith, *Reagan and Thatcher*, 197.

59. Reagan, "American Bar Association," APP.

60. Ronald Reagan Diary, April 7 and 9, 1986, *Reagan Diaries* (vol. 2), 586–587.

61. Letter, Ronald Reagan to Margaret Thatcher, transmitted within cable, John Poindexter to Robert Armstrong, "Response to Libyan Terrorism," April 8, 1986, folder "Libya–El Dorado Canyon [1 of 10]," Box 91747, James Stark Files, RRPL.

62. Aldous, *Reagan and Thatcher*, 209; Moore, *Margaret Thatcher* (vol. 2), 507–508; Margaret Thatcher, *The Downing Street Years* (London: HarperCollins, 1993), 443.

63. Moore, *Margaret Thatcher* (vol. 2), 514.

64. Letter, Ronald Reagan to Margaret Thatcher, transmitted within cable, John Poindexter to Charles Powell, April 9, 1986, folder "Libya–El Dorado Canyon [1 of 10]," Box 91747, James Stark Files, RRPL; Moore, *Margaret Thatcher* (vol. 2), 508–509.

65. Memo, Poindexter to Reagan, "Next Steps: Libya," April 9, 1986, RRPL; Moore, *Margaret Thatcher* (vol. 2), 509–511; Thatcher, *The Downing Street Years*, 444.

66. Moore, *Margaret Thatcher* (vol. 2), 510–511.

67. Memcon, Arnold Raphel and John Kerr, "UK Comments on Draft Presidential Speech on Libya," April 14, 1986, folder "Libya (Fortier File) [9 of 12]," RAC Box 8, Donald Fortier Files, RRPL; Thatcher, *The Downing Street Years*, 445–446.

68. Note, Rod McDaniel to John Poindexter, April 14, 1986, folder "Libya (Fortier File) [9 of 12]," RAC Box 8, Donald Fortier Files, RRPL.

69. Ronald Reagan, "Address to the Nation on the United States Air Strike against Libya," April 14, 1986, APP, https://www.presidency.ucsb.edu/documents/address-the-nation-the-united-states-air-strike-against-libya.

70. White House Talking Points, "U.S. Action against Libyan Terrorists," April 16, 1986, folder "U.S. Action in Libya, 1986 (3/4)," Box 91747, James Stark Files, RRPL.

71. "CBS News Special Report – Attack on Libya – April 14, 1986," 31 min., 53 sec., https://www.youtube.com/watch?v=cIvc8alwQIY&t=994s; Cable, Oliver Wright to Geoffrey Howe, "Libya Crisis: Shultz/Weinberger Press Conference," April 15, 1986, MTF, https://www.margaretthatcher.org/document/149551.

72. Aldous, *Reagan and Thatcher*, 211.

73. Memo, Poindexter to Reagan, "Next Steps: Libya," April 9, 1986, RRPL.

74. Ronald Reagan Diary, April 14, 1986, *Reagan Diaries* (vol. 2), 589.

75. Reagan, "Address to Nation on Libya," APP.
76. Cable, George Shultz to US embassies around the world, "Post Libya: Addressing U.S. Relations with Arab World," April 24, 1986, folder "U.S. Action in Libya, 1986 (1/4)," Box 91747, James Stark Files, RRPL.
77. Cable, Charles Price to Ronald Reagan, April 21, 1986, folder "United Kingdom—1986—04/21/1986-04/24/1986," RAC Box 4, Peter Sommer Files, RRPL; Cable, Charles Price to George Shultz, "Libya Raid: UK Perspective Two Weeks On," April 29, 1986, folder "Post April 14 [1986] Action (2)," Box 1, Elaine Morton Files, RRPL; Aldous, *Reagan and Thatcher*, 212-213.
78. Margaret Thatcher, House of Commons Speech on the US Bombing of Libya, April 16, 1986, MTF, https://www.margaretthatcher.org/document/106363.
79. Cable, Price to Shultz, "Libya Raid," April 29, 1986, RRPL; Aldous, *Reagan and Thatcher*, 214-215; Moore, *Margaret Thatcher* (vol. 2), 518.
80. Letters, Ronald Reagan to Richard Lugar and Robert Dole, April 22, 1986, folder "United Kingdom—1986—04/21/1986-04/24/1986," RAC Box 4, Peter Sommer Files, RRPL.
81. Ronald Reagan, "Radio Address by the President to the Nation," May 31, 1986, folder "United Kingdom—1986—05/29/1986-06/02/1986," RAC Box 4, Peter Sommer Files, RRPL.
82. Memo, Peter Sommer to John Poindexter, "Your Meeting with Sir Robert Armstrong," April 2, 1986, folder "United Kingdom—1986—04/01/1986-04/20/1986," RAC Box 4, Peter Sommer Files, RRPL; Memo, Nicholas Platt to John Poindexter, "US-UK Supplementary Extradition Treaty," May 12, 1986, folder "United Kingdom—1986—04/25/1986-05/15/1986," RAC Box 4, Peter Sommer Files, RRPL; Draft Presidential Statement, "Statement on U.S.-UK Extradition Treaty," attached to memo, Oliver North and Robert Earl to John Poindexter, "Presidential Statement on the U.S.-UK Extradition Treaty," May 19, 1986, folder "United Kingdom—1986—05/16/1986-05/20/1986," RAC Box 4, Peter Sommer Files, RRPL.
83. Memcon, "President's Meeting with Prime Minister Thatcher," May 4, 1986, folder "United Kingdom Meeting on Libya/Syria—05/28/1986 (1 of 2)," Box 91750, James Stark Files, RRPL.
84. Memo, Nicholas Platt to John Poindexter, "Libyan Economic Sanctions," May 1, 1986, folder "Next Steps (1/2)," Box 91747, James Stark Files, RRPL.
85. Memo, "Public Diplomacy Action Plan: Countering Libyan Support for Terrorism," undated, folder "Terrorism—Libya Public Diplomacy (05/01/1986-05/09/1986)," Box 91721, Judyt Mandel Files, RRPL.
86. Cable, US embassy in Paris to George Shultz, "Mitterrand Advisor on Tokyo Summit, Terrorism, Libya, and the Problems of Cohabitation Foreign Policy," April 29, 1986, folder "U.S. Action in Libya, 1986 (1/4)," Box 91747, James Stark Files, RRPL.
87. Memcon, "President's Meeting with Thatcher," May 4, 1986, RRPL; Talking Points, "Private Meeting with Sir Percy Craddod and Sir Anthony Acland," May 28, 1986, folder "United Kingdom Meeting on Libya/Syria—05/28/1986 (2 of 2)," Box 91750, James Stark Files, RRPL.
88. Memo, Poindexter to Reagan, "Next Steps: Libya," April 9, 1986, RRPL.
89. Memo, "Next Steps to Deter Further Libyan Terrorism," undated, folder "Libya Sensitive 1986 [3 of 7]," Box 91668, Howard Teicher Files, RRPL; Memo, Don Fortier to John Poindexter, "Libyan Planning," April 28, 1986, folder "Libya Sensitive 1986 [7 of 7]," Box 91668, Howard Teicher Files, RRPL.
90. Memo, Graham Fuller to William Casey and Robert Gates, "A Successor to Qadhafi," April 15, 1986, folder "Libya Sensitive 1986 [3 of 7]," Box 91668, Howard Teicher Files, RRPL; Memo, CIA Directorate of Intelligence, "LIBYA: What If Qadhafi Is Ousted?" April 30, 1986, folder "Libya Sensitive 1986 [2 of 7]," Box 91668, Howard Teicher Files,

RRPL; Memo, CIA Directorate of Intelligence, "LIBYA: Qadhafi's Political Position since the Airstrike," July 17, 1986, folder "Libya (1)," Box 91095, James Stark Files, RRPL.

91. NSPG Meeting Minutes, August 14, 1986, folder "NSPG 0137, 14 Aug. 1986 (2/2)," Executive Secretariat, NSC: Records, NSPG 137, RRPL.

92. Bob Woodward, "Gadhafi Target of Secret U.S. Deception Plan," *Washington Post*, October 2, 1986, folder "NSPG 0137, 14 Aug. 1986 (2/2)," Executive Secretariat, NSC: Records, NSPG 137, RRPL; Ronald Reagan Diary, May 11 and 26, 1987, *Reagan Diaries* (vol. 2), 720, 727; Stanik, *El Dorado Canyon*, 223–226; Bob Woodward, *Veil: The Secret Wars of the CIA, 1981–1987* (New York: Simon and Schuster, 1987), 471–477.

93. Ronald Reagan Diary, August 14, 1986, *Reagan Diaries* (vol. 2), 629.

94. Shultz, *Turmoil and Triumph*, 244; Joshua Sinai, "Libya's Pursuit of Weapons of Mass Destruction," *The Nonproliferation Review* 4, no. 3 (Spring/Summer 1997): 93.

95. Ronald Reagan Diary, November 9, 1988, *Reagan Diaries* (vol. 2), 975.

96. Sinai, "Libya's Pursuit of Weapons of Mass Destruction," 92.

97. Målfrid Braut-Hegghammer, *Unclear Physics: Why Iraq and Libya Failed to Build Nuclear Weapons* (Ithaca, NY: Cornell University Press, 2016), 189–190; Sinai, "Libya's Pursuit of Weapons of Mass Destruction," 92–94. For more on Libya's failed efforts to acquire nuclear weapons, see Braut-Hegghammer, *Unclear Physics*, 127–217.

98. Reagan, *An American Life*, 704.

99. Shultz, *Turmoil and Triumph*, 244–245.

100. Ronald Reagan Diary, December 21, 1988, and January 9, 1989, *Reagan Diaries* (vol. 2), 998, 1005.

101. NSPG Meeting Minutes, May 5, 1988, Case File 8890403, Office of the Assistant to the President for National Security Affairs: Chron File, RRPL; Memo, Rozanne Ridgway to George Shultz, "Your Bilateral with Soviet Foreign Minister Shevardnadze in Paris, January 8 at 1430 Hours," with attachment "Chemical Weapons," December 30, 1988, folder "Briefing Book re: Shultz Bilateral with Soviet FM Shevardnadze, Paris CW Conference, 01/08/1989," RAC Box 2, Lisa Jameson Files, RRPL; Shultz, *Turmoil and Triumph*, 245.

102. George H. W. Bush, "The President-elect's News Conference Announcing Five Cabinet Nominations," December 22, 1988, APP, https://www.presidency.ucsb.edu/documents/the-president-elects-news-conference-announcing-five-cabinet-nominations.

103. George H. W. Bush, "Remarks and a Question-and-Answer Session with Students at James Madison High School in Vienna, Virginia," March 28, 1989, APP, https://www.presidency.ucsb.edu/documents/remarks-and-question-and-answer-session-with-students-james-madison-high-school-vienna.

104. Michael R. Gordon, "Plant Said to Make Poison Gas in Libya Is Reported on Fire," *New York Times*, March 15, 1990; George H. W. Bush, "Interview by Jim Angle of National Public Radio," March 16, 1990, APP, https://www.presidency.ucsb.edu/documents/interview-jim-angle-national-public-radio; "Libya: Mystery Blaze at Rabta," *Time*, March 26, 1990; Sinai, "Libya's Pursuit of Weapons of Mass Destruction," 94.

105. "Pan Am 103 Bombing," Federal Bureau of Investigation (FBI), accessed January 10, 2025, https://www.fbi.gov/history/famous-cases/pan-am-103-bombing; Henriksen, *America and the Rogue States*, 151; Naftali, *Blind Spot*, 202; Stanik, *El Dorado Canyon*, 232.

106. Naftali, *Blind Spot*, 203–204.

107. "Pan Am 103 Bombing," FBI; William P. Barr, *One Damn Thing after Another: Memoirs of an Attorney General* (New York: William Morrow, 2022), 108–112; Naftali, *Blind Spot*, 206–207, 211, 219–220.

108. "Pan Am 103 Bombing," FBI; Barr, *One Damn Thing after Another*, 112–114; Henriksen, *America and the Rogue States*, 151, 156; Naftali, *Blind Spot*, 220–221; Stanik, *El Dorado Canyon*, 232–236. The convicted Libyan was released from prison in 2009 when he was believed to be near death from cancer, but he lived for nearly three more years. The

FBI continued the investigation into the Lockerbie bombing and charged a third person (a former senior Libyan intelligence officer and bomb maker for the Qadhafi regime) on December 21, 2020—thirty-two years to the day after the terrorist attack. "Pan Am 103 Bombing," FBI; Press Release, "Former Senior Libyan Intelligence Officer and Bomb-Maker for the Muamar Qaddafi Regime Charged for the December 21, 1988, Bombing of Pan Am Flight 103," US Department of Justice, December 21, 2020, accessed January 10, 2025, https://www.justice.gov/opa/pr/former-senior-libyan-intelligence-officer-and-bomb-maker-muamar-qaddafi-regime-charged; Barr, *One Damn Thing after Another*, 114, 420–421.

109. Stanik, *El Dorado Canyon*, 2, 228–230.

110. Ronald Reagan Diary, January 4, 1989, *Reagan Diaries* (vol. 2), 1003. Reagan had earlier commented on the variety of spellings of the Libyan dictator's name, explaining, "I notice I use the last one I've read so this book has it a dozen ways." Ronald Reagan Diary, January 15, 1986, *Reagan Diaries* (vol. 2), 561.

111. Stanik, *El Dorado Canyon*, 231.

112. Reagan, "Radio Address," May 31, 1986, RRPL.

113. Ronald Reagan, "The President's News Conference," January 7, 1986, APP, https://www.presidency.ucsb.edu/documents/the-presidents-news-conference-961

114. Memo, CIA Directorate of Intelligence, "LIBYA: Qadhafi's Political Position since the Airstrike, Appendix C: Prospect for Libyan Terrorism," July 17, 1986, folder "Libya (1)," Box 91095, James Stark Files, RRPL.

115. Naftali, *Blind Spot*, 206–207, 219–220.

116. Memo, Howard Teicher and Rod McDaniel, "Terrorism/Libya Topics Discussed at the Summit," May 9, 1986, folder "Libya Sensitive 1986 [2 of 7]," Box 91668, Howard Teicher Files, RRPL.

117. NSPG Meeting Minutes, February 24, 1987, folder "NSPG 0146, 2/24/87 (1)," Executive Secretariat, NSC: Records, NSPG 146, RRPL.

3. THE CRIMINAL ROGUE

1. Ronald Reagan, "Remarks at the Annual Convention of the American Bar Association," July 8, 1985, American Presidency Project digital archive (APP), https://www.presidency.ucsb.edu/documents/remarks-the-annual-convention-the-american-bar-association.

2. For example, see Thomas H. Henriksen, *America and the Rogue States* (New York: Palgrave Macmillan, 2012); Michael Klare, *Rogue States and Nuclear Outlaws: America's Search for a New Foreign Policy* (New York: Hill and Wang, 1995); Robert S. Litwak, *Rogue States and U.S. Foreign Policy: Containment after the Cold War* (Washington, DC: Woodrow Wilson Center Press, 2000).

3. Reagan, "American Bar Association," APP; George H. W. Bush, "Remarks at the Aspen Institute Symposium in Aspen, Colorado," August 2, 1990, APP, https://www.presidency.ucsb.edu/documents/remarks-the-aspen-institute-symposium-aspen-colorado.

4. For example, see Hal Brands, *From Berlin to Baghdad: America's Search for Purpose in the Post–Cold War World* (Lexington: University Press of Kentucky, 2008), 41–46; Hal Brands, *Making the Unipolar Moment: U.S. Foreign Policy and the Rise of the Post–Cold War Order* (Ithaca, NY: Cornell University Press, 2016), 149–150; Jeffrey A. Engel, *When the World Seemed New: George H. W. Bush and the End of the Cold War* (Boston: Houghton Mifflin Harcourt, 2017), 250–253, 306–308; Thomas H. Henriksen, *America's Wars: Interventions, Regime Change, and Insurgencies after the Cold War* (New York: Cambridge University Press, 2022), 15–32. Even George Bush and Brent Scowcroft chose to leave the Panama crisis and military operation out of their memoir on US foreign affairs from 1989–1991: George Bush and Brent Scowcroft, *A World Transformed* (New York: Alfred A. Knopf, 1998).

5. Officials who played central roles in the Panama crisis during both the Reagan and Bush administrations included George Bush (vice president under Reagan, then president), James Baker (secretary of the treasury under Reagan, secretary of state under Bush), Colin Powell (national security advisor under Reagan, chairman of the JCS under Bush), and Mike Kozak (Reagan's chief negotiator with Noriega who remained in his post as a senior official in the State Department's Bureau of Inter-American Affairs under Bush), among others at lower levels.

6. Russell Crandall, *Gunboat Democracy: U.S. Interventions in the Dominican Republic, Grenada, and Panama* (Lanham, MD: Rowman and Littlefield, 2006), 174–179, 183–186; Engel, *When the World Seemed New*, 250–251; Peter Huchthausen, *America's Splendid Little Wars: A Short History of U.S. Engagements: From the Fall of Saigon to Baghdad* (New York: Penguin Books, 2003), 114; Herbert S. Parmet, *George Bush: The Life of a Lone Star Yankee* (New York: Scribner, 1997), 201–202; Robert A. Strong, *Character and Consequence: Foreign Policy Decisions of George H. W. Bush* (Lanham, MD: Lexington Books, 2020), 57.

7. Crandall, *Gunboat Democracy*, 187–189; Parmet, *George Bush*, 201–205; Strong, *Character and Consequence*, 50–51.

8. Memo, Charles Hill to Robert McFarlane, "Resignation of President of Panama," February 18, 1984, folder "Panama (2/16/84–4/27/84)," Box 33, Executive Secretariat, NSC: Country File, Ronald Reagan Presidential Library (RRPL); Crandall, *Gunboat Democracy*, 187–188; Parmet, *George Bush*, 201–203; Colin L. Powell with Joseph E. Persico, *My American Journey* (New York: Random House, 1995), 415; George P. Shultz, *Turmoil and Triumph: My Years as Secretary of State* (New York: Charles Scribner's Sons, 1993), 1052. Powell wrote of his first time meeting Noriega in 1983, "I immediately had the crawling sense that I was in the presence of evil.... Cold War politics sometimes made for creepy bedfellows." Powell with Persico, *My American Journey*, 415. Even Oliver North, no stranger to distasteful characters during his service on the NSC staff, commented that he felt he "just wanted to go home and take a shower" after meeting with Noriega in the early and mid-1980s. Oliver L. North with William Novak, *Under Fire: An American Story* (New York: HarperCollins, 1991), 226.

9. Crandall, *Gunboat Democracy*, 187–188; Jeane Kirkpatrick, "Dictatorships and Double Standards," *Commentary* 68, no. 5 (November 1979): 34–45; Parmet, *George Bush*, 279; Powell with Persico, *My American Journey*, 415; Louise Richardson, *When Allies Differ: Anglo-American Relations during the Suez and Falklands Crises* (New York: St. Martin's Press, 1996), 121–122; Strong, *Character and Consequence*, 52–54.

10. Brands, *From Berlin to Baghdad*, 41–42; Huchthausen, *America's Splendid Little Wars*, 116–117.

11. Crandall, *Gunboat Democracy*, 189–191; Huchthausen, *America's Splendid Little Wars*, 116–117; Strong, *Character and Consequence*, 53–54.

12. Ted Gup, "Backing Away from a Latin Dictator," *Time*, September 7, 1987, folder "National Security: Panama, September 1987," Box 759, Edwin Meese Papers, Hoover Institution Library and Archives (HILA).

13. Press Release, US Department of Justice, February 5, 1988, folder "Noriega Cases, 1988," Box 720, Edwin Meese Papers, HILA; Crandall, *Gunboat Democracy*, 191–192; Shultz, *Turmoil and Triumph*, 1052, 1063. The Justice Department unsealed and made public the indictments the next day, February 5, 1988.

14. Brands, *From Berlin to Baghdad*, 42; Crandall, *Gunboat Democracy*, 191–192.

15. Crandall, *Gunboat Democracy*, 192–193; Shultz, *Turmoil and Triumph*, 1053; Strong, *Character and Consequence*, 54–55.

16. Ronald Reagan Diary, January 23, 1987, August 4, 1987, and January 4 and 19, 1988, *The Reagan Diaries*, unabridged ed., vol. 2, *November 1985–January 1989*, ed. Douglas Brinkley (New York: HarperCollins, 2009), 680, 759, 821, 827.

17. Ronald Reagan Diary, January 4, 1988, *Reagan Diaries* (vol. 2), 821; Strong, *Character and Consequence*, 54.

18. Ronald Reagan Diary, February 10, 23, and 26, 1988, *Reagan Diaries* (vol. 2), 839, 844, 846.

19. Ronald Reagan Diary, March 10, 1988, *Reagan Diaries* (vol. 2), 851.

20. NSPG Meeting Minutes, March 10, 1988, NSPG 179: Panama, The Reagan Files digital archive, https://www.thereaganfiles.com/880310.pdf.

21. George H. W. Bush, "VP Statement on Panama," February 26, 1988, folder "PRG—Panama," OA/ID 19865-035, Samuel Watson Files, Country Files, Office of National Security Affairs, Bush Vice Presidential Records, George H. W. Bush Presidential Library (GBPL).

22. Ronald Reagan, "Statement on Economic Sanctions against Panama," March 11, 1988, APP, https://www.presidency.ucsb.edu/documents/statement-economic-sanctions-against-panama; Ronald Reagan Diary, March 11 and 13, 1988, *Reagan Diaries* (vol. 2), 852; Memo, Colin Powell, "Deployment of Marine FAST Team," March 13, 1988, folder "Memorandum for the Record (CLP)," RAC Box 1, Colin Powell Files, RRPL.

23. Crandall, *Gunboat Democracy*, 193; Shultz, *Turmoil and Triumph*, 1053; Strong, *Character and Consequence*, 55.

24. Shultz, *Turmoil and Triumph*, 1053–1054.

25. Memo, George Shultz to Ronald Reagan, "Panama," March 30, 1988, folder "Panama (2)," Box 4, Howard Baker Files, RRPL.

26. Ronald Reagan Diary, March 31, 1988, and April 7 and 8, 1988, *Reagan Diaries* (vol. 2), 863, 865; Executive Order, Ronald Reagan, "Prohibiting Certain Transactions with Respect to Panama," April 8, 1988, folder "Panama," OA/ID CF00083-005, Country Files, National Narcotics Border Interdiction System, Bush Vice Presidential Records, GBPL.

27. Ronald Reagan Diary, April 21, 1988, *Reagan Diaries* (vol. 2), 873; Shultz, *Turmoil and Triumph*, 1054–1056.

28. Shultz, *Turmoil and Triumph*, 1054–1056.

29. NSPG Meeting Minutes, March 10, 1988, Reagan Files.

30. Peter T. Kilborn, "U.S. Preparing to Relax Some Panama Sanctions," *New York Times*, April 26, 1988; Shultz, *Turmoil and Triumph*, 1054–1057.

31. Ronald Reagan Diary, April 29, 1988, *Reagan Diaries* (vol. 2), 878; Shultz, *Turmoil and Triumph*, 1056–1058.

32. President's Daily Diary, May 9 and 10, 1988, RRPL, https://www.reaganlibrary.gov/public/digitallibrary/dailydiary/1988-05.pdf; Ronald Reagan Diary, May 9 and 10, 1988, *Reagan Diaries* (vol. 2), 882–883; Shultz, *Turmoil and Triumph*, 1051, 1058.

33. Shultz, *Turmoil and Triumph*, 1058–1060.

34. Letters, E. Clay Shaw to Ronald Reagan and Benjamin Gilman et al. to Ronald Reagan, May 12, 1988, folder "Briggs/Noriega [Panama]," OA/ID 19876-003, Thomas Collamore Files, Foreign Issue Files, Office of Operations, Administration, and Staff Secretary, Bush Vice Presidential Records, GBPL; Shultz, *Turmoil and Triumph*, 1059.

35. Ronald Reagan Diary, May 13, 1988, *Reagan Diaries* (vol. 2), 885.

36. Cable, George Bush to Ronald Reagan, May 14, 1988, folder "Panama (1)," Box 4, Howard Baker Files, RRPL; Shultz, *Turmoil and Triumph*, 1061–1062. "Irangate" was an alternate name, more commonly used at the time, for what is now generally known as the Iran-Contra affair.

37. Ronald Reagan Diary, May 16, 1988, *Reagan Diaries* (vol. 2), 886; Shultz, *Turmoil and Triumph*, 1064. The minutes of the meeting record Reagan telling his advisors to "present the matter to Noriega that he was 'madder than hell.' [If Noriega] did not go through with the deal, then we would invade Panama and bring him back to trial." Closing the meeting, Reagan explained his reasoning that "this is a deal for Noriega to step down

from power, and leave his country." Short of military action, "The alternative is for him to stay in office and continue running drugs." Memo, "Meeting on Panama," May 16, 1988, folder "Panama (1)," Box 4, Howard Baker Files, RRPL.

38. Cable, Bush to Reagan, May 14, 1988, RRPL; George H. W. Bush, "Excerpts of Remarks for Vice President George Bush, Los Angeles Police Academy," May 18, 1988, folder "PRG—Panama," OA/ID 19865-035, Samuel Watson Files, Country Files, Office of National Security Affairs, Bush Vice Presidential Records, GBPL; Memo, George Bush to Ronald Reagan, "Noriega," May 18, 1988, folder "Panama (1)," Box 4, Howard Baker Files, RRPL; David Hoffman, "Bush Splits with Reagan on Handling of Noriega," *Washington Post*, May 19, 1988; Crandall, *Gunboat Democracy*, 193; Parmet, *George Bush*, 331–332; Powell with Persico, *My American Journey*, 387–388; Shultz, *Turmoil and Triumph*, 1063–1064, 1066–1067.

39. Ronald Reagan Diary, May 17 and 19, 1988, *Reagan Diaries* (vol. 2), 887–888; Hoffman, "Bush Splits with Reagan on Handling of Noriega"; Crandall, *Gunboat Democracy*, 193–194; Shultz, *Turmoil and Triumph*, 1066–1067.

40. Ronald Reagan Diary, May 20, 1988, *Reagan Diaries* (vol. 2), 888–889; Shultz, *Turmoil and Triumph*, 1067–1069.

41. Ronald Reagan Diary, May 19 and 21, 1988, *Reagan Diaries* (vol. 2), 888–889.

42. Parmet, *George Bush*, 330.

43. Powell with Persico, *My American Journey*, 387.

44. James A. Baker III with Thomas M. DeFrank, *The Politics of Diplomacy: Revolution, War, and Peace, 1989–1992* (New York: G. P. Putnam's Sons, 1995), 179–180.

45. Cable, Bush to Reagan, May 14, 1988, RRPL.

46. Shultz, *Turmoil and Triumph*, 1062–1063.

47. Ronald Reagan Diary, May 19 and 21, 1988, *Reagan Diaries* (vol. 2), 888–889.

48. Ronald Reagan Diary, May 21, 1988, *Reagan Diaries* (vol. 2), 889; Shultz, *Turmoil and Triumph*, 1067, 1070–1075.

49. Ronald Reagan Diary, May 21 and 22, 1988, *Reagan Diaries* (vol. 2), 889–890; Shultz, *Turmoil and Triumph*, 1062, 1075.

50. Ronald Reagan Diary, May 25, 1988, *Reagan Diaries* (vol. 2), 891; Shultz, *Turmoil and Triumph*, 1075–1078. Reagan was prepared to announce the terms of the negotiated settlement with Noriega in a public statement on May 25, in which he planned to emphasize that "the indictments now pending against Noriega will be dismissed when Noriega is gone from the Panama Defense Forces, and only then. Dismissal of these indictments to secure Noriega's departure promotes our policy to restore democracy in Panama and to remove the influence of drug traffickers over the Panamanian government." He never had the chance to deliver the statement. Ronald Reagan, "Presidential Statement on Panama," May 25, 1988, folder "Panama (2 of 5)," CFOA 1308, C. Dean McGrath Files, RRPL.

51. Crandall, *Gunboat Democracy*, 194.

52. Ronald Reagan Diary, July 6, 1988, *Reagan Diaries* (vol. 2), 912; Lou Cannon and Joe Pichirallo, "U.S. Covert Action Seeks to Discredit Noriega," *Washington Post*, July 28, 1988; Strong, *Character and Consequence*, 55.

53. George P. Shultz, "Terrorism and the Modern World," October 25, 1984, folder "'Terrorism and the Modern World,' 10-25-84," Box 1969, George P. Shultz Papers, HILA.

54. Brands, *From Berlin to Baghdad*, 42; Crandall, *Gunboat Democracy*, 193, 195.

55. Cannon and Pichirallo, "U.S. Covert Action Seeks to Discredit Noriega."

56. Baker with DeFrank, *The Politics of Diplomacy*, 177–178, 180.

57. Powell with Persico, *My American Journey*, 415–416. A paper prepared by the administration's interagency Policy Coordinating Committee on Panama in April 1989 reflected the same menu of options that the Reagan administration had considered and debated the year before, including waiting Noriega out, accommodating to his regime,

mounting a military operation to "remove Noriega and neutralize [the] PDF," launching a "snatch operation to seize Noriega," spurring a PDF coup against Noriega through covert operations, or using coercive diplomacy to reach a negotiated settlement that would force Noriega to relinquish power. The paper also included a discussion of whether to pursue the indictments against Noriega. Panama Policy Coordinating Committee Paper, "Strategic Alternatives" and "The Dilemma of the Indictments," April 25, 1989, folder "Panama (U.S. Policy) [1]," OA/ID 29878-018, William Pryce Files, Subject Files, NSC, Bush Presidential Records, GBPL.

58. Baker with DeFrank, *The Politics of Diplomacy*, 180.

59. Memo, George Bush to Dan Quayle et al., "Panama," undated, folder "NSC/DC 019—April 11, 1989—NSC/DC Meeting on Panama," OA/ID 90009-019, H-Files, NSC/DC Meetings Files, NSC, Bush Presidential Records, GBPL; Crandall, *Gunboat Democracy*, 195; Strong, *Character and Consequence*, 55.

60. Baker with DeFrank, *The Politics of Diplomacy*, 177–178, 180–181.

61. Baker with DeFrank, *The Politics of Diplomacy*, 182–183; Crandall, *Gunboat Democracy*, 195–196; Engel, *When the World Seemed New*, 250; Strong, *Character and Consequence*, 56.

62. George H. W. Bush, "Remarks and a Question-and-Answer Session with Reporters on the Situation in Panama," May 11, 1989, APP, https://www.presidency.ucsb.edu/documents/remarks-and-question-and-answer-session-with-reporters-the-situation-panama; Panama Policy Coordinating Committee Options Paper, "Panama Economic Sanctions," August 7, 1989, folder "NSC/DC 043—August 09, 1989—NSC/DC Meeting on Panama Economic Sanctions," OA/ID 90010-022, H-Files, NSC/DC Meetings Files, NSC, Bush Presidential Records, GBPL; Timeline, "History of Diplomatic Efforts to Resolve the Panamanian Crisis," December 19, 1989, folder "Panama," OA/ID 29878-004, William Pryce Files, Subject Files, NSC, Bush Presidential Records, GBPL; Baker with DeFrank, *The Politics of Diplomacy*, 182–183; Brands, *From Berlin to Baghdad*, 43; Crandall, *Gunboat Democracy*, 196–197; Strong, *Character and Consequence*, 56–57.

63. Baker with DeFrank, *The Politics of Diplomacy*, 184–185; Engel, *When the World Seemed New*, 251; Strong, *Character and Consequence*, 56. The Policy Coordinating Committee on Panama explained that the administration's policy rested on two points: first, the US government would not reestablish normal diplomatic relations with Panama "for so long as Noriega remains in power," and second, "We will maintain our policy of mounting pressure across the board until Noriega departs." Panama Policy Coordinating Committee Paper, "Panama under Noriega after September 1, 1989," August 28, 1989, folder "NSC/DC 047—August 30, 1989—NSC/DC Meeting on Panama," OA/ID 90010-026, H-Files, NSC/DC Meetings Files, NSC, Bush Presidential Records, GBPL.

64. Baker with DeFrank, *The Politics of Diplomacy*, 184.

65. Baker with DeFrank, *The Politics of Diplomacy*, 185; Crandall, *Gunboat Democracy*, 198; Parmet, *George Bush*, 412; Powell with Persico, *My American Journey*, 418; Strong, *Character and Consequence*, 57–58.

66. Baker with DeFrank, *The Politics of Diplomacy*, 185–186; Crandall, *Gunboat Democracy*, 197; Parmet, *George Bush*, 412; Powell with Persico, *My American Journey*, 414, 417–419; Strong, *Character and Consequence*, 56, 58.

67. Baker with DeFrank, *The Politics of Diplomacy*, 185–186; Crandall, *Gunboat Democracy*, 198; Strong, *Character and Consequence*, 58. Controversy lingers over the extent of the involvement of US forces in support of Giroldi's coup attempt, as well as President Bush's attitude toward an active US role. Baker asserts that Bush, more than any of his advisors, was "open to a U.S. role," and that consequently "U.S. troops blocked the exit from Fort Amador and the Bridge of the Americas across the canal, the action that had been requested of us." However, he also notes, "By the time we had enough information to order

U.S. troops to block a key reinforcement route, the coup had already failed." Presumably this second statement refers to a separate route from those already blocked. Baker with DeFrank, *The Politics of Diplomacy*, 185–186.

Powell, however, paints a markedly different picture. In his telling, Bush resolutely decided to keep out of the coup plot: Bush "had made up his mind. Giroldi had still said nothing about democracy. And we would not support him unless he made a commitment to restore civilian rule.... He repeated that the plotters had to express a clear intention to restore democracy 'or we don't commit.'" Powell says nothing of US forces blocking PDF reinforcement routes as Giroldi had requested. Powell with Persico, *My American Journey*, 418–419. The historian Jeffrey Engel likewise writes that US troops "never left their barracks" and that "none of the requested roadblocks went up to hinder Noriega's troops." Engel, *When the World Seemed New*, 251.

A comparison of these sources indicates the likelihood that US forces, with Bush's authorization, did in fact block the two routes that Giroldi had requested, as Baker records in detail. The administration also considered—but rejected for lack of information and for the reasons that Powell explains—further military steps that would support the coup. It was these additional, more active steps to which Bush decided not to commit. As it turned out, neither US forces nor the PDF engaged the other in combat during the coup, as the PDF found alternate routes to reach the Comandancia and rescue Noriega. Contemporaneous news reports confirm this sequence of events. Andrew Rosenthal, "Panama Crisis: Disarray Hindered White House," *New York Times*, October 8, 1989, folder "Panama," Box 1747, George P. Shultz Papers, HILA.

68. Baker with DeFrank, *The Politics of Diplomacy*, 186; Crandall, *Gunboat Democracy*, 198; Engel, *When the World Seemed New*, 251; Parmet, *George Bush*, 412–413; Powell with Persico, *My American Journey*, 418–419; Strong, *Character and Consequence*, 58.

69. Baker with DeFrank, *The Politics of Diplomacy*, 186–187; Brands, *From Berlin to Baghdad*, 43–44; Crandall, *Gunboat Democracy*, 199; Engel, *When the World Seemed New*, 251–253; Parmet, *George Bush*, 413–414; Powell with Persico, *My American Journey*, 418–420; Strong, *Character and Consequence*, 58–59.

70. Baker with DeFrank, *The Politics of Diplomacy*, 181, 187; Brands, *From Berlin to Baghdad*, 43–44; Crandall, *Gunboat Democracy*, 197–198, 200; Engel, *When the World Seemed New*, 251; Parmet, *George Bush*, 414; Powell with Persico, *My American Journey*, 416, 420–421, 426; Strong, *Character and Consequence*, 57, 59.

71. Baker with DeFrank, *The Politics of Diplomacy*, 188; Crandall, *Gunboat Democracy*, 200–201; Strong, *Character and Consequence*, 49, 59.

72. George Bush Diary, December 17, 1989, quoted in Jon Meacham, *Destiny and Power: The American Odyssey of George Herbert Walker Bush* (New York: Random House, 2015), 388; Brent Scowcroft interview, November 12–13, 1999, George H. W. Bush Oral History Project, Presidential Oral History Program, Miller Center, University of Virginia, https://millercenter.org/the-presidency/presidential-oral-histories/brent-scowcroft-oral-history-part-i; Baker with DeFrank, *The Politics of Diplomacy*, 188–189; Strong, *Character and Consequence*, 59–60, 63.

73. George H. W. Bush, "The President's News Conference in San Jose, Costa Rica," October 28, 1989, APP, https://www.presidency.ucsb.edu/documents/the-presidents-news-conference-san-jose-costa-rica; Powell with Persico, *My American Journey*, 422, 427–428, 491.

74. Baker with DeFrank, *The Politics of Diplomacy*, 189–190; Crandall, *Gunboat Democracy*, 201–202; Powell with Persico, *My American Journey*, 423–425; Strong, *Character and Consequence*, 60. Those present at the December 17 meeting reported different impressions over whether Bush had already made his final decision to authorize the invasion before the meeting began. Baker, who was personally closer to Bush than any other advisor,

wrote that he "knew the President had already decided on his course of action," and Chief of Staff John Sununu agreed. Powell, on the other hand, felt that the decision was in doubt until the end of the meeting. Likewise, Robert Gates, the deputy national security advisor, thought that Bush was responding to the immediate provocations of December 16 rather than giving a predetermined order to go ahead. Baker with DeFrank, *The Politics of Diplomacy*, 189; Strong, *Character and Consequence*, 62–64.

75. Brands, *From Berlin to Baghdad*, 45; Huchthausen, *America's Splendid Little Wars*, 119.

76. George H. W. Bush, "Address to the Nation Announcing United States Military Action in Panama," December 20, 1989, APP, https://www.presidency.ucsb.edu/documents/address-the-nation-announcing-united-states-military-action-panama.

77. Baker with DeFrank, *The Politics of Diplomacy*, 191; Powell with Persico, *My American Journey*, 430–431; Strong, *Character and Consequence*, 60–61.

78. Baker with DeFrank, *The Politics of Diplomacy*, 191–193; Brands, *From Berlin to Baghdad*, 45; Crandall, *Gunboat Democracy*, 206–207; Engel, *When the World Seemed New*, 307; Parmet, *George Bush*, 418–419; Powell with Persico, *My American Journey*, 433; Strong, *Character and Consequence*, 60–61.

79. Baker with DeFrank, *The Politics of Diplomacy*, 193–194.

4. NO GOOD DEMON

1. Ronald Reagan Diary, June 11, 1981, *The Reagan Diaries*, unabridged ed., vol. 1, *January 1981–October 1985*, ed. Douglas Brinkley (New York: HarperCollins, 2009), 47.

2. See Bruce W. Jentleson, *With Friends Like These: Reagan, Bush, and Saddam, 1982–1990* (New York: W. W. Norton, 1994); Kenneth R. Timmerman, *The Death Lobby: How the West Armed Iraq* (Boston: Houghton Mifflin, 1991).

3. Saddam Hussein's name has puzzled English-language style guides since he first became a regular subject of US news outlets. Neither "Saddam" nor "Hussein" is a surname in the Western sense; indeed, his regime outlawed Arabic surnames to promote loyalty to the state rather than to a familial tribe, and he never used his own tribal surname (al-Tikriti) while in power. To complicate matters further, "Saddam," meaning "one who confronts," may have been more of a self-bestowed title than a given name, though sources disagree as to when or whether he adopted this moniker himself. US officials, most notably Presidents George H. W. Bush and George W. Bush, referred to the Iraqi dictator as "Saddam," prompting some observers to wonder whether this was a subtle show of disrespect. Many news outlets, including the *New York Times*, referred to him as "Mr. Hussein" to avoid this criticism, though "Hussein" was not his surname. Since the Iraqi leader was known universally throughout Iraq and the Middle East as simply "Saddam" (a choice that he endorsed and encouraged), this is the most logical way to refer to him here. For further discussion, see "What's the Name of Saddam Hussein?" *Slate*, November 16, 1998, https://slate.com/news-and-politics/1998/11/what-s-the-name-of-saddam-hussein.html; Brian Whitaker, "Saddam Who?" *Guardian*, September 22, 2000, https://www.theguardian.com/world/2000/sep/22/israel; Blair Shewchuk, "Saddam or Mr. Hussein?" CBC News Online, February 2003, https://www.cbc.ca/news2/indepth/words/saddam_hussein.html.

4. Hal Brands, *Making the Unipolar Moment: U.S. Foreign Policy and the Rise of the Post–Cold War Order* (Ithaca, NY: Cornell University Press, 2016), 235–236; Lawrence Freedman, *A Choice of Enemies: America Confronts the Middle East* (New York: PublicAffairs, 2008), 152, 154–155; Peter L. Hahn, *Missions Accomplished? The United States and Iraq since World War I* (New York: Oxford University Press, 2012), 60, 70–73; Thomas H. Henriksen, *America and the Rogue States* (New York: Palgrave Macmillan, 2012), 32.

5. Freedman, *A Choice of Enemies*, 156–157; Hahn, *Missions Accomplished?*, 72, 76.

6. George P. Shultz, *Turmoil and Triumph: My Years as Secretary of State* (New York: Charles Scribner's Sons, 1993), 236.

7. Memo, Charles Hill to Robert McFarlane, "DOD Concept Paper: Contingency Planning for Escalation in the Iran-Iraq War," June 12, 1984, folder "NSDD-141 Responding to Escalation in the Iran-Iraq War (1 of 8)," Executive Secretariat, NSC: Records, NSDD-141, Ronald Reagan Presidential Library (RRPL).

8. Memo, Frank Carlucci to George Shultz et al., "Operation Staunch," February 26, 1987, folder "NSPG 0144, 12 Feb. 1987," Executive Secretariat, NSC: Records, NSPG 144, RRPL; Brands, *Making the Unipolar Moment*, 237; Shultz, *Turmoil and Triumph*, 236–237; Joseph Stieb, *The Regime Change Consensus: Iraq in American Politics, 1990–2003* (New York: Cambridge University Press, 2021), 17. The United States partly undermined its own policy in Operation Staunch by covertly selling arms to Iran from 1985 to 1986 in what became known as the Iran-Contra affair.

9. Brands, *Making the Unipolar Moment*, 236–237; Paul Thomas Chamberlin, *The Cold War's Killing Fields: Rethinking the Long Peace* (New York: HarperCollins, 2018), 518–520; Hahn, *Missions Accomplished?*, 77; Henriksen, *America and the Rogue States*, 32–33. In fact, some officials in the administration, such as Paul Wolfowitz of the State Department, felt the situation was so dire in mid-1982 that the United States could no longer count on Iraq to be "an effective shield against Iran." Wolfowitz argued that "only we . . . can be such a shield" and the United States should therefore take a more direct role in protecting the moderate Arab states in the Gulf region against Iranian expansion. Memo, Paul Wolfowitz to Alexander Haig, "Thoughts on the Iraq-Iran Conflict Memo," May 5, 1982, folder "Iran/Iraq, Jan.–Jun. 1982," Box 2, Geoffrey Kemp Files, RRPL.

10. Memo, CIA Directorate of Intelligence, "Possible Outcomes and Implications of the Iran-Iraq War," May 17, 1982, folder "Iran/Iraq, Jan.–Jun. 1982," Box 2, Geoffrey Kemp Files, RRPL.

11. Memo, William Clark to Ronald Reagan, "An Iranian Invasion of Iraq: Considerations for US Policy," undated, folder "Iran/Iraq, Jan.–Jun. 1982," Box 2, Geoffrey Kemp Files, RRPL.

12. Karen DeYoung, *Soldier: The Life of Colin Powell* (New York: Alfred A. Knopf, 2006), 192.

13. Shultz, *Turmoil and Triumph*, 237.

14. Memo, CIA, "Possible Outcomes," May 17, 1982, RRPL; Memo, Clark to Reagan, "Iranian Invasion," undated, RRPL. The CIA repeated these concerns in early 1984, when momentum on the battlefield again shifted in favor of Iran: "If Iraqi forces suffer a major defeat, the consequences could be dire. . . . [This outcome] could trigger a series of events possibly leading to the overthrow of Iraqi President Saddam Husayn and his replacement by a fundamentalist Shia regime controlled by Tehran. . . . A radical Shia regime in Baghdad would have profound implications for the political equilibrium in much of the Middle East and would threaten US interests in the region." Memo, CIA, "Iran-Iraq: Consequences of an Iranian Breakthrough at Al Basrah," March 23, 1984, folder "Iran-Iraq War, 1983–4/31/84 (2)," RAC Box 36, Executive Secretariat, NSC: Country File, RRPL.

15. Memo, Geoffrey Kemp to Robert McFarlane, "Talking Points for Meeting with Ambassador Eagleton," January 30, 1984, folder "Iraq (January–March 1984)," RAC Box 37, Executive Secretariat, NSC: Country File, RRPL; National Security Decision Directive (NSDD) 139, "Measures to Improve U.S. Posture and Readiness to Respond to Developments in the Iran-Iraq War," April 5, 1984, folder "NSDD-139 Measures to Improve U.S. Posture and Response to Developments in the Iran-Iraq War (2 of 3)," Executive Secretariat, NSC: Records, NSDD-139, RRPL.

16. Donald Rumsfeld, *Known and Unknown: A Memoir* (New York: Sentinel, 2011), 4.

17. Shultz, *Turmoil and Triumph*, 235.

18. Brands, *Making the Unipolar Moment*, 237–238; Hahn, *Missions Accomplished?*, 77–78; Henriksen, *America and the Rogue States*, 33. Both Shultz and the NSC staff supported the resumption of diplomatic relations with Iraq, despite their recognition of "Iraq's support for terrorism and use of chemical agents in the war." They argued that "upgrading diplomatic relations does not imply approval of Iraqi policy, merely that full diplomatic contacts make resolving problems between Iraq and the U.S. easier." Memo, Geoffrey Kemp to Robert McFarlane, "Iraqi Minister's Request to Call on the President to Announce Resumption of Relations," September 26, 1984, folder "Iraq (April–September 1984)," RAC Box 37, Executive Secretariat, NSC: Country File, RRPL.

19. Brands, *Making the Unipolar Moment*, 267–268; Hahn, *Missions Accomplished?*, 79–80; Henriksen, *America and the Rogue States*, 73.

20. Caspar W. Weinberger, *Fighting for Peace: Seven Critical Years in the Pentagon* (New York: Warner Books, 1990), 388–391.

21. Memo, Robert Oakley to Frank Carlucci, "Engaging the Allies on Persian Gulf Security," June 2, 1987, folder "Persian Gulf 1987 (01/01/1987–06/04/1987)," RAC Box 14, Near East and South Asia Directorate, NSC: Records, RRPL.

22. Shultz, *Turmoil and Triumph*, 926.

23. NSPG Meeting Minutes, February 12, 1987, folder "NSPG 0144, 12 Feb. 1987," Executive Secretariat, NSC: Records, NSPG 144, RRPL; NSPG Meeting Minutes, May 18, 1987, folder "NSPG 0152, 18 May 1987," Executive Secretariat, NSC: Records, NSPG 152, RRPL; Brands, *Making the Unipolar Moment*, 268; Hahn, *Missions Accomplished?*, 79–80, 82; Henriksen, *America and the Rogue States*, 73; Stephen F. Knott and Jeffrey L. Chidester, *Presidential Profiles: The Reagan Years* (New York: Facts on File, 2005), 79.

24. Letter, Saddam Hussein to Ronald Reagan, undated, folder 'Iraq, 1987–1988 (1 of 2)," RAC Box 1, William Burns Files, RRPL; Shultz, *Turmoil and Triumph*, 927; Weinberger, *Fighting for Peace*, 403.

25. Shultz, *Turmoil and Triumph*, 927.

26. NSPG Meeting Minutes, May 18, 1987, RRPL; Memo, Robert Oakley to Frank Carlucci, "Saddam Hussein's Message to Families of USS Stark Victims," May 21, 1987, folder "Iraq, 1987–1988 (1 of 2)," RAC Box 1, William Burns Files, RRPL; Weinberger, *Fighting for Peace*, 403.

27. NSPG Meeting Minutes, May 18, 1987, RRPL; Letter, George Shultz to George Bush, May 20, 1987, folder "Persian Gulf 1987 (01/01/1987–06/04/1987)," RAC Box 14, Near East and South Asia Directorate, NSC: Records, RRPL; Memo, Richard Murphy to George Shultz, "USS *Stark*: Results of the Joint Investigation Group's Sessions in Baghdad," June 1, 1987, folder "Persian Gulf 1987 (01/01/1987–06/04/1987)," RAC Box 14, Near East and South Asia Directorate, NSC: Records, RRPL; Shultz, *Turmoil and Triumph*, 243.

28. Ronald Reagan Diary, February 23, 1988, *The Reagan Diaries*, unabridged ed., vol. 2, *November 1985–January 1989*, ed. Douglas Brinkley (New York: HarperCollins, 2009), 844.

29. Memcon, Colin Powell and Tariq Aziz et al., December 6, 1987 folder "Iraq, 1987–1988 (1 of 2)," RAC Box 1, William Burns Files, RRPL; Letter, Colin Powell to Jack Davis, March 8, 1988, folder "Iraq, 1987–1988 (2 of 2)," RAC Box 1, William Burns Files, RRPL.

30. Shultz, *Turmoil and Triumph*, 238.

31. Report, Defense Intelligence Agency, "The Iran-Iraq War: A Reference Aid," September 1988, folder "Gulf War (1 of 2)," RAC Box 3, William Burns Files, RRPL; Brands, *Making the Unipolar Moment*, 241; Freedman, *A Choice of Enemies*, 152–163; Henriksen, *America and the Rogue States*, 33. A report issued by the Defense Intelligence Agency in September 1988 noted that Iraq's first major use of chemical weapons occurred in July 1982 and recurred regularly and with more lethal effect beginning in late 1983.

32. Memo and Press Statement, Charles Hill to Robert McFarlane, "Press Statement on Iraqi Use of Chemical Weapons," March 5, 1984, folder "Iraq (January–March 1984)," RAC Box 37, Executive Secretariat, NSC: Country File, RRPL; Cable, William Eagleton to George Shultz, "Iraqi Production of Chemical Weapons: Third Conversation with FRG Ambassador," April 3, 1984, folder "Iraq (April–September 1984)," RAC Box 37, Executive Secretariat, NSC: Country File, RRPL; Shultz, *Turmoil and Triumph*, 238–239.

33. Interagency Intelligence Memo, CIA, "Impact and Implications of Chemical Weapons Use in the Iran-Iraq War," April 1988, FOIA, CIA CREST digital archive.

34. David G. Newton interview, November 1, 2005, Foreign Affairs Oral History Project, Association for Diplomatic Studies and Training. Aziz also ominously asserted that "if we had nuclear weapons we'd use those too."

35. Cable, George Shultz to US embassy in Jordan, "Chemical Weapons: Meeting with Iraqi Chargé," April 6, 1984, Electronic Briefing Book no. 82, Document 54, National Security Archive; Brands, *Making the Unipolar Moment*, 241–242; Freedman, *A Choice of Enemies*, 163–164.

36. Shultz, *Turmoil and Triumph*, 243.

37. Shultz, *Turmoil and Triumph*, 240–241.

38. Ronald Reagan Diary, April 27, 1988, and July 28, 1988, *Reagan Diaries* (vol. 2), 876, 923.

39. Shultz, *Turmoil and Triumph*, 241.

40. Brands, *Making the Unipolar Moment*, 269; Chamberlin, *The Cold War's Killing Fields*, 534; Shultz, *Turmoil and Triumph*, 932–935.

41. Brands, *Making the Unipolar Moment*, 270–271; Freedman, *A Choice of Enemies*, 213–214.

42. Memo, William Burns to John Negroponte, "CIA Analysis on Impact of US Economic Sanctions on Iraq," September 23, 1988, folder "Iraq, 1987–1988 (2 of 2)," RAC Box 1, William Burns Files, RRPL; Statement of Administration Policy, "H.R. 5337—To Provide for the Imposition of Sanctions on Iraq," September 26, 1988, folder "Iraqi Sanctions," Box CF1321, Economic Policy Council: Records, RRPL; Letter, J. Edward Fox to Dante Fascell, September 30, 1988, folder "Iraqi Sanctions," Box CF1321, Economic Policy Council: Records, RRPL; Hahn, *Missions Accomplished?*, 80–81; Bruce W. Jentleson, "Iraq: The Failure of a Strategy," in *Reversing Relations with Former Adversaries: U.S. Foreign Policy after the Cold War*, ed. C. Richard Nelson and Kenneth Weisbrode (Gainesville: University Press of Florida, 1998), 133–134, 137; Zachary Karabell and Philip D. Zelikow, "Iraq, 1988–1990: Unexpectedly Heading toward War," in *Dealing with Dictators: Dilemmas of U.S. Diplomacy and Intelligence Analysis, 1945–1990*, ed. Ernest R. May and Philip D. Zelikow (Cambridge, MA: MIT Press, 2006), 170–171; Shultz, *Turmoil and Triumph*, 241–242.

43. Report, State Department Bureau of Intelligence and Research, "INR Estimate: Iran after the War," September 1988, folder "Iran [1987–1988] (5 of 5)," RAC Box 1, William Burns Files, RRPL.

44. Memo, Richard Murphy, Alan Larson, and Richard Schifter to George Shultz, "Export-Import Financing for Iraq," December 29, 1988, collection "Iraqgate: Saddam Hussein, U.S. Policy, and the Prelude to the Persian Gulf War, 1980–1994," Digital National Security Archive (DNSA); Brands, *Making the Unipolar Moment*, 271.

45. Shultz, *Turmoil and Triumph*, 243.

46. Memo, Murphy, Larson, and Schifter to Shultz, "Export-Import Financing," December 29, 1988, DNSA; James A. Baker III with Thomas M. DeFrank, *The Politics of Diplomacy: Revolution, War, and Peace, 1989–1992* (New York: G. P. Putnam's Sons, 1995), 262; Shultz, *Turmoil and Triumph*, 243.

47. Elaine Sciolino with Michael Wines, "Bush's Greatest Glory Fades as Questions on Iraq Persist," *New York Times*, June 27, 1992; Jentleson, "Iraq," 137–138; Karabell and Zelikow, "Iraq, 1988–1990," 171–172; Shultz, *Turmoil and Triumph*, 243.

48. Ronald Reagan, *An American Life* (New York: Simon and Schuster, 1990), 704.

49. George Bush and Brent Scowcroft, *A World Transformed* (New York: Alfred A. Knopf, 1998), 305.

50. Bush and Scowcroft, *A World Transformed*, 305.

51. Baker with DeFrank, *The Politics of Diplomacy*, 263; Karabell and Zelikow, "Iraq, 1988–1990," 173.

52. Dick Cheney with Liz Cheney, *In My Time: A Personal and Political Memoir* (New York: Threshold Editions, 2011), 181.

53. Cable, Lawrence Eagleburger to US embassies in the Middle East and Europe, "Reaffirmation of U.S. Persian Gulf Policy," February 11, 1990, folder "Iraq Pre 8/2/90 [1]," OA/ID CF01937-001, Richard Haass Files, Working Files, NSC, Bush Presidential Records, George H. W. Bush Presidential Library (GBPL).

54. Karabell and Zelikow, "Iraq, 1988–1990," 175.

55. National Security Directive (NSD) 26, "U.S. Policy toward the Persian Gulf," October 2, 1989, folder "Iraq Pre 8/2/90 [1]," OA/ID CF01937-001, Richard Haass Files, Working Files, NSC, Bush Presidential Records, GBPL.

56. Baker with DeFrank, *The Politics of Diplomacy*, 262–263; Karabell and Zelikow, "Iraq, 1988–1990," 173, 176–177.

57. Baker with DeFrank, *The Politics of Diplomacy*, 264; Bush and Scowcroft, *A World Transformed*, 305.

58. Baker with DeFrank, *The Politics of Diplomacy*, 261–262; Bush and Scowcroft, *A World Transformed* 306; Karabell and Zelikow, "Iraq, 1988–1990," 175–176. The administration's complacent assessment of Saddam's intentions was reinforced by a National Intelligence Estimate (NIE) on Iraq, prepared by the CIA and circulated in the fall of 1989. The NIE argued that he would generally behave rationally and predictably, and that despite his penchant for saber-rattling he would focus on economic reconstruction rather than external expansionism for the next several years. This assessment "reflected the general view among U.S. government experts on Iraq." Karabell and Zelikow, "Iraq, 1988–1990," 185–187.

59. Baker with DeFrank, *The Politics of Diplomacy*, 263; Bush and Scowcroft, *A World Transformed*, 306; Karabell and Zelikow, "Iraq, 1988–1990," 178.

60. Memo, Nicholas Rostow to Brent Scowcroft, "Iraq, Agriculture Department Guaranties, and the BNL Bank Fraud Case," May 21, 1990, folder "Desert Shield/Desert Storm (May 1990) [2]," OA/ID 91143-004, Desert Shield/Desert Storm Files, Chron Files, Brent Scowcroft Collection, Bush Presidential Records, GBPL; Baker with DeFrank, *The Politics of Diplomacy*, 265; Karabell and Zelikow, "Iraq, 1988–1990," 179–180.

61. Baker with DeFrank, *The Politics of Diplomacy*, 266–267; Bush and Scowcroft, *A World Transformed*, 306; Karabell and Zelikow, "Iraq, 1988–1990," 181, 183–185.

62. Baker with DeFrank, *The Politics of Diplomacy*, 262; Brands, *Making the Unipolar Moment*, 271; Karabell and Zelikow, "Iraq, 1988–1990," 167, 185–187.

63. Brands, *Making the Unipolar Moment*, 270, 299.

64. Letter, Bob Dole to George Bush, April 17, 1990, folder "Desert Shield/Desert Storm (May 1990) [1]," OA/ID 91143-003, Desert Shield/Desert Storm Files, Chron Files, Brent Scowcroft Collection, Bush Presidential Records, GBPL; Cable, April Glaspie to James Baker, "Saddam's National Day Speech: Warning to OPEC Over-Producers," July 18, 1990, folder "Iraq Pre 8/2/90 [3]," OA/ID CF01937-003, Richard Haass Files, Working Files, NSC, Bush Presidential Records, GBPL; Baker with DeFrank, *The Politics of Diplomacy*, 265–266; Brands, *Making the Unipolar Moment*, 271–272, 299–300.

65. Baker with DeFrank, *The Politics of Diplomacy*, 267; Bush and Scowcroft, *A World Transformed*, 307; Karabell and Zelikow, "Iraq, 1988–1990," 187, 189–190.

66. Baker with DeFrank, *The Politics of Diplomacy*, 267–268; Bush and Scowcroft, *A World Transformed*, 306–307; Karabell and Zelikow, "Iraq, 1988–1990," 189–190.

67. Bush and Scowcroft, *A World Transformed*, 307.

68. Memo, Peter Rodman to Brent Scowcroft, "Iraq," April 5, 1990, folder "Desert Shield/Desert Storm (April 1990)," OA/ID 91143-002, Desert Shield/Desert Storm Files, Chron Files, Brent Scowcroft Collection, Bush Presidential Records, GBPL.

69. Baker with DeFrank, *The Politics of Diplomacy*, 267–269.

70. Letter, George Bush to Hosni Mubarak, May 14, 1990, folder "Desert Shield/Desert Storm (May 1990) [2]," OA/ID 91143-004, Desert Shield/Desert Storm Files, Chron Files, Brent Scowcroft Collection, Bush Presidential Records, GBPL; Letter, Brent Scowcroft to Bob Dole, May 22, 1990, folder "Desert Shield/Desert Storm (May 1990) [1]," OA/ID 91143-003, Desert Shield/Desert Storm Files, Chron Files, Brent Scowcroft Collection, Bush Presidential Records, GBPL; Baker with DeFrank, *The Politics of Diplomacy*, 269–270; Bush and Scowcroft, *A World Transformed*, 306; Karabell and Zelikow, "Iraq, 1988–1990," 191–192.

71. Memo, Brent Scowcroft to George Bush, "Response to Mr. Niedermeyer on the Status of the Iraqi CCC Program," June 4, 1990, folder "Desert Shield/Desert Storm (May 1990) [2]," OA/ID 91143-004, Desert Shield/Desert Storm Files, Chron Files, Brent Scowcroft Collection, Bush Presidential Records, GBPL; Baker with DeFrank, *The Politics of Diplomacy*, 270–271; Bush and Scowcroft, *A World Transformed*, 307; Karabell and Zelikow, "Iraq, 1988–1990," 191–197.

72. Baker with DeFrank, *The Politics of Diplomacy*, 267–268, 270; Karabell and Zelikow, "Iraq, 1988–1990," 192.

73. Letter, H. James Saxton to George Bush, April 12, 1990, folder "Desert Shield/Desert Storm (May 1990) [1]," OA/ID 91143-003, Desert Shield/Desert Storm Files, Chron Files, Brent Scowcroft Collection, Bush Presidential Records, GBPL; Stieb, *The Regime Change Consensus*, 19.

74. Brian Duffy et al., "The World's Most Dangerous Man," *U.S. News and World Report* 108, no. 22 (June 4, 1990).

75. Baker with DeFrank, *The Politics of Diplomacy*, 271; Brands, *Making the Unipolar Moment*, 299; Bush and Scowcroft, *A World Transformed*, 308–309; Karabell and Zelikow, "Iraq, 1988–1990," 197–198.

76. Memo, Richard Haass to Brent Scowcroft, "Gulf Contingency Planning," July 25, 1990, folder "Iraq Pre 8/2/90 [1]," OA/ID CF01937-001, Richard Haass Files, Working Files, NSC, Bush Presidential Records, GBPL; Baker with DeFrank, *The Politics of Diplomacy*, 271–272; Bush and Scowcroft, *A World Transformed*, 309; Karabell and Zelikow, "Iraq, 1988–1990," 199–200; Stieb, *The Regime Change Consensus*, 20.

77. Cable, Lawrence Eagleburger to April Glaspie, "President Bush's Response to Saddam Hussein's Message," July 28, 1990, folder "Iraq Pre 8/2/90 [1]," OA/ID CF01937-001, Richard Haass Files, Working Files, NSC, Bush Presidential Records, GBPL; Baker with DeFrank, *The Politics of Diplomacy*, 271–272; Bush and Scowcroft, *A World Transformed*, 310–312; Karabell and Zelikow, "Iraq, 1988–1990," 198–202; Stieb, *The Regime Change Consensus*, 20–21. Baker had sent general policy guidance to US embassies across the Middle East that informed Glaspie's discussion with Saddam: "While we take no position on the border delineation issue raised by Iraq with respect to Kuwait, or on other bi-lateral disputes, Iraqi statements suggest an intention to resolve outstanding disagreements by the use of force, an approach which is contrary to UN-Charter principles." Cable, James Baker to US embassies in the Middle East, "US Reaction to Iraqi Threats in the Gulf," July 24, 1990, folder "Iraq Pre 8/2/90 [1]," OA/ID CF01937-001, Richard Haass Files, Working Files, NSC, Bush Presidential Records, GBPL.

78. Cable, April Glaspie to James Baker, "Iraq Blinks—Provisionally," July 26, 1990, folder "Iraq Pre 8/2/90 [1]," OA/ID CF01937-001, Richard Haass Files, Working Files, NSC, Bush Presidential Records, GBPL; Baker with DeFrank, *The Politics of Diplomacy*, 268, 274; Brands, *Making the Unipolar Moment*, 299–300; Bush and Scowcroft, *A World Transformed*, 311–313; Karabell and Zelikow, "Iraq, 1988–1990," 198–202; Stieb, *The Regime Change Consensus*, 20–21. For further analysis of Saddam Hussein's decision to invade Kuwait, see Hal Brands and David Palkki, "'Conspiring Bastards': Saddam Hussein's Strategic View of the United States," *Diplomatic History* 36, no. 3 (June 2012): 625–659; Daniel Chardell, "The Origins of the Iraqi Invasion of Kuwait Reconsidered," *Texas National Security Review* 6, no. 3 (Summer 2023): 51–78; Steve Coll, *The Achilles Trap: Saddam Hussein, the C.I.A., and the Origins of America's Invasion of Iraq* (New York: Penguin Press, 2024), 156–174.

5. THE FORMATIVE PRECEDENT

1. George H. W. Bush, "Remarks at the Aspen Institute Symposium in Aspen, Colorado," August 2, 1990, American Presidency Project digital archive (APP), https://www.presidency.ucsb.edu/documents/remarks-the-aspen-institute-symposium-aspen-colorado.

2. George Bush and Brent Scowcroft, *A World Transformed* (New York: Alfred A. Knopf, 1998), 302.

3. Speech Drafts, "Presidential Remarks: The Aspen Institute," July 31 and August 1, 1990, folder "Aspen Institute 40th Anniversary, 8/2/90 [1]," OA/ID 13538-001, Speech File Draft Files, Chron File, 1989–1993, White House Office of Speechwriting, Bush Presidential Records, George H. W. Bush Presidential Library (GBPL); Bush, "Aspen Institute Symposium," APP; Bush and Scowcroft, *A World Transformed*, 318.

4. Philip Zelikow and Condoleezza Rice, *To Build a Better World: Choices to End the Cold War and Create a Global Commonwealth* (New York: Twelve, 2019), 359.

5. George H. W. Bush, "Remarks and an Exchange with Reporters on the Iraqi Invasion of Kuwait," August 2, 1990, APP, https://www.presidency.ucsb.edu/documents/remarks-and-exchange-with-reporters-the-iraqi-invasion-kuwait-1.

6. Bush and Scowcroft, *A World Transformed*, 315.

7. NSC Meeting Minutes, August 2, 1990, folder "Iraq—August 2, 1990–December 1990 [4]," OA/ID CF01478-026, Richard Haass Files, Working Files, NSC, Bush Presidential Records, GBPL; Bush and Scowcroft, *A World Transformed*, 315; Jon Meacham, *Destiny and Power: The American Odyssey of George Herbert Walker Bush* (New York: Random House, 2015), 425; Colin L. Powell with Joseph E. Persico, *My American Journey* (New York: Random House, 1995), 462–463.

8. Jeffrey A. Engel, *When the World Seemed New: George H. W. Bush and the End of the Cold War* (Boston: Houghton Mifflin Harcourt, 2017), 384–385; Lawrence Freedman, *A Choice of Enemies: America Confronts the Middle East* (New York: PublicAffairs, 2008), 219.

9. Memo, Paul Wolfowitz to Robert Gates et al., "US Security Relations, Commitments, and Interests in the Persian Gulf," July 26, 1990, folder "Iraq Pre 8/2/90 [4]," OA/ID CF01937-004, Richard Haass Files, Working Files, NSC, Bush Presidential Records, GBPL; Dick Cheney with Liz Cheney, *In My Time: A Personal and Political Memoir* (New York: Threshold Editions, 2011), 184; Peter L. Hahn, *Missions Accomplished? The United States and Iraq since World War I* (New York: Oxford University Press, 2012), 94; Thomas H. Henriksen, *America and the Rogue States* (New York: Palgrave Macmillan, 2012), 38–39.

10. NSC Meeting Minutes, August 2, 1990, GBPL; Richard B. Cheney interview, March 16–17, 2000, George H. W. Bush Oral History Project, Presidential Oral History Program, Miller Center, University of Virginia, https://millercenter.org/the-presidency/presidential-oral-histories/richard-b-cheney-oral-history; Bush and Scowcroft, *A World*

Transformed, 317; Bartholomew Sparrow, *The Strategist: Brent Scowcroft and the Call of National Security* (New York: PublicAffairs, 2015), 389.

11. Meacham, *Destiny and Power*, 425.

12. George Bush Diary, August 3, 1990, quoted in Meacham, *Destiny and Power*, 425; Bush and Scowcroft, *A World Transformed*, 317–318; Sparrow, *The Strategist*, 385.

13. NSC Meeting Minutes, August 2, 1990, GBPL; Bush and Scowcroft, *A World Transformed*, 317; Sparrow, *The Strategist*, 387.

14. Bush and Scowcroft, *A World Transformed*, 321–322; Richard N. Haass, *War of Necessity, War of Choice: A Memoir of Two Iraq Wars* (New York: Simon and Schuster, 2009), 62.

15. Cheney with Cheney, *In My Time*, 186.

16. Telcon, George Bush and King Fahd, August 2, 1990, folder "Telcons—August 1990–December 1990: August 1990 [1]," OA/ID CF01731-020, Presidential Telcon Files, NSC, Bush Presidential Records, GBPL; Telcon, George Bush and Margaret Thatcher, August 3, 1990, folder "Telcons—August 1990–December 1990: August 1990 [1]," OA/ID CF01731-020, Presidential Telcon Files, NSC, Bush Presidential Records, GBPL; Meacham, *Destiny and Power*, 424–425.

17. Bush and Scowcroft, *A World Transformed*, 318.

18. Charles Moore, *Margaret Thatcher: The Authorized Biography*, vol. 3, *Herself Alone* (London: Penguin Books, 2019), 599; Margaret Thatcher, *Margaret Thatcher: The Autobiography* (New York: Harper Perennial, 2010), 698.

19. Moore, *Margaret Thatcher* (vol. 3), 602.

20. George H. W. Bush, "Remarks and a Question-and-Answer Session with Reporters in Aspen, Colorado, Following a Meeting with Prime Minister Margaret Thatcher of the United Kingdom," August 2, 1990, APP, https://www.presidency.ucsb.edu/documents/remarks-and-question-and-answer-session-with-reporters-aspen-colorado-following-meeting; Moore, *Margaret Thatcher* (vol. 3), 602, 604.

21. Bush, "Question-and-Answer Session in Aspen with Thatcher," APP.

22. Bush and Scowcroft, *A World Transformed*, 303, 314.

23. George H. W. Bush, "Address before a Joint Session of the Congress on the Persian Gulf Crisis and the Federal Budget Deficit," September 11, 1990, APP, https://www.presidency.ucsb.edu/documents/address-before-joint-session-the-congress-the-persian-gulf-crisis-and-the-federal-budget.

24. George Bush Diary, August 3, 1990, quoted in Meacham, *Destiny and Power*, 428; Sparrow, *The Strategist*, 388.

25. NSC Meeting Minutes, August 3, 1990, folder "Iraq—August 2, 1990–December 1990 [8]," OA/ID CF01478-030, Richard Haass Files, Working Files, NSC, Bush Presidential Records, GBPL; Bush and Scowcroft, *A World Transformed*, 318, 322–323; Haass, *War of Necessity, War of Choice*, 62.

26. Memo, Peter Rodman to Brent Scowcroft, "Iraq Crisis: Long-Term Implications," August 8, 1990, folder "Desert Shield/Desert Storm (August 1990) Part I," OA/ID 91143-006, Desert Shield/Desert Storm Files, Chron Files, Brent Scowcroft Collection, Bush Presidential Records, GBPL.

27. NSC Meeting Minutes, August 3, 1990, GBPL.

28. Powell with Persico, *My American Journey*, 464–466; Sparrow, *The Strategist*, 389. Curiously, this significant incident, which Powell recounts at length in his memoir, is missing from the NSC meeting minutes as released from the Bush Presidential Library. The minutes do, however, still include redactions for classified national security material. Moreover, the cautionary tone of Powell's remarks that are documented in the meeting minutes, as quoted here, reflects a similar spirit, if not the same phrasing, as his question "if it was worth going to war to liberate Kuwait."

29. NSC Meeting Minutes, August 3, 1990, GBPL.
30. Engel, *When the World Seemed New*, 393.
31. Bush and Scowcroft, *A World Transformed*, 324; Haass, *War of Necessity, War of Choice*, 63.
32. NSC Meeting Minutes, August 4, 1990, folder "Iraq—August 2, 1990–December 1990 [8]," OA/ID CF01478-030, Richard Haass Files, Working Files, NSC, Bush Presidential Records, GBPL; Bush and Scowcroft, *A World Transformed*, 323–324, 327–328.
33. George Bush Diary, August 5, 1990, quoted in Meacham, *Destiny and Power*, 432; George H. W. Bush, "Remarks and an Exchange with Reporters on the Iraqi Invasion of Kuwait," August 5, 1990, APP, https://www.presidency.ucsb.edu/documents/remarks-and-exchange-with-reporters-the-iraqi-invasion-kuwait-0; Bush and Scowcroft, *A World Transformed*, 329, 332–333.
34. Bush, "Remarks and Exchange on Iraqi Invasion," APP; J. Danforth Quayle interview, March 12, 2002, George H. W. Bush Oral History Project, Presidential Oral History Program, Miller Center, University of Virginia, https://millercenter.org/the-presidency/presidential-oral-histories/-danforth-quayle-oral-history.
35. Powell with Persico, *My American Journey*, 466–467.
36. Margaret Thatcher, "Speech to the Aspen Institute ('Shaping a New Global Community')," August 5, 1990, Margaret Thatcher Foundation digital archive (MTF), https://www.margaretthatcher.org/document/108174.
37. Moore, *Margaret Thatcher* (vol. 3), 607, 609–610; Thatcher, *Margaret Thatcher*, 700–701.
38. NSC Meeting Minutes, August 5, 1990, folder "Iraq—August 2, 1990–December 1990 [8]," OA/ID CF01478-030, Richard Haass Files, Working Files, NSC, Bush Presidential Records, GBPL; Moore, *Margaret Thatcher* (vol. 3), 611; Thatcher, *Margaret Thatcher*, 703.
39. Moore, *Margaret Thatcher* (vol. 3), 604, 607–609. It was the historian Jean Edward Smith's 1992 book *George Bush's War* that popularized the notion that it was during their meeting at Aspen that Thatcher told Bush, "Remember, George, this is no time to go wobbly." Jean Edward Smith, *George Bush's War* (New York: Henry Holt, 1992), 68. In fact, the context was the enforcement of sanctions against Iraq and the embargo of Iraqi oil exports in late August 1990, not the initial overall response to the crisis. Moreover, the "wobbly" comment was not directed against Bush's actions but rather at the need to head off external pressures to pursue a more conciliatory course of action toward the Iraqi regime. Agreeing with Bush's statement on a phone call on the night of August 25–26 (not August 2) that "we must not vacillate" and "had the authority to act and we should act" to stop Iraqi shipping, Thatcher asserted, "*The key was not to go wobbly now*" [emphasis added]. Bush responded that "he did not think there was any pressure for that yet, in the United States or internationally." Moore, *Margaret Thatcher* (vol. 3), 616–618; Thatcher, *Margaret Thatcher*, 703.
However, President Bush himself contributed to the confusion over the context of the statement. Presenting the Presidential Medal of Freedom to Thatcher in March 1991, shortly after the end of the Gulf War, he told the story of Thatcher's comment as a statement of caution against his decision on August 22 to allow an Iraqi tanker to pass through the blockade, pending UN authorization to use force to enforce the sanctions. Bush's memoir makes this same mistake in more detail. In this context, Thatcher's comment would have constituted clear criticism of the president's decision, which it was not. George H. W. Bush, "Remarks upon Presenting the Presidential Medal of Freedom to Margaret Thatcher," March 7, 1991, APP, https://www.presidency.ucsb.edu/documents/remarks-upon-presenting-the-presidential-medal-freedom-margaret-thatcher; Bush and Scowcroft, *A World Transformed*, 352.
40. George H. W. Bush, "Address to the Nation Announcing the Deployment of United States Armed Forces to Saudi Arabia," August 8, 1990, APP, https://www.presidency.ucsb

.edu/documents/address-the-nation-announcing-the-deployment-united-states-armed-forces-saudi-arabia.

41. Bush and Scowcroft, *A World Transformed*, 340.

42. Bush and Scowcroft, *A World Transformed*, 353–354. Secretary of State Baker and General Powell shared the view that from late August into October 1990 US policy was "drifting" and that firmer measures were required to push Saddam out of Kuwait, though neither was yet as willing as Bush to resort to military action. James A. Baker III with Thomas M. DeFrank, *The Politics of Diplomacy: Revolution, War, and Peace, 1989–1992* (New York: G. P. Putnam's Sons, 1995), 302.

43. Bush and Scowcroft, *A World Transformed*, 353–354.

44. Both Jeffrey Engel and Kristina Spohr compare Bush's speech to Wilson's famous Fourteen Points address before Congress in January 1918, as well as to the vision set out by Franklin Roosevelt for the United Nations at the end of World War II. See Engel, *When the World Seemed New*, 415–419; Kristina Spohr, *Post Wall, Post Square: Rebuilding the World after 1989* (London: William Collins, 2019), 349.

45. Bush, "Address before Congress on Persian Gulf Crisis," APP.

46. George Bush Diary, August 22, 1990, and September 22, 1990, quoted in Meacham, *Destiny and Power*, 439, 442; George H. W. Bush, "Remarks at a Republican Fundraising Breakfast in Burlington, Vermont," October 23, 1990, APP, https://www.presidency.ucsb.edu/documents/remarks-republican-fundraising-breakfast-burlington-vermont; Bush and Scowcroft, *A World Transformed*, 340, 374–375; Engel, *When the World Seemed New*, 398; Spohr, *Post Wall, Post Square*, 353.

47. George Bush Diary, September 4, 1990, quoted in Meacham, *Destiny and Power*, 440; Bush and Scowcroft, *A World Transformed*, 374–375, 389; Engel, *When the World Seemed New*, 398–400.

48. Svetlana Savranskaya and Thomas Blanton, eds., *The Last Superpower Summits: Conversations That Ended the Cold War*, vol. 2, *Gorbachev and Bush* (Budapest: Central European University Press, 2020), Document 39.

49. George H. W. Bush, "Remarks at a Fundraising Luncheon for Gubernatorial Candidate Clayton Williams in Dallas, Texas," October 15, 1990, APP, https://www.presidency.ucsb.edu/documents/remarks-fundraising-luncheon-for-gubernatorial-candidate-clayton-williams-dallas-texas; George H. W. Bush, "Remarks at a Republican Campaign Rally in Manchester, New Hampshire," October 23, 1990, APP, https://www.presidency.ucsb.edu/documents/remarks-republican-campaign-rally-manchester-new-hampshire; Baker with DeFrank, *The Politics of Diplomacy*, 331–332.

50. Baker with DeFrank, *The Politics of Diplomacy*, 331; Bush and Scowcroft, *A World Transformed*, 375, 388–389; Engel, *When the World Seemed New*, 399; Powell with Persico, *My American Journey*, 491.

51. George Bush Diary, January 13, 1991, quoted in Meacham, *Destiny and Power*, 455; George H. W. Bush, *All the Best, George Bush: My Life in Letters and Other Writings* (New York: Scribner, 2013), 497; Bush and Scowcroft, *A World Transformed*, 375.

52. George Bush Diary, September 13, 1990, quoted in Bush and Scowcroft, *A World Transformed*, 372; George Bush Diary, October 17, 1990, in Bush, *All the Best, George Bush*, 482–483; Powell with Persico, *My American Journey*, 470; Robert A. Strong, *Character and Consequence: Foreign Policy Decisions of George H. W. Bush* (Lanham, MD: Lexington Books, 2020), 109–110.

53. George Bush Diary, October 17, 1990, quoted in Bush and Scowcroft, *A World Transformed*, 382; Bush and Scowcroft, *A World Transformed*, 382.

54. George Bush Diary, August 16, 1990, quoted in Meacham, *Destiny and Power*, 441; Bush and Scowcroft, *A World Transformed*, 354; Engel, *When the World Seemed New*, 396.

55. Powell with Persico, *My American Journey*, 470, 479–480.

56. Bush and Scowcroft, *A World Transformed*, 380–381; Engel, *When the World Seemed New*, 403–404; Strong, *Character and Consequence*, 109–110.

57. Bush and Scowcroft, *A World Transformed*, 354, 392.

58. Memo, Richard Haass to Brent Scowcroft, "October 30, 3:30 pm Mini-NSC on the Gulf," October 29, 1990, folder "Iraq—October 1990 [3]," OA/ID CF01584-033, Richard Haass Files, Working Files, NSC, Bush Presidential Records, GBPL; Memo and Talking Points, Brent Scowcroft to George Bush, "Meeting on the Gulf," October 30, 1990, folder "Iraq—October 1990 [3]," OA/ID CF01584-033, Richard Haass Files, Working Files, NSC, Bush Presidential Records, GBPL; Bush and Scowcroft, *A World Transformed*, 391–393; Powell with Persico, *My American Journey*, 487–488; Strong, *Character and Consequence*, 110–111.

59. Background Paper, "The Gulf Crisis: Possible Futures," October 30, 1990, folder "Iraq—October 1990 [3]," OA/ID CF01584-033, Richard Haass Files, Working Files, NSC, Bush Presidential Records, GBPL; Powell with Persico, *My American Journey*, 469–470, 479–480, 488.

60. Memo, Scowcroft to Bush, "Meeting on the Gulf," October 30, 1990, GBPL; Background Paper, "Gulf Crisis," October 30, 1990, GBPL; Strong, *Character and Consequence*, 110–111.

61. Talking Points, October 30, 1990, GBPL.

62. Robert M. Gates interview, July 23–24, 2000, George H. W. Bush Oral History Project, Presidential Oral History Program, Miller Center, University of Virginia, https://millercenter.org/the-presidency/presidential-oral-histories/robert-m-gates-deputy-director-central; Spencer D. Bakich, *The Gulf War: George H. W. Bush and American Grand Strategy in the Post-Cold War Era* (Lawrence: University Press of Kansas, 2024), 74–76; Bush and Scowcroft, *A World Transformed*, 394–395; Powell with Persico, *My American Journey*, 488–489; Strong, *Character and Consequence*, 112–113.

63. Engel, *When the World Seemed New*, 404.

64. Baker with DeFrank, *The Politics of Diplomacy*, 302–303.

65. Spohr, *Post Wall, Post Square*, 354; Strong, *Character and Consequence*, 114.

66. Bush and Scowcroft, *A World Transformed*, 489.

67. Cable, James Baker to George Bush, "Memorandum for the President: Moscow, November 8," November 9, 1990, folder "Iraq—November 1990 [2]," OA/ID CF01584-029, Richard Haass Files, Working Files, NSC, Bush Presidential Records, GBPL.

68. Baker with DeFrank, *The Politics of Diplomacy*, 327–328.

69. George Bush Diary, November 28, 1990, quoted in Bush and Scowcroft, *A World Transformed*, 418; George Bush Diary, January 4, 1991, quoted in Meacham, *Destiny and Power*, 453; H. W. Brands, "George Bush and the Gulf War of 1991," *Presidential Studies Quarterly* 34, no. 1 (March 2004): 127–130; Bush and Scowcroft, *A World Transformed*, 397–398, 418, 441, 446; Meacham, *Destiny and Power*, 451–453.

70. George H. W. Bush, "Address to the Nation Announcing Allied Military Action in the Persian Gulf," January 16, 1991, APP, https://www.presidency.ucsb.edu/documents/address-the-nation-announcing-allied-military-action-the-persian-gulf; Bush and Scowcroft, *A World Transformed*, 448–451.

71. "Excerpts from Saddam's Speech with AM-Gulf Rdp, Bjt," *AP News*, January 6, 1991; George Bush Diary, January 19, 1991, and February 24, 1991, quoted in Meacham, *Destiny and Power*, 460, 464; Bush and Scowcroft, *A World Transformed*, 485–486; Meacham, *Destiny and Power*, 458, 466.

72. National Security Directive (NSD) 54, "Responding to Iraqi Aggression in the Gulf," January 15, 1991, GBPL, https://bush41library.tamu.edu/files/nsd/nsd54.pdf; Bush, "Address Announcing Allied Military Action," APP; Bush and Scowcroft, *A World Transformed*, 463.

73. NSD-54, GBPL.

74. Bush, "Address Announcing Allied Military Action," APP.

75. Memo, Richard Haass to Brent Scowcroft, "Responding to Iraqi CW Use," January 29, 1991, folder "Persian Gulf Conflict—January 1991 [1 of 2]," OA/ID CF00946, Robert Gates Files, NSC, Bush Presidential Records, GBPL; George Bush Diary, February 23, 1991, quoted in Meacham, *Destiny and Power*, 463; Bush and Scowcroft, *A World Transformed*, 477; Powell with Persico, *My American Journey*, 468. Saddam was indeed prepared to use chemical and biological weapons against coalition forces and cities in Saudi Arabia and Israel, and he directed his commanders to prepare for such WMD attacks prior to the outbreak of the war; however, he decided not to carry them out, likely deterred by the threat of massive retaliation, perhaps with nuclear weapons, from the United States. Steve Coll, *The Achilles Trap: Saddam Hussein, the C.I.A., and the Origins of America's Invasion of Iraq* (New York: Penguin Press, 2024), 194–195, 201.

76. Powell with Persico, *My American Journey*, 468, 503–504.

77. Powell with Persico, *My American Journey*, 507.

78. Memo, Scowcroft to Bush, "Meeting on the Gulf," October 30, 1990, GBPL; Bush and Scowcroft, *A World Transformed*, 392, 447.

79. Margaret Thatcher argued in support of threatening to use chemical weapons in response to an Iraqi WMD attack in at least two meetings with Bush and Cheney in the fall of 1990. She "believed it would be justified for the United States to use CW [chemical weapons] against Iraq armoured formations in Kuwait if the Iraqis themselves used it first." She argued against considering the use of nuclear weapons against Iraq. Memcon, Margaret Thatcher and Dick Cheney, "Prime Minister's Meeting with the United States Defence Secretary," October 15, 1990, MTF, https://www.margaretthatcher.org/document/206250; Nigel Ashton, *False Prophets: British Leaders' Fateful Fascination with the Middle East from Suez to Syria* (London: Atlantic Books, 2022), 229–230.

80. Bush and Scowcroft, *A World Transformed*, 463; Powell with Persico, *My American Journey*, 468.

81. Meacham, *Destiny and Power*, 463.

82. NSD-54, GBPL; Bush and Scowcroft, *A World Transformed*, 463; Cheney with Cheney, *In My Time*, 220–221; Powell with Persico, *My American Journey*, 504.

83. NSD-54, GBPL.

84. Baker with DeFrank, *The Politics of Diplomacy*, 436–438; Bush and Scowcroft, *A World Transformed*, 433, 463–464; Meacham, *Destiny and Power*, 458–459; Powell with Persico, *My American Journey*, 490. One early proponent of seeking regime change in Iraq was Richard Haass of the NSC staff. In a series of memos in mid- and late August 1990, he argued that a diplomatic solution to the crisis that "leaves Saddam in power and Iraq's industrial and war-making capability intact" would not be "a viable much less optimal outcome." Such an outcome "all but ensures that in a few years we will have a much more aggressive and capable Iraq (with biological and nuclear weapons) on our hands," one that "would likely return to threaten us another day." "All agree," he asserted of his colleagues in the administration, that if Iraq attacked Saudi Arabia "we would not stop until we had effectively decapitated Iraq and destroyed its key military and related targets." Memo, Richard Haass, "The Gulf Crisis: Thoughts, Scenarios, and Options," August 19, 1990, folder "Iraq—August 2, 1990–December 1990 [2]," OA/ID CF01478-024, Richard Haass Files, Working Files, NSC, Bush Presidential Records, GBPL; Memo, Richard Haass to Brent Scowcroft, "What Next in the Gulf?" August 27, 1990, folder "Iraq—August 2, 1990–December 1990 [2]," OA/ID CF01478-024, Richard Haass Files, Working Files, NSC, Bush Presidential Records, GBPL.

85. Baker with DeFrank, *The Politics of Diplomacy*, 437–438; Bush and Scowcroft, *A World Transformed*, 433, 463–464, 489; Meacham, *Destiny and Power*, 459; Powell with Persico, *My American Journey*, 490.

86. NSD-54, GBPL; Memcon, George Bush, James Baker, and Hans-Dietrich Genscher, March 1, 1991, folder "Memcons—January 1991–June 1991: March 1991," OA/ID CF01728-009, Presidential Memcon Files, NSC, Bush Presidential Records, GBPL; Baker with DeFrank, *The Politics of Diplomacy*, 435; Bush and Scowcroft, *A World Transformed*, 488–489; Meacham, *Destiny and Power*, 459.

87. NSC Meeting Minutes, August 6, 1990, folder "Iraq—August 2, 1990–December 1990 [8]," OA/ID CF01478-030, Richard Haass Files, Working Files, NSC, Bush Presidential Records, GBPL; George Bush Diary, January 17 and 20, 1991, quoted in Meacham, *Destiny and Power*, 461; George Bush Diary, January 31, 1991, quoted in Bush and Scowcroft, *A World Transformed*, 464; Memcon, Bush, Baker, and Genscher, March 1, 1991, GBPL.

88. Meacham, *Destiny and Power*, 462.

89. George Bush Diary, February 28, 1991, quoted in Meacham, *Destiny and Power*, 467. Bush was referring to the formal surrender ceremony for Japan aboard the American battleship USS *Missouri* in Tokyo Bay on September 2, 1945, which marked the official end of World War II.

90. Thatcher, *Margaret Thatcher*, 706–707.

91. Memo, Brent Scowcroft to George Bush, "Restoring Liberated Kuwait," February 8, 1991, folder "Iraq—February 1991 [2]," OA/ID CF01584-004, Richard Haass Files, Working Files, NSC, Bush Presidential Records, GBPL; Bush and Scowcroft, *A World Transformed*, 472, 488–489. Meacham, *Destiny and Power*, 459, 464. After World War II, victorious Allied forces divided Germany into four sectors that were placed under military occupation, unlike their decision to restore self-rule in liberated France under a sovereign provisional government.

92. Målfrid Braut-Hegghammer, *Unclear Physics: Why Iraq and Libya Failed to Build Nuclear Weapons* (Ithaca, NY: Cornell University Press, 2016), 75, 103, 117–123; Coll, *The Achilles Trap*, 195–196; Vipin Narang, *Seeking the Bomb: Strategies of Nuclear Proliferation* (Princeton, NJ: Princeton University Press, 2022), 246–250; Giordana Pulcini and Or Rabinowitz, "An Ounce of Prevention—A Pound of Cure? The Reagan Administration's Nonproliferation Policy and the Osirak Raid," *Journal of Cold War Studies* 23, no. 2 (Spring 2021): 36–38.

93. Memo, Brent Scowcroft to George Bush, "Current Status of the Iraqi Nuclear Program," March 30, 1990, folder "Desert Shield/Desert Storm (March 1990)," OA/ID 91143-001, Desert Shield/Desert Storm Files, Chron Files, Brent Scowcroft Collection, Bush Presidential Records, GBPL.

94. Baker with DeFrank, *The Politics of Diplomacy*, 441.

95. United Nations Security Council (UNSC) Resolution 687, April 3, 1991, United Nations Digital Library (UNDL), https://digitallibrary.un.org/record/110709.

96. George H. W. Bush, "White House Statement on Weapons of Mass Destruction," March 7, 1991, APP, https://www.presidency.ucsb.edu/documents/white-house-statement-weapons-mass-destruction.

97. George H. W. Bush, "The President's News Conference," November 30, 1990, APP, https://www.presidency.ucsb.edu/documents/the-presidents-news-conference-19.

98. Margaret Thatcher, *Statecraft: Strategies for a Changing World* (London: HarperCollins, 2002), 228.

99. Baker with DeFrank, *The Politics of Diplomacy*, 441.

CONCLUSION

1. George P. Shultz, "The Ecology of International Change," in *US Foreign Policy in the 1990s*, ed. Greg Schmergel (New York: St. Martin's Press, 1991), 3–5, 9–11. Though published after the Gulf War, the text of Shultz's essay makes clear that he wrote it shortly after the 1988 presidential election.

2. Jessica Tuchman Mathews, "Redefining Security," *Foreign Affairs* 68, no. 2 (Spring 1989): 162–177.

3. Letter, George Bush to the nation, November 22, 1990, folder "Persian Gulf Conflict—Pre-1991," OA/ID CF00946, Robert Gates Files, NSC, Bush Presidential Records, George H. W. Bush Presidential Library (GBPL).

4. Ronald Reagan, "Remarks at the Annual Convention of the American Bar Association," July 8, 1985, American Presidency Project digital archive (APP), https://www.presidency.ucsb.edu/documents/remarks-the-annual-convention-the-american-bar-association.

5. George H. W. Bush, "Remarks at the Aspen Institute Symposium in Aspen, Colorado," August 2, 1990, APP, https://www.presidency.ucsb.edu/documents/remarks-the-aspen-institute-symposium-aspen-colorado.

6. Bill Clinton, "Remarks to Future Leaders of Europe in Brussels," January 9, 1994, APP, https://www.presidency.ucsb.edu/documents/remarks-future-leaders-europe-brussels.

7. Thomas H. Henriksen, *America and the Rogue States* (New York: Palgrave Macmillan, 2012), 22.

8. Anthony Lake, "Confronting Backlash States," *Foreign Affairs* 73, no. 2 (March/April 1994): 45–55.

9. Richard N. Haass, *The Reluctant Sheriff: The United States after the Cold War* (New York: Council on Foreign Relations Books, 1997), 6.

10. Madeleine Albright, "Interview on NBC-TV 'The Today Show' with Matt Lauer," February 19, 1998, https://1997-2001.state.gov/statements/1998/980219a.html.

11. For fuller discussion and analysis of the George W. Bush administration's use of coercive diplomacy against Iraq, see Robert Draper, *To Start a War: How the Bush Administration Took America into Iraq* (New York: Penguin Press, 2020); Melvyn P. Leffler, *Confronting Saddam Hussein: George W. Bush and the Invasion of Iraq* (New York: Oxford University Press, 2023).

12. See Joseph Stieb, *The Regime Change Consensus: Iraq in American Politics, 1990–2003* (New York: Cambridge University Press, 2021).

13. For discussion of how the post–9/11 context prompted the George W. Bush administration to adopt preemptive or preventive military force as a key part of its national security strategy, see John Lewis Gaddis, *Surprise, Security, and the American Experience* (Cambridge, MA: Harvard University Press, 2004), 69–113; Rachel Elizabeth Whitlark, *All Options on the Table: Leaders, Preventive War, and Nuclear Proliferation* (Ithaca, NY: Cornell University Press, 2021), 119–121, 140–153.

Bibliography

ARCHIVES

CIA CREST. Digital archive, https://www.cia.gov/library/readingroom/document-type/crest.
George H. W. Bush Presidential Library. Texas A&M University, College Station, TX.
Hoover Institution Library and Archives. Stanford University, Stanford, CA.
Margaret Thatcher Foundation. Digital archive, https://www.margaretthatcher.org.
National Security Archive. George Washington University, Washington, DC. Digital archive, https://nsarchive.gwu.edu/virtual-reading-room.
The Reagan Files. Digital archive, https://www.thereaganfiles.com.
Ronald Reagan Presidential Library. Simi Valley, CA.
United Nations Digital Library. Digital archive, https://digitallibrary.un.org.

PUBLISHED PRIMARY SOURCES

American Presidency Project. Digital archive, https://www.presidency.ucsb.edu.
Bush, George H. W. *All the Best, George Bush: My Life in Letters and Other Writings*. New York: Scribner, 2013.
Foreign Affairs Oral History Project. Association for Diplomatic Studies and Training. Digital archive, https://adst.org/oral-history/oral-history-interviews/.
Foreign Relations of the United States, 1981–1988. Vol. 13, *Conflict in the South Atlantic, 1981–1984*. Edited by Alexander R. Wieland. Washington, DC: US Government Publishing Office, 2015.
George H. W. Bush Oral History Project. Presidential Oral History Program, Miller Center, University of Virginia. Digital archive, https://millercenter.org/the-presidency/presidential-oral-histories/george-h-w-bush.
Reagan, Ronald. *The Reagan Diaries*. Unabridged ed. 2 vols., edited by Douglas Brinkley. New York: HarperCollins, 2009.
Ronald Reagan Oral History Project. Presidential Oral History Program, Miller Center, University of Virginia. Digital archive, https://millercenter.org/the-presidency/presidential-oral-histories/ronald-reagan.
Savranskaya, Svetlana, and Thomas Blanton, eds. *The Last Superpower Summits: Conversations That Ended the Cold War*. 2 vols. Budapest: Central European University Press, 2020.

MEDIA, NEWSPAPERS, AND MAGAZINES

AP News, New York.
CBC News Online, Ottawa.
CBS News, New York.
Chicago Tribune, Chicago.
The Guardian, London.
The New York Times, New York.
Newsweek, New York.
Slate, New York.
The Sunday Times, London.

Time, New York.
U.S. News and World Report, Washington, DC.
The Washington Post, Washington, DC.

MEMOIRS

Baker, James A. III, with Thomas M. DeFrank. *The Politics of Diplomacy: Revolution, War, and Peace, 1989-1992.* New York: G. P. Putnam's Sons, 1995.

Barr, William P. *One Damn Thing after Another: Memoirs of an Attorney General.* New York: William Morrow, 2022.

Bush, George, and Brent Scowcroft. *A World Transformed.* New York: Alfred A. Knopf, 1998.

Carter, Jimmy. *Keeping Faith: Memoirs of a President.* New York: Bantam Books, 1982.

Cheney, Dick, with Liz Cheney. *In My Time: A Personal and Political Memoir.* New York: Threshold Editions, 2011.

Gates, Robert M. *From the Shadows: The Ultimate Insider's Story of Five Presidents and How They Won the Cold War.* New York: Simon and Schuster, 1996.

Haass, Richard N. *War of Necessity, War of Choice: A Memoir of Two Iraq Wars.* New York: Simon and Schuster, 2009.

Haig, Alexander M. Jr. *Caveat: Realism, Reagan, and Foreign Policy.* New York: Macmillan, 1984.

Haig, Alexander M. Jr., with Charles McCarry. *Inner Circles: How America Changed the World: A Memoir.* New York: Warner Books, 1992.

North, Oliver L., with William Novak. *Under Fire: An American Story.* New York: HarperCollins, 1991.

Powell, Colin L., with Joseph E. Persico. *My American Journey.* New York: Random House, 1995.

Reagan, Ronald. *An American Life.* New York: Simon and Schuster, 1990.

Rumsfeld, Donald. *Known and Unknown: A Memoir.* New York: Sentinel, 2011.

Shultz, George P. *Learning from Experience.* Stanford, CA: Hoover Institution Press, 2016.

Shultz, George P. *Turmoil and Triumph: My Years as Secretary of State.* New York: Charles Scribner's Sons, 1993.

Thatcher, Margaret. *The Downing Street Years.* London: HarperCollins, 1993.

Thatcher, Margaret. *Margaret Thatcher: The Autobiography.* New York: Harper Perennial, 2010.

Weinberger, Caspar W. *Fighting for Peace: Seven Critical Years in the Pentagon.* New York: Warner Books, 1990.

Weinberger, Caspar W., with Gretchen Roberts. *In the Arena: A Memoir of the 20th Century.* Washington, DC: Regnery, 2001.

BOOKS

Aldous, Richard. *Reagan and Thatcher: The Difficult Relationship.* London: Hutchinson, 2012.

Arquilla, John. *The Reagan Imprint: Ideas in American Foreign Policy from the Collapse of Communism to the War on Terror.* Chicago: Ivan R. Dee, 2006.

Ashton, Nigel. *False Prophets: British Leaders' Fateful Fascination with the Middle East from Suez to Syria.* London: Atlantic Books, 2022.

Ashton, Nigel, and Bryan Gibson, eds. *The Iran-Iraq War: New International Perspectives.* London: Routledge, 2013.

Bacevich, Andrew J. *America's War for the Greater Middle East: A Military History.* New York: Random House, 2016.

Baker, Peter, and Susan Glasser. *The Man Who Ran Washington: The Life and Times of James A. Baker III*. New York: Doubleday, 2020.
Bakich, Spencer D. *The Gulf War: George H. W. Bush and American Grand Strategy in the Post-Cold War Era*. Lawrence: University Press of Kansas, 2024.
Barton, Mary S. *Counterterrorism between the Wars: An International History, 1919–1937*. New York: Oxford University Press, 2020.
Bass, Warren. *A Surprise Out of Zion? Case Studies in Israel's Decisions on Whether to Alert the United States to Preemptive and Preventive Strikes, from Suez to the Syrian Nuclear Reactor*. Santa Monica, CA: RAND Corporation, 2015.
Brands, H. W. *Reagan: The Life*. New York: Doubleday, 2015.
Brands, Hal. *From Berlin to Baghdad: America's Search for Purpose in the Post-Cold War World*. Lexington: University Press of Kentucky, 2008.
Brands, Hal. *Making the Unipolar Moment: U.S. Foreign Policy and the Rise of the Post-Cold War Order*. Ithaca, NY: Cornell University Press, 2016.
Brands, Hal, ed. *The New Makers of Modern Strategy: From the Ancient World to the Digital Age*. Princeton, NJ: Princeton University Press, 2023.
Brands, Hal. *What Good Is Grand Strategy? Power and Purpose in American Statecraft from Harry S. Truman to George W. Bush*. Ithaca, NY: Cornell University Press, 2014.
Braut-Hegghammer, Målfrid. *Unclear Physics: Why Iraq and Libya Failed to Build Nuclear Weapons*. Ithaca, NY: Cornell University Press, 2016.
Brown, Archie. *The Human Factor: Gorbachev, Reagan, and Thatcher, and the End of the Cold War*. New York: Oxford University Press, 2020.
Cannon, Lou. *President Reagan: The Role of a Lifetime*. Rev. ed. New York: PublicAffairs, 2000.
Carr, Jack, and James M. Scott. *Targeted: Beirut: The 1983 Marine Barracks Bombing and the Untold Origin Story of the War on Terror*. New York: Emily Bestler, 2024.
Chamberlin, Paul Thomas. *The Cold War's Killing Fields: Rethinking the Long Peace*. New York: HarperCollins, 2018.
Chidester, Jeffrey L., and Paul Kengor, eds. *Reagan's Legacy in a World Transformed*. Cambridge, MA: Harvard University Press, 2015.
Coleman, Bradley Lynn, and Kyle Longley, eds. *Reagan and the World: Leadership and National Security, 1981–1989*. Lexington: University Press of Kentucky, 2017.
Coll, Steve. *The Achilles Trap: Saddam Hussein, the C.I.A., and the Origins of America's Invasion of Iraq*. New York: Penguin Press, 2024.
Crandall, Russell. *Gunboat Democracy: U.S. Interventions in the Dominican Republic, Grenada, and Panama*. Lanham, MD: Rowman and Littlefield, 2006.
Crist, David. *The Twilight War: The Secret History of America's Thirty-Year Conflict with Iran*. New York: Penguin Press, 2012.
Davis, Brian L. *Qaddafi, Terrorism, and the Origins of the U.S. Attack on Libya*. New York: Praeger, 1990.
DeYoung, Karen. *Soldier: The Life of Colin Powell*. New York: Alfred A. Knopf, 2006.
Draper, Robert. *To Start a War: How the Bush Administration Took America into Iraq*. New York: Penguin Press, 2020.
Dueck, Colin. *Hard Line: The Republican Party and U.S. Foreign Policy since World War II*. Princeton, NJ: Princeton University Press, 2010.
Engel, Jeffrey A. *When the World Seemed New: George H. W. Bush and the End of the Cold War*. Boston: Houghton Mifflin Harcourt, 2017.
Ferguson, Niall, Charles S. Maier, Erez Manela, and Daniel J. Sargent, eds. *The Shock of the Global: The 1970s in Perspective*. Cambridge, MA: Belknap Press of Harvard University Press, 2010.
Fischer, Beth A. *The Reagan Reversal: Foreign Policy and the End of the Cold War*. Columbia: University of Missouri Press, 1997.

Freedman, Lawrence. *A Choice of Enemies: America Confronts the Middle East*. New York: PublicAffairs, 2008.

Freedman, Lawrence. *The Official History of the Falklands Campaign*. Vol. 1, *The Origins of the Falklands War*. London: Routledge, 2005.

Freedman, Lawrence. *The Official History of the Falklands Campaign*. Vol. 2, *War and Diplomacy*. London: Routledge, 2005.

Freedman, Lawrence, and Efraim Karsh. *The Gulf Conflict, 1990–1991: Diplomacy and War in the New World Order*. Princeton, NJ: Princeton University Press, 1993.

Fuksman-Sha'al, Moshe, ed. *Israel's Strike against the Iraqi Nuclear Reactor, 7 June 1981: A Collection of Articles and Lectures*. Jerusalem: Menachem Begin Heritage Center, 2003.

Fuller, Christopher J. *See It/Shoot It: The Secret History of the CIA's Lethal Drone Program*. New Haven, CT: Yale University Press, 2017.

Gaddis, John Lewis. *Strategies of Containment: A Critical Appraisal of American National Security Policy during the Cold War*. Rev. ed. New York: Oxford University Press, 2005.

Gaddis, John Lewis. *Surprise, Security, and the American Experience*. Cambridge, MA: Harvard University Press, 2004.

Gavin, Francis J. *Nuclear Statecraft: History and Strategy in America's Atomic Age*. Ithaca, NY: Cornell University Press, 2012.

Haass, Richard N. *The Reluctant Sheriff: The United States after the Cold War*. New York: Council on Foreign Relations Books, 1997.

Hahn, Peter L. *Missions Accomplished? The United States and Iraq since World War I*. New York: Oxford University Press, 2012.

Hänni, Adrian, Thomas Riegler, and Przemyslaw Gasztold, eds. *Terrorism in the Cold War: State Support in Eastern Europe and the Soviet Sphere of Influence*. London: I. B. Tauris, 2021.

Hänni, Adrian, Thomas Riegler, and Przemyslaw Gasztold, eds. *Terrorism in the Cold War: State Support in the West, Middle East, and Latin America*. London: I. B. Tauris, 2021.

Hayward, Steven F. *The Age of Reagan: The Conservative Counterrevolution, 1980–1989*. New York: Crown Forum, 2009.

Helfont, Samuel. *Iraq against the World: Saddam, America, and the Post–Cold War Order*. New York: Oxford University Press, 2023.

Henriksen, Thomas H. *America and the Rogue States*. New York: Palgrave Macmillan, 2012.

Henriksen, Thomas H. *America's Wars: Interventions, Regime Change, and Insurgencies after the Cold War*. New York: Cambridge University Press, 2022.

Herring, George C. *From Colony to Superpower: U.S. Foreign Relations since 1776*. 2nd ed. Vol. 2, *The American Century and Beyond: U.S. Foreign Relations, 1893–2015*. New York: Oxford University Press, 2017.

Huchthausen, Peter. *America's Splendid Little Wars: A Short History of U.S. Engagements: From the Fall of Saigon to Baghdad*. New York: Penguin Books, 2003.

Hunt, Jonathan R. *The Nuclear Club: How America and the World Policed the Atom from Hiroshima to Vietnam*. Stanford, CA: Stanford University Press, 2022.

Hunt, Jonathan R., and Simon Miles, eds. *The Reagan Moment: America and the World in the 1980s*. Ithaca, NY: Cornell University Press, 2021.

Inboden, William. *The Peacemaker: Ronald Reagan, the Cold War, and the World on the Brink*. New York: Dutton, 2022.

Jentleson, Bruce W. *With Friends Like These: Reagan, Bush, and Saddam, 1982–1990*. New York: W. W. Norton, 1994.

Johns, Andrew L., ed. *A Companion to Ronald Reagan*. Malden, MA: Wiley Blackwell, 2015.

Keefer, Edward C. *Caspar Weinberger and the U.S. Military Buildup, 1981–1985*. Washington, DC: Historical Office, Office of the Secretary of Defense, 2023.
Kengor, Paul. *The Crusader: Ronald Reagan and the Fall of Communism*. New York: Harper Perennial, 2006.
Klare, Michael. *Rogue States and Nuclear Outlaws: America's Search for a New Foreign Policy*. New York: Hill and Wang, 1995.
Knott, Stephen F., and Jeffrey L. Chidester. *Presidential Profiles: The Reagan Years*. New York: Facts on File, 2005.
Leffler, Melvyn P. *Confronting Saddam Hussein: George W. Bush and the Invasion of Iraq*. New York: Oxford University Press, 2023.
Leffler, Melvyn P. *For the Soul of Mankind: The United States, the Soviet Union, and the Cold War*. New York: Hill and Wang, 2007.
Litwak, Robert S. *Rogue States and U.S. Foreign Policy: Containment after the Cold War*. Washington, DC: Woodrow Wilson Center Press, 2000.
Lüthi, Lorenz M. *Cold Wars: Asia, the Middle East, Europe*. New York: Cambridge University Press, 2020.
Martin, David C., and John L. Walcott. *Best Laid Plans: The Inside Story of America's War against Terrorism*. New York: Harper and Row, 1988.
Matlock, Jack F. Jr. *Reagan and Gorbachev: How the Cold War Ended*. New York: Random House, 2004.
Meacham, Jon. *Destiny and Power: The American Odyssey of George Herbert Walker Bush*. New York: Random House, 2015.
Miller, Nicholas L. *Stopping the Bomb: The Sources and Effectiveness of US Nonproliferation Policy*. Ithaca, NY: Cornell University Press, 2018.
Monteiro, Nuno P., and Fritz Bartel, eds. *Before and After the Fall: World Politics and the End of the Cold War*. New York: Cambridge University Press, 2021.
Moore, Charles. *Margaret Thatcher: The Authorized Biography*. Vol. 1, *Not for Turning*. London: Penguin Books, 2013.
Moore, Charles. *Margaret Thatcher: The Authorized Biography*. Vol. 2, *Everything She Wants*. London: Penguin Books, 2015.
Moore, Charles. *Margaret Thatcher: The Authorized Biography*. Vol. 3, *Herself Alone*. London: Penguin Books, 2019.
Morris, Roger. *Haig: The General's Progress*. New York: Playboy Press, 1982.
Naftali, Timothy. *Blind Spot: The Secret History of American Counterterrorism*. New York: Basic Books, 2005.
Nakdimon, Shlomo. *First Strike: The Exclusive Story of How Israel Foiled Iraq's Attempt to Get the Bomb*. Translated by Peretz Kidron. New York: Summit Books, 1987.
Narang, Vipin. *Seeking the Bomb: Strategies of Nuclear Proliferation*. Princeton, NJ: Princeton University Press, 2022.
National Commission on Terrorist Attacks upon the United States. *The 9/11 Commission Report: The Attack from Planning to Aftermath*. 2nd ed. New York: W. W. Norton, 2011.
Natsios, Andrew S., and Andrew H. Card Jr., eds. *Transforming Our World: President George H. W. Bush and American Foreign Policy*. Lanham, MD: Rowman and Littlefield, 2020.
Parmet, Herbert S. *George Bush: The Life of a Lone Star Yankee*. New York: Scribner, 1997.
Richardson, Louise. *When Allies Differ: Anglo-American Relations during the Suez and Falklands Crises*. New York: St. Martin's Press, 1996.
Sargent, Daniel J. *A Superpower Transformed: The Remaking of American Foreign Relations in the 1970s*. New York: Oxford University Press, 2015.
Sarotte, Mary Elise. *1989: The Struggle to Create Post–Cold War Europe*. Princeton, NJ: Princeton University Press, 2009.

Smith, Geoffrey. *Reagan and Thatcher.* New York: W. W. Norton, 1991.
Smith, Jean Edward. *George Bush's War.* New York: Henry Holt, 1992.
Sparrow, Bartholomew. *The Strategist: Brent Scowcroft and the Call of National Security.* New York: PublicAffairs, 2015.
Spohr, Kristina. *Post Wall, Post Square: Rebuilding the World after 1989.* London: William Collins, 2019.
Stanik, Joseph T. *El Dorado Canyon: Reagan's Undeclared War with Qaddafi.* Annapolis, MD: Naval Institute Press, 2003.
Stieb, Joseph. *The Regime Change Consensus: Iraq in American Politics, 1990–2003.* New York: Cambridge University Press, 2021.
Strong, Robert A. *Character and Consequence: Foreign Policy Decisions of George H. W. Bush.* Lanham, MD: Lexington Books, 2020.
Taubman, Philip. *In the Nation's Service: The Life and Times of George P. Shultz.* Stanford, CA: Stanford University Press, 2023.
Thatcher, Margaret. *Statecraft: Strategies for a Changing World.* London: HarperCollins, 2002.
Timmerman, Kenneth R. *The Death Lobby: How the West Armed Iraq.* Boston: Houghton Mifflin, 1991.
Toaldo, Mattia. *The Origins of the US War on Terror: Lebanon, Libya, and American Intervention in the Middle East.* New York: Routledge, 2013.
Tucker, David. *Skirmishes at the Edge of Empire: The United States and International Terrorism.* Westport, CT: Praeger, 1997.
Westad, Odd Arne. *The Cold War: A World History.* New York: Basic Books, 2017.
Westad, Odd Arne. *The Global Cold War: Third World Interventions and the Making of Our Times.* New York: Cambridge University Press, 2005.
Whitlark, Rachel Elizabeth. *All Options on the Table: Leaders, Preventive War, and Nuclear Proliferation.* Ithaca, NY: Cornell University Press, 2021.
Wills, David C. *The First War on Terrorism: Counter-Terrorism Policy during the Reagan Administration.* Lanham, MD: Rowman and Littlefield, 2003.
Wilson, James Graham. *The Triumph of Improvisation: Gorbachev's Adaptability, Reagan's Engagement, and the End of the Cold War.* Ithaca, NY: Cornell University Press, 2014.
Woodward, Bob. *The Commanders.* New York: Simon and Schuster, 1991.
Woodward, Bob. *Veil: The Secret Wars of the CIA, 1981–1987.* New York: Simon and Schuster, 1987.
Zelikow, Philip, and Condoleezza Rice. *To Build a Better World: Choices to End the Cold War and Create a Global Commonwealth.* New York: Twelve, 2019.
Zoller, Silke. *To Deter and Punish: Global Collaboration against Terrorism in the 1970s.* New York: Columbia University Press, 2021.

JOURNAL ARTICLES, BOOK CHAPTERS, DISSERTATIONS, AND THESES

Aldrich, Richard J. "British Intelligence and the Anglo-American 'Special Relationship' during the Cold War." *Review of International Studies* 24, no. 3 (July 1998): 331–351.
Auffant, Marino. "Oil for Atoms: The 1970s Energy Crisis and Nuclear Proliferation in the Persian Gulf." *Texas National Security Review* 5, no. 3 (Summer 2022): 59–82.
Brands, H. W. "George Bush and the Gulf War of 1991." *Presidential Studies Quarterly* 34, no. 1 (March 2004): 113–131.
Brands, Hal. "Choosing Primacy: U.S. Strategy and Global Order at the Dawn of the Post–Cold War Era." *Texas National Security Review* 1, no. 2 (March 2018): 8–33.
Brands, Hal, and David Palkki. "'Conspiring Bastards': Saddam Hussein's Strategic View of the United States." *Diplomatic History* 36, no. 3 (June 2012): 625–659.

Chardell, Daniel. "The Origins of the Iraqi Invasion of Kuwait Reconsidered." *Texas National Security Review* 6, no. 3 (Summer 2023): 51–78.
Chiampan, Andrea. "Running with the Hare, Hunting with the Hounds: The Special Relationship, Reagan's Cold War, and the Falklands Conflict." *Diplomacy and Statecraft* 24, no. 4 (December 2013): 640–660.
Evans, Alexandra Tejblum. "An Early Test: The Reagan Administration and the Osirak Raid of 1981." MA thesis, University of Virginia, 2015.
Evans, Alexandra Tejblum. "Reagan's Middle East: Lebanon and the Evolution of U.S. Strategy, 1981–1985." PhD diss., University of Virginia, 2018.
Feldman, Shai. "The Bombing of Osiraq—Revisited." *International Security* 7, no. 2 (Fall 1982): 114–142.
Garrity, Patrick J. "The Falklands Factor." *Claremont Review of Books* (April 24, 2013). https://claremontreviewofbooks.com/digital/the-falklands-factor.
Hanhimäki, Jussi M. Introduction to H-Diplo Roundtable XXIII-4 on *Engaging the Evil Empire: Washington, Moscow, and the Beginning of the End of the Cold War*, by Simon Miles (September 27, 2021). https://hdiplo.org/to/RT23-4.
Jentleson, Bruce W. "Iraq: The Failure of a Strategy." In *Reversing Relations with Former Adversaries: U.S. Foreign Policy after the Cold War*, edited by C. Richard Nelson and Kenneth Weisbrode, 126–163. Gainesville: University Press of Florida, 1998.
Karabell, Zachary, and Philip D. Zelikow. "Iraq, 1988–1990: Unexpectedly Heading toward War." In *Dealing with Dictators: Dilemmas of U.S. Diplomacy and Intelligence Analysis, 1945–1990*, edited by Ernest R. May and Philip D. Zelikow, 167–202. Cambridge, MA: MIT Press, 2006.
Kirkpatrick, Jeane. "Dictatorships and Double Standards." *Commentary* 68, no. 5 (November 1979): 34–45.
Lake, Anthony. "Confronting Backlash States." *Foreign Affairs* 73, no. 2 (March/April 1994): 45–55.
Leffler, Melvyn P. "Ronald Reagan and the Cold War: What Mattered Most." *Texas National Security Review* 1, no. 3 (May 2018): 76–89.
Mathews, Jessica Tuchman. "Redefining Security." *Foreign Affairs* 68, no. 2 (Spring 1989): 162–177.
Pulcini, Giordana, and Or Rabinowitz. "An Ounce of Prevention—A Pound of Cure? The Reagan Administration's Nonproliferation Policy and the Osirak Raid." *Journal of Cold War Studies* 23, no. 2 (Spring 2021): 4–40.
Shultz, George P. "The Ecology of International Change." In *US Foreign Policy in the 1990s*, edited by Greg Schmergel, 3–13. New York: St. Martin's Press, 1991.
Sinai, Joshua. "Libya's Pursuit of Weapons of Mass Destruction." *The Nonproliferation Review* 4, no. 3 (Spring/Summer 1997): 92–100.
Wilson, James Graham. "How Grand Was Reagan's Strategy, 1976–1984?' *Diplomacy and Statecraft* 18, no. 4 (December 2007): 773–803.
Zelikow, Philip. "Offensive Military Options." In *New Nuclear Nations: Consequences for U.S. Policy*, edited by Robert D. Blackwill and Albert Carnesale, 162–195. New York: Council on Foreign Relations Press, 1993.

Index

Abrams, Elliott, 82, 84
Abu Nidal terrorist organization, 50–51, 112
Achille Lauro, 50, 56
Acland, Sir Antony, 144–45
Afghanistan, Soviet invasion of, 14–15, 22, 107
Airborne Warning and Control System (AWACS), 22, 25
airplane hijackings, 43–44, 50, 51. *See also* Pan Am Flight 103 bombing
Albright, Madeleine, 188
Allen, Richard, 16–17, 17*f*, 18, 20, 21
Argentina
  and Falklands War, 12–13, 25–37, 39, 40, 189, 203–5nn48–49, 51, 60, 75–76
  nuclear program of, 203n48
Armitage, Richard, 83
Aspen Institute Symposium, 137–38, 139, 144, 147, 151, 152–53
Aziz, Tariq, 22, 112, 116, 118, 130, 134, 222n34

backlash states, 187. *See also* rogue states
Baker, Howard, 87, 88, 91
Baker, James
  and Gulf crisis and war, 124, 134, 163*f*, 165–67, 178, 224n77
  with national security team, 17*f*, 123*f*
  and Osirak strike, 20
  and Panama crisis, 86, 88, 90, 91, 92*f*, 95, 96, 97, 98, 99–100, 101, 104, 105, 214n5, 217n67, 218n74
  and US relations with Iraq, 126, 127, 128, 129, 131–32, 160, 161–62, 228n42
Banca Nazionale del Lavoro (BNL), 128
Bazoft, Farzad, 131
Begin, Menachim, 12, 18–20, 21, 24
Beirut, terrorist attacks in, 44–47. *See also* US Marine barracks, bombing of
Berlin Wall, 104
biological weapons, 126, 127, 157, 171–72, 173, 178, 180, 186, 230n75. *See also* weapons of mass destruction (WMD)
Britain
  counterterrorism against Libya, 42–43, 60–62
  and Falklands War, 25–27, 189, 204n49
  and Iraqi invasion of Kuwait, 144–47, 151–53, 166
  and Lockerbie bombing, 71–72, 74, 75, 212n108
  and US counterterrorism efforts, 54–57, 64–65, 66
  See also Thatcher, Margaret
Bush, George H. W.
  on aggression against Kuwait, 13
  approaches to rogue state threat, 3, 4, 9, 10–11, 185, 188–90
  Aspen Institute speech, 137–38
  counterterrorism strategy and task force, 51–52, 72
  and escalating confrontation with Libya, 59*f*, 70–73
  and Gulf War as precedent for defining global security, 179–80
  and international treaty on chemical warfare, 117
  lasting impact of response to Iraqi invasion of Kuwait, 154–68
  "New World Order" speech, 156–58
  and Osirak strike, 20, 24
  and Panama crisis, 76–77, 83, 87, 88, 89–91, 92*f*, 94–104, 102*f*, 214n5, 217n67, 218n74
  reshaping of national security under, 183–84
  resolution to Gulf War, 168–79, 170*f*, 191
  response to Iraq's invasion of Kuwait, 123*f*, 139, 140–54, 146*f*, 163*f*
  strategy toward Iraq, 122–35, 224n77, 228n42
  summit with Reagan and Gorbachev, 1–2, 2*f*, 192, 192*f*
  Thatcher's counsel to, regarding Iraq, 152–53, 227n39
  during TWA Flight 847 hijacking crisis, 52*f*
  and US relations with Iraq, 107
Bush, George W., 189, 190, 191–92, 199n9

Carlucci, Frank, 75, 83, 86, 114
Carter, Jimmy, 14–15, 24, 28, 78, 96, 183
Casey, William, 17–18, 20, 63*f*

241

INDEX

Chad, 68–69
chemical weapons
  developed by Libya, 68–71
  and Gulf War, 171–73
  held / used by Iraq, 116–18, 119, 131, 177, 186, 221n31, 230n75
  Shultz on, 182–83
  Thatcher on use of, against Iraq, 230n79
  See also weapons of mass destruction (WMD)
Cheney, Dick
  background of, 143–44
  and Bush's attempt to remove Noriega, 102f
  on destruction of Pharma 150, 71
  and Gulf crisis and war, 125, 142, 143, 149, 152, 162, 163f, 170f, 172–73
  with national security team, 123f
Churchill, Winston, 52f, 60
Clark, William, 17, 17f, 20, 37, 111
Clinton, Bill, 186–87
coercive diplomacy, 164, 165, 188–90
Cold War
  Carter and, 14–15
  and emergence of rogue states, 3, 4–6
  end of, 1–3, 6–7, 104
  international system during, 6
  perceptions of, 10
  Reagan and, 13–18, 25, 38–40
  scholarship on, 9–10, 11
Commodity Credit Corporation (CCC), 128–29, 132
counterterrorism
  aftermath of US bombing of Libya, 64–68
  evolution of US views on, 43–47
  forging and acceleration of US strategy, 50–59
  and Libya's development of WMD, 68–71
  and Lockerbie bombing, 71–72, 212n108
  recalibration of US strategy, 73–75
  and US bombing of Libya, 41–43, 59–64
  US seeks international support for, 64–66
  See also terrorism
Crowe, William, 58, 59f, 84, 125

Darman, Richard, 142
Davis, Arthur, 96
Deaver, Michael, 20
Delvalle, Eric, 82–83
Drug Enforcement Administration (DEA), 79–80
drug trafficking, 81–83, 86, 89, 90–91, 93, 105, 183

Eagleburger, Lawrence, 125, 148–49
Eagleton, William, 117, 202n35

Endara, Guillermo, 96, 103
Export-Import Bank, 128–29

Fahd, King, 144
Falklands War, 12–13, 25–37, 39, 40, 189, 203–5nn48–49,51,60,75–76
Fitzwater, Marlin, 70
Ford, Billy, 97
"freedom of navigation" (FON) exercises, 48, 57–58, 113

Gabriel, Charles, 63f
Gaddafi, Muammar. *See* Qadhafi, Muammar
Galtieri, Leopoldo, 28
Gates, Robert, 17–18, 102f, 123f, 163f, 165, 170f, 218n74
Genscher, Hans-Dietrich, 69
Germany, reunification of, 138
Giroldi, Moises, 98–99, 217n67
Glaspie, April, 134–35, 224n77
global security
  Bush on threats to, 137–38
  emerging threats to, 3, 4–5, 182–83
  Gulf War as precedent for defining, 179–81
  post–Cold War, 6, 7
  Soviet Union as threat to, 16, 18
  See also counterterrorism; drug trafficking; terrorism
Global War on Terror, 189, 190, 191
Gorbachev, Mikhail, 1–2, 2f, 104, 138, 144, 159, 166–67, 192, 192f
grand strategy, 4, 10–11, 184, 197n4
Gulf of Sidra, freedom of navigation exercises in, 48, 57–58
Gulf War, 3, 137–40
  lasting impact of US response in, 154–68
  as precedent for defining global security, 179–81
  and reshaping of national security, 183–84
  resolution and aftermath of, 168–79, 186, 191
  US's initial response, 139, 140–54

Haass, Richard
  and Gulf crisis and war, 134, 142, 143, 148, 149–50, 230n84
  and US policy toward Iraq, 125, 131, 132
  on US's international role, 188
Haig, Alexander
  on Argentina's nuclear program, 203n48
  and Falklands War, 28–30, 31–32, 33, 35f, 204n60
  and Osirak strike, 18–19, 20, 22, 24

as secretary of state, 15–16, 17f, 39–40
on terrorism, 44
Halabja, Iraq, 119
Herres, Robert, 115f
Hezbollah, 44–46, 50
Hill, Charles, 79, 110–11
Hussein, Saddam. *See* Saddam Hussein

Inman, Bobby Ray, 203n48
International Atomic Energy Agency (IAEA), 21, 22–23
international security. *See* global security
Iran
  Islamic revolution in, 107
  as rogue state, 7–8, 199n9
  support for terrorism, 44–46
Iran-Contra affair, 74–75, 220n8
Iran-Iraq War, 107, 109, 110–12, 113, 116–19, 129, 220n14
Iraq
  agricultural credits for, 112, 127–29, 132
  Bush's strategy toward, 122–35, 224n77, 228n42
  chemical weapons held / used by, 116–18, 119, 131, 177, 186, 221n31, 230n75
  and "constructive engagement," 124–35
  invades Kuwait, 136, 183–84
  Israeli strike on Osirak, 12, 18–25, 39, 40
  nuclear program of, 133, 177–78
  Reagan's strategy toward, 108–22
  as rogue state, 4–5, 8, 135–36, 199n9
  US occupation of, 191–92
  US relations with, 106–7, 221n18, 230n84
  See also Gulf War; Saddam Hussein
Iraq War, 190, 191
Israel, 12, 18–25, 39, 40, 131, 132, 202n38

Kelly, Thomas, 102f
Khalilzad, Zalmay, 121
Khomeini, Ayatollah, 110, 112, 120
Kirkpatrick, Jeane, 19, 20, 25, 28, 30, 32, 79
Kohl, Helmut, 66, 69
Kozak, Mike, 85, 86, 87 91, 92–93, 92f, 96, 214n5
Kurds, 119
Kuwait, 113, 116–17, 133–35, 136, 183–84. *See also* Gulf War

La Belle discotheque bombing, 58–60
Lake, Anthony, 187
Leach, Sir Henry, 27
Lebanon, 44–47
Lewis, Samuel, 24

Libya
  air battle over Tobruk, 72–73
  economic boycott of, 53–55
  and forging of US counterterrorism strategy, 50–56
  and Lockerbie bombing, 71–72, 74, 75, 212n108
  naval confrontation with, 57–59
  regime change in, 66–67
  retaliatory strikes against, 54–55, 57, 60–61
  as rogue state, 4–5, 8, 47–50, 105
  US bombing of, 41–43, 59–68
  weapons of mass destruction developed by, 68–71
  See also Qadhafi, Muammar
Lockerbie bombing. *See* Pan Am Flight 103 bombing

Mathews, Jessica Tuchman, 183
Meese, Edwin, 20, 81, 87, 88, 91, 92f
Mitterrand, François, 66
Mubarak, Hosni, 132

national security
  and evolution of US views on terrorism and counterterrorism, 43–47
  reshaping of, for post–Cold War world, 2–3, 7, 9, 183–87
  See also counterterrorism; terrorism
National Security Decision Directives (NSDD), 36–38, 46, 51
National Security Directives (NSD), 125–26, 127, 132, 170, 171, 172, 173, 174–75
new world order, 155–57, 165–66, 190
"New World Order" speech, 156–58
Nixon, Richard, 15, 44
Noriega, Manuel
  Bush's strategy for removal of, 94–104, 217n67, 218n74
  history with United States 78–80, 94–95
  Newsweek cover, 82f
  and possibility of deposing Saddam Hussein, 174
  Reagan's strategy for removal of, 80–94, 215n37, 216nn50,57, 217n63
  similarities between Qadhafi and, 78, 105
  US officials' views on, 214n8
  See also Panama
North, Oliver, 57, 67, 75, 214n8
North Korea, 7, 199n9
Nuclear Non-Proliferation Treaty (NPT), 21, 202n38
nuclear weapons
  and Gulf War, 172–73

244   INDEX

nuclear weapons (*continued*)
   Iraq and, 133, 177–78
   Libya and, 69
   and National Security Decision Directive (NSDD) 32, 38
   Reagan on, 202n38
   See also Osirak strike; weapons of mass destruction (WMD)

Oakley, Robert, 56–57
Operation Desert Shield, 153–54, 162, 164
Operation Desert Storm, 168, 169, 170–71, 173, 178, 186
Operation El Dorado Canyon, 63–64, 73
Operation Just Cause, 100, 102–3, 105
Operation Staunch, 111, 220n8
Organization of American States, 97
Osirak strike, 12, 18–25, 39, 40

Palestinian Liberation Front, 50
Panama
   Bush's strategy for regime change in, 94–104, 217n67, 218n74
   fraudulent election in, 96–97
   history with United States, 78–80, 94–95
   versus Iran as rogue state, 8
   officials playing central roles in crisis, 214n5
   Reagan's strategy for regime change in, 80–94, 215n37, 216nn50,57, 217n63
   as rogue state, 4–5, 7, 76–78, 105
   US invasion of, 101–3
   See also Noriega, Manuel
Panama Defense Forces (PDF), 79, 86, 96, 97, 98, 99, 100
Pan Am Flight 103 bombing, 71–72, 74, 75, 212n108
pariah states, 5. *See also* rogue states
Pharma 150. *See* Rabta, Libya, chemical weapons plant
Pickering, Thomas, 147
Poindexter, John, 41, 53, 59*f*, 66, 67, 74–75
Powell, Charles, 54, 62, 144–45, 151–52
Powell, Colin
   and Gulf crisis and war, 141, 142, 149, 150, 151, 160, 162, 163–65, 163*f*, 170*f*, 173
   on Iran-Iraq War, 111
   on Iraqi attacks on US ships, 116
   with national security team, 123*f*
   and Panama crisis, 79, 86, 89*f*, 90, 91, 92*f*, 95, 98, 100, 101, 102*f*, 214n5, 214n8, 217n67, 218n74
   on policy toward Iraq, 228n42
Price, Charles, 65

Provisional Irish Republican Army (IRA), 49, 54, 55

Qadhafi, Muammar
   and Libya's emergence as rogue state, 47–50
   and Lockerbie bombing, 71–72
   Newsweek cover, 48*f*
   similarities between Noriega and, 78, 105
   terrorist acts sponsored by, 41, 42
   US seeks regime change in Libya, 66–67
   weapons of mass destruction developed by, 68–71
   See also Libya
Quayle, Dan, 123*f*, 151

Rabta, Libya, chemical weapons plant, 68–71, 73
Reagan, Ronald
   and aftermath of US bombing of Libya, 64–68
   air battle with Libya over Tobruk, 72–73
   approaches to rogue state threat, 3, 4, 9, 10, 11, 76
   bombing of Libya, 59–64, 63*f*
   and coercive diplomacy, 188–90
   Cold War as foreign policy priority of, 13–18, 25, 144
   counterterrorism against Libya, 41–43, 59*f*
   and emergence of rogue state threats, 3, 38–40
   and Falklands War, 28, 31–36, 35*f*
   legacy regarding rogue states, 184–86
   and Libya's development of WMD, 68–70, 71
   and Libya's emergence as rogue state, 47–50
   and National Security Decision Directive (NSDD) 32, 36–38
   nonproliferation goals of, 202n38
   and Osirak strike, 18, 19, 20–21, 22, 23–25
   and Panama crisis, 76–77, 80–94, 89*f*, 92*f*, 215n37, 216nn50,57, 217n63
   reshaping of national security under, 13, 17*f*, 183–84
   strategy toward Iraq, 107, 108–22, 115*f*
   summit with Bush and Gorbachev, 1–2, 2*f*, 192, 192*f*
   during TWA Flight 847 hijacking crisis, 52*f*
   and US counterterrorism strategy, 44–47, 50–59, 73–75
Regan, Don, 59*f*, 63*f*
Rodman, Peter, 131, 148
rogue states
   Bush and, 185–86

characteristics of, 5–6, 197n5
Clinton on, 187
emergence of, 3, 4–5, 6, 104–5
Libya's emergence as, 42, 47–50
Reagan and, 76, 184–85
United States' approach to, 3–4, 7, 183–87, 188–90
Rome airport attack, 50–51, 52
Rumsfeld, Donald, 112, 120

Saddam Hussein
background of, 110
chemical weapons use, 230n75
comparisons between Hitler and, 144, 154, 158–60, 158, 175–76, 180
concerns regarding, 126–27, 133, 158–60, 223n58
crisis with Kuwait, 133–35
deposing of, 174–77, 179, 180, 191
following Iran-Iraq War, 129
and Israeli strike on Osirak nuclear reactor, 12, 19, 21, 23
name of, 219n3
Newsweek cover, 108f
paranoia of, 130–31
power abuses of, 106
Reagan's strategy toward, 108–22
and resolution to Gulf War, 169
on United States, 129–30
US pursuit of relations with, 106–7
See also Gulf War; Iraq
Saudi Arabia
and Iraqi invasion of Kuwait, 142, 144, 150, 152
sale of Airborne Warning and Control System to, 22, 25
Schwarzkopf, Norman, 162, 172
Scowcroft, Brent
and Bush's Aspen Institute speech, 138
and Iraqi invasion of Kuwait, 142, 143, 144, 148, 150, 151
on Iraqi nuclear capability, 178
and lasting impact of Gulf War, 155–56, 163f
with national security team, 123f
and Panama crisis, 101, 102f
on policy toward Iraq, 124, 132, 161, 162
on resolution to Gulf War, 176
on Saddam Hussein, 126–27, 130, 131, 160
on weapons of mass destruction in Gulf War, 172
September 11, 2001, terrorist attacks, 190
Shamir, Yitzhak, 180
Shevardnadze, Eduard, 70

Shultz, George
approach to rogue state threat, 9, 64, 182–83, 185
on attack on USS *Stark*, 116
background of, 40
on bombing of US Marine barracks, 45
and chemical weapons, 117, 118
on counterterrorist strikes, 45–46, 58
on Falklands War, 36
on Iran as threat, 8
on Iran-Iraq War, 110, 111–12, 118, 120
on Iraq as threat, 136
on Iraqi attacks on Kurds, 119
and Panama crisis, 79, 81, 82, 83, 84–86, 89, 89f, 91, 92f, 93, 100, 105
on terrorism, 46–47
during TWA Flight 847 hijacking crisis, 52f
and US bombing of Libya, 55–56, 63, 63f, 67, 68, 69, 70
and US policy toward Iraq, 107, 114, 121, 221n18
Soviet Union
invades Afghanistan, 14–15, 22, 107
and lasting impact of Gulf War, 156
as threat to national security, 16, 18, 36–38
See also Cold War
Spadafora, Hugo, 80
Sununu, John, 123f, 170f, 218n74

Tanker War, 113–14
Teicher, Howard, 61
terrorism
defined, 198n8
drug trafficking and, 93, 105, 183
escalation in, 50
Global War on Terror, 189, 190, 191
and Libya's emergence as rogue state, 47–50
September 11, 2001, terrorist attacks, 190
Thatcher on, 61–52
See also counterterrorism
Thatcher, Margaret
attempted assassination of, 49, 54
and Falklands War, 26–27, 28, 29, 34–35, 35f, 36, 204n51
and Gulf crisis and war, 144–47, 146f, 151–53, 166, 176, 227n39, 230n79
influence on Reagan, 40, 185
and Osirak strike, 21
on Saddam Hussein, 180
and US counterterrorism strategy, 51, 54–55, 60–62, 64–65, 66
Thurman, Maxwell, 98
Torrijos, Omar, 78–79

Truman, Harry S., 176
TWA Flight 847, hijacking of, 50, 51

United Kingdom. *See* Britain
United Nations, 33–34, 62–63
United Nations Security Council, 25, 147–48, 166, 167, 174, 178
United Nations Special Commission (UNSCOM), 178
US Marine barracks, bombing of, 44–45, 46. *See also* Beirut, terrorist attacks in
USS *John F. Kennedy*, 72
USS *Stark*, 114–16

Vienna airport attack, 50–51, 52

Walters, Vernon, 62
weapons of mass destruction (WMD)
  defined, 198n8
  developed by Libya, 68–71
  and Gulf War, 171–73
  held / used by Iraq, 109, 116–18, 119, 131, 177–78, 180, 186, 221n31, 230n75
  US policy concerning, 178, 182–83
  See also biological weapons; chemical weapons; nuclear weapons
Weinberger, Caspar
  on attack on USS *Stark*, 115–16, 115*f*
  and counterterrorist strikes against Hezbollah, 45–46
  and dealing with rogue states, 58, 185
  and Falklands War, 28, 30–32, 33
  and Osirak strike, 20, 24
  on protection of Kuwaiti shipping, 113–14
  as secretary of defense, 16, 17*f*
  and US bombing of Libya, 59*f*, 60
West Germany, 69, 70, 117
Whitehead, John, 55
Wilson, Woodrow, 156
Wolfowitz, Paul, 142, 220n9
World War II, 158, 175–76, 180

www.ingramcontent.com/pod-product-compliance
Lightning Source LLC
Chambersburg PA
CBHW031353230426
43670CB00006B/527